The Political Economy of NGOs

# THE POLITICAL ECONOMY OF NGOs

## State Formation in Sri Lanka and Bangladesh

Jude L. Fernando

**Pluto**Press
www.plutobooks.com

First published 2011 by Pluto Press
345 Archway Road, London N6 5AA

www.plutobooks.com

Distributed in the United States of America exclusively by
Palgrave Macmillan, a division of St. Martin's Press LLC,
175 Fifth Avenue, New York, NY 10010

Copyright © Jude L. Fernando 2011

The right of Jude L. Fernando to be identified as the author of this work
has been asserted by him in accordance with the Copyright, Designs and
Patents Act 1988.

British Library Cataloguing in Publication Data
A catalogue record for this book is available from the British Library

ISBN    978 0 7453 2172 1    Hardback
ISBN    978 0 7453 2171 4    Paperback

Library of Congress Cataloging in Publication Data applied for

This book is printed on paper suitable for recycling and made from fully
managed and sustained forest sources. Logging, pulping and manufacturing
processes are expected to conform to the environmental standards of the
country of origin.

10  9  8  7  6  5  4  3  2  1

Designed and produced for Pluto Press by Chase Publishing Services Ltd
Typeset from disk by Stanford DTP Services, Northampton, England
Simultaneously printed digitally by CPI Antony Rowe, Chippenham, UK and
Edwards Bros in the United States of America

# Contents

# Acknowledgements

When I survey the vast field of generous people and institutions that have assisted me in my work, I feel compelled to single out a succession of institutions, teachers, friends, and colleagues as the ones ultimately responsible for motivating me to complete this book. The project began with the doctoral dissertation fieldwork I conducted in Bangladesh and Sri Lanka from 1996 to 1998, and the work continued until the end of 2009. The Social Science Research Council and the Aspen Institute generously funded my research. I also owe a debt to those who shaped my intellectual development, especially Professors Alan Heston and David Ludden, Drs. Jayadeva Uyangoda, Arjun Appadurai, Vinoth Ramachandra, Carolyn Beck, S.W.R.D. Samarasinghe, Samuel Escobar, and Van Weigal, Rev. Fr. Stephen Abraham and Mr. Sunil Sirisena. I am also grateful to my friends Simon Batterbury, Harsha Athurupana, Kanthi Gamage, Ian Barnes, Duncan Earle, Lawrence Were, Sarah Belisea-Abrams, Asha Singh, Angela Schroll and David Fullerton, whose editorial assistance, support, and suggestions were extremely instrumental in producing this volume. The book was also enriched by students of Clark University who took my class on Theory and Practice of NGO Management. Finally, this work would not have seen the light if not for the patient comments and editorial assistance of my former colleague Dr. Kali Tal.

# Preface

"If I have seen further it is by standing on the shoulders of Giants."

Isaac Newton

During the period in which I wrote this book, post-Cold War optimism about social, economic, political, and environmental improvements gave way to a widespread pessimism about growing and seemingly intractable problems in those areas. The prosperity in developed countries associated with the dot-com bubble was short-lived. During this period, few developing countries achieved sustainable levels of economic growth. Instead, they became even more vulnerable to corporate exploitation and the vicissitudes of the wider global economy. In light of the crises precipitated by the spectacular collapse of real estate, commodity, and financial markets in 2007 and 2008, even capitalism's most vocal advocates began to express doubts about the free market's resiliency. Capitalism's effects on developed and developing countries are suddenly becoming more alike.

The plight of capitalist institutions is now so grave that they beg the state for historically unprecedented "bailout" loans and regulatory interventions. Yet no one cites conspiracy theories or the "war on terror" as the cause of this deplorable state of affairs. Nor have the usual suspects, communism and socialism, been blamed. To the contrary, communist countries such as China and Vietnam have spearheaded the post-Cold War economic recovery, their socialism used as a means of creating the material and social conditions for capitalist development. It is as though capitalism is unraveling before our eyes. More than ever, the free market's "invisible hand" is at the mercy of the government's all-too-visible manipulation. While some might continue to accuse governments of greed and corruption, most still espouse the political economy of capitalism. And, while both dominant and subordinate classes vie for public resources, the state continues to consolidate its power. The emerging solidarity between national governments seems geared more toward bolstering global capitalism and less toward the resolution of the social, economic, political, and environmental problems faced by their citizens. Paradoxically, amid rapid globalization, everyone seems to have embraced the notion of democracy, but no one has presented a framework for its achievement on a global scale. Instead, transnational institutions fail regularly to prevent states from embracing the socially exclusive forms of "nativism" and ethnoreligious nationalism which so often result in military coups and violence against marginalized social groups. The ability of any particular society to hold the state and corporations accountable, and to imagine alternatives to capitalism, seems to be diminishing rapidly.

These global trends raise serious doubts about the promise of nongovernmental organizations (NGOs) to compensate for the shortcomings of the state and of corporations while contributing to sustainable development and environmental justice. The relevance, efficiency, and sustainability of NGOs are all in question, now more than ever before. On the one hand, NGOs are simultaneously facing drastic funding cuts and new state sanctions. On the other hand, they also face a growing number of allegations of mismanagement, corruption, and irresponsibility. NGOs are thus under immense pressure to reinvent themselves vis-à-vis the state if they are to make good on their claim to be the last "free agents" of social change.

Equally troubling is the widespread ideological confusion among social theorists regarding the causes of, and solutions to, our current problems. The euphoria over diverse alternative paths to social change, stimulated by many postmodernist, feminist, poststructuralist, postcolonialist, and postdevelopmentalist ideologues, is dissipating as we enter the "end game of globalization."[1] We now face not only the practical challenge of finding solutions to multiple concrete problems, but also the theoretical challenge of rethinking our most basic assumptions. In this respect, the crisis of social theory and the crisis of political economy are mutually constitutive.

Despite the gravity of the situation, doomsday is not yet here. Far from being passive victims of globalization and development, many people are creative and reflective enough to find ways out of undesirable circumstances. On this point, I concur with Marx that excessive materialistic determinism—"vulgar materialism"—underestimates the power of human thought and action. Drawing inspiration from the Judeo-Christian tradition, Marx questioned how man could "emancipate himself" if he was a "product of material conditions."[2] Ultimately, he firmly believed in the capacity of people to transform the conditions shaping their lives: "The materialistic doctrine that men are products of circumstances and upbringing, and that, therefore, changed men are the product of other circumstances and changed upbringing, forgets that it is men that change circumstances and that the educator himself needs education."[3]

According to Marx, the human will trumps "circumstances and upbringing," for "it is not consciousness that determines their being, but, on the contrary, their social being determines their consciousness."[4] Social being, moreover, is "an active agency capable of shaping the environments within which they live."[5] Recent scholarship provides many examples of the transformative power of the human will. For example, Anthony Bebbington's exploration of "islands of sustainability" in the rural Andes shows how successful environmentally sustainable and socially equitable development practices can be.[6] And Thomas Ponniah and William Fisher's reflections on the 2001 World Social Forum in Porto Alegre, Brazil, have sparked new hope for potentially counterhegemonic pedagogical and political spaces, particularly those spearheaded by NGOs around the world.[7] Although these examples are at once highly localized and scattered, and although they may be difficult to replicate on a macroeconomic scale, they offer powerful new visions for social transformation. In fact, they provide a more accurate description of human agency, and create hope as opposed to hopelessness among those concerned with making society better. At the same time, while my critical agenda resembles those of Bebbington, Ponniah, and Fisher, I find their use of the term "globalization" too broad, flattening the hierarchical nature of forces of social change. That is because the word implicitly downplays the centrality of the capitalist state in structuring contemporary social trajectories. They are, of course, not alone in using language that downplays the capitalist state's role. Even Michael Hardt and Antonio Negri's optimistic analysis, identifying the militant "multitude" as the new revolutionary subject capable of challenging capitalism, fails to provide an adequate account of capitalism's ability to coordinate and discipline the multitude.[8] Similarly, the political effect of using the term "neoliberalism" so often in radical political practice is the mystification of capitalism's materiality. While the foregoing terms should not be abandoned in critical discourse, we should be aware of the capitalist context from which they derive their deeper meaning. The tendency of ostensibly counterhegemonic discourse to downplay capitalism's exploitation of the language and practices of its critics is a theme I address throughout this book.

Postdevelopmentalist critics sympathetic to postcolonialism and poststructuralism too often dismiss development as a Western construct while blaming it for any number of the Third World's social and economic ills. Such scholarship sheds much-needed light on conventional thinking about development, but the basic claim is both historically inaccurate and grossly oversimplified. Failing to provide an adequate account of the relationship between capitalism and development, such scholarship cannot explain the origins of either. Yet it is the process of social development that needs to be understood in terms of its expansionary and reproductive logic. Uneven development in both developed and developing countries has everything to do with the ways in which capitalism appropriates and internalizes space for the reproduction of capital.

The emergence of a hyperactive identity politics of diversity, in place of the more subdued class politics of redistribution, has also been counterproductive to society's quest for equality and justice. Indeed, identity politics, as both a discourse and a practice, has proven to be the most creative instrument of capitalist expansion and the continuing exploitation of the underdeveloped global south by the developed global north. For example, postcolonial and post-structuralist feminist theorists have contributed a great deal to the mainstreaming of gender equality in development, but their fixation on and privileging of gender at the expense of class has led to the appropriation and exploitation of feminist politics by capitalist forces. The problem with all of these "alternative" social theories is that they not only fail to identify capitalism as the central force of social change, but they also fail to consider their own place in the history of capitalist development. Consequently, these theories cannot explain how capitalism survives multiple crises by co-opting the languages and practices of its opponents.

Yet I still believe in the possibility of a better world. Uncompromising pessimism is not only fatalistic but also shortsighted. It undermines, as C.L.R. James noted in his discussion of the slaves in the French colonies,[9] the historically proven capacity of human beings to appropriate and subvert the hegemonic ideas and practices that oppress them. It is because I believe that a better world is possible that I wish to re-examine the role of NGOs in social change, in a broader historical context.

It is possible that the post-Cold War expansion of NGOs is a response to society's disenchantment with conventional theories and practices of social transformation, and represents a meaningful search for viable alternatives. But we must grapple with our concerns and doubts about the potential of NGOs to reshape society, particularly in light of the growing tendency of states to ignore public opinion and violate well-established international laws. We must consider the meaning of the correspondence between neoliberal capitalism's rise over the past three decades and the ascendance of NGOs. Have NGOs succumbed to the very forces that they purport to oppose? How and why have NGOs, with their diverse progressive agendas, reproduced the same sociopolitical institutions and relationships that they set out to change? Should we begin to theorize a post-NGO world? Current NGO scholarship has, across the board, downplayed or failed to address the ways in which NGOs can be co-opted, disciplined, and reproduced within the ideological parameters of capitalist modernity. Furthermore, the role of the state in this process has not yet been thoroughly examined even though it is the most important determinant of NGO agency. It imposes limits to the autonomy of NGOs, and determines their very institutional nature, agenda, and politics.

Let me be clear: it is too soon to dismiss NGOs altogether. They have played, and will continue to play, a central role in producing new ideas and leadership for politically meaningful social transformation. In many instances, where all other democratic means have been exhausted, NGOs are the only institutions through which marginalized groups have been able to voice their concerns and organize their struggles. The evidence of their co-optation by adversaries should not blind us to the continuing importance of their interventions. Ultimately, it would be difficult, if not impossible, to explain social change without taking into account the vital role played by NGOs. However, while current scholarship is primarily concerned with determining the relative advantages and disadvantages of NGOs vis-à-vis the state and for-profit organizations (FPOs), I seek to refocus the debate on their constitutive role in effecting social change under modern capitalism. The relationship between NGOs and the state cannot meaningfully be explained outside the historical context of capitalist development; capitalism heightens the tensions between them. Some may find this theoretical approach reductionist and overly simplistic, but it is not: it reflects a political and moral choice. At the current juncture in the history of the global political economy, meaningful hope for social and environmental justice requires direct engagement with capital, and demands that we offer radical alternatives. Hence the primary focus of my analysis and of my claims on the charting of macrosocial patterns of relations between NGOs and the state, and the social, economic, and political conditions that shape those relations.

My aim is to contribute to a more reflective and politically engaged understanding of the role of NGOs in social change. Although the ideology of neoliberal capitalism has become dominant, the potential of NGOs to bring about substantive social transformation is undiminished. At the same time, one cannot ignore the shortcomings of current NGO theory and practice. We are presently experiencing a collective failure of imagination and a lack of political willingness to contemplate alternatives to capitalism and adjust our own lives accordingly. As the book makes clear, this lack of imagination is one result of the 'colonization' of progressive minds by the political economy of the NGO-industrial complex. I hope that this study will provide a resource for scholars and practitioners still concerned with democracy and with social and economic justice.

Jude L. Fernando
Clark University
February 2010

# Introduction: Theorizing Social Change—Beyond the Impasse

"It is necessary over and over again to engage in the critique of these fundamental concepts, in order that we may not unconsciously be ruled by them."

Albert Einstein[1]

This book explores the role of nongovernmental organizations (NGOs) in social change, focusing on what they do and how they are organized, and assesses their impact on state formation in Sri Lanka and Bangladesh under capitalist modernity. I examine the important ideas that emanate from NGOs, and the various practices that shape their agency and their ties with each other and the state. Using the NGO–state relationship as a focus, I provide an analysis of theories of social change in general, and development theory in its "postmodern" and "postcolonial" phases in particular, employing a historically grounded critical perspective on current claims about the progressive transformative potential of NGOs as "third sector" institutions.

The history of NGO activities also provides insights into nationalist and colonial historiographies, subjecting them to critical scrutiny—an essential prerequisite for achieving counterhegemonic social change. A broad focus on the continuities and discontinuities of NGO–state relations makes clear the process by which political actors exploit the NGO phenomenon, using NGOs as an arena in which popular versions of national history are produced, reconfigured, and contested to suit ideological ends. I find that NGOs play both a material and ideological role in social change ("NGOism"), and I offer some suggestions as to how we might re-imagine the social roles of NGOs to make the world a better place.

Institutions both large and small—from states, international corporations, and global NGOs, to neighborhood organizations, schools and local unions—are primary actors in the drama of social change. Social theory seeks to explain the agents, causes, and consequences of change, but theories are themselves the products of particular locations and histories, and are themselves embedded in the "life worlds" of institutions. The totality of institutions, as

1

constituted by the relations between them, makes up the social order: institutional change affects the evolution of society over time, connecting its past, present, and future. Similar institutions take on different meanings in different contexts, and studying them can provide a fruitful path to understanding the reasons for spatial differentiation in social development.

At the beginning of the new millennium, debates over the analytical and prescriptive frameworks applied to understanding and bringing about intentional social change appear to have arrived at an impasse. Existing theories and the solutions provided by modern forms of knowledge have proven insufficient and unsustainable. "Self-evident truths" are being seriously challenged, most notably by postmodernist/poststructuralist scholars, on the grounds that their theoretical foundations are flawed. These concerns were buttressed as post-Cold War optimism regarding a prosperous and peaceful social order began to give way to increasing levels of poverty, inequality, violence, and political uncertainty worldwide. These indicate a crisis of public and private institutions, highlighting an urgent need for new perspectives and approaches in order to make them more effective.

Hegemony involves the production, dissemination, and legitimization of norms, values, and practices that facilitate a social group's—or multiple social groups'—view and understanding of the world. Ideology achieves hegemonic status when it becomes widely accepted as a description of the past, present, and future, and induces social agents to act in one manner rather than in another. The term "NGO" is now a hegemonic category in social theory and practice, employed to organize and disseminate knowledge about a wide range of phenomena. It is even, one may argue, an ideology. NGO interventions in social development provide alternative descriptions of the history and future of the existing social order, leading actors to articulate and legitimize their ideas and practices accordingly. Today there are hardly any areas of social, cultural, or political life in which NGOs are not implicated. The current claim that NGOs function as a "third sector" in relation to the state and for-profit organizations (FPOs) demonstrates that an old state of affairs has been superseded by a new one.

## CRISIS OF IDENTITY: THE STATUS OF NGO–STATE RELATIONS

The definition of the term "NGO" is contested. Its ambiguity has long fascinated scholars, and it has received many rich and varied interpretations. In terms of substantive characteristics, the origins of NGOs in Bangladesh and Sri Lanka, for example, can be traced back to at least the precolonial period. The diversity of organizations identified as NGOs has surely increased, and controversy persists over the criteria for inclusion or exclusion in this grouping. Yet many discussions treat NGOs as though they belong to a unified institutional category, endowed with distinct characteristics relative to other institutions, all presumed to be consistent across time and space. This is simply not the case.

The UN Charter explicitly recognizes NGOs as partners. Article 71 states:

> The Economic and Social Council [ECOSOC] may make arrangements for consultation with non-governmental organizations, with [. . .] matters within its competence. Such arrangements may be made with international organizations and, where appropriate, with national organizations after consultation with the Member of the United Nations concerned.

According to Steinberg, the term "NGO" was deeply embedded in Cold War politics, "largely an afterthought stimulated by the Soviet Union's attempt to put a government-organized non-governmental organization (GONGO) on par with the International Labour Organization (ILO)."[2] To gain NGO status, the goals of the organizations had to be within the "UN economic and social ambit." Membership was decided by the Committee on Non-Governmental Organizations, elected each year by the ECOSOC from among its member governments.

The UN definition includes "any international organization which is not established by a governmental entity or intergovernmental agreement."[3] However, NGOs "with consultative status with the ECOSOC are accredited for participation in UN fora, by merely expressing their interest to participate to become accredited and [. . .] other NGOs wishing to participate can apply through the respective conference secretariat." The role of governments in decisions on membership was retained, as "it was decided that accreditation processes are the prerogative of member states exercised through the respective preparatory committee."[4] The World Bank, which has increased its dialogue with NGOs, prefers environmental NGOs to trade unions, docile outfits to grassroots groups, and libertarian NGOs to socialist or communitarian ones.[5] Despite soliciting the services of NGOs, states remain the Bank's main partners in the implementation of its projects.

There is no consensus, even among NGOs, about their institutional identity. Their preference for different designations has resulted in the use of more than twelve terms, each of which modifies states' definitions and represents an attempt to recontextualize state–NGO relations. Regardless of these differences, legal definitions impose a certain degree of homogeneity on the sector as a whole. Even in the international domain, the laws of individual nation-states bind NGOs. Generally, organizations outlawed by states are not recognized by international donor bodies, even when their substantive characteristics are similar to those of typical NGOs. The identification of a given organization as an NGO is determined not so much by its internal characteristics as by its external relationships and political affiliations.

The claim that the difference between NGOs and other organizations is legally absolute limits the possibilities for evaluating NGOs' role in development. The abstract nature of legal definitions obscures relations of power and domination. Clifford Geertz aptly observed: "Law is local knowledge, not placeless principle."[6] Although law appears to be abstract and determinate, it is, nonetheless, a social artifact, articulated and interpreted by social actors in varying contexts.[7] Legal recognition may not be a good indicator of the unequal distribution of power between NGOs with respect to the state and society; studies based on legal definitions are misleading unless they are grounded in an analysis of the institutional and power relationships from which those definitions arise.

David Korten divides the evolution of NGOs into four generations: relief and welfare, community development, sustainable systems development, and people's movements.[8] He is not the only one to develop a typology of NGOs,[9] but the differences between Korten's categories are not entirely clear. Rigid historical periodization is misleading and imposes an artificial homogeneity on categories of NGOs. R.L. Stirrat, referring to development NGOs, counters:

[A] striking feature of the emerging new orthodoxy of participatory development is the sharing of similar objectives, expressed in words such as "empowerment," "social mobilization," and "participatory development," by international financial agencies, governments and NGOs in describing their respective policy agendas. Such words are not value free: language is not easily transparent.[10]

Most literature derives the common institutional characteristics of NGOs by comparing their substantive features with those of FPOs. According to legal stipulations, NGOs cannot earn profits. But this doesn't prevent them from engaging in profit-making ventures or from forming partnerships with FPOs. Growing pressure on NGOs to be financially self-sufficient has forced them to function increasingly like FPOs. While surplus for NGOs may be different from profit for FPOs, the organizational culture of the for-profit sector has a significant influence on the overall activities of non-profits. When we focus on the relationships between NGOs and individual corporations, the broader meaning and implications of their counterhegemonic economic practices is obscured, and we cannot understand the impact of NGO interventions in microfinance, good governance, and corporate social responsibility.

Current practices suggest that NGOs increasingly model their programs according to a policy framework shared by neoliberal donors, particularly governments and commercial banks. Some donors of international aid also transfer funds to NGOs indirectly by stipulating that beneficiary governments use NGOs as subcontractors. But availability of resources and the possibility of increased activity by NGOs do not necessarily mean that they have the freedom to make decisions about their own programs, or even to ensure that their programs reflect their interests. These practices, coupled with pressure on NGOs to embrace financial self-sufficiency and market-friendly development programs, have blurred the (contextually specific and highly negotiable) ideological and institutional boundaries between states, markets, and NGOs. The outcomes of NGO activity are largely determined by the forces that shape "policy coordination" between these institutional actors.

An important characteristic of NGOs is their ability to "mobilise social energy and resources through the mechanisms of shared values and expectations."[11] Volunteers now play a marginal role in the activities of NGOs in most developing countries and traditional forms of voluntarism have declined. NGOs employ fewer volunteer staff and experience less success in mobilizing local voluntary contributions for their activities than ever before. According to one of the field workers of Sarvodaya:

Poor people are not willing to provide voluntary labour unless the NGOs offer tangible benefits. These same poor people are more willing to provide voluntary labour to organizations directly associated with political parties, as such organizations are more promising in terms of tangible benefits in the long run.[12]

Voluntary social mobilizations are based on existing social norms, values, and power relations, and have consequences that extend beyond specific projects into larger political contexts. As Robert Wirsing points out in his study *Voluntary Associations in Nagpur,* "The history of politics in significant ways has [always] been the history of the politics of voluntary associations." Commenting on the relationship between hierarchically structured village society and voluntary associations, Wirsing noted that voluntary associations, regardless of their stated intentions, are "traditional agencies in modern garb—that protect and enrich privilege, [and] exploit, manipulate and hold subservient the poor."[13] The above suggests that terms such as governmental, commercial, and voluntary cannot help us to distinguish NGOs from other institutions.

The many different taxonomic systems applied to NGOs are "instruments of cognition and communication which are the precondition for the establishment of meaning and the consensus on meaning."[14] Definitions become ideological constructions that reflect and shape relations of power and domination. Understanding the institutional identity of NGOs is an integral part of exploring the wider issues concerning them. As David Lewis puts it, "Each term [is] clearly rooted in different cultural, historical and economic conditions. [Any given term] sometimes reflects genuine difference while at other times it simply generates conceptual confusion."[15] Such problems cannot be overcome by inventing new terms because each is influenced by the politics of the definer and includes some organizations at the expense of others, based on particular notions of their commonalities and differences.

Despite their limitations, legal definitions applied to NGOs in their specific locations appear to be useful, in so far as they are applied consistently to all organizations in those areas. NGOs can function as legal entities only within the institutional parameters set by the state. While these definitions do not reveal the full complexity of the relationships between NGOs and other institutions, the strategic mobilization of these definitions—by NGOs themselves and others—is important because definitions affect the outcomes of NGO activities. Typologies and legal definitions are most useful for examining NGOs when one takes into account the meanings and power relations implicitly reflected in them. The state has the legal power to define NGOs, and it also has the power to interpret definitions according to its own interests. Those definitions and interpretations are often inconsistent and even incoherent across time and space.

The central challenge for social theory, then, is to explain how these ideologically and operationally diverse organizations, which do not command resources or social constituencies comparable to those of the state, are represented as a unified institutional category and believed to present the state with a significant challenge. The proponents of the NGO phenomenon have described it as an "association revolution" spreading around the world in the late twentieth century.[16] NGOs have rapidly become the new institutional means by which society seeks to express a wide variety of demands for equality, justice, human rights, and sustainable development.[17] As agents of social transformation and providers of welfare and social services, NGOs have facilitated an ideological shift in the focus of social change from "radical revolution" to "empowerment." Their increasing visibility and involvement in social service delivery has validated neoliberal claims about the limitations of the state, and many observers claim that NGOs have succeeded in translating their agendas into public policy, redefining the trajectories and boundaries of political change in their respective societies and on an international level. There is widespread optimism about the potential of NGOs to shift state policy toward social responsiveness, accountability, and transparency. (Similar arguments are also made on behalf of the for-profit sector.) Anthony Giddens claims that these trends signify the rise of "third way" politics and provide a framework for thinking about and formulating policies that transcend the limitations and excesses of both socialism and neoliberal capitalism.[18]

As noted above, claims about the role of NGOs in social change tend to focus on their relationships with states and FPOs. NGOs, according to their proponents, are better equipped to effect meaningful change in the areas of sustainable development, environmental justice, humanitarian assistance and human rights, good governance, conflict resolution, and peacebuilding. NGOs are credited with bringing these themes into public fora, institutionalizing them as legitimate goals of social development, and implementing them either independently or in direct collaboration with states and for-profit organizations.

Although the precise nature of the relationship between NGOs and the state is unclear, it is generally accepted that NGOs must to some extent be defined in terms of that relationship. According to Lester M. Salamon, the director of the Center for Civil Society Studies at Johns Hopkins University, "There has been a general questioning of the capacity of the state to carry out a whole host of functions [. . .]. [The] NGO sector represents another way of organizing the common business of society."[19] States are under increasing pressure to incorporate NGOs into their programs and must reckon with them as a powerful political force. As already noted, the incorporation of NGOs into governmental activities is often a condition attached to foreign aid, and NGOs are frequently entrusted with the responsibility of creating the conditions for good governance as well as promoting the development of civil society.

For some, the astonishing growth of NGOs signals a new kind of global revolution. "It is reshaping politics and economics both at the domestic and global levels," observed Salamon. "I believe it is as important a development to the latter part of the 20th century as the rise of the nation-state was at the end of the 19th century."[20] These claims are buttressed by the role played by NGOs in the events leading to the defeat of apartheid in South Africa, the end of dictatorship in Chile, the political transformation of the Philippines, the overthrow of communist regimes in Central Europe, the gradual withdrawal of the state from direct intervention in social development, and the creation of the World Social Forum in January 2001 in Porto Alegre. NGO participation in struggles for basic freedoms and social justice have been instrumental in current attempts to rethink state-centric citizenship, and in the formulation of key social concepts such as "transnationalism," "post-Westphalianism," and "international citizenship."[21]

The growth of NGOs in response to the diminishing role of the state in social development, and the concomitant expansion of the role of civil society, is touted as evidence of a shift in the locus of social change, away from the state and markets and toward society. The transition from welfare capitalism to neoliberal capitalism, in which the state plays a lesser role, is now viewed as a fundamental break from, instead of a response to, an internal crisis of capitalism at a particular moment in time. Shifts from progressive to regressive taxation, and from social welfare expenditure to the subsidization of private industry, are mistakenly interpreted as signs of the state's declining power over the economy. These claims ignore the ways in which state power is exercised through new regulatory regimes in order to facilitate the mobility of capital. As James Petras has noted, "In a deeper sense, the welfarists failed to recognize the underlying drive of capital to understand how democracy would be subverted from within—by increasing influence of non-elected officials and powerful national and international financial institutions."[22] And Sassen points out: "Even though transnationalism and deregulation have reduced the role of the state in the governance and economic processes, the state continues to remain as the guarantor of the rights of capital whether national or foreign."[23] The reduction of investments by the state in social development does not necessarily mean a diminishing of state power.

In some analyses, the question is not the strength or weakness of the state, but rather of its bases of power—that is, of the interests that it serves: "Is the capitalist state the instrument of the particular ruling-class groups that occupy positions within its machine of government, or is the state able to look after the interest of capitalism because it is structurally set up to do so?"[24] But this question is not grounded in a sound theory of state power in relation to the reproduction of capital. Instead, it retains a conventional view of the "autonomy of the state"—a political state somehow independent of economy and society. Current analyses of the NGO–state relationship fail to answer three important questions: How is the autonomy of the state articulated and reproduced? What is its impact on the development of capitalism and therefore its implications for the NGO–state relationship? And what are the ideological and institutional characteristics of the state that NGOs must advocate if they wish to prevent their agendas from being co-opted by state actors? If we remember that NGO history dates to the precolonial period, we understand that their evolution cannot be entirely explained in terms of the failure of the nation-state; many organizations have come into being for reasons other than state failures. Current studies take the difference between the state and NGOs for granted, and only analyze NGOs' comparative advantage in responding to social issues. We must instead theorize the state and the NGOs as mutually constitutive within a larger process of social transformation.

## CIVIL SOCIETY AND NGOs

Civil society is often thought to be the site of progressive democratic political activity which many critics expect will birth a "new hegemonic project, that of the liberal conservative discourse which seeks to articulate the neoliberal defense of the free market economy with [the] profoundly anti-egalitarian cultural and social traditionalism of conservatism."[25] The project offers "engagement, deeper commitment, more participation and heightened solidarity [than] seem desirable in any social order—particularly one plagued by cheapened politics and civic decline."[26] In the European context, it is the "bourgeois public sphere [which] evolved in the tension-charged field between state and society," and thus "it remained itself a part of the private realm."[27] In the public sphere, private individuals, though motivated by personal interests, can enter into and create social transformation by "viewing themselves as persons capable of entering 'purely human' relations with one another."[28] Through the rational-critical debates that take place in the "world of letters," individualistic bourgeois subjectivity becomes intra-subjective, what Habermas calls "audience oriented."[29] Proponents of civil society argue that it will revive communities, provide a moral alternative to the relentless pursuit of self-interest, enhance the accountability and transparency of government agencies and reinvigorate the public sphere as an effective arena of positive social change.

The main problem with the above definition of civil society is that it remains an "unavoidably nebulous concept and elastic conception that does not lend itself to a great deal of precision."[30] It can appeal to a broad spectrum of different ideological and operational orientations.[31] While a vibrant civil society is sometimes regarded as a panacea for a multiplicity of social ills, it potentially serves as a source of both freedom and oppression. As John Ehrenberg notes, as important perhaps as the normative and structural clarity of the concept of civil society is an understanding of the economic and political forces that constitute it.[32]

The need for strong civil society in developing countries is allegedly demonstrated by the weakness, inefficiency, and failures of government. Neoliberal capitalist logic begins with the claim that development needs sound policies and accountable and transparent institutions to implement them. Accountability and transparency "depends upon the existence of autonomous centres of economic and social power that can act as the watchdogs over the activities of the politicians and government authorities."[33] But there is no sound empirical research that proves that in their advocacy roles NGOs are more effective than any given government:

In certain ways, ironically, [. . .] advocacy by the government on behalf of the citizens was better than that of NGOs, in that it gave detailed instructions to the public on exactly what government workers or contractors should and should not be doing.[34]

The unique feature of civil society is its intermediaries between the state and families—numerous associations enjoying "autonomy from the state." Each of these associations has "one important role to play among others to influence the state on behalf of their members."[35] Blair warns that civil society is not an unmitigated blessing when diverse interest groups are making diverse demands on the state: "A debilitated state continuously pummeled by conflicting special groups may [. . .] become feeble to act in the interest of the citizens as a whole."[36] In order to develop a better understanding of civil society, we must question the *ceteris paribus* assumption in economics. As Blair asks:

> What are the *ceteris* (other things), and what are the *paribus* (equal) for democratic development, and what kind of policies are needed to ensure their maintenance? Pluralism in politics is similar, in that it appears to be the best way to enable citizens to tell governments what they want and for government to respond. However, if we are to promote democratic pluralism we need to know a great deal more about what it really does for the polity, about determining just what the *ceteris* are, and about ensuring that they remain *paribus*.[37]

In its more radical formulations, civil society is envisioned as a site for the launching of protests against neoliberal capitalist economic restructuring by the state. But current studies have not paid much attention to the possibility that the institutional diversity of civil society and patron–client networks can be exploited by the state in order to divert any direct opposition against it. The functioning of civil society and the channeling of social dissent into a multiplicity of institutions, including NGOs, can lead to the reproduction of state power. According to Rob Jenkins, there is a risk of "robbing pro-democracy movements of their force; in [civil society's] obsession with maintaining the autonomy from the centers of social and economic power, it jeopardizes the healthy development of 'political society'"[38]

If one considers the context in which the notion of civil society is articulated, then *ceteris paribus* seems to underpin neoliberal capitalist political economy. NGOs do not have the legal mandate to challenge these fundamental ideological underpinnings and institutions and, unsurprisingly, they are rarely willing to do so. As Geoffrey Woods points out, "the preoccupation with privatization and markets on the one hand and good governance on the other do not easily sit side by side."[39] However, in the scholarly literature, the definition of good governance remains ambiguous, particularly in the context of the relationship between good governance, the imperatives of the neoliberal political economy, and empowerment goals advocated by NGOs.

Current studies of civil society are mostly concerned with its role in responding to the urgent economic and political issues in developing countries. Less emphasis is given to the analytical relevance, normative significance, and political implications of the rediscovery of civil society for NGOs in those countries. The fundamental limitation of these studies is the assumption that the crucial determinants of civil society are different from the basic determinants of markets and the state. We must subject civil society to an analysis based on the general determinants of social change, because "any civil society can be created, supported, manipulated, or repressed by any state, and it is profoundly misleading to conceptualize apart from political power."[40] Therefore, the relevance of civil society for contemporary politics can be grasped only by analyzing what its "constituent structures do, how they are organized, and what political and economic forces are at work— no matter how strenuously some theorists try to describe it as an autonomous sphere of democratic activity."[41]

## GLOBALIZATION AND NGOs

More and more NGOs have begun to operate in transnational fora, thereby tying their local activities to global ones. NGOs are now the main force behind the transnationalization of local issues, such as the water crisis in Cochabamba, Bolivia, the Narmada Dam project in India, and human rights abuses in East Timor, and have brought such issues visibility and organizational reach well beyond the boundaries of their respective nation-states. Consequently, within the United Nations and other transnational bodies, NGOs enjoy consultative status. They are even permitted to question the governments of their countries of origin. NGOs have earned praise for their role in producing a number of successful international treaties on the environment, human rights, and sustainable development. They have been at the center of protests against US and UK involvement in Iraq and have highlighted the risk of national security legislation undermining civil liberties. In 1992, a campaign to ban land mines initiated by a coalition of six NGOs led to the Mine Ban Treaty which was finally put into effect in 1997. In June of 2003, a group of NGOs affiliated with the World Court Project warned the leaders of the Canadian and British governments that the prosecutor of the International Criminal Court (ICC) would investigate their actions if they used illegal force against Iraq.[42] Perhaps the most influential role played by NGOs involves framing agendas for international treaties and pushing governments to address issues that they would otherwise neglect.

The increasingly transnational character of NGOs is further evidence of the erosion of state sovereignty under globalization, and forces us to take a fresh look at conventional theories that regard the state as the central organization of the "world system." The movement of the world away from the nation-state system towards a "global village" is apparent in the rapid and aggressive movement of capital, commodities, ideas, and persons across national boundaries. States are relinquishing direct ownership of industry, participation in economic development, and the delivery of services. The protests against globalization, too, have embraced a minimalist notion of the state. As David Slater has noted:

> Terms such as "globalization," the "global–local nexus," "critical globalism," the "global condition," all reflect a widening sensibility of the need to go beyond the national boundaries. Stretching across these boundaries and making global connections have been a characteristic of some of the new forms of mobilization of resistance and movement that have acquired a high degree of fluidity and flexibility across national boundaries.[43]

Because transnational capitalism reconfigures modes of production "in ways that are parasitic on the nation-state and its institutions, but rely on disempowered citizenry [...] it continues to exploit labor, but redefines and differentiates who that labor is in terms of gender, race and nation."[44] Hence, those who consider globalization to be the defining characteristic of the current political economy argue that contemporary social change needs to be theorized at the transnational level rather than that of the nation-state. It is between these two levels that NGOs play an influential role.

The reality of globalization and corresponding claims about the decline of the nation-state are subject to criticism from a wide variety of perspectives. Peter Gowan writes: "An enormous outpouring of academic literature has failed to provide an agreed [upon] view of [globalization's] physiognomy or its location and some reputable academics of Right and Left even question its very existence."[45] Despite increasing economic interdependence internationally, domestic markets, savings, and industry continue to be crucial for capital formation, economic growth, and employment. Trends in global financial flows show a phenomenon that appears closer to "triadization"—a high concentration of financial flows in Europe, North America, and Japan—than to full-scale globalization.[46] While world markets determine economic policies, countries' competitiveness depends above all on their national policies. In response to this growing importance of the state to the global economy, the term internationalization seems a more appropriate descriptor than globalization.

NGO participation in transnational networks and fora and their increasing influence over social, economic, and political change are seen as evidence of an emerging "transnational society" or "world polity."[47] The World Social Forum, established in January 2001 in Porto Alegre, is a case in point.[48] Participants at this gathering sought to oppose neoliberal capitalist globalization. They focused on common themes and they brought different organizations together from different parts of the world. Such meetings and movements are unique in that they are located outside the boundaries of the nation-state and are not directly subordinated to its interests. The implications of these organizations for the world order have rejuvenated old debates in international relations theory between realists, neorealists, and Grotians.

In contrast to classical realists, who maintain that the world order is anarchic, and that only "states and international organizations" matter internationally, the neorealists conceptualize international order within a web of international institutions or "networks of interdependence."[49] The argument is that, while these transnational institutions effectively influence the state, especially when it is weak, they can also be explained as a functional necessity of the state. Thus the primacy of the state is maintained. For realists and neorealists, international institutions can only prescribe "principles, rules, and procedures," but state actors must ratify these and the state is conceptualized as pursuing self-interest voluntarily.[50]

Boli and Thomas argue that both the realist and the neorealist positions are inadequate because both positions dismiss culture as irrelevant. Boli and Thomas's ideas emphasize two aspects of culture: its organizational function, and its global scale.[51] They point out that "international actions came, to a considerable extent, from [the] transnational INGO [international NGO] sector." As states entered the process, they responded not only to their own or societal interests but also to concepts and principles promoted by INGOs. At times, "states were more explicit agents of INGO authority."[52]

In contrast to state authority, the authority of the INGOs is "neither coercive nor commanding; above all it is cultural." The power and legitimacy of INGOs are derived from what Boli and Thomas call "world cultural authority." Their description of this authority is normative and ambiguous: "It depends on widely and deeply legitimated theories of the ultimate source of sovereignty, the proper constitution of rational action, the worthwhile ends of human endeavors, and the proper organization of collective structures to solve world problems."[53] However, they do not clarify the meanings of "proper organization" and "rational action." These are simply considered as an "essentially cultural process, and the exercise of cultural authority is difficult to observe." Employing the concept of culture without contextualizing it within the capitalist economy, Boli and Thomas fail to establish a fundamental difference between their account and those of the realists and neorealists.

Several articles in Boli and Thomas's volume attempt to take into account the role played by INGOs within the context of global capitalism. The authors demonstrate that while the "capitalist pursuit of profit is legitimated by the standardization projects" of INGOs, "they [the INGOs] are circumscribed by a meaning structure that is not reducible to the world economic system." They argue, however, that the imperatives of capitalist ideology are, in the final analysis, subordinated to more universal goals of "[the] welfare and comfort of the human species and, as a necessary component of this goal, the health of the planet and all its life forms."[54] Therefore INGOs have managed to lock states into a subordinate role, as INGO legitimacy derives from hypothetically universal norms and values. In this process, the "states take the back seat, and the deadly struggles between the states are not permitted to shape the products of global standards organisations."[55]

Arguments regarding the foundation of the role of INGOs in "cultural principles" are also unconvincing. Their claims about INGOs' capacity to use cultural principles to limit the negative effects of capitalism are based on an a priori distinction between economic and cultural principles and an assignation of superior moral status to the latter. They do not systematically analyze the complex ways in which capitalism uses culture as a means of profit maximization or the impact of the interplay between culture and profit maximization on state formation. They mistakenly assume that cultural principles are a privileged site from which INGOs derive the ability to overpower state actors, without asking how it is possible for states and INGOs to use the same cultural forces in different ways. Similarly, they assume that the economic vision associated with INGOs' culturally derived legitimacy is somehow different from the economic organization that characterizes the capitalist state. Such assumptions have led to the erroneous claim that INGOs are "exercising a surprising degree of authority in the contemporary world. This authority is neither coercive nor commanding. Above all, it is cultural."[56] INGOs are thus ascribed a superior moral status capable of transcending diverse social, political, and economic contexts and serving the common good.

An emphasis on the formal institutions of the state does not explain the "multilayered complexity of political reality"[57] that informs the organization and exercise of state power. It does not help us understand what Robert Cox referred to as the "internationalization of the state," whereby the state disciplines society through myriad "monetary and fiscal policies, industrial regulation, social policies, the restructuring of the welfare state, and even the reconstitution of social obligations; for example, an ideological attack on alternative lifestyles, and prioritization of traditional values through social policy initiatives."[58] The ways in which the formal and substantive characteristics of the state and NGOs have been redefined and reconfigured in the context of globalization are too often overlooked, but an examination of these issues raises serious questions about the role of NGOs. As Stephen Cummins has noted:

> To put it in stark terms, they are becoming the delivery agency for a global soup kitchen, handing out meager comfort amidst harsh economic changes and complex political emergencies, in a world that is characterized by global economic integration and the social exclusion of low income communities, as well as continuing and widespread levels of civil strife.[59]

Critics continue to argue that NGOs are not comparable to state actors in terms of their respective roles in social change. Success stories are few and far between and have certainly not been replicated on a global scale. Skeptics characterize NGOs as an "elusive promise" and an "unattainable panacea."[60] Even some former advocates for NGOs are questioning the extent of the contributions they can actually make to development, and NGOs are increasingly viewed as counterproductive and even potentially retrograde social agents. Some recent failures only contribute to these growing doubts. NGOs were unable to persuade the United States and some other countries to ratify international conventions such as the Mine Ban Treaty, the ICC, and the Kyoto Convention. The pressure exerted by the governments of some advanced industrialized countries has forced the ICC to limit its jurisdictional powers to prosecute crimes against humanity, effectively shielding those states from scrutiny by multilateral institutions. Barbara Crosette wrote of Washington's ICC policy:

> The U.S. Bush administration's obsession with the new International Criminal Court shows no signs of abating any time soon, and anger is rising around the United Nations at the apparent willingness of Washington to undermine all international peacekeeping if that is what it takes to curtail the tribunal's jurisdiction—and not just over Americans.[61]

On July 1, 2003, the White House announced that it was cutting off military aid to Colombia and 34 other countries because they had refused to grant American citizens immunity from prosecution by the new ICC.[62] And despite NGO opposition, the rapid nuclear buildup in Pakistan, India, Iran, and China continues. The parochial interests of these states, rather than the objectives of international treaties and laws, continue to frustrate and undermine the possibility of ending the nuclear arms race in the foreseeable future.

In another defeat for NGOs, the main players in the 2003 war against Iraq ignored worldwide protests and calls for greater accountability. International outcry by NGOs against human rights abuses by the Taliban became a serious concern of the US government only after the attacks of September 11, 2001. Prior to that date, US government and transnational oil corporations' good relations with Taliban officials were unaffected.[63] The United States' and Britain's success in mobilizing the patron–client model to solicit the support of other states for the Iraq invasion once again underscored the importance of state power in international affairs and revealed a complete disregard for NGO demands for accountability and transparency. The Iraq war demonstrates the political will of powerful states to ignore international norms pertaining to the conduct of war, human rights, humanitarian assistance, and freedom of expression. The military appropriated the functions of humanitarian assistance (i.e., military humanitarianism) and also provided the frameworks in which humanitarian NGOs and media (i.e., embedded journalism) were to function.

The NGOs' abilities to compel states to compromise their neoliberal capitalist economic policies and national security practices in favor of commonly shared human rights, sustainable development, and environmental justice are in serious doubt. Now more than ever before, anti-NGO rhetoric by state representatives and others is having a powerful ideological impact on NGO–state relations.

The NGO-mediated "new social contracts," between citizens of different polities on the one hand and new structures of authority at different levels of the world system on the other, are viewed with much suspicion and concern by state actors. Tensions between states and NGOs in many parts of the world have increased to a point where governments now demand greater control and oversight. In June 2003, the American Enterprise Institute, a Washington think tank that was particularly influential with the George W. Bush administration, held a conference entitled "Non-Governmental Organizations: Growing Power of an Unelected Few." The name was justified as follows:

> While non-governmental organizations [. . .] such as Amnesty International, Greenpeace, and Oxfam have made significant contributions to human rights, the environment, and development, they are using their growing prominence and power to pursue a "liberal" agenda at the international level that threatens U.S. sovereignty and free-market capitalism.

The conferees warned: "The extraordinary growth of advocacy NGOs in liberal democracies has the potential to undermine the sovereignty of constitutional democracies, as well as the effectiveness of credible NGOs."[64]

In June 2003, India's Home Ministry blacklisted more than 800 NGOs in north eastern India for alleged links to antigovernment separatist groups.[65] NGOs have also proven their ineffectiveness at alleviating human rights violations, starvation, and malnutrition in Zimbabwe, where Robert Mugabe's government banned several key organizations including Save the Children and Oxfam, and proposed new legislation to bring under government control those NGOs that they accuse of aiding opposition political forces.[66] In 2002, less than 24 hours after the departure of US Secretary of State

Colin Powell, and following a promise by Israel's government to ease movement restrictions on Palestinians as a "goodwill gesture," the Israeli Defense Forces imposed a full closure over the entire Gaza Strip. In 2004, the Coordinator of Government Activities in the Eretz Territories Office informed international NGOs that they were prohibited indefinitely from entering the Strip.[67] And since 2008, the Sri Lankan government has withstood calls from NGOs both for a ceasefire and for the release of detainees, and has refused to grant NGOs access to conflict areas.

Government regulation and expulsion of NGOs has increased the administrative expenses of their operations and made it difficult for them to function independently. NGOs have been silenced by government allegations that they are undermining national security and sovereignty. Their ability to influence states and protect human rights has, subsequently, been progressively eroded. The balance of power between powerful states does not show signs of shifting in response to NGO demands that they better serve human well-being and environmental justice.

Some critics doubt that NGOs have halted the convergence of state interests and the advance of neoliberal capitalism. The once popular claim that globalization will trigger the demise of the nation-state no longer enjoys intellectual currency, and the state has once again been placed at the center of social theory.[68] The current global economic crises inaugurated by the collapse of markets have made NGOs around the world extremely vulnerable to the failure of the private-sector financial institutions upon which they depend for their continued existence. While reducing funding for NGOs, including those providing essential services to the underprivileged, governments have increased by trillions of dollars subsidies to the very companies whose corruption and mismanagement hastened the economic downturn. There is no evidence that NGOs can withstand the discriminatory actions of the state. The likelihood that a government will concede to the demands of any particular NGO is entirely determined by strategic economic and political relationships between states, rather than by values of human rights or social and environmental justice. Governments alternate between dismissing and justifying the claims and interventions of NGOs, skillfully linking NGO activities with institutionalized memories of colonialism and imperialism. Such state exploits, while providing legitimization for claims of its "national culture-based" autonomy, also replace the old tyrannies of universalism with new tyrannies of cultural relativism. The repeated failures and internal crises of NGOs have tarnished their public image and weakened them politically, leading to an identity crisis of sorts for the sector.[69]

There is still a great deal to be said about NGOs. Indeed, as an institutional formation, they remain significantly undertheorized. Jenny Pearce's comment sums up the chief problem with current scholarship:

> [NGOs] are appearing in a world in which the collapse of intellectual and political reference points has prompted an eclectic outpouring of ideas and views, without organized and coherent debate. As a result, good thinking and writing is lost; much is duplicated and reinvented; people talk but do not listen; people write but do not read; and vice versa. At the beginning of the millennium, development debates—if they can be called that—are like concentric circles, orbiting without touching.[70]

Yet one cannot ignore the intellectual challenges that NGOs present to our established knowledge and practices. They continue to evolve in creative and unpredictable ways as they confront the crises of capitalist modernity. If politically engaged social theorists are to face these intellectual challenges, and assist NGOs in accomplishing their important social goals without becoming a casualty of their excesses, they should question the prevailing view of NGOs as progressive "third sector" institutions.

There is good reason to be skeptical of the claim that the great ideological and operational diversity of the organizations is the main reason for the shortcomings of current NGO scholarship. The theoretical and political claims for the progressive potential and agency of NGOs are, in a word, overstated. Critical blindness on this point has everything to do with the current impasse in social theory. Theory's progress is hindered by a number of factors. Most importantly, theorists lack practical experience of the social processes and power relationships embodied in NGOs. In turn, they misunderstand how these are implicated in the concrete social phenomena of everyday life. Claims about NGOs often define them in opposition to the state and markets, when, in fact, the contrary is the case. The positive outcomes of activism are often attributed to NGOs, while the negative outcomes are attributed to the state and markets.

The lack of studies of NGO–state–market relations has only perpetuated such misperceptions. For example, the evaluation of programs for the empowerment of women through microcredit loans may measure success on the basis of final loan repayment rates. However, these results are tied to long-term investments by the state in education and agricultural subsidies. On the whole, microloans do not affect larger social processes that are oppressive to women.[71] How do we make forceful claims about the outcomes of NGO activities without understanding the interaction of many different institutions and players with diverse ideological, operational, resource, and power differentials? A more practical approach would entail examination of the complex interactions between structure, agency, and power in the shaping of NGO agency.

## CAPITAL, STATE, NGOs, AND SOCIAL CHANGE: A THEORETICAL FRAMEWORK

It is necessary to theorize the interconnected roles of NGOs and the state if one wishes to understand the ways in which they both constitute and are constituted by their respective trajectories of social change. This book considers the vexed roles played by NGOs in Bangladesh and Sri Lanka and their implications for current debates about social change. It explores the agency of NGOs and rethinks dominant theories of social change, bringing together debates about NGOs and state formation and resituating them in the historical context of capitalist modernity.

A concise political economy of NGOs—as both a concept and a process—must be understood in terms of their involvement in social change. The separation of the economic and the political is theoretical rather than practical, and this study both historicizes and theorizes the appearance of such distinctions. The political economy approach explains NGO practices both in terms of their ideals and their practices. In pursuing their goals, NGOs enter into a variety of relations with other institutional actors who hold diverse ideological and operational orientations and among whom the distribution of resources and power is often uneven. The outcomes of these relationships range from compliance and compromise to conflict and resistance, and the choices available are historically and contextually determined.

Among these actors the state remains the central institution, and the different roles that NGOs assume in different locations need to be theorized in terms of their relationships with states. In NGO agendas, the state is identified simultaneously as a target of influence and change, a collaborator, and an institution that provides legal legitimacy. Differences in state formation and the varying intersections of states and NGOs in diverse historical and geographical settings are too often ignored. When these relationships are discussed, they are usually mentioned merely as outcomes of accumulated practices or actions, rather than in terms of their concreteness as constitutive agents of social reproduction. Moreover, state–NGO relationships are generally analyzed with excessive emphasis on the formal institutions of the state; scant attention is given to the complexities involved in the exercise of state power over society.

Let me explain why I prefer to use the term "state formation" instead of simply "the state." States are evolving institutions; they are "never formed once and for all."[72] The term state formation captures the inherently historical and relational character of the state, which I think is useful for theoretical and substantive analysis. State formation is a complex and ongoing process. As Timothy Mitchell notes:

> [I]t is unreasonable to separate the material forms of the state from the ideological, or the real from the illusory. The state idea and the state system are better seen as two aspects of the same process [. . .] [The] networks of institutional arrangements and political practice that form the material substance of the state are diffused and ambiguously defined at its edges, whereas the public imagery of the state as an ideological construct are more coherent.[73]

Mitchell's insight recalls Foucault's notion of "governmentality," which implies that the state should not be understood as the sum of its parts but as a method of governance that takes people and economies as its objects. Governmentality takes into account the administration of nature and society by the state through the production, simplification, legitimization, and manipulation of knowledge.[74] The notion of governmentality is extremely useful for understanding the state because it explores the daily practices of government in their complex relations to the various ways in which "truth" is produced in social, cultural, and political spheres.[75] It is a conceptual tool with which to problematize and deconstruct widely accepted accounts of the state. It is, at the same time, subject to a number of limitations. Foucault avoids the "ideological" aspect of government and instead focuses primarily on the technical and knowledge-based practices that directly shape subjectivity. He attempts to explain political processes without identifying political actors.[76] Similar concerns are raised about the distinctions between the "governmentalised state" and the "interventionalist state," between the "governmental" and the "political," and between the "state" and the "non-state" in governmentality studies.[77]

I approach the role of NGOs in state formation by viewing them and the state less as autonomous actors and more as co-evolving institutional formations within the context of capitalist development. I seek to understand how an ideologically and operationally diverse set of organizations came to terms with capitalist modernity and what impact that relationship has had on state formation in Bangladesh and Sri Lanka since the latter part of the eighteenth century. I theorize the seemingly dualistic relationship between NGOs and states and its implications for understanding the role of NGOs in social change. This study demonstrates that, while the ideological positions espoused by different NGOs may be diverse, they are ultimately embedded within the same social, cultural, economic, and political processes operating in society at large. I attempt to clarify the relationship between NGOs and the process of state formation by considering their complicity in the reproduction of state power. Sri Lanka and Bangladesh are home to some of the largest and most highly regarded NGOs in the world and their rise has profoundly shaped current views.

Social change is an ongoing process of "the metabolism between man and nature." The metabolism is the social production of life, which Marx called the mode of production. He wrote:

> In the social production of their life, men enter into definite relations that are indispensable and independent of their will, relations of production, which correspond to a definite stage of development of their material productive forces. The sum total of these relations of production constitutes the economic structure of society, the real foundation, on which raises a legal and political superstructure and to which correspond definite forms of social consciousness. The mode of production of material life conditions the social, political and intellectual life process in general. It is not the consciousness of men that determines their being, but, on the contrary, their social being that determines their consciousness.[78]

Mode of production here refers to a combination of forces and relations of production—a specific historically occurring set of factors in the way that human beings organize their production.[79] It cannot be reduced to a material activity, because it is a *social* activity which takes place within the realm of natural human relations. Since meeting basic human needs is a social process, human nature is "social and intra-subjective."[80] The individual and society cannot be "two mutually exclusive entities" because "each concept includes within itself certain moments of the other."[81] Analysis of the relations between the two allows us to understand the link between being and consciousness. Marx condemns "old materialism" as "vulgar materialism" because in the case of the latter "the object, the reality, sensibility, is conceived only in the form of the object or of perception, but not as sensuous human activity, practice, not subjectively."[82] The concept of mode of production is a useful way of understanding "major variations in political and economic arrangements and calls us to visualize their effect."[83]

One way in which social experience varies across different modes of production is by the wide array of institutions that give meaning and structure to our thoughts and actions. Hence, institutional or structural variation is central to understanding social change, which, in turn, is always embedded in a mode or modes of production. Notably, *institution* is a broader term than *organization*, since the former includes norms, values, and ideologies that shape the practices of the latter.[84] If changes in the mode of production are dynamic and proliferative, so, too, are changes in institutions and organizations. The capitalist mode of production is one among several, and historically has been far more spatially expansive and colonizing of social life than other modes. The historical development of capitalism shows evidence of the reconfiguration and incorporation of non-capitalist modes of production rather than their complete demise. NGOs are an institutional expression of these diverse modes of production and their mutations within the capitalist mode of production.

NGOs and the state co-evolved within a developing capitalism. Situating capitalism as the central force of social change allows us to examine NGOs as a unified institutional totality. The state is conceptualized as an arena of class struggle defined by the accumulation and legitimization crises of capitalism. Its crises and management strategies are experienced in and through a multiplicity of institutions. While these institutions did not originate solely in capitalism, their determinants lie within its reproductive logic. The unique position of the state among other institutions was not achieved by accident. Rather, it has been constituted by the historical development of the capitalist mode of production. When capitalism is considered to be an exclusively economic or Western phenomenon, the process of state formation is often misunderstood. The evolution of the international nation-state system is an integral part of the geographical expansion of capital. As such, it must be explained in terms of its expansion, rather than simply as a Western imposition on the rest of the world. The Western ideal of the state, which overdetermines most development theories, tends to mystify the state's capitalist nature. However, the historically specific cultural meanings and representations of capital do not substantively alter its internal logic, which has no preference or bias towards any one culture or geographical location.

Mainstream economics errs when it views capital simply as either a thing or a factor of production. Capitalism is, in fact, a social system based on a social relation. As a social system, it is defined and bounded by a process of capital circulation and reproduction. As a social relation, it requires continually increasing surplus value created by maximizing the economic inequality between those who control capital and those who provide the labor required to translate capital into wealth. The essence of the social relation in capitalism is the essence of the class relation. Growth—the motif of capitalist history—takes place when nature and society are aligned with the logic of profit or surplus value. Accumulation of surplus value— the ongoing self-realization of capital—entails commodification of the forces and relations of production. The logic of commodification maximizes the difference between use values and exchange values, thereby maximizing surplus value through the economic and ideological control of workers and their society. The fact that the extraction of surplus value depends on perpetual inequality between capital and labor means that capitalism is always prone to two overlapping crises. The crisis of accumulation refers to the difficulty of maintaining continuing expansion of surplus value. A crisis of legitimization involves the obstacles to securing the stable social acceptance of accumulation in response to the social, economic, and environmental crises it generates.

Understanding capital's central role in social change requires analyzing how it manages its ongoing crises. Institutions voluntarily and involuntarily become sites of crisis management. Institutions take multiple forms in their encounter with capital and reproduce class relations, making them key loci of social change. Jon Elster explains the essence of Marx's notion of class: "A class relation is a group of people who by virtue of what they possess are compelled to engage in the same activities if they want to make the best use of their endowments."[85] Class relations can be reproduced through a multiplicity of seemingly noneconomic social relations. What matters to capitalists is the effect of class relations—the generation of surplus value, rather than the process through which it is produced or its human consequences.

Marx and Engels argued that class "has an independent existence as against individuals," framing the "conditions under which we make ourselves, regardless of our conscious identity, will, or effort."[86] Class relations function as a constraining force for the behavior of institutions, as Marx noted. It "establishes definite social and cultural limits and opportunities for individuals, and imposes substantial costs for deviation from expected roles."[87] When productive forces develop and free labor becomes more self-conscious, this engenders a "more diverse intermediate class and fluid multi-sided class relations."[88] Crucially, the fluidity of social relations, or what Marx referred to as the "melting of everything that is solid into the thin air,"[89] cannot be understood outside the logic of class relations. As capitalism expands, class relations become more fluid. Fluidity is a result of the never-ending transformation of the forces and relations of production, which, in turn, are internalized as a means of reproducing class relations. Fluidity tends to suppress, disperse, and distort class consciousness, forestalling working-class solidarity and a final showdown between the proletariat and the bourgeoisie.[90] When Marx wrote that "the history of all hitherto existing society is the history of class struggles,"[91] he did not mean that social conflict between labor and capital will necessarily be perceived as class-based. Rather, he intended to underscore the centrality of class relation in social conflicts under the conditions of the capitalist mode of production.

Class relation makes the extraction of surplus value possible. The expansion of surplus value is a self-limiting process: "The more the productivity develops, the more it comes into conflict with the narrow basis on which the relations of consumption rest."[92] By improving technology and exploiting labor and nature, capital drives towards a crisis of overproduction and underconsumption, further precipitating the accumulation crisis as the slow growth in purchasing power fails to absorb the rapid expansion of productive capacity. The crisis of accumulation arises from contradiction in the system. That contradiction involves, on the one hand, the maximization of exchange value, which always produces "systemic scarcities" of commodities in the marketplace by making them available to consumers only according to their ability to pay the highest possible price. On the other hand, it involves another problem: the system also has to increase the effective demand for commodities, making them appear to be absolute necessities for the survival of humans and the environment. The capitalist system will always be incapable of profitably disposing of the enormous volumes of commodities it produces. The reason for the crisis of overproduction is not simply the lack of consumer purchasing power, but also the consumer's demand for socially and environmentally friendly consumption, i.e., the ever-changing social and cultural meanings of commodities. Ultimately, the survival of the capitalist system depends chiefly on its ability to endlessly create new needs.

Class relations are implicated in and managed by a multiplicity of institutions. The state is only one among many mediating institutions that influence the dynamic of accumulation and class struggle worldwide.[93] Yet the state occupies a central position in facilitating the geographical expansion of capital and provides society with some semblance of order and permanence at any given moment. It appears as the institution that bears the primary responsibility for achieving the formal equality and freedom critical for the expansion of accumulation, while at the same time keeping in check the exercise of freedoms that could undermine the reproductive logic of capital. Equality, however, while guaranteed in the sphere of exchange by political institutions, is not guaranteed in the sphere of production, specifically in the workplace. This is why the formal equalities that are guaranteed politically are always undermined by numerous inequalities in the domain of economics. Both civil society and the state are structured by and cannot escape the logic of capital: the limits of civil society are also the limits of the state. "Civil society's network of particular material interests structured the state and seriously compromised its ability to serve as mankind's 'ethical whole.'"[94] Ehrenberg clarifies:

> Where Hegel theorized the state as freedom from the antagonisms of civil society, Marx's materialism led him to criticize the state as part of a more general criticism of civil society [. . .] [T]he rule of law and the moral state could not eliminate pauperism because the market processes of civil society that give rise to inequality are beyond direct political remedy.[95]

Making civil society an instrument of radical political activity involves making it an object of that activity, because the formal separation of civil society from the state has not weakened the state's hold over civil society: "The emancipation of the state from religion is not the emancipation of the real man from religion."[96]

The appearance of civil society as a distinct space where people can exercise their freedoms is an illusion, to the extent that such freedoms are constrained by the separation of the social order into the distinct domains of economics and politics. The formal equalities promised in the former are always undermined by the inevitable inequalities of the later.

For example, in the NGO world, the legal freedom and "security" guaranteed in civil society do not protect people from hunger, poverty, and deprivation. They primarily guarantee the sanctity of property and "rights" defined as individual property rights. This, in turn, guarantees the right of capital to exploit labour. Therefore, security is not understood as the security of people or of individuals but specifically as the security of property and the right to use property for the exploitation of labour. Thus, none of the so-called human rights of man extend beyond egoistic man, man as he exists in civil society as an individual, driven by his private interests and whims and separated from the community. In other words, for Marx, civil society is the realization of the principle of individualism that violates the model of man as a social being. Such individualism implies "man as an entity whose social relations are only a means towards his own private ends." Such an individualistic model of human beings cannot, by its very nature, develop a collective model of human being.[97]

The fragmentation of civil society pluralizes the management of accumulation and legitimization crises, and often marginalizes class inequalities as a focus of society's political dissent. The subordination of civil society to the legal apparatus of the state ensures that such fragmentation does not destabilize either entity. Civil society is thus disciplined to ensure conditions for the overall stability and expansion of the capitalist system. The ideas that civil society is free from state oppression and that the state is the primary guardian of substantive freedoms are both illusions to the extent that they are circumscribed by the expansionary logic of capital.

The dominance of the state over civil society provides evidence of, on the one hand, capital's success in bringing about a massive concentration of social, economic, and political power that is eventually concentrated in the ideological, legal, and coercive apparatus of the state.[98] On the other hand, it provides evidence of the formal separation between society and the state: "Since the state is the form in which individuals of a class assert their common interests and in which the whole civil society of an epoch is epitomized, it follows that common institutions are set up with the help of the state and are given in a political form."[99] In the final analysis, the task of regulating the public sphere falls upon the state. The state, then, inevitably becomes a target of dissent against capitalism since "the commodification of the public sphere stands behind the legitimation crises of a political order that is unable to provide the rational justification for state power that it once could."[100]

Capitalism, as it expands, threatens to strip workers of "every trace of national character" as they become "subject to the unified rule of capital."[101] Class struggle then becomes global, but, somewhat paradoxically, the state continues to hold an important position as chief manager of the political economy. In fact, under the conditions of globalization, the state's role in resolving capitalist crises is more crucial than ever. Grounding a theory of the state in the logic of capital accumulation presupposes that the state is a site of class struggle, by virtue of its trusteeship over basic institutions such as property, finance, law, and governance, in accordance with the needs of capitalism. While the character of the state at any given moment reflects a balance of social forces, the following questions remain: How is it possible for the state to present itself as the autonomous guardian of both universal and particular interests simultaneously? How can it claim to represent various social classes with conflicting interests, i.e., the ruling class and the subordinate classes? How has it maintained the illusion that it acts in the general interest while clearly functioning as the "executive committee for managing the common affairs of the whole bourgeoisie"?[102] How does it derive its legitimacy by negotiating disputes between competing social institutions over which it wields ultimate authority? How can we explain the simultaneous centralization and decentralization of state power in its everyday business?[103]

These questions all focus on the way in which the state is manifested amid conflicting tendencies within capitalist modernity. If the state is fundamentally capitalistic, can we ultimately reduce it to a function of capital? Not exactly. As Simon Clarke has pointed out, the state is not, in the strictest sense, necessary for the reproduction of capitalism, nor can it be "logically derived from the requirements of the capitalist social reproduction."[104] It is not a formal or abstract necessity, but rather a historical one, and "developed logically out of the requirements of capital as it has developed historically out of the class struggle."[105] The problem of conceptualizing the state hinges on properly conceptualizing the class struggle that results from capitalism's internal dynamics.

The nature of the state must be theorized as a "moment of capital relation" where "capital is not a thing, but rather a definite social relation, belonging to a definite historical formation of society, which is manifested in a thing and lends this thing a specific social character."[106] Such an analysis does not require reducing the state to either material or economic determinants. Capital as a value form arises from relations of production. These relations are "constituted by the valorization process, relations of a total process of social production."[107] Theorizing the state arising under capitalist relations is not an attempt to reduce the state to economic determinants, but rather to historicize it.[108]

Under capitalism, the state appears as an autonomous entity due to the formal separation of economic and political spheres into "distinct forms of social relations."[109] This is neither an accidental nor a fixed separation. It is, rather, continually reproduced.[110] This process channels social activity, especially protests, away from the economic and into the political sphere. Conflicts between labor and capital are thus mediated by various particularized political categories which do not pose direct challenges to the reproductive workings of the system. Direct class conflict, in other words, appears to derive from different social identities. Through politics, social identities are reconstituted.[111] In parliamentary systems that involve elections, "the population is treated as an undifferentiated mass of 'voters,' and 'constituents,' defined according to arithmetical numbers rather than as a member of class or community." The very act of voting by secret ballot is nothing more than a "supreme expression of the privacy of political opinion."[112]

The economic basis for this lies in the separation of production and circulation into two different spheres, through the universalization of relations of exchange. It is through exchange that the principle of equality is guaranteed in the sphere of circulation.[113] The apparent separation of politics and economics authorizes the view that the former may guarantee certain fundamental rights. The notion of "citizen," "judicial person," and "individual" are liberated from their original dependencies and are "all apparently free to collide with another and to engage in exchange within this freedom."[114] The notion of private property "ensures that the individual can gain command over use values only through ownership or exchange." In the marketplace, all individuals are "free and equal" to engage in the common practice of exchange. This means that the "free individual and equality are also socially determined—they can only be achieved within the conditions laid down by society and through means provided by the society."[115]

Equality and freedom under capitalism are fundamental preconditions for, and limited to, the free exchange of property, commodities, and labor power to maximize surplus value. The pure ideas of equality idealized in the law and the justice system, then, "are merely the basis of a higher power."[116] The functional separation of economics from politics transforms the state into an arena in which conflicting private interests get reconfigured in the public sphere. Economic struggles thereby become political struggles, resulting in the popular and perhaps necessary illusion of state neutrality. Political parties actively recast economic struggles as political ones, capable of resolution merely by the election of a new government. Some view this as state inefficiency, and mistakenly attribute it to institutional failure.[117]

As Simon Clark's work illustrates, the expansion and the continuity of the capitalist system depend on the state maintaining its nature by changing its form to manage the space and time specific accumulation and legitimization crisis of capitalism. Yet, the state cannot achieve lasting social stability by promising political solutions to social problems, as these "solutions" are always undermined by the instability deriving from economic inequality. The state therefore avoids debilitating disorder through dynamic, creative economic and social policies that are reflected in periodic changes in the *form* of the state. The ideologies that legitimize the state thus become necessary for the reproduction of capital. The "bourgeois state did not arise as some automatic reflection of capitalist social relations." It had to be "painfully constructed" through strategic intervention.[118] It is not a limited goal, but an ongoing process. Management of accumulation and legitimization via the structures of the state requires extensions of state power to multiple social, cultural, and political domains. The incorporation of these into class relations means that "[p]rovisions must be made for representing and satisfying non-class relations and demands."[119] This process may indicate "that a basic feature of the capitalist type of state is the constitutive absence of class from its explicit organizational principles."[120] All of this complicates state forms, and makes analysis of their class character difficult. The main limitation of political realism and current theories of globalization is that they obscure the fact that state policies result from the presence of a "calculating subject," i.e., the class subject.[121]

As John Gledhill notes, the "neo-liberal discourse of the minimalist state might be seen as a mask for expanded state domination, and its accompanying programs of deregulation, privatization, and 'outsourcing' as new and more effective techniques for managing a social body dismembered by capitalist restructuring."[122] In this context, the politics of multiculturalism and identity within the parameters of the neoliberal state are a "regulatory agency under late capitalist conditions, whose language of recognition of difference as difference [. . .] becomes a vehicle of subordination through individualization, normalization and regulation, even as it strives to produce visibility and acceptance."[123] That is why it is far from convincing

> that a politics of rights focused on other kinds of identities—specific forms of injury, discrimination and social subordination on grounds of race or sexuality or preference, for example—is any more emancipating. Seeking redress through the law 'fixes the identities of the injured' as victims of injustice and casts the law in particular and the state more generally as neutral arbiters of injury.[124]

The politics of identity and the politics of distribution are two sides of the same coin; they are dialectically related. The appearance of a growing gap between them results from state practices of crisis management, social legitimization, and capital accumulation. Increasing unemployment due to the technological and geographical displacement of work reinforces the politics of identity and forestalls direct confrontation between capital and labor by attributing job loss and lowered standards of living to "bad" immigration policies rather than to the dynamics of capital accumulation. The state then moves to change these "bad" policies and rearticulate its social platform by appeal to primordial identities, thereby deflecting public opinion away from its neglect of fundamental social ills. Cultural discourses might sanction these policies by demanding fair treatment of immigrants or renewed emphasis on the integrity of national culture and identity. As Michael Kearney notes, "formation of transnational migrant populations problematizes the regulation of their identities by bureaucratic and disciplinary apparatuses of national states, but the unequal powers embedded in different national states still structure their lives in important ways."[125] And, as Gledhill argues, the attempt to champion national culture will only exacerbate conflicts between communities, because "what is happening in the old industrial zones of the world economy is an intelligible consequence of the need to manage economic decline within the framework of preserving an existing class structure and maintaining the incomes of its upper strata."[126]

In current liberal identity politics discourses, "categorical equivalence can be just as individualist in [its] foundations as the more obvious 'individualism' of the culture of consumerism promoted by capitalist corporations."[127] Multiculturalism and identity-based politics also find a companion in neoliberal social policies and NGOs that advocate self-help, self-reliance, and self-empowerment as alternatives to state paternalism. Practices resulting from these policies fit neatly into neoliberal restructuring and prevent people from achieving well-being while forcing them to participate in the market economy. They result in continued expansion of the informal sectors that absorb the economic, social, and political costs of adjustments made to the formal economy to increase the market for commodities and provide cheap labor. Neoliberal institutions accommodate investments in the informal sector and empower marginalized social groups through programs such as microcredit. Microcredit empowers women by offering access to scarce start-up capital, and at the same time it facilitates the expansion and stability of the capitalist system. "Social capital," social norms, values, social relationships, and networks in the society are tolerated and actively mobilized as long as it does not destabilize neoliberal economic policies.

The growing interdependencies between the formal and the informal sectors compel the state to extend its regulatory authority into the informal sector, managing the political economy without undermining the ability to resolve various conflicts. When the underground and informal economies become both necessary and destabilizing, the state incorporates them into the formal sectors, portraying them as threats to "public security." In the final analysis, the state expands its power and inhibits the politicization of social conflict along class lines.

As capitalism evolves, the limits to increased surplus value within national boundaries, and the inability to increase economic growth and employment, force the state to become more complacent about the spatial relocation of capital beyond its borders and the penetration of non-national capital into the domestic economy. Paradoxically, the state also assumes the sole responsibility for managing the political and economic consequences, domestically and internationally, resulting from that relocation of capital. Given the primary duty of the state to protect domestic capital's interests, such interventions inevitably mean violating international norms of free trade, environmental justice, sustainable growth, human rights, freedom of expression, and so on. Interstate competition over investments and markets does not leave much room for negotiations and diplomacy, which cause delays and missed opportunities for economic growth. Gradually, the possibility of transnationalism and multilateralism gives way to bilateralism shaped by the strategic relations between the states concerned.

The expansion and survival of national capital is increasingly dependent on the capital and labor of other nations, making substantive sovereignty (i.e., political and economic sovereignty) impossible. Transnational neoliberal institutions rely on formally sovereign states to manage the crises locally. Collectively, these trends tend to escalate social tensions and crises and make national security a primary project of the state. The ability of states to secure conditions for national and global security is constrained when the security mechanisms themselves become the means of capitalist development, through the rise of a military industrial complex. The militarization of the social order cannot succeed without wide social legitimacy. It achieves this through the ideologies of nationalism and national security. This results in, or intensifies, domestic tensions between social groups which are included and those which are excluded or otherwise marginalized. As the state assumes management of these domestic crises, it also demands immunity from international human rights laws. States, embedded in the global military industrial complex and transnational capital, simply do not have the freedom to act alone; they require assistance from other states.

Collectively, these trends force the state to reconcile the needs of local and transnational capital and the military industrial complex. This is where the war against terrorism and ethnoreligious nationalism act as interdependent ideologies, the latter legitimizing the former, and allow transnational capital to retain the state as chief agent responsible for creating the conditions for its own survival. The commodification of the mass media combined with the suppression of free expression under the pretext of national security further limit dissent against the state. These measures allow the state and the various interest groups controlling its power to extend their authority over society, resulting in violations of human rights and civic freedoms. The ideal of "good governance" emerged as the ostensible cure for all economic problems precisely at a moment when capital began to demobilize class-based social protests and reconfigure them as problems that have political solutions. The good-governance agenda of neoliberal capitalist institutions incorporates human rights and environmental justice, and therein civil society, as long as those projects do not disrupt the stability of the capitalist system. Good governance involves disciplining the state, and other institutions under its authority, to stabilize the accumulation and legitimization crises of capital.

The foregoing discussion demonstrates how capitalism drives the production of a wide range of state *forms*, and how a historically capitalist nature is reproduced through the state's assimilation of different social institutions (Clark, 1991). Capitalism favors no particular state form as long as its reproductive needs are met. This dialectical articulation of form and nature via the incorporation of various social relations invariably reproduces class relations. E.P. Thompson describes this situation as the reproduction of class relations in "cultural terms," which often take myriad forms since they involve "embodied traditions, value systems, ideas and institutional forms."[128] He added, "We can see this in the responses of similar occupational groups undergoing similar experiences, but we cannot predicate any law." Differently put, "class eventuates." Human beings participating in productive processes undergo experiences that give rise to consciousness, expressed within the "ensemble of social relations, with their inherited culture and expectations, and as they handled these experiences in cultural ways." Class experiences are expressed in a variety of ways, and are therefore a key analytic concept."[129] Failure to understand how culture disrupts the relationship between class location and class expression results in debilitating cultural amnesia.[130]

It is widely accepted that power relations, including relations between individuals and the state, are dispersed throughout society, and that such relations entail the possibility of resistance from various locations. The challenge is to analyze the processes by which different relations of power and resistance crystallize to produce what David Harvey refers to as "structured permanence." Society experiences structured permanence as hegemonic ideologies embedded in the practices of the state. Hegemony is itself an ideological construct formulated through coercion and consensus, a complex process involving the articulation and legitimization of the principles organizing the relations between nature and society. The production and legitimization of hegemony is an institutional process. Institutions are themselves "produced spaces." In the most obvious sense, they are "territorializations—territories of control with powers of control and surveillance, terrains of jurisdiction, and domains of organizing and administration."[131]

The capacity of any institution to effectively articulate a particular hegemonic project is based on its structural "privileges" (i.e., material and social capital) within a given institutional ensemble. These privileges include how they are placed in relation to other institutions, their ability to set the parameters of debates over alternative ways of structuring the social order, and their ability to support these activities. The more expansionary the hegemonic project, the greater the need to create a balance between the universal and the particular, or, in Bob Jessop's words, to bring macrosocial stability in the midst of microsocial diversity.[132] Hegemonic projects require "setting bounds" or "setting limits" for how we should act or think. It does not "cause" us to act or think in some causal manner.[133]

The expression of capitalist hegemony within the nation-state is important precisely because of the need to discipline "postmodern conditions" of production in order to preserve or create conditions conducive to the accelerating accumulation of surplus. This is an ongoing requirement in capitalist development, as Marx and Engels noted in the *Communist Manifesto*: "constant revolutionizing of production, uninterrupted disturbance of all social conditions, everlasting uncertainty and agitation distinguish [the] bourgeois [epoch] from earlier epochs." Contrary to the claims of Hardt and Negri, for example, capitalist hegemony brings about social order within the bounds of the nation-state according to the reproductive needs of capital. The question also remains of whether the "multitude" can ever evolve as a counterhegemonic force without a coherent alternative ideology and political economy capable of countering the growing powers of the state under globalization. The counterhegemonic, social transformative potential of the multitude and the social movements associated with it are questionable because they are rooted in ahistorical readings of capitalist modernity which see civilization as a uniquely Western project.

The state provided the institutional relations necessary for the expansion and popular acceptance of capitalist production, along with class relations and property rights: "[I]n order to lay down permanent spatial roots, that is to achieve a fixed territorial definition, early societies must develop to the point where they can begin to emancipate themselves from space."[134] The attempts of precapitalist state formations to either accommodate the emerging capitalist mode of production within their territorial domains or "to prevent such incorporation by any of their rivals" resulted in the "complete disintegration of the medieval system of rule" and the post-Westphalian system of nation-states.[135] At that point, the nation-state became necessary. Nationalism was thus not simply a "civilizing mission" but also a political response to an economic problem. The state grouped together the people in a fixed territorial unit and, for the first time, "divided the people for public purposes, not by kinship but by common place of citizens."[136] Legitimizing the state's power in universal terms also required the arbitration of class conflict in favor of the ruling class while presenting the state as the guardian of the common good. The notion of citizenship was imposed on society as a whole to create a common social identity, but this pertains only to political rights, not to communal identity understood in terms of economic rights and privileges.

The accumulation and legitimization crises of capitalism in Europe were the main cause of the diffusion of capitalist modernity and the modern nation-state system throughout the "postcolonial world." The social, political, and economic upheavals in Europe in response to these crises were not much different from those that had been caused by capitalist development in the colonies. They too were shaped by religion, ethnicity, territoriality, language, and so on. The objectives of the institutionalization of state power within the territorial boundaries of the countries of the colonizers and those of the colonized were not radically different. In the mother countries and the colonies alike, the morality of capitalism and the nation-state was represented in terms of universal categories promising self-determination, progress, and freedom. The investors and interest groups who engineered the expansion of capitalist production to the colonies promised cheap labor, raw materials, larger markets, and better standards of living for the citizens of their home countries. This expansion did not follow from a democratic mandate determined by a majority. Rather, in the metropolitan countries, it was a particular class that controlled the state and which faced fierce criticism from its own lower strata, who themselves suffered many of the same consequences of capitalism as their counterparts in the colonies.

In imperial nation-states, critiques of capitalist modernity and imperialism emerged in the later part of the nineteenth century, if not earlier, and were then exported to the colonies. Different manifestations of nationalism directly addressed class conflict, among other concerns. Paradoxically, nationalism continues to drive the transnationalization of the capitalist system, since the *form* and *nature* of the state are determined by the ruling classes. The very constitution of the state in terms of formally universal principles, such as self-determination, sovereignty, and progress, motivated social classes to address their demands to the state. This conflated the reproduction of class relations on a global scale with the social relations that make up state power in individual nation-states. Development, far from being an orientalist project imposed by the West on non-Western countries, is primarily a global response to the accumulation and legitimization crises of capitalism. During the Cold War, development projects oscillated between paradigms of capitalism and socialism. As capitalism enters its neoliberal phase, the increasing colonization of society by capital is matched by the state's growing responsibility to create the conditions for capital's reproduction and the management of its resultant crises and conflicts. That is the context in which this book re-examines the rise of neoliberalism, national security ideology, and parochial nationalism.

Chapters 1 through 4 provide a social history of NGOs in Bangladesh and Sri Lanka from the pre-independence period to the present. A broad social historical perspective is essential for theorizing the agency of NGOs. Critical claims about their social roles not only invoke their history but also function as one of the chief means by which social groups reconfigure and reconstruct the past in order to serve their own political and economic interests in the present. An examination of NGOs, and their institutional cultures and representations in particular, provides some insights into the politics of hegemonic and subaltern histories, and those histories' impacts on trajectories of social change. It also permits a critical appraisal of the ways in which history is invoked today to buttress such claims, continuities, discontinuities, and transformations. I have been selective rather than exhaustive in discussing NGO case studies in order to call attention to some of the less-understood aspects of NGO involvement in state formation.

Capitalism has long functioned as the driving force of social change, providing ideological justification for both NGOs and states. I argue that the ideologically and operationally diverse activities of NGOs and their critics since the British colonial period have enabled the state to perpetually consolidate its capitalist *nature* by continuously changing its *form,* and I demonstrate that although NGOs may be more or less independent vis-à-vis the states under which they operate, they are no more or less "free" than any other agent in the global capitalist marketplace. Both NGOs and nation-states are ideologically underwritten by capitalism. This becomes apparent when one considers, from a historical perspective, the close correspondence between transformations in NGO–state relations and transformations in the global marketplace. As this study explains, the former has generally followed the latter. In other words, as market forces shift, so, too, do NGO–state relationships.

The following analysis focuses on the political and developmental aspects of these relations throughout the period of capitalist modernity, drawing on primary as well as secondary sources. I have selected organizations, ideas, and practices that best illustrate the links between NGOs and state formation. Though I look at organizations across different historical periods, they all share the characteristics of contemporary NGOs and they have all been considered by the state to be nongovernmental. Because NGO political economy evolved in tandem with capitalist political economy, it is possible to characterize NGOs by historical period. Despite their great diversity and multiplicity, three distinctly different historical types of NGO political economies can be distinguished: native, missionary, and contemporary, associated respectively with the precolonial, colonial, and postcolonial periods. Ultimately, what distinguishes different NGO political economies, both from each other and from the state, are differences in their stances toward capitalism.

Chapter 1 begins with a discussion of the native and Christian organizations that shaped the pre-independence state in Sri Lanka and Bangladesh. I discuss the ways in which precolonial NGOs in Bangladesh differed from precolonial NGOs in Sri Lanka. In Sri Lanka the activities of these organizations reveal a national history that is radically different from the populist ethnonationalist versions of that history produced by both the state and NGOs. Christian missionary organizations, in particular, were NGO prototypes and provided the basis for the emergence of similar associations and for the emergence of the native ruling bloc. I emphasize the progressive thrust of the missionary organizations, which contributed to the revitalization of local cultures by broadening opportunities for participation in public fora and by creating the conditions for counterhegemonic social movements. These associations set the stage, and determined the structures, for the consolidation of the colonial state and the transition from the colonial to the postcolonial period, establishing relationships between NGOs and the state that continue today.

The relatively lower density of NGOs in the eastern parts of Bengal led to a higher incidence of peasant uprisings until the independent state of Bangladesh was created in 1971. Despite their diverse and exclusionary politics, organizations in Bangladesh facilitated broader national movements that culminated in independence struggles against the colonial powers of Britain and Pakistan. In contrast to Sri Lankan NGOs, Bangladeshi NGOs place a higher premium on the notion of secularism. Underlying these differences, as I explain, are important variations in the ways in which these two states incorporated capitalism into their domestic economies in relation to dominant colonial powers.

Chapter 2 considers how post-independence economic nationalism in Sri Lanka revitalized and supported NGOs, bringing them under its control even though they were critical of the state. Relations between the state and NGOs became openly contentious, however, after the introduction of an open economy, 25 years of ethnic conflict between the government and Tamil militants, and growing disenchantment among progressive intellectuals and activists with both socialist and capitalist paradigms of change. In contrast to Bangladesh, Sri Lanka has been less concerned with NGO interventions in development and more concerned with their involvement in human rights and peacebuilding work, particularly as they pertain to the current ethnic conflict. State-sanctioned criticism of NGOs, so prevalent in the popular press, obscures the basic fact that NGOs have ultimately enabled the state to consolidate its power.

Chapter 3 illustrates how, during the post-independence period, the culture of NGOs in Bangladesh evolved as a kind of "parallel state," with powers over the social and economic development of the country rivaling those of the national government. Some of these NGOs are among the largest in the world and they function as "nonprofit corporate franchises," with their own retail businesses, universities, and banks. I consider why such powerful NGOs, in the midst of the severe economic turmoil caused by the government's economic policies, have not overthrown their national government. I also discuss the state's increasingly close connections to religious nationalists. As I argue, the relationship between NGOs and the state is better understood as mutually constitutive, in the context of international capitalism.

In contrast to the Sri Lankan organizations, Bangladeshi NGOs are in a more precarious position since many of their religious nationalist critics have formed their own NGOs with the help of Islamic countries suspected by the West of being terrorist-friendly. Ethnoreligious nationalist and national security paradigms in both countries shape, albeit in different ways, the context for the ongoing development of capitalism. Throughout this book, I grapple with the questions of how and why NGOs have, despite their best intentions, failed to challenge the dominant capitalist hegemonies of their national governments. Instead, they have effectively substituted a critique of cultural relations for the critique of class relations. At the same time, NGOs concerned with empowerment, charity, self-sufficiency, humanitarian assistance, good governance, conflict resolution, and peacebuilding continue to function as vital spaces in which capitalist class relations are simultaneously interrogated and affirmed.

Finally, Chapter 4 describes the diverse activities of NGOs, as well as the ideas that shape them and their relationships with states in the context of capitalist modernity, and introduces the term "NGO-industrial complex." The chapter offers a metanarrative, a general theory of the ways in which ideologically and operationally diverse NGOs influence, and have been influenced by, state formation in Sri Lanka and Bangladesh over the past three centuries. Centuries of NGO activity, both radical and conservative, have contributed to the "centralization" and "domestication" of the state's capitalist *nature* through changes in state *forms*. These historically specific forms are characterized as precolonial, colonial, pre-independence, post-independence, neoliberal, ethnonationalist, and national security. Their continuities and discontinuities are also discussed. These states have not only subverted and exploited the counterhegemonic agendas of NGOs by appropriating their language and practices, but they have also progressively narrowed the scope for radical social change. Although NGOs, both historically and contemporaneously, dominate public discourse, they should not be viewed as counterhegemonic forces to the extent that they function according to, and operate within, the same fundamental logic and institutional boundaries as neoliberal capitalism.

# 1
# The Emergence of the Unified Nation-State: Precolonial NGOs in Bangladesh and Sri Lanka

"[A]uthoritarianism, chauvinism, and inequity were as much constitutive of middle-class modernity as democracy, secularism, and egalitarianism."

Sanjay Joshi[1]

"Whatever little chance there may have been of a genuinely 'Ceylonese' nationalism growing up in time was aborted almost at conception. The unitary state, freed from the strait-jacket of imperial order, became the battle-ground of competing nationalisms which convulse the country to this day."

Adrian Wijemanna[2]

Contemporary Bangladesh and Sri Lanka are heirs to a rich legacy of organizations exhibiting characteristics typical of NGOs, and they are also home to some of the largest and most innovative of these organizations. The histories of these organizations date back to the precolonial period and continue to shape NGO–state relations today. While most studies of Bangladeshi NGOs begin in 1971, with independence, the story in fact begins much earlier. Likewise, in Sri Lanka, "NGOs have emerged out of a long history of people's participation and self-help, a history that stretches back as far as the times of ancient Sri Lankan kings."[3] These premodern social organizations, known by many different names, were embedded in the symbiotic relationship between religion, the state, and society, and although they were transformed by colonial rule and capitalist development, the associational traditions they established continue to inform the practices of NGOs in both countries. The culture of NGOs underwent significant changes following the era of Christian missionary organizations which predate the colonial state. Ever since, the relationship between Christianity and NGOs has continued to play an important role in shaping the relationship between NGOs and the state, and determining how NGOs are mobilized by the state as sources of its power and legitimacy.

Analysis of NGO-precursor activities in Bangladesh and Sri Lanka offers us a way to explore the trajectories of social change—the processes of living as a community. Proto-NGOs were among the most fundamental institutions shaping community processes, predating the modern nation-state. Local, regional, and national associations were integral to the evolutionary trajectories of state formation in both the precolonial and colonial periods. In fact, they were the instruments through which various nongovernmental social groups sought to consolidate their power by soliciting state patronage and vying for economic advantage.

Contemporary social histories of NGO–state relationships are too often based on simplistic binaries and selective readings of a country's history, a problem found in the work of NGO proponents and opponents alike. In Bangladesh and Sri Lanka, popular perceptions and written histories of NGOs have distorted the complexity of their role in shaping the antagonistic and reciprocal relations between local elites and the colonial state. These distortions are rooted in highly contested revisionist histories of these countries. Since independence, the invocation of these revisionist histories has continued to play an important part in both countries' economic and political processes.

This chapter illustrates the impact of NGOs on state formation in Bangladesh and Sri Lanka during the precolonial and colonial periods, in terms not only of their respective activities but also the discourse surrounding them. Such analysis is of critical importance for this study since the postcolonial relations between NGOs and the state are significantly impacted by the revisionist histories. In fact, one may meaningfully refer to NGOs themselves as a "discursive formation" when certain of their common ideas and practices are configured in a coherent framework. While the reference points of this discourse are NGO activities, those framing it may be far removed from such activities. In these cases, discourse functions ideologically, as "NGOism." NGOism conceals more than it reveals about the realities of NGOs and their impact on state formation. As an ideology, NGOism acquires political power through linkage with history. NGOism is an important part of nation building, particularly in terms of how the state mobilizes the nation and its history in order to concentrate and legitimize its power. Current controversies surrounding NGOs are not only about NGOs themselves, they also concern history, and how history informs a sense of belonging in multicultural states as they undergo capitalist development. A nuanced understanding of history is important not only because history informs the relationship between NGOs and the state today, but also because NGOs can achieve positive social change only if they are willing to critically engage with the past.

## BANGLADESH

Any truly useful history of NGOs in Bangladesh must begin with an inquiry into the history of precolonial Bengal, and postcolonial East and West Bengal. Without an examination of this early period, we cannot understand the evolution of modern NGO culture, or the forces that have shaped its development and the relationships between NGOs and the state to this day. Such an inquiry is necessary to counter the distortion of NGO history that I discussed above.

The territory of Bengal, out of which Bangladesh was later carved, was conquered by the British in 1757. Lying within the Ganges delta, Bengal's eastern and western regions were inhabited primarily by Bengali-speaking Muslims and Hindus, respectively, although many ethnic, tribal, linguistic, and religious groups are scattered throughout the region. When India was partitioned in 1947, Pakistan incorporated the eastern part of Bengal and became an independent state unified by faith in Islam. In 1971, civil war in East Pakistan, sparked by discrimination against the Bengali-speaking population, resulted in Bangladeshi independence. Since then, political boundaries have remained more or less stable, even though they have been challenged by Chakmas living in the northern part of the country. Despite the fact that 90 percent of the country's population identify as Muslim, the national identity is defined by the ongoing contest between secularism and Islam. NGOs play an influential role in this process by providing ideas, mobilizing financial and social support, and functioning as fora for public debates.

During the precolonial period in Bengal, particularly in the urban centers, a diverse array of traders, artisans, and welfare and religious organizations flourished, particularly during the vibrant Husain Shai period (1496–1583). Among them guilds such as the *pundit sabhas* (assemblies of scholars) and the *Kavyagosthi's* (associations of poets) were common.[4] But the most dominant form of association (although more widespread in western than eastern Bengal) was the *panchayat* system, under which were *dallas* (family groupings). *Panchayats* provided the means by which members of the *dallas* negotiated their respective interests and status in society. These associations were rarely interested in changing the status quo, and operated under the imperatives of revenue accumulation in the economy of the Mughal Empire (1526–1725). Christian missionary associations, on the other hand, promoted reforms and challenged the social status of elites, and also provided those same elites with new ideas and structures within which to organize their activities. This new type of association became a means by which elites managed the diverse regimen of accumulation that allowed them to simultaneously monopolize the opportunities provided by British colonial rule, legitimize their authority as indigenous leaders, and manage threats to their authority from subordinate classes. The tensions between these different kinds of organizations, between elite and lower classes, and between these organizations and the state have shaped the development of Bangladesh.

In eastern Bengal, as I mentioned above, the topographical, social, cultural, and political characteristics were not as conducive to the development of village organizations like *panchayats,* or the councils that encompassed entire villages in other parts of the subcontinent. The upper delta lacked nucleated villages, though the British and Mughals continued to use the term *muza,* a term commonly used to refer to a village. While there is scattered evidence that social groupings like *bamsa* and *gosthi* are of common matrilineal descent, they did not have the same "cohesiveness or social significance as the endogamous *baradaries* among the Muslims of the upper delta." They were "much less endogamous[than the] *jati* of [the] fully developed Hindu caste society."[5]

Village communities in eastern Bengal were diverse and stratified. They were built along the creeks and riverbanks and were scattered as amorphous clusters, which makes it difficult to identify clear boundary demarcation patterns.[6] The relations between them, and with local and imperial functionaries, were not merely maintained by feudal type relations. They also involved a complex array of interpersonal relationships. The homesteads maintained multiple ties between local and imperial authorities without depending on the mediation of a single designated person or organization. The widespread use of cash for transactions made it easier for the central authorities and local interest groups to bypass tradition and provide flexibility to "deal with groups of different cultures."[7]

Groups in eastern Bengal, particularly in the areas dominated by agriculture, were closely associated with Samaj (worship assemblies) and *Jamaat* (Islamic organizations). Their mosques and shrines were administered by individual *mullahs* (heads of mosques) and *pirs* (holy men), and were the focal "social institutions" of group solidarity and mobilization. More than one of these institutions existed in an area that can be identified as a village. A single Samaj did not claim the monopoly of authority over a given locality. It was the mosque and its constituency, rather than the *muza*, that was the physical embodiment of social relationships and the expression of social identity as group solidarity.[8] Broad-based manifestations of group solidarity were limited to occasional religious functions such as Friday prayers and annual religious events. Authority over religious and social matters was divided between the *mullahs* and local authorities known as *matababdars,* who drew their authority from a series of networks and patronage. However, the "social order was unstable as, for centuries, in the lower delta, authority was poorly organized; centers of officialdom were few and widely scattered. Islam and Vaisnasvis functioned to provide authority in anarchic frontier society, and they did so through loosely constituted religious organizations."[9]

Throughout the Mughal Empire, agriculture and Islamic institutions developed in parallel. A revenue-maximizing regime, the Mughals used their reciprocal relations with local institutions to achieve the conversion of forests into arable land. Land grants (*waqf*) were given to *pirs* to develop Islamic institutions in return for their participation in state-centered agricultural development.[10] Mughals issued document called *sanads* as titles for the transfer of land from the crown to the *pirs*, granting "tax-free lands directly to the trustees (mutawalli) of mosques or shrines [...] Hence grantees became the de facto and de jure land lords of territories alienated from the support of institutions under their administrative control." The *pirs* "combined religious piety with the organizational skills necessary for forest clearing and land reclamation; hence they were remembered not only for establishing mosques and shrines but also for mobilizing communities to cut the forest and settle the land."[11] The *waqf* endowments prohibited personal land use, as they were reserved for the support of Muslim institutions such as schools, hospitals, shrines, and mosques. In 1770, the British found that in Chittagong two thirds of the land grants were used by charities.[12] In this process, "forest land became rice fields and indigenous inhabitants became rice-cultivating peasants, at once the economic and religious clients of a new gentry,"[13] a trend that continued into the second quarter of the nineteenth century. During the Mughal period, Bengal urban society had cosmopolitan characteristics and the state actively patronized numerous institutions. Trade and commerce, and a cash economy, helped spread this cosmopolitanism from urban centers outward. The Bengali frontier regions accommodated even the growth of Christian institutions. In 1713, the French Jesuit Père Barbier encountered a Christian community in the Noakhali district organized around the authority of a local patriarch.[14] But the development of associations in the eastern part of Bengal began much later than in western Bengal for several reasons, the first of which was the relative distance between the center and the periphery. During the Sultanate (1345–1575), elites in Bengal had been integrated into local culture and were close to local groups. The gap between the Ashrafs (aristocratic Muslims with roots outside of India, who often had expertise in Persian and Islamic law) and non-Ashrafs widened as Ashrafs increasingly identified with the central administration, and Ashrafs maintained a considerable degree of social distance from the rest of society.

*Mullahs* were subordinate to the Ashrafs,[15] enforcing revenue collection on behalf of the imperial state, and they did not have a harmonious or stable relationship with the peasants who were frequently forced into debt and flight[16] due to constantly increasing revenue demands, wedding expenses, the purchase of cattle, and expenses involving dispute settlement.[17] These eastern traditional ruling elites—who were directly dependent on, and functioned on behalf of, the state—did not see the necessity of forming associations to legitimize their status in society.

A second reason for the relatively late development of associations in the east was the decentralization of revenue accumulation, and the resolution of conflicts through religious, caste, and other traditional institutions, although the landlords did mobilize state power when it became necessary to curb peasant unrest. The expansion of a revenue-maximizing regime was articulated through tradition that, on the one hand, strengthened religious identities, and, on the other hand, intensified the differences between classes.

Third, there was a relative absence of intermediary organizations and a middle class that could provide them with leadership, which may help explain the widespread concentration of peasant uprisings in the eastern part of Bengal as compared to West Bengal. Peasant authority did not extend beyond local religious leaders (*pirs*). To the bureaucrats and the administrative class, the *pir* and the peasants didn't matter, since neither *pir* nor peasant could influence their status and power. This disjuncture opened a space for "class" consciousness to emerge as a form of peasant resistance. When recalcitrant *pirs* and peasants disturbed the flow of revenue, Mughal authorities directly intervened in rural settlements. The relationship between the religious gentry and the Mughal authorities was not always peaceful, since "a pir's natural ties of authority and patronage generally lay with the masses of peasants beneath him and not with the governors and bureaucrats in the distant Dhaka." People looked up to the *pir* as a leader who "guided and did not pay the rent to the Nawabs [provincial governors]." Religious institutions were more involved in addressing peasant discontent in East Bengal than in other parts of the Indian subcontinent. During the second quarter of the nineteenth century, Faraidi and Taraqh-I-Muhammadiya,[18] two religious reformers of the Faraizi movement (founded by Haji Shariatullah), incorporated agrarian issues into their campaign to establish an orthodox Islam by dispelling extraneous influences. The grievances of peasants, and their remedies, were articulated within an orthodox Islamic world view and *faraizis* devoted much time and effort to stimulating political consciousness and the mobilization of peasantry. According to them, "God made earth common to all man" and the "payment of rent is contrary to his law." Dadu Miyan, son of Shariatullah, used a "small-group approach," dividing many parts of eastern Bengal into units of 300 to 400 peasant families for the purposes of education and social mobilization.

Radical social movements in Bengal during this period were distinctively local and noncommunal in their outlook: Faraizis were "much disliked by Hindus, by the orthodox Muhammadans and by the Europeans."[19] Subsequently, as Faraizi ideals were incorporated into nineteenth-century political movements, the issues faced by peasants became secondary to the interests of the greater Muslim community, which extended beyond Bengal. Bengali Muslim nationalist leaders such as Fazlul Huq of Barisal, Maulana Bhashani of Mymensingh, and the first prime minister of Bangladesh, Sheikh Mujibur Rahman, were directly influenced by the Faraizi movement.[20] As I shall demonstrate later, the expansion of NGOs since independence coincided with the decline of radicalism of peasant and tribal communities and the demise of organizations associated with them, bringing them under the direct control of transnational capital, and thereby contributing to the extension of state control over these communities.

Though Christian missionaries were more active in western Bengal than in eastern Bengal during the British colonial period, they were present as a force on the Indian subcontinent as far back as the sixteenth century. Missionary agencies, throughout their history, demonstrated many characteristics of NGOs. Missionaries of different denominations shared the common goal of converting natives to Christianity and transforming the prevailing social structure, which they saw as an impediment to the spread of the gospel. They considered the caste system to be incompatible with Christianity.

After the Indian Rebellion of 1857, missionaries took a more aggressive stand and began demanding that the state adopt "a new Christian policy" toward caste inequalities. But missionaries were not always in agreement with each other. Some called for an assault on everything idolatrous; others, more moderate, adopted a more secular and civil approach to fighting inequality by presenting caste as an obstacle to progress, intellectual liberty, social advancement, and charity; still others had a hands-off policy, because the renunciation of caste by converts was usually ineffective and costly. Many Indian Christians maintained their caste affiliations as well as their new church affiliations.[21] Missionary challenges to the caste system brought resistance from the upper classes as converts began to think critically about traditional authority.

In 1860, mass conversions led to popular movements in villages where cohesion and stability were disturbed. These movements sometimes led to the renunciation of caste by converts, but more often strengthened caste solidarity. For example, in some cases converts sought to maintain a degree of autonomy from the missionaries by maintaining their existing social relations.[22] There was little agreement among missionaries about how to deal with mass-based movements when they challenged larger systemic forces. The government feared that if missionaries were allowed to continue with mass conversions it could ignite another rebellion. Grants-in-aid to missionary schools were blamed for the problem and a colonial administrator demanded an end to such assistance, enforcing the official policy of separation between church and state in order to restore the confidence of the people and the stability of the Raj.[23]

After the debates of the Theological Conference of 1879 in Calcutta, the missionary position on caste changed. Christians suddenly began viewing caste as another opportunity to spread the gospel. Caste, they realized, "provided a system of social cohesion which was still useful and alive among mass movement converts and its lines of communication could as easily lead to conversion as to apostasy."[24] The change came about when high-caste Indian Christians complained that missionaries were unsympathetic towards indigenous culture and undermined indigenous expressions of faith.[25] Although missionary activities eventually led to legislative reforms, those reforms frequently had unintended results. For example, their efforts to uplift the lower castes and facilitate communication with the government ultimately encouraged "a sense of caste solidarity and intensified inter-caste rivalry."[26] Caste thus became a basis of political mobilization.

Missionaries also challenged the *zamindari* system, regarding it as a violation of Christian ethics and an obstruction to the spread of Christianity.[27] *Zamindars* were local elites who gained their land rights by promising to collect taxes for the British government. Typically, the highest bidder was granted land tenure and the farmers and peasants who had previously owned the land were either evicted or transformed overnight into tenants. *Ryots* (hereditary peasant tenants) then became responsible for paying the zamindar in cash. Pressure to pay was always great since a zamindar would lose his title to the land if he couldn't deliver the promised sum to the authorities. If a zamindar or a tenant came up short, he had to turn to the *mahajan* (moneylender). Missionaries, meanwhile, worked to make ryots aware of their rights and privileges and to advocate for legislative reforms. Ryots looked to the missionaries for leadership and protection as they were often able and willing to act as mediators.[28] Missionaries appealed to Christian newspapers, the Landholders Society, the Bengal British India Association, and the educated classes to improve the situation of the ryots. When those tactics failed, they offered guidance and limited support.[29]

Between 1763 and 1800, the chief agents of political turmoil in rural Bengal were organized bands of "holy men" known as *sannyasis* and *fakirs*. While it is difficult to determine the specific agendas of these groups, the evidence suggests that poverty-stricken peasants rallied around them, especially in the aftermath of the famine of 1770. The best-known instances of uprisings before 1793 reveal the class character of such social mobilizations.[30] In that year, as a result of the Permanent Settlement, incentives were granted to the zamindars, including effective ownership of their lands and a fixed land tax that was intended to prevent exploitation by British administrators. However, the changes had unintended consequences. Zamindar-owned land became more valuable. So, because British land taxes were based on the value of the land, zamindars often went into debt and eventually lost their land in auctions presided over by notoriously corrupt government bureaucrats. Zamindars thus found themselves caught between a revenue-maximizing state and recalcitrant peasants. State policies oscillated between the ideals of free trade and mercantilism. At the same time, the state provided more legal protection to zamindars by authorizing them to take legal action against tenants that would otherwise have been prohibited by custom, such as eviction.[31] Recommendations by British officers to address peasant grievances were not implemented by colonial state administrators because the interests of the zamindars were joined with those of the indigo planters.[32]

The collaboration between British and Indian elites finally broke down in 1836 when native elites demanded equality for Indians in the eyes of the law. In 1837, the Zamindari Association was formed, in opposition to the Raj's decision to resume rent-free land ownership and the sale of zamindari holdings in case of failure to pay revenues. The Association's objective was to safeguard the interests of landlords, and it was later renamed the Landlords' Society. Zamindars sought assistance from the Society and the colonial government, but the peasants had greater success with tactics of desertion and migration: "Refusal to fulfill indigo contracts after taking advances—what planters and pro-planter magistrates referred to as 'deliberate fraud'—was the usual early form of resistance against an unremunerative forced cultivation."[33]

Between 1830 and 1840, peasant uprisings against the zamindaris and the Landlords' Society were widespread in Bengal. Although these movements were inspired by religious ideology, Muslim landlords were not spared. For example, violence erupted on the Bengal–Bihar border during the Santal rebellion. Both men and women took part in the violence, which targeted foreigners and moneylenders, and the level of cooperation among the Santal poor, regardless of tribal affiliation, demonstrated evidence of class consciousness.[34]

Missionary activists found their organizations increasingly politicized as they protested this system and came into direct conflict with powerful segments of the Bengali community. This was particularly evident in the wake of the Indigo Revolt of 1859, which the government suppressed by force. Ryots lacked the institutional means to represent themselves, and in response to Hindu, Muslim, and Christian ryot requests for assistance, 24 missionary organizations intervened in the crisis.[35] In 1860, when petitions and negotiations repeatedly failed to bring about change, hundreds of ryots from indigo plantation districts flooded into the city to submit a petition to the Lieutenant Governor. The petition subsequently led to the formation of the Indigo Commission, where ryots were represented by Reverend Richard Sale.

Planters accused missionaries of fomenting rebellion among both the educated classes and the ryots. In many instances, zamindars and other landowners sided with the peasants and did not openly criticize the missionaries, because the crisis provided them with the opportunity to extract more rent from planters by promising to take action against the ryots. While these groups were locked in struggle, others were silent.[36] According to Hardiman: "Big landlords were quite happy to let the white planters do what they liked with the ryots so long as they themselves were not threatened."[37] The government began dissociating itself from the planters when it realized the costs of supporting them. It simply could not afford to allow the indigo protests to become a mass rebellion. At the same time, profits from indigo plantations declined considerably, decreasing the government's incentive to protect them.

Reverend James Long was sentenced to prison for his alleged role in translating Nil Darpan, a Bengali play by Dinabandhu Mitra, which influenced the Indigo Revolt. His conviction improved missionary relations with the natives. As Long noted: "I have been surprised to see whenever I go among the natives the Nil Darpan case has given me an open door."[38] Missionary involvement in the Indigo Revolt was successful because it strengthened relations with the natives as well as with the colonial government. And yet, when issues of politics and governance came into play, missionaries often tended to stayed aloof. This distance, spurred by the church's interest in self-reliance and continuity, severely limited missionary involvement in the independence movement.

Some missionaries believed that nationalism was a natural outcome of Christian education. Others, in favor of British rule, feared that uniting patriotism, revivalism, and militancy would jeopardize the Christian mission. Those who took a neutral view held that the nationalist movement was sectarian and would eventually be beneficial to evangelism.[39] When the nationalist movement gained momentum, the close association between missionaries and the government, along with the lack of leadership by the former, frustrated patriotic Indian Christians and the intelligentsia on whom the missionaries had pinned all their hopes of converting India. Even those who opposed the idea of home rule were concerned that the church would become an alien, minority institution. The dilemmas posed by the nationalist movement compelled Christian agencies to act as a unified body, leading to the formation of the National Missionary Council (NMC) in 1912.[40]

The nineteenth century may be best understood as an age of public associations. Calcutta was emerging as an economic, administrative, and cultural center. The new middle classes (*bhadraloks*) were engaged in a struggle to gain control of public space as a means of asserting their leadership,[41] and public associations were instrumental in shaping their ideological and political practices. Bhadraloks were drawn from the middle and lower echelon of the rent-receiving hierarchy. Their "forbears in another age worked as scribes at the Moguls and Nawabi courts or had formed part of the traditionally literate caste elites."[42] The decline of the rentier economy and the diminishing prospects for traditional vernacular education affected their standard of living and social status. Some returned to the countryside, while others remained in the city and sought to regain their status through opportunities provided by the colonial regime.[43] The diversity of their associations was reflected in the continuous conflicts which took place over resources and power. Although the majority of them did not directly perform political functions, they established institutional prerequisites for political mobilization and entry into public life.[44]

Any discussion of the relationship between the bhadraloks and the public associations in Bengal must begin with the *dal*, the primary system of social organization. Later voluntary associations combined dallas with Western forms of association. The dallas emerged as a means of defending the traditional social order and as a way for different groups to legitimize their social positions. They were hierarchically structured and maintained a strict code of conduct among their members. Dallas that were based upon family groupings within specific caste groups were relatively more stable than supra-dallas, which were largely unsuccessful. For example, in 1830, Dharma Sabah, an association of orthodox Hindus in Calcutta who opposed the government abolition of *sati* (immolation of widows), did not incorporate all dallas. By 1840, it had split into three groups.

In 1867, the National Society was formed to unite dallas "for a common purpose" and bring together "different sections and classes of the Hindu community ... into a harmonious whole."[45] However, as the editor of *Sadharani* noted, by 1874 it had become nothing more than an extension of the dal that centered on the Tagore family of Jorasanko.[46] Similarly, in 1869, Sanatana Raksini Saber, sponsored by the junior branch of the Deb family, was established to offer advice on Hindu law. It failed, however, to gain a corporate identity and became merely an extension of the Deb family. The dallas were unable to exercise much influence beyond the areas they inhabited. They lacked common interests or agendas to create widespread unity among them.

Brahmo Samaj, which was organized in opposition to the prevailing system of dallas, and which pioneered religious, social, and educational advancement in the Hindu community, continued to fulfill many of the traditional functions of the dallas. In 1866, Debendra Nath Tagore's attempts to resolve the differences between conservative and radical factions led to a split in the organization. One segment, Rahmo Samaj of India, split again after a debate over the status of women.[47] An outcome of this conflict-driven evolutionary process was that native voluntary associations adopted Western organizational forms.

Between 1816 and 1857, bhadralok families participated in only twelve large-scale associations. But between 1857 and 1885, the number grew to 59. Several factors contributed to this, such as the growing demand for an end to European intervention in local affairs. Increasing attention was also being paid to Bengali language and literature, spurring the rise of cultural and literary organizations like the Bengali Social Science Association (1867), the Calcutta Book Society (1857), the Hindu Literary Society (1875), and the Calcutta Literary Society (1876). Furthermore, the bhadraloks gained skills and experience managing associations in collaboration with Europeans, and by 1867 began to assume control of those set up by the missionaries.[48] Soon, the bhadraloks countered the missionaries' challenges by forming their own associations and incorporating Christian methods of evangelism in the propagation of Hinduism.[49]

Of the 475 bhadraloks who assumed key leadership positions in the voluntary associations, the majority were drawn from 18 different castes. Twenty-eight percent were Radhi Brahmans. Twenty-six percent were Daksina Radhi Kayasthas. And 19 percent were Saptagram Suvarnaika. Sadharan Brahmos and Christians were underrepresented in relation to their actual numbers. Thirty-two percent of the organizers were either landlords or merchants. The rest were government servants, lawyers, medical practitioners, and educators. Not surprisingly, 36 percent came from rentier aristocrats, "whereas the rest were, of course, middle class."[50] It is important to note that the character of the leadership also changed between 1857 and 1885. In 1857, 54 percent of individual leaders were orthodox Hindus, while the rest were unorthodox, Brahmos, or Christians.[51]

N.G. Chandavakar (1855–1923), a prominent Brahmin reformer, said, "It is, I know, the fashion in some quarters to cry down the missionaries. To the Christian Missionary is due to a great extent the credit of the religious and social awakening of which the school of 'hindoo Protestantism' of the present day is the fruit." [52] And Raja Ramohan Roy stated in *The Precept of Jesus* (1820), "I found the doctrines of Christ more conducive and better adapted for the use of rational beginnings than any other which have come to my knowledge." [53] Though praising Christianity, he prevented the doctrine from winning over new adherents by keeping Hinduism relevant, through reinterpretation and purification. Tattvabodhini Sabha was established in 1839 to counter the progress of Christianity bya new reading of Hindu scriptures. The Brahma Samaj journal, *Tattvabodhini Patrika*, presented a debate. On the one hand, it argued for arresting the march of Christianity. On the other hand, it presented Hinduism as compatible with the Western ideals of reason and progress.

While the Hindu associations were expediting the anti-Christian crusade, Muslims showed indifference. Muslims considered Islam superior to Christianity and they generally declined to utilize opportunities provided by the colonial government. Their response to Hindu organizations revealed resentment toward Hindu revivalism and its convergence with Indian national identity, from which they felt excluded. [54]

As a result of Western education and the opportunities provided by the colonial economy, a large number of men from landowning families entered the professions. Declining income in urban areas, particularly for small zamindars, encouraged this trend. [55] Those in more traditional professions, such as pundits (scholars), were confronted with challenges presented by the newly educated elites from the missionary schools and their associations. Modes of knowledge in the areas of medicine, industry, and agriculture challenged the traditional occupational associations such as the *vaidyas* (traditional physicians). Professional associations of all kinds were established by the newly emerging professional groups and were later instrumental in transmitting the institutional practices of capitalist development. They also furthered the interests and increasing involvement of the professional classes throughout society.

Many among this emerging group of young urban professionals had been students at Westernized colleges. The important Young Bengal Group (YBG), founded by students associated with Hindu

College, was preceded by the Academic Association, which had been critical of religious practices. In 1830, Academic Association students brought out the *Parthenon*, a short-lived paper discussing controversial topics like colonization and the education of females. It was closed down and its founder, the young teacher H.L.V. Derozia, was expelled from the faculty. After Derozia's death in 1831 the organization disbanded, but was soon succeeded by the Society for the Acquisition of General Knowledge.

In the sole issue of *Parthenon*, one student wrote: "If there is anything that we hate from the bottom of our heart it is Hinduism"[56] These sentiments alarmed Christian missionaries, who condemned Derozia as an "atheist and universal skeptic." The solution for both Hindu conservatives and Christian missionaries was to found educational establishments in order to counter radical student activism.[57] The Reverend Alexander Duff founded a Higher Christian Institute in Calcutta, and the Hindus established many institutions in the early 1830s, such as Hindu Free School, Hindu Benevolent Institution, Oriental Seminary, and Hindu Liberal Academy.[58] His institution in Feringhi Kamal Bose cultivated a spirit of intellectual enquiry and helped spread European ideals of Enlightenment among Bengalis, leading to what later became known as the Young Bengal Movement and the Bengal Renaissance.

The YBG was initially interested in intellectual pursuits, but soon became involved in political campaigns, such as the repeal of press regulation (1835), the extension of the jury system to civil suits (1835), and the banning of exports of coolies from Mauritius (1838). In 1842, with the arrival of George Thompson, an anti-slavery activist and member of the British Parliament, the YBG underwent significant changes. Thompson urged YBG to form a new political association to advocate the extension of human rights to all classes. Of Thompson's role, Bholanauth Chunder said: "Thomson has planted the first seed of native political education in the country."[59]

Although the YBG never gained much support among the bhadraloks, one outcome of their active involvement in politics was the formation of the British India Association (BIA) in 1851, the forerunner of the Indian National Congress. Although it was an association of the landlords, it was comprised of members of the urban middle class, and its main objective was to protect the interests of the rentier classes. Its activities reflected a growing sense of class identity and interest in national politics. Members of BIA and the Landholders' Society came from the same class. The activities of the associations were controlled by a few influential families, such as the Debs, the Tagores, the Singhs, and the Ghosals. The BIA became an important site of interaction between the town and the countryside and a platform for political activity and the nationalist movement in particular.[60]

The founders of these associations did not call for the end of British rule, but wanted an "enlargement of its basis and [the] liberalization of its attitude."[61] The three associations mentioned above—the Landholders' Association, the YBG, and the BIA—were well developed. They had established procedures, paid staff, and constitutions. The BIA had two branches, the India Reform Society and the London Indian Society. Their transnational character was evident in ongoing collaborations with the East Indian Association and the Aborigines Protection Society in London. They were the most active associations in Bengal and the best established in representing the interests of the natives.

Initially, the impetus for growth in these associations was the need to counter Christianity, either by defending orthodox Hinduism or by "purifying" Hindu ideals. Natives themselves drew comparisons between Christianity and Hinduism, arguing that a lack of initiative would result in mass conversions to Christianity. A local newspaper commented on the lack of local efforts among natives during a famine:

> [I]t is to be regretted, that while the Americans and the Germans are collecting funds for the relief of famine-stricken people of this country, well-to-do natives are themselves so indifferent and close-fisted as to contribute nothing towards the relief of their fellow countrymen, but on the contrary raise a hue and cry when the missionaries provide aid to the helpless widows and children and complain that they are propagating their religion.[62]

Partly in response to such criticism, both the Hindu Orphan Relief Movement in 1857 and a similar movement in the Muslim community were established.

With the awakening of nationalist consciousness, public associations became an important means through which conflicting views about national identity were expressed and employed to mobilize the masses for collective action. Broadly, one could identify two different groups. First, there were those who represented a "bourgeois democratic" notion of nationalism, such as the Asiatic Society, the Bethune Society, the Family Literary Society, the Bengal Scientific Association, the Sadharani Sabha, and the Indian Reform

Association. Second, there were those who gravitated towards religion-based nationalism. These included the associations started by both Hindu traditionalists and modernists. The modernists, including Brahmo Sanaj, held utilitarian and rationalist ideals which did not undermine Hindu identity.

The activities of these associations revealed different class interests. For example, one of the main points of contention was the use of public associations for political purposes. In 1857, Ranjendra Lal Mitra, a spokesperson for rentiers, demanded that the Bengal Social Science Association remain politically neutral. When the move was rejected, "rentier aristocrats and their clients withdrew from the Association."[63] Another example may be found in Kailas Chandra Bose's attempt to create more opportunities for political debate within the Bethune Society. That attempt was severely criticized by the *Hindoo Patriot*, a leading rentier newspaper, when, in 1878, the BSSA applied for permission to hold public meetings at the town hall in Calcutta. The author wrote: "If things are allowed to go in the same way as heretofore, [we] shall not be surprised to find our washerman and barbours [sic] clamoring for the concession of holding their Punchayets there."[64]

Although their platforms were generally complex and often contradictory, the interests of traditionalist and modernist associations tended to converge "at the level of popular appropriation." Hindu revivalism was the unifying force compelling radical anti-traditionalists to subsume their interests in the larger struggle until the state was liberated from "alien rule," and it inspired the majority of social reformers and national independence associations.[65] When modernists challenged tradition, it was usually in the name of returning to a mythical golden age of Hinduism. For example, Ram Mohun Roy, a leading modernist, acknowledged Lord William Bentinck's early nineteenth-century efforts to prohibit *sati* by claiming that "the heinous sin of cruelty to females" would be forbidden if Hinduism could return to "the ancient and purest system" which would "no longer be set at naught by the Hindus themselves."[66]

Public associations in Calcutta benefited the landlords and the Hindu middle classes. The 1905–1908 Swadeshi (self-sufficiency) movement, which focused on undermining British power through economic protests and local production, highlighted Hindu neglect and insensitivity towards Muslim grievances as class consciousness was overwhelmed by religious and communal identities. The primacy of the notion of a "great Hindu community" led the bhadraloks to become inward-looking and parochial.[67] Because of this, the diversity and vitality of their associations faded as virtually everyone gave in to the interests of the freedom movement. In fact, most of the associations mentioned above became frontline organizations for the nationalist cause. In the process, differences between various bhadralok groups and rural gentry became less distinct.[68] By the 1920s, the bhadraloks had reached out to rural areas and formed associations throughout the country. The Bengal Province Hindu Mahasabha and the Bengal Branch of Rashtriya Swayam Sevak Sangham (RSS) patronized these associations, which had distinctly anti-Muslim agendas. As Bengali nationalist leader Bipin Chandra Pal noted, "In those days Hindus regarded Muslims and Christians as foreigners."[69]

The beginning of the Islamic Renaissance in the latter part of the nineteenth century coincided with the redefinition of Islamic identity, in opposition to Hindu identity, in the Indian National Congress. This trend extended far beyond Calcutta, where Muslims began joining Hindu-run organizations in greater numbers as well as founding organizations of their own. This attitude toward Muslims had already spurred the establishment of the Muslim League in 1906, after the colonial government gave in to Hindu demands and established Hindi as the official language of the largest Indian state. Essentially, Muslims feared that their interests would be ignored. But the growth of Muslim organizations was slowed by the predominantly agrarian social structure of East Bengal society. The Muslims' immediate and overwhelming concern was the threat of Hindu domination. This concern also influenced the emergence of Muslim peasant associations. Their political demands were moderate. They asked for rent reductions and debt remissions while focusing less on economic and more on religious issues.

In 1921, an Italian missionary in the district of Nadia formed Kisan Samiti (peasant societies). Subsequently, Kishan Sabhas (the peasants' front of the Communist Party [CP] of India) were formed in response to peasants' growing opposition to the hardships they endured under the zamindars. The intellectuals and the leaders of the *sabhas* had already come under the influence of the Russian Revolution of 1917, and *samitis* were introduced all over Bengal, especially in the eastern parts like Jessor, Rangpur, Mymensingh, Kulna, Chittagong, and Dinajpur. This development led to the formation of the Peasants and Workers Party in Bogra in 1925, which agitated against landlords and moneylenders. The fact that their meetings were held next to mosques led government officials to complain that the "wild nature" of these meetings did not represent "the true Islam."[70]

After 1929, the Nikhil Bangla Praja Samiti (All Bengal Peasants Association) developed a national following. The 1935 Government of India Act was supposed to grant Indian provinces autonomy, establish an Indian Federation, and introduce direct elections while reserving "discretionary powers" and "special responsibilities" for the British authorities. However, it was opposed by both the Indian National Congress and the Muslim League. In the wake of the Act, samitis became the "public space" for Muslim political activism. Samitis mobilized peasants against zamindars, indebtedness, unfair rent, and forced labor. Small groups formed to discuss peasant issues and radical change. Despite the fact that the majority of the leaders of Kishan Sabhas were Hindu, the *jotedars* and zamindars were not entirely successful in exploiting communalism to sabotage peasant activities. Nor were communal overtones entirely absent in debates between the Kishan groups and the predominantly Hindu landlords and moneylenders. Although Muslim peasants were led primarily by the Hindu leaders, the local bhadralok Hindus continued to view the situation as a Muslim-versus-Hindu struggle. For example, in Jessor, when Muslim and Namasudra groups jointly attacked Hindu zamindars, the Bengal Congress interpreted it as an anti-Hindu campaign. In Noakhali, Krishak Samiti members were accused of killing cows belonging to Hindu zamindars.[71]

Gradually, the associations that had formed to address the grievances of the peasantry gave way to political parties. Sporadic movements and scattered associations were, subsequently, brought under party control. During the 1937 elections, the Krishak Praja Party (KPP), which had spun off from the Nikhil Bangla Praja Samiti (All Bengal Tenants' Association) after the India Act of 1919, campaigned to resolve peasant grievances against the zamindars. However, its lack of initiative in challenging the interests of the majority Muslim *jotedars* prevented KPP from effectively addressing those demands. Similarly, since most zamindars in East Bengal were Hindus from West Bengal, anti-landlord agitation stalled when it took on communal overtones. As the differences between Muslims and Hindus became more apparent, Muslim leadership began to seek its support base among the Muslim populace.[72]

Voluntary associations played an important role in the Tebhaga movement, which arose during the Bengal famine of 1943.[73] Kisan Sabha was very active at this time. Subhajyoti Ray countered Ranajit Das Gupta by pointing out that the role of communist organizers in these protests "was important not so much to raise the consciousness of the workers, as Marxist historians tend to emphasize, or even to manipulate the workers for narrow political aims, as the colonial officials believed." Rather, Ray maintained, communist activists provided peasants with a "sense of the dissolution of existing authority and its replacement by an alternative."[74] Mahila Atma Rasksha Samiti (Women's Self-Defence League, or MARS) succeeded in mobilizing six million peasants. This was a notable, if not entirely surprising, accomplishment, since, as Binia Agarwal points out, "poor rural women were amongst the worst sufferers" during famines.[75]

Although many objected to the participation of women in Kishan Samiti, the women replied: "It does not hurt your sense of propriety when we sow harvest in the fields along with you. How does it become objectionable when we want to attend Kishan meetings?"[76] After that, older peasants withdrew their objections.[77] In Nindagram, women "would open up their veils and burkas and start demonstrating in front of the jotedars."[78] *Naribahani* (women's militia movements) emerged in opposition to state and police oppression, as spontaneous and localized responses to peasant grievances: "Unlike the Kishan Samiti, Nari Bahinis were untrained in tactics of guerrilla warfare, and they were mostly equipped with what might be called household equipment."[79] Resistance was so widespread that "the practice of *purdah* (seclusion of women) started to lose its hold under the influence of these movements."[80]

Women's associations in Bengal predated the Tebhaga movement, but, until the arrival of the missions, native women did not have the institutional means to carry out their agendas. Christian missionary organizations were dedicated to reforming the status of women, though not necessarily to emancipating them. Sir Herbert Risley described the Christian and colonial basis of women's reform: "A society which accepts intellectual inanition and moral stagnation as the moral condition of its womankind cannot hope to develop the high qualities of courage, devotion and self-sacrifice which go to the making of nations."[81] Thus, the first Women's Christian Associations were concerned with education, although attempts were sporadic and lacked the continuity of boys' schools. Although a few Hindu religious leaders and educators, such as Radhakanta Deb and Gaurmohun Vidyalankar, promoted schools for women, most Indian reformers preferred home schooling for females. Women showed enthusiasm for education in the public sphere, but rigid social conditions prevented most of them from attending public schools, hindering their ability to form their own associations, though not stopping them entirely.

The formation of Anjumn-i-Khawateen-i-Islam (Muslim Women's Association in Calcutta) led to the Muslim Education Conference in 1886, and the Muslim Ladies' Conference in 1905. These samitis took a stand against child marriage, *mohar* (excessive dowry), and pageantry at wedding ceremonies. After 1900, women's rights protests became commonplace.[82] Ashrafs such as Nawab Abdul Lateef, Syeed Ameer Ali, Mirza Delwar Hussain, and Maulvi Abdul Hamid initiated reforms to bring Muslims back into the mainstream. Activists were typically high-ranking officers in the Mughal administration, members of affluent families in the jute trade, administrators, and landowners, and the freedom of women in their families to acquire education enabled them to form their own associations.

As a result of conditions that had, until the twentieth century, prevented female education from gaining favor among Muslims, women turned increasingly to Hindu men's organizations. The most important of those associations was the Brahmo Samaj, which initially included the female family members of its Hindu leaders. Through these associations, women made several important appeals to the state regarding various laws which they considered unjust. For example, in 1883, Brahmo Samaj women presented a memorandum supporting the Ilbert Bill, which allowed Indian judges the right to try British offenders. After Brahmo Samaj split in 1866, Brahmo Samaj of India, led by K.C. Sen, started the women's branch, Bramika Samaj, in 1865.[83] The Samaj taught Brahmo values, religion, and vocational skills to women. K.C. Sen established the first Brahmo Samaj School for Girls, and his leadership enabled the passage of the Native Marriage Act of 1872, despite powerful opposition. He subsequently started a women's journal and formed Sadharan (General) Brahmo Samaj, which created many associations for women.

In 1878, when Brahmo Samaj split into two factions, each established women's branches. Nava Bidhan Brahm was led by K.C. Sen and supported by Arya Samaj. It did not favor higher education for women. Banga Mahila Samaj adopted a more liberal attitude towards women, offering them prominent positions in the association's activities.[84] All of these reforms were intended to prepare ideal counterparts for modern bhadralok society, although they were a product of the "Christianization and Westernization" of Hinduism. The ultimate effect was the articulation and legitimization of the traditional social order, the affirmation of the dominant religious and cultural ideologies shaping caste, class, and community differences. At the same time, they facilitated upward social mobility for women.[85]

Hindu associations were concentrated in Calcutta, and Muslim participation in them was limited. Shah Din, the father of Begum Jahan Ara Shah Nawaz, who later became leader of many women's associations, feared that Muslim women would fall behind Hindu women if reforms were not introduced. The initiatives taken up by this family subsequently laid the foundation for the Muslim Women's Association in 1915 and the All India Women's Conference (AIWC) in 1927.[86] From the nineteenth century onwards, a number of philanthropic associations, including Antopur Stri Shikkha Shobha (1870), Kouliniya Shongshodhoni O'Konya Bikroy Nibaroni Shoba of Faridhpur (1871), Bidhoba Bibaho Shobha of Dhaka (1871), and Muslim Shurid Shommiloni of Dhaka (1882), endeavored to make education more easily attainable for women. During this period, as women completed their educations, they began to organize themselves.

The evolution of public associations among women is associated with the emergence of *bhadramahila*, a term that, as Brothwick explains, initially described female members of bhadralok families. The term eventually came to embody a Brahmo ideal, namely, a woman possessing upper-class qualities and leading an upper-class lifestyle. In this context, it denoted an "Enlightened, Muhammadan lady or sister."[87] These women were "consciously welded into a body with a progressive image and seen as pioneers of a new way of life to be adopted by other non-Brahmo women."[88] Traditional indigenous notions were interwoven with the Victorian ideal of humanitarian service to the poor. In 1882, after Colonel Olcott's visit to Calcutta, Swarnakumari Devi, of the Tagore family, established a Ladies' Theosophical Society. In 1886, Shahi Samiti was established so that "women in respectable families [could] have the opportunity of mixing with each other and devoting themselves to the cause of social welfare."[89]

The activities of women's associations were not intended to mark a radical departure from the traditional ideal of womanhood. To the contrary, they were rooted in revivalist claims about Hindu and Islamic traditions. In the process, women became active participants in and embodiments of their respective nation-states. Sister Nivedita explained, "In India, the sanctity and sweetness of Indian family life have been raised to the rank of a great culture. Wifehood is a religion; motherhood, a dream of perfection; and the pride and protectiveness of men are developed to a very high degree."[90] The articulation of women's interests within traditional religious ideology served the interests of men as well as the class interests of elite women by providing a means through which they could legitimize their leadership. Annie Besant and Sarojini Naidu argued that women's direct participation in India's national development was essential for improving their status in society. By referring to the high status of women in traditional society, they advocated their uplift in the name of reviving the greatness of India's past, its "golden age."[91]

By the early 1910s, these associations began to exert their influence on a national scale. In 1910, Sarala Devi Choudrani founded the Bharat Stri Mahamandal; in 1917, the Women's India Association (WIA) was founded by Annie Besant; and, in 1925, the National Council of Women in India was founded by Lady Aberdeen. The leaders of these associations were members of the elite classes. Their activities created links among different elite groups throughout the country, establishing networks which soon enabled women to influence government decision making at the level of policy reforms. At the same time, the middle-class character of the women's associations was an obstacle to the realization of women's interests in general. Even radical female activists agreed that their cause could only be served within the parameters of national interests, which were primarily articulated within Hinduism.

As Gandhi began to play a leading role in Indian politics, women's organizations incorporated his ideals of womanhood and nonviolence, reinforcing sex stereotypes and the traditional division of labor. Gandhi asserted: "Equality between sexes does not mean equality of occupations. Nature has created the sexes as complements to each other."[92] AIWC leaders argued that their task was to develop the "special capacities and virtues of womanhood so as to give her the training for participation in general culture."[93] Social reforms such as widow remarriage, polygamy, and property rights were primarily the concerns of the middle class, as they only affected "the first two castes."[94]

By the 1930s, the AIWC began advocating equal rights for women via state reforms in the areas of marriage, divorce, and equal inheritance between men and women. They also demanded economic equality between the sexes. In 1940, Bameshwari Nehru explained that without economic rights in the home women would continue to be the suppressed sex and dependent on the generosity, patronage, and sentimentality of the artificially-made superior sex, and she cannot have self-respect or self reliance but imbibes an inferiority complex, thinking also that her great hard work of mothering and caring for the race is her curse instead of her worthy vocation.[95]

Gandhi emphasized self-development but had little to say in favor of modern notions of sexual equality.

Theosophists like Annie Besant and Maria Helena Blavatsky also protested against widow burning and child marriage and advocated women's rights in India, but unlike missionaries they romanticized Indian society, and claimed that there had been greater equality for women in precolonial India than in Western Christian society. Theosophists also gave precedence to the interests of nationalist elites, deeming it "tactically necessary not to press too much of women's rights of women's education."[96] Theosophist reforms gave the elite classes (both in Sri Lanka and India) the means to maintain their dominance while simultaneously monopolizing the fruits of capitalist modernity. Theosophy undermined the potential of both socialist and Christian worldviews to present meaningful challenges to existing social hierarchies. This is one reason why the ideals of a radical reformer like M.N. Roy, who condemned India's "feudal-patriarchal society" as an "ugly ghost of the past" and criticized Gandhi's views on celibacy and opposition to birth control as "traditional ideals put forward by nationalist leaders", did not command popular acceptance.[97] Roy, who had previously argued that the modernization of India was a structural necessity, eventually succumbed to the pressures of nationalism.

Nor were women's organizations united in their demands. For example, women in the WIA were politically divided. In the 1937 elections, the AIWC moved to the forefront of the women's rights movement, and a number of its members were elected to political office, but radical factions of women were also represented. New associations of workers and peasants involved a large number of women, and these organized women threatened the elites whose economic base was derived from land ownership. Kamaladevi Chattopadhyaya claimed that elections were of no use in a capitalist society; she ran as a socialist candidate in 1937 but was defeated. Radicals were energetically suppressed by middle-class reformers with the cooperation of the colonial government. Missionaries, too, distanced themselves from female radicalism.

Some female members of the Muslim League resigned from the AIWC after it became involved in national politics because its activity was dominated by the Hindus. Many progressive women resigned, too, protesting the AIWC's decision to align itself with a political party instead of representing the interests of all women. Despite their religious diversity, these dissenters were branded the "Muslim Bengal Group," implying that they represented only a minority of Indians.[98] Thereafter, the AIWC, in its official rhetoric, declared that its members were "[n]ot feminist, not suffragettes, and did not want to start a sex war with men." The organization sought to maintain its distance from Western feminists, whose arguments and reputations might undermine the nationalist cause.[99]

Until independence in 1947, tradition and religion were not serious obstacles to women's participation in the public sphere. On March 17, 1943, thousands of women from Chittagong, Pabna, and Dinajpur gathered in Calcutta to protest against food price increases. In radical social uprisings, women provided housing and care to male insurgents, spread propaganda, collected funds, and transported and sometimes even used weapons. Pritilatha Waddekar, who led a group of men to the Chittagong Club, wrote a letter before she committed suicide:

> Why should there be any distinction between males and females in a fight for the cause of the country's freedom? If our brothers can join a fight for the cause of the motherland why can't sisters? Instances are not rare that Rajput ladies of hallowed memory fought bravely in the battlefields and did not hesitate to kill their country's enemies. The pages of history are replete with high admiration for the historic exploits of these distinguished ladies. Then, why should not modern Indian women join this noble fight to redeem our country from foreign domination? If sisters can stand side by side with the brothers in the Satyagraha movement, why are they not so entitled in a revolutionary movement?[100]

By 1947, these women's associations had a long history as frontline organizations mobilizing women in broad-based social movements. They enabled both Muslim and Hindu women to successfully blend religious themes and social interests under the banner of larger social and political movements like Hindu revivalism, "Indian Nationalism," and the Non-Cooperation Movement. When the Muslim League established its women's wing in 1935, the AIWC became an important part of the struggle for Pakistani independence. But, in the end, the nationalist movement subsumed them. Women's issues did not disappear from public debate during the high point of the struggle, but, as Partha Chatterjee has argued, nationalists simply would not "make the women's question an issue of political negotiation with the colonial state."[101] Gail Pearson points out: "The role of female participants was to provide the basis for the universalization of the whole movement."[102] Leadership in the women's movement initially came from the new middle class, which unequivocally supported British rule, until they developed aspirations of their own. Those aspirations soon led to the freedom movement, but a majority from the middle classes, following independence, aligned with dominant interests. Ultimately, those middle-class groups were conservative and sought legitimization through religious-ethnic ideologies.

## INTERNATIONAL ORGANIZATIONS, VOLUNTARY ASSOCIATIONS, AND THE STATE

Toward the middle of the nineteenth century, the colonial government began introducing laws and regulations to control the activities of the voluntary associations. It was the duty of district officers to organize charities to undertake "private works to stimulate private charity collection of subscriptions. In managing these organizations, the government believed that the effectiveness of relief operations would depend very largely on the use of non-official agencies."[103] The government recognized that its interference would be resented by relief organizations and charities, and district officers were told that "[they] should not in any way interfere in the management of such works."[104]

In the 1850s, charity collectors took personal initiative to promote rural welfare through Ferry Funds Committees and District Red Cross Committees. They organized small villages into samitis, introduced Village Development Funds, Village Halls, and Model Villages, and mobilized voluntary labor for eradicating water hyacinths and excavating canals.[105] With the emergence of the freedom movement, politicians grew hostile to such activities. They soon sought to undermine the power and influence of collectors,[106] who may have been motivated to intervene in rural development to increase their sphere of influence among the population. The British government was also apprehensive that voluntary associations would lead mass mobilizations against the colonial state, a sentiment that increased as the independence movement gained momentum.

The colonial administration was not convinced that local institutions could manage delegated tasks. They believed that East Bengal, in contrast to other parts of the subcontinent, lacked the "self-government institutions appropriate for government's administrative tasks." The Annual Bengal Administration Report of 1871 states:

> In the plains of Bengal these institutions seem to have been very much weakened even prior to British rule and in the last one hundred years of British rule [...] they have almost disappeared. It cannot be said that in the more important provinces of this administration, there are absolutely no self-government institutions. Some traces yet remain; some things are in some places regulated by village panchayats and by Headmen, elders. But more and more, the Zamindari agents supplant the old model and the landlord takes the place of indigenous self-rule.[107]

It is also likely that the colonial government's hesitation to incorporate local institutions such as Samaj and Salish was reinforced by the dominance of Hindu landlords in the region, the preponderance of Hindus in higher positions in the government, and the apparently slow progress of Muslims in utilizing the opportunities provided by the colonial government.

By 1880, however, in the face of deteriorating law and order and increasing poverty, the government began to recognize the importance of voluntary associations. The Famine Commission pointed out that the government lacked the resources and administrative capacity to carry out relief and rehabilitation programs. The usefulness of a government-developed administrative system that would not be perceived as "alien" by the natives was no longer in doubt. The goal of post-famine relief and rehabilitation programs was to help the victims resume their lives and reduce dependence upon aid. Credit constituted a significant component of relief assistance, acting as a "moral strategy to give confidence to the people, and also with the object of stimulating agricultural efforts."[108] The government's initiatives in mobilizing local resources and participation enabled it to place the many charitable funds and voluntary associations under the supervision of the Revenue Department, further solidifying its hold over them.[109] Public funds were allocated to various private institutions in the form of grants-in-aid, and government officers monitored the process. District officers organized charities and non-official agencies to undertake collection of subscriptions, for the government believed that "the effectiveness of relief operations would depend very largely on the use of non-official agencies."[110]

At the beginning of the nineteenth century, in response to the crisis presented by the disaffection of the local intelligentsia, missionaries debated changing their approach to evangelism. The theological tradition that evolved during this debate came to be known as the "theology of fulfillment" and was popularized by John Nicol Farquhar. Its guiding principle was that Christ's coming fulfills Christian beliefs, and also completes the world's great religions. Christ was described therein as the "crown" of Hinduism. Reverend T.E. Slater argued that Christianity needed to be explained in light of the fundamental principles of Hinduism, as opposed to the earlier approach of rapprochement and condemnation. Otherwise, Hindus simply would not listen.[111] These views were adopted by the church and also by international Christian lay organizations like the Young Men's Christian Association (YMCA).The theology of fulfillment gained widespread acceptance as India experienced a political awakening. Missionaries were astonished at the resilience of the social system that they sought to transform. Yet they remained optimistic, despite their apparent inability to impose their value systems.[112]

The international Christian voluntary associations that evolved during this period assumed an increasingly nonsectarian and non-denominational outlook. The church began to stress an ecumenical rather than a directly evangelical approach to social change, and an increasing number of lay persons joined the associations. Both missionaries and the public doubted the capacity of government agencies to carry out social development programs. There was general agreement that the government could not be trusted "either with control of private wealth or reformation of the society."[113] Organizations emerged which drew their membership and financial assistance from multiple denominations and varied individuals, as opposed to the fixed constituencies which had supported earlier missionary work. The YMCA is an excellent example of such an organization, and a short history is in order.

George Williams, a Christian businessman, established the YMCA in the United States in 1844 to provide for the needs of young men who had migrated to cities from rural areas and found urban living very difficult. The organization's objective was to develop a "total person" by emphasizing both spiritual and physical needs. Worldwide, the YMCA was known for giving particular emphasis to sports or physical education. Revivalists thought that "muscular

Christianity might be the means of salvation for errant youth."[114] In 1890, the YMCA came to India. Within a short period, branch associations were established throughout the country. The aim was to build "self-directing, self-supporting and self-propagating" local organizations that would undertake a variety of social welfare programs.

In 1910, 1926, and 1938, the International Missionary Council discussed the role of missionary aid in rural development. They needed to address the difficulties faced by converts in obtaining employment in the absence of traditional social and economic networks. In the 1930s, the YMCA introduced a number of programs designed to reconstruct rural societies in order to foster self-reliance and self-sufficiency. Their goals were not achieved, and, by the 1940s, their programs were entirely US-funded. They ended, at last, when the money ran out. However, the YMCA became a model for the development of several local associations, such as the Young Men's Hindu Association, the Young Women's Hindu Association, and the Young Men's Muslim Association.

The YMCA was not immune to geopolitical developments. As noted by Rekha Mehra: "Like other American agencies in India at that time, the YMCA had few doubts about whether it should combat Communism."[115] It provided pro-capitalist and pro-democratic literature to compete with similar propaganda from the USSR and China, and hoped that, in the "competition for the minds of the educated classes in India, the YMCA [could] play a significant role."[116] In addition to providing direct aid, the YMCA was seen by its funders as an opportunity to build democracy in India, as "a spiritual rock, social welfare agency and bulwark against communism."[117] It became even more important to Westerners after China adopted communism in 1949.

## SECOND COLONIZATION, 1947–1971

Pakistan was established as an independent state in 1947. The "intermediate regime" that yielded power lacked a broad social base. It had derived its authority from positions within the civil administration and the armed forces, both of which were disproportionately dominated by Indians of Punjabi descent. Revenues were extracted from different provinces and only marginally invested in social development. Such investment was generally inequitable across regions, and typically produced a slow and highly skewed pattern of growth. The weakness of the state in consolidating its authority, coupled with the geopolitical realities of the Cold War era, made it heavily dependent on foreign aid from Western countries, particularly the United States.[118] In its quest to broaden its social base, the state embraced Islam as its national ideology.

In the process of state formation, particularly in west Pakistan, associations based on religious identities appeared as the most significant players in the voluntary sector.[119] The *mullah* lobby within the Muslim League organized the *ulema* (body of mullahs) of Deoband, Majlis-I-Ahrar and Khaksars. It was also the first group to agitate for an Islamic Constitution. Akhwan-ul-Muslimeen was established mainly as a bid to legitimize state power in the greater Islamic world at a time when Jamait-ul-Ulema-I-Islam desired to establish links with Islamic parties around the world. During the period of Ahmediya issue, state patronage was extended to Islamic religious groups, including Jamait-I-Islam, the Jamait-ul-Ulema-I-Pakistan and the Jamait-ul-Ulema-I-Islam.[120] The relationship between religious groups and political actors was always paradoxical. On the one hand, social groups competing for state power sought to minimize the explanatory power of religion. On the other hand, political parties competed for the support of various religious groups. The end result was the irreversible establishment of Islam as a powerful political force.

In contrast to the vast area that became India after partition, the territory that became Pakistan did not undergo many radical changes during the colonial period. Historically, a large illiterate rural population, a small middle class, and the monopoly of educational activities by the religious authorities had limited the prospects of public associations like those seen in Bengal. In Pakistan, there was no need for landlords, already allied with the ruling classes, to form such associations as a means of legitimization. The Pakistani ruling alliance adopted various measures to suppress associations consisting of intellectuals, journalists, and trade unionists, which seemed to be a potential threat to the state and the landowning class.

In the process of expanding government control over collective action, waqf were brought under the power of government imams and *khatibs* (preachers), and placed on the government payroll.[121] In east Pakistan, the departure of Hindu landlords, and the progressive deterioration of the economic and political positions of Bengali Muslims caused by the discriminatory policies of the Pakistani state, rendered most philanthropic associations powerless.

After partition in 1947, development progressively became an integral part of nation-building, a process in which the state assumed a leading role. In the area that came to be known as Pakistan, colonial governments had shown relatively little interest in revitalizing existing rural institutions and involving them in social development. However, after independence, the vastness of the rural population was a problem for the highly centralized administrative system. This compelled the state to look for new institutions through which it might decentralize its functions. The government initiated local government reforms, integrated rural and community development, and established cooperative organizations with the objective of creating a spirit of self-help, initiative, leadership, and cooperation among the villagers. The hope was that this might become the foundation of independent, healthy, and self-supporting economic, political, and social progress.[122] These programs were dependent primarily on government aid and were under the supervision of government officers. They were generally implemented on an ad hoc basis and lacked continuity, and, in the final analysis, their activities contributed more to the development and extension of large bureaucracies than anything else. Those bureaucracies then charted the courses of local institutions.[123]

A number of studies have shown that the objective of decentralization was vitiated by a tendency toward political centralization, resulting in the broadening of the state's rural power base and opening the way for competition between old and new claimants to political power. In the process, the benefits of government programs were monopolized by a small group of elites, and government agencies became distributors of patronage.[124] Sixty to sixty-five percent of the elected members of these associations each owned seven or more acres of land, in a country where average landholdings were less than two and a half acres. Participation in voluntary associations, combined with political patronage and personal wealth, enhanced landowners' direct power over property relations, increased their access to credit, entitled them to government subsidies on agricultural inputs, and gave them exclusive employment opportunities.[125]

Large international foundations also helped Pakistan to consolidate its power. Between 1890 and 1920, a new kind of institution had evolved, changing the character of nonprofit associations, not only in the US but around the world: the nonprofit foundation. As Peter Hall pointed out, the evolution of nonprofit organizations is intimately connected to the evolution of the for-profit sector. Foundations and endowments "served as a mechanism of capital formation and proved to be an effective means for members of the business community who were politically in the minority to exert their influences over education, profession and culture."[126] The period in which foundations evolved was characterized by mass poverty, social disorder, labor crises, periodic financial crises, and political challenges to capitalism by communist revolutions. Business communities redefined their relationship with the state and society and searched for private-sector alternatives to state-funded welfare capitalism,[127] one of which was private-sector intervention in welfare policy and activities. Large-scale business enterprises needed

> social, political and economic intelligence, for both the purposes of long-range planning and for defining the historically unprecedented relations between the corporate giants and the immense accumulation of wealth that they produced and the Christian and democratic ideals of the American Society (which were shared by the businessmen themselves).[128]

In 1936, charitable contributions became tax-deductible in the US, and this became a major incentive for personal and corporate investments in the nonprofit sector. As a result, local recipients of international foundation funds were directly tied to international capital, despite the fact that their autonomy was still embedded in national laws. Well-endowed foundations thus became key players in shaping public policy.

After 1947, the Rockefeller Foundation, in India since 1916, widened its interests from medicine to include agricultural as well as cultural affairs. The Ford Foundation, founded in 1936, opened its first international office in India in the early 1950s. It was especially interested in population control, since it felt that lowering the population would improve living conditions for the people of underdeveloped nations. It began funding pilot projects in India and Pakistan in 1959 and 1961, respectively.

Initially, the Rockefeller Foundation believed that industrialization was the key to India's development, and it worked closely with the government toward that end, giving less emphasis to agricultural development. By 1980, its interest in supporting NGOs increased, as did Ford's. In contrast to other donor agencies, the Ford Foundation in Bangladesh gave financial assistance to diverse types of programs, with occasionally conflicting objectives. Bangladeshi intellectuals and NGOs generally agreed that the Ford Foundation had a more liberal political position than the Rockefeller Foundation. Ford played a crucial role in shaping the Association of Development Agencies (ADAB) and other prominent NGOs in Bangladesh.

Because of the skewed pattern of social, economic, and political development in the regions presided over by the central and the provincial governments,[129] East Bengal, which suffered the most, presented a serious challenge to the Punjabi-dominated state. That challenge, of course, culminated in the emergence of Bangladesh in 1972.[130] Student organizations played a leading role in the protests of trade unions and communist organizations which advanced the cause of an independent Bangladesh. There was little opposition to those protests, in part because all segments of the population felt disadvantaged. Even business magnates, such as M.A. Ispahani, who dominated the jute trade, became disenchanted with the West Pakistani government after Malik Firoz Khan Noon, a member of the Punjabi landowning family, was appointed as governor of the province.

Voluntary associations during this period were mainly confined to urban areas and included organizations such as Mahila Parishads, All Pakistan Women's Association (APWA), Youth Welfare Councils, and East Pakistan Welfare Association. Mahila Parishads' programs, in particular, were extended to rural areas and improved the social conditions of women.[131] Membership of these organizations mostly consisted of government officers and their wives, who, in their spare time, helped the destitute and performed cultural functions while furthering their professional interests.[132] The growing discontent between West and East Pakistan meant that Bengali Muslims generally steered clear of these associations.

While most of these associations were not directly involved in politics, in 1955 the APWA campaigned against the existing family and marriage laws, bringing it into conflict with the Ulema Board (Muslim leadership) and placing the state in a precarious position.[133] As a result, the Family Laws Ordinance of 1961 was passed, setting a minimum age limit for marriage and placing restrictions on men's previously unilateral rights to both polygamy and divorce. *Khula* (the Islamic right of women to divorce or separate) was also made easier for women to enforce, but, even within APWA, there were disagreements regarding family law. By 1969 the Family Laws Ordinance came under fire along with the Ayub regime in general. Opposition continued under Zulfiqar Ali Bhutto. Consequently, APWA activism declined. During this period, oil-producing countries in the Middle East and North Africa showed interest in providing financial assistance to voluntary associations that were based on Islamic ideals. These opportunities did not, however, lead to an upsurge of Islamic NGOs in East Pakistan, both because funds were controlled by the West, and because Bengalis failed to take advantage of those opportunities. State officials misappropriated external resources with ease, since they were the only sources through which donors could disburse their funds. With the emergence of Bengali nationalism, with its secularist overtones, the activities of Islamic NGOs in East Pakistan declined further as they became increasingly identified with the West Pakistani state.

When the first five-year plan was formulated, there was no bureaucracy to administer voluntary agency activity. Those agencies thus functioned mostly as independent organizations or in collaboration with government ministries. They were exclusively based on government grants-in-aid, and most employees were paid wages. Volunteers were also compensated for their expenses and were able to use the facilities of their employers free of charge to further their personal interests.[134] On December 2, 1961, a new ordinance was introduced entitled the Registration and Control of Voluntary Agencies Act. The Act required organizations to register with the director of social welfare. The regulation did not prevent officials of voluntary organizations from holding office in other bodies, so the same politically influential persons were at once patrons and functionaries of many organizations. One commentator noted that, after the promulgation of martial law and the introduction of Basic Democracies, welfare organizations became a refuge for disgruntled politicians as well as a springboard for new political aspirants.[135]

Church-based NGOs were active in many parts of what is now Bangladesh during the period of Pakistani rule and there is no substantial evidence of conflicts between them and the government of West Pakistan. The visibility of NGOs in East Pakistan increased with the escalation of military suppression by West Pakistan and the cyclone of 1970. For example, the Heartland Emergency Life-Saving Project (HELP), an NGO formed by American doctors, intervened to assist cyclone victims. They were well-trained, experienced, and able to mobilize international resources, while Bengali-speaking Muslims, whose economy and social structure had been in disarray since partition, were not. These organizations also functioned as neutral mediators whose activities were less likely to be challenged given their international connections.

As relief and rehabilitation efforts began, the Pakistani army was intensifying its efforts to curb emerging protests, and the West

Pakistan government was coming under severe criticism from the international community for neglecting those affected by the cyclone. When the army arrived, it demanded that organizations turn over to them their relief activities. In one instance, HELP refused to function under the conditions laid down by the military. It solicited the assistance of Steve Baldvi, the director of the Ford Foundation in India. Baldvi flew to Dhaka and implored the military to allow HELP to continue its relief work. In response, the military removed the uncooperative officer and appointed another one, giving him specific orders to work with HELP.

The government took control of NGO rehabilitation activities and mandated that all projects be carried out on the Comilla cooperative model. Cooperatives held public meetings, elected officers, and remained responsible for their basic functions. NGOs formed several co-ops to distribute relief and agricultural supplies and to build boats, but the power structure of the villages often undermined the cooperative ideal of equality. For example, an open lottery system was introduced to distribute cattle during famines. However, the lists of lottery winners were clearly being manipulated. Father R.W. Timm wrote: "One co-op has all Hindu names. Another lists members of one of the biggest families on the island in the top four positions."[136]

On March 7, 1971, Sheikh Mujibur Rahman delivered his famous speech to a crowd of over 1 million people at Ramna Park. He claimed, "The struggle this time is the struggle for freedom; the struggle this time is the struggle for independence." This was followed by the movement of Pakistani troops, disguised as civilians, to Dhaka via Sri Lanka. The massacre that followed is now regarded as one of the most gruesome episodes in South Asian military history. Hindus were the most obvious targets, because the war was not isolated from foreign policy relations between Pakistan and India after partition. NGOs attempted to protect the victims and played a crucial role in documenting the violence and reporting it to the international community. The SEATO doctors, another group operating in Dhaka alongside CORR (Christian Organization for Relief and Rehabilitation), Caritas, and HELP, had formed a lobby group in Washington DC to explain conditions to the US Senate. Reports from Bangladeshi NGOs were read at the Senate proceedings. Pressure from the US government brought a temporary halt to military operations. NGO lobbying efforts were not entirely successful due to close military and foreign policy collaboration between Pakistan's government and the United States, but NGO efforts continued, and in some cases won important concessions. For example, during the war many international NGOs, such as Irish Concern, Oxfam, and Red Cross, along with the United Nations, undertook relief and rehabilitation work.

As early as the 1970s, significant ideological shifts within NGOs became apparent. These took place on a transnational scale and came about primarily from the interaction of the churches with the capitalist and socialist systems of South America and the Philippines. Cooperative models were adopted by most NGOs as a way of organizing long-term development programs. Those models assumed the basic need for increased productive capacity among the poor. Organizations like the Mennonite Central Committee, the Young Women's Christian Association, the Irish Concern, Oxfam, and the Community Health Care Project (CHCP) focused on income generation activities for women involved in the jute industry. The evidence suggests that villagers were not opposed to working in NGO programs. In 1976, women were organized into small groups and "came together for the first time for united action; they made decisions by themselves about the work and the use of their income; they excluded men from their projects."[137] The ideals of self-sufficiency and self-reliance, and the strategies of small groups and microcredit, were well established by the end of the decade.

Until East Bengal merged with Pakistan, peasant interests had dominated association culture there. With the departure of Hindu landlords and Muslim peasants from East Bengal, the Muslim elite consolidated their position over the land. Yet East Bengal's economy remained under the control of the East Pakistan government. The 1956 election had seen the demise of the Muslim League and the resurgence of linguistic and communitarian mobilization among the intelligentsia, but the class character of resistance among subordinate groups was more apparent than communitarian solidarity. The latter languished until 1972.

Historically, a diverse spectrum of voluntary associations carried out a wide range of activities in Bengal and Bangladesh, most of which ultimately bolstered the dominance of the landowning and middle classes—i.e., the hegemonic bloc—over the state and society. Religion, nationalism, and communalism proved to be effective tools in the ongoing competition for state power. In the process, the radical agendas of public associations were subverted and brought under the control of the state. Public associations then became the instruments of political parties, which remained the main organs of social mobilization. The subversion of radical associations was primarily due to their failure to articulate a notion of the state that was different in kind from the prevailing one.

While NGOs ostensibly sought to change power structures, their ideological and institutional strategies were vague. For example, Caritas, the Catholic relief organization, had been restructured as a result of Vatican II, when Catholic aid efforts adopted a broader focus. It opened its first office in Pakistan in 1966. Its new approach was shaped by its direct encounter with both the poor and with Marxist revolutionary groups.[138] Within the NGO community there was widespread reluctance to accept radical approaches to social change when they were articulated along Marxist lines. Jos Van Beurden and Jenneke Arens were commissioned by CORR to conduct a one-year study of rural development in Bangladesh, with the aim of assisting CORR's development interventions. The first chapter of their report underlined the importance of eliminating "village oppressors through people's courts" and the study included a lengthy appendix on Marx and Lenin's theories on the role of women in development. References to Vietnam and China were also highlighted. Father Timm refused to endorse the appendix and handed over the manuscript to the secretary of rural development and the president's chief advisor, Khurshed Alam and Mahbub Alam Chasi, respectively. Both of them rejected the report. Still, Van Beurden and Arens refused to publish the book with the amendments suggested by Caritas, and they were finally forced to find a publisher based outside of the country. The preface to the publication indicated that it was too sensitive to publish in Bangladesh.

Timm reflected on the experience:

> Up to then I had been attracted more and more toward socialism as a more idealist system for benefiting the poor, but after having my fingers burned I became more cautious and critical and observed that the acceptance of socialism in Catholic circles was based more on religious and emotional grounds than on well-reasoned theoretical grounds or on historical experience. I also concluded that dialogue is difficult with people whose theorists (Lenin) encouraged deception in the name of the cause.[139]

Timm pointed out the nature of the ideological conflict within the NGO community: while NGOs may have stood for justice and equality, and while many employed Marxist analyses, their ideological commitment has, historically, been weak. (A strong commitment to ideological Marxism on the part of an NGO leads to political action that will likely bring the organization into conflict with the state and put its existence at risk.) The rejection of Marxism by the NGO community reassured the government, Bangladesh's ruling class, and the international community that NGOs were not allied with political parties. NGOs maintained their distance from parties and for-profit organizations and focused on uncompromisingly defending the rights of the poor. This pragmatic orientation attracted exiles and expatriates from London, Calcutta, and West Pakistan, some of whom founded organizations in East Pakistan to organize rehabilitation efforts. Some of the founders of those organizations subsequently became the leaders of contemporary NGOs, such as the Bangladesh Rural Advancement Committee (BRAC), Najira Kori, the Association for Social Development, and ADAB.

During the colonial period, the native middle classes adopted the organizational models of the missionaries to meet challenges to their authority by "subaltern groups," as well as by missionaries and the colonial government. These associations, in turn, provided the basic structure of the "Bengal Renaissance," the social reform and independence movements, and determined the shifting forms of the state during the nineteenth and early twentieth centuries. These associations were transnational in so far as they borrowed ideas and material resources from many different parts of the world. Both the colonial government and the indigenous middle classes subverted the radicalism of missionary organizational models—suppressing and emulating them—and used them for their own ends. The history of missionary and native associations, their sometimes complementary and sometime competing agendas, illustrates the formation of the class basis of the colonial state. The activities of these associations played an important role in shaping the character of the elite politics that Ranajith Guha described as dominance without hegemony:

> where one representing the bourgeois colonial rulers, who gained political dominance in India by coercion, and the other, the Indian elite bourgeois nationalists "spawned and nurtured" by colonialism itself, who led a passive nationalist movement in order to succeed to the ruling power in the borrowed robes of their colonial mentors.[140]

Missionaries, native organizations, and the government all conducted activities that contributed to the institutionalization of the state as the leading actor in social development and the maintenance of law and order. They reconfigured social problems as political problems which needed to be resolved through the state apparatus, making the colonial state the primary target of social discontent. The state in turn constrained the space for NGOs as it consolidated its hold over social development, often emulating the models that NGOs had provided. At the end of each colonial period (British and Pakistani), many from the economically prosperous elites (e.g., Hindu and Pakistani landlords, industrialists, and money lenders) abandoned the country and went into exile, depriving the country of an entrepreneur class with capital. Similarly, the Pakistan government was more interested in plundering the East Bengal economy than investing in its development. The interventions of the governments of Pakistan, India, and Western countries were motivated by their respective geopolitical interests, rather than by a genuine interest in the country's condition. The relative neglect of the region by the superpowers during the Cold War period, and the destruction of the East Pakistan economy, combined with the economic weakness of the Bangladeshi state since its independence in 1971, opened a far greater space for NGO intervention in social development than many other developing countries offered. The result was that NGOs almost comprised a parallel government.

The openness of Bangladesh to NGOs with diverse ideological orientations, and its vulnerability to their exigencies, is also a result of the cosmopolitan and secular ethos of the middle class in East Bengal, and the oppression the population had suffered under the Pakistan government and the Hindu zamindars. At the same time, decades-long neglect of social development also meant that traditional village organizations, centered on the religious establishment, also remained intact. After independence in 1971, the confrontation between secularism and Islamic nationalism came to be the critical determinant of state formation and of the state's relationship with NGOs.

## SRI LANKA

Sri Lanka emerged as a unified nation-state under British rule in 1815. Prior to that, it was a confederation of social collectivities divided along the lines of religion, race, class, caste, and kin. Its social order has always been diverse and dynamic. With the possible exception of the Vaddahs (indigenous community), who are the only "organic people" on the island, all other ethnic groups, including the Sinhalese, Tamils, Muslims, Burgers, Malays, Indians, and so on, and their respective religions, are foreign to the country.

Since precolonial times, Sri Lanka has experienced many waves of migration and invasion. These have been partly the result of internal political disorder and the decisions of local rulers to seek external assistance for the legitimization of their authority. The distorted social histories invented by majority Sinhalese and minority Tamils continue to suppress and obscure deeper social complexities which, though erased in competing colonial and ethnonationalist historiographies, were evident in the activities of a broad range of institutions comparable to contemporary NGOs. The evolution of state forms since the precolonial period has been shaped by the state's accommodation of these institutions through reciprocal relations, reconfiguration, suppression, and domination.

Sri Lankan historians often make sweeping statements about the antiquity of NGOs. For example: "[A]s we know today NGOs have emerged out of a long history of people's participation and self-help, a history that stretches back as far as the times of ancient Sri Lankan kings."[141] The consensus among historians is that indigenous institutions once had a symbiotic relationship with Buddhism, the state, and society, but that this relationship was destroyed by colonialism and capitalism. Dr. A.T. Ariyarathna, the founder and leader of the Sarvodaya Shramadana Movement, Sri Lanka's largest NGO, asserts that traditional morality was eroded "with the advent of the colonial powers beginning with the Portuguese followed by the Dutch and finally the British."[142] It is unclear whether or not other NGOs share this view, but they have not openly challenged it.

Before the colonial period, the basic unit of Sri Lankan social organization was the *gama*. The term initially referred to systems of land tenure rather than administrative units,[143] but it eventually came to mean "village." A significant number of Sri Lankan gamas were inhabited by single castes and divided along occupational lines. Such homogeneous caste-based segmentation did not lead to social and economic equality among the inhabitants of a given community. Inequalities were perpetuated by a skewed pattern of internal differentiation based on social status and property ownership. Order was enforced by strict rules which were maintained through systems of patriarchy and endogamy.[144]

Ancient Sri Lanka was a hydraulic-powered civilization, and the mechanisms of power and control evolved accordingly. In traditional society, the *gamsabhava* (village council) held political power in village committees. It was comprised of village elders who commanded respect due to the age, learning, and influence of its members. Their powers extended from the maintenance of law and order to the general administration of village life, and were authorized by the hierarchical and centralized state administrative system. Their specific responsibilities included the maintenance of village roads, water tanks, temples, and property, as well as the publication of royal decrees issued by the monarch.[145] Gamsabhavas maintained the exclusiveness of the village and its "jurisdiction correspondingly concentrated on the transgression of rules regulating social and sexual relations between persons belonging to different *varige* [clans] and castes."[146] They administered local justice and, according to Paranavithana, "were authorized to deal with cases of murder, violence, theft, robbery and other offences against the community."[147] They imposed severe punishment on offenders and adjudication typically involved restrictions of land ownership and water use. During the reign of the Kandyan Kings (1492–1815), gamsabhavas had been exclusively responsible for maintaining law and order. None of the existing accounts refers to them performing extra-judicial functions.[148] After the colonial period, the government sought to revitalize the gamsabhavas because they had been an effective means of carrying out government programs.

Buddhism was introduced to Sri Lanka in the third century BC. According to historians, after King Devanampiyatissa (307–267 BC) was converted to Buddhism, a symbiotic relationship developed between rulers, the masses, and the *sangha* (communities of monks). Since then, as the story goes, Buddhism has helped to underwrite the regime's authority. However, the Indian emperor Asoka, who ruled from 273–232 BC, contemporaneously described his own religious policies. His work presents a different picture, not only from those presented in the Ceylonese chronicles and the Pali commentaries, but also from those presented in the works of later historians, such as G.C. Mendis. As Hanz Bechert suggests: "[T]his rewriting of history by the monastic literati of the Therevada tradition in Ceylon established the prototype of a Buddhist Monarch and a Buddhist State which was to become the model for the policies of Theravada Buddhist Kings."[149] Although Buddhism flourished under state patronage, its importance in shaping political relations remains unclear. What is clear is that the Asokan model of development had decisive implications for the political development of the country and for Buddhist nationalism during the colonial period.[150]

Although the king's patronage legitimized its authority, the sangha's participation in political affairs was severely constrained.[151] The political activity of monks was most visible during times of crisis and change, but periodic reforms of *Sasana* (the teachings of the Buddha) enabled the kings to limit the influence of the sangha to the sphere of everyday life.[152] Existing polytheistic religious practices were incorporated into Buddhist cosmology, which formed a hierarchical pantheon of gods. In that pantheon, the Buddha occupied the highest position, followed by a host of lesser deities, demons, and spirits. Within the hierarchy, each figure performed a specific function.[153] The introduction of Buddhism to Sri Lanka did not radically transform patterns of unequal distribution. Instead, Buddhism helped to legitimize existing systems of social stratification.

The Buddhist establishment in Sri Lanka was not centralized. From its inception, it was fragmented along the lines of caste, territory, and property ownership. Internal differences and conflicts among monks, kings, and the aristocracy shaped the rise and fall of kingdoms. In addition to functioning as spiritual and scholarly centers, temples were also institutions for the unrestricted accumulation of wealth. In a system known as "monastic capitalism," monks who owned temples were known as "monastic landlords."[154] According to some scholars, Buddhism was in practice "hierarchically structured and in consonance with a social structure based on a hierarchy of caste, an anathema of canonical Buddhism."[155]

In the *rajakariya* system, the traditional system of land tenure until the early nineteenth century, tenants provided agricultural labor and services to the temples. The law was enforced by temple lords, officials, and the king. The customary tithe of sharecroppers also played a pivotal role. Slavery was widely practiced and legitimized on religious grounds, even though the Buddha had expressly prohibited it.[156] As Hans Dieter Evers noted, few tenants complied with temple service requirements out of religious conviction.[157] Few tenants, in fact, were even conscious of their oppression.[158] For example, the peasant rebellion in 1861 was sparked only because the state arbitrarily decreed that peasants had to provide services to two landowners instead of one.[159]

Monarchs played an important role in perpetuating divisions within the sangha by playing one monastic order against another, and in legitimizing the power of rulers in the context of ongoing civil wars, invasions, political fragmentations, and shifts of administrative centers.[160] Although the state's central authority was weak, the provincial administrative system remained strong.

Perhaps that is why the hydraulic social system survived for centuries. Political succession was determined mostly through wars and the assassination of incumbents, rather than through peaceful transfers of power. K.M. de Silva writes: "Political instability and fragmentation of Sri Lankan polity, the bane of Sri Lankan history throughout the period, had a debilitating effect on Sri Lanka's economy, which suggests deterioration of the economy prior to the advent of the colonial period."[161]

Thereafter, the much celebrated hydraulic civilization "began its slide down to oblivion" and the administrative machinery that maintained the complex irrigation systems disintegrated. Agro-irrigation complexes were abandoned as the political crisis deepened.[162] By the thirteenth century, "cumulative disintegration" had "reached a point of no return" and the ancient civilization collapsed.[163] Towards the latter part of the fifteenth century, the monarchical system began to fall apart. In the sixteenth and seventeenth centuries, during the Portuguese and Dutch periods, the hierarchical system and central authority within the Buddhist establishment also collapsed. Colonization did nothing to unify different Buddhist sects. Instead, each sect sought to establish pragmatic relations with the new rulers. But even before the colonial period, there had been a "very noticeable deterioration in the morale and discipline of the Sangha."[164] Measures taken to restore the authority of Buddhist monks were unsuccessful primarily due to political instability and turmoil. In any case, the social and political conditions for the establishment of British colonial rule were present long before the British arrived.

Colonial power was consolidated through coercion and consensus. The fall of the Kandyan kingdom, which led to the unification of the country in 1815, was facilitated by divisions among the Kandy and by the support of some in the sangha and the aristocrats themselves. In return, the British promised to uphold aristocratic privileges and safeguard the interests of Buddhism.[165] The 1815 Kandyan Convention declared: "The religion of Boodhoo professed by the chiefs and inhabitants of these provinces is declared inviolable, and its rites, ministries and places are to be maintained and protected."[166] Monks accepted these provisions and, at a conference in 1847, took the position that the "Queen is the head of our religion, and we wish it to be; that is what you promised and you are bound to do."[167] The Temple Land Registration Ordinance No. 6 of 1840 provided absolute rights of property to temples, which were not supervised by the state as they had been by the king. This altered the traditional relationship between Buddhism, the state, and society. The withdrawal of direct state patronage meant that the sangha either had to be self-supporting or dependent on charity.[168]

British rule was based on a relationship between rulers and social groups that had evolved during the Dutch period. The administration maintained its social control by securing the loyalty and cooperation of the mudaliyar (administrative class). This was achieved "by placating them with grants, honors and privileges and by continuing many Dutch institutions." In particular, the mudaliyar were recruited by the British administrative service.[169] It was from this class that the landowning elites and professionals emerged. These were to play leading roles in public associations. Mudaliyar were subjects of a colonial state that was caught between creating the conditions for colonial capitalist expansion and subordinating the colony's practices of accumulation to metropolitan interests, as local elites negotiated with the state. These elites sought to find ways in which they could both benefit from the colonial economy and maintain their traditional bases of authority.

The crisis of the monastic orders resulted from shifts in the *form* of the state. The centralizing drive of the colonial state required indigenous sources of legitimacy, but local elites wanted to maximize the gains they made from the colonial economy. The revitalization of monastic authority and its accumulative practices required redefinition of its relationship to both state and society as traditional hierarchies were fractured. This crisis of tradition and the drive towards modernity needs to be understood in relation to colonial modes of accumulation based on plantation economics.

As in Bangladesh, missionary organizations in Sri Lanka during the British colonial period provided models for present-day NGOs, and played a decisive role in creating the social conditions for the emergence of public and private modern organizations. Although missionary agencies arrived in Sri Lanka as early as 1505, they gained a strong political foothold in the country only after the Baptists, led by James and Ann Cater, arrived from Serampore, Calcutta, in 1812. Missionaries played an important role in shaping government social policy, but their relations with the state were complicated.[170] The state depended on the missionaries to create the social conditions necessary for its rule by creating, sustaining, and supporting the middle-class institutions and values required to maintain the colonial state's economy. At the same time, missionaries received "no systematic support from the State, though individual governors gave intermittent assistance."[171]

The main strategy for propagating Christianity was education, which missionaries believed would make evangelism "self-supporting, self-governing and self-propagating."[172] After 1833, missionary schools began receiving government grants-in-aid which they used to build new schools, even while many missionaries opposed government policies mandating that English remain the language of instruction. Past experience had taught the missionaries that the vernacular, not English, was the most efficient means of promoting the gospel to the heathens.[173] Some natives took advantage of this situation by establishing vernacular schools themselves.[174] By 1856, as government grants were reduced, most missions had either abandoned English schools or stopped teaching in English.[175]

In the face of reduced government aid, missionaries tried various approaches to make their schools self-sufficient and self-reliant, but the policy of self-support had disastrous consequences. Enrollment and attendance dropped when school fees increased, some schools were closed, and the number of teachers was reduced. But as Priyantha notes, "the inculcation of a spirit of self-help and self-reliance" was one of the most valuable contributions made by the missionaries, despite its negative impact on enrollment and attendance, and such values were the basis for the establishment of native educational institutions.[176]

In Ceylon, as in India, "Female education in the first half of the nineteenth century was the child of no one but the missionaries."[177] The missionaries' emphasis on female education received much encouragement from the government. Chief Justice Sir Richard Ottley, on the opening of the schools, stated: "Nothing would possibly help to so uplift a nation as the education and moral upbuilding of the mothers of generations to come."[178] The missionaries considered the "idolatrous mother" as the main "repository of superstition of the land." Some pointed out that a "heathen wife is a source of constant trial to her husband, and not infrequently ruin to the children. The experience of American missionaries proves to themselves at least, that pious wives are the safety, and with the blessing of God will be the life and stability of the rising Church."[179] Particularly within Tamil society, educating a woman was viewed as spoiling "her modesty, endangering her chastity, and rendering her insubordinate to the other sex," and many natives objected to educating women. Opponents warned that education would lead to female pride, "and make it difficult for husbands to manage them; it will only make it necessary for men to resort to more and more whipping."[180]

The first day school for women opened in Galle in 1819. It was short-lived due to the general reluctance of parents to allow women to appear in public. Thereafter, missionaries used a system of boarding schools as the main institutional framework for female education in Sri Lanka, beginning with the Central Boarding School at Uduvil, Jaffna, in 1824. Initially, most of the students were drawn from the ranks of the poor or lower castes, but the progress these women made gradually persuaded wealthier high-caste parents to send their daughters to schools.[181]

Poverty was an obstacle for both male and female children seeking education, and missionary schools were especially interested in taking in indigent or orphaned children from high-caste families. In an article published by *Bibliotheca* and the American Bible Society in 1854, the missionaries explained:

> Vellalas [agriculturalists and traders] are empathetically our people; and, notwithstanding the losses they have sustained by the freedom of their slaves, and by the introduction of the principles of liberty and equality in society, yet, combining the advantages of Christian instruction and of a superior education with the advantages which they inherited from their fathers, they will long continue to be the most thriving, energetic, intelligent and best behaved portion of the Tamil population.[182]

The caste system in Sri Lanka is not derived from the Hindu Varna system, and is relatively flexible in terms of caste group mobility, although it was more strictly adhered to in Tamil areas than in Sinhalese ones. Except in Tamil sectors, caste did not pose an immediate threat to missionary activities since villages were predominantly single-caste. Nevertheless, even the Sinhalese faced the threat of being ostracized after conversion to Christianity, and they responded proactively. For example, in Moratuwa, "Christian converts threatened to form themselves into a new caste, the Christian caste, embracing all who love Christ."[183]

While missionaries were determined to change the system, they had to proceed with caution.[184] The rationale was that interventions could wait until the people were convinced of the injustice of caste.[185] Missionaries did not recognize caste distinctions within the Christian educational institutions, but they adopted a cautious policy in their private and social lives and expected that education would gradually bring about change. They encouraged converts to live among their "heathen" relatives and friends, in order to test their sincerity and to show Hindus that conversion to Christianity would not require the severing of family ties. They hoped in this way to use converts to gain more converts.

Colonial policies toward missionary education varied from one governor to another and were shaped by individual personalities as well as prevailing geopolitical considerations. For example, Sir Edward Barnes was prejudiced against American missions, as he saw "no necessity of having recourse to a foreign nation for the instruction or conversion of the natives."[186] Barnes refused to increase the number of missions, denied a charter to a proposed Mission College, and refused to permit James Garrett, who was sent from America, to live on the island. After recommendations from the Colebrook-Cameron Royal Mission, he withdrew some restrictions. By then local elites had successfully established a number of schools, although a majority of them continued to send their children to those operated by the missionaries.

The Protestant missionaries' educational dominance did not go entirely unchallenged, for Roman Catholics were strongly opposed to it. Protestants, in their attempts to convert Catholics to Protestantism, called attention in pamphlets to the alleged errors of Catholicism. The Catholics, in turn, asked their flock to destroy all American books and tracts and even petitioned the government to act to prevent Protestant attacks on their religion.[187] Primarily because of such interdenominational conflicts, particularly those between Wesleyans, Anglicans, and Catholics, the colonial government became disillusioned with the School Commission. This disillusionment intensified with the revival of Buddhism and Hinduism, when native elites began regarding the colonial state as a patron of the missionaries. When Goegly realized that his efforts to end the influence on the Commission of "economy-minded administrators and bigoted Anglicans" were coming to an end, he wrote in despair: "So much bitter hostility had been manifested by the chaplains of the Anglican Church to the Wesleyans in reference to this question that I feel inclined to recommend that we depend altogether on our own resources for our native schools."[188] Consequently, the School Commission was deprived of its administrative powers, and its role was reduced to an advisory one. All powers were handed over to the colonial Secretary, C.J. Macarthy, who was "no friend of missionary interests in general. Macarthy was to function as the chairman of the Commission."[189] Thereafter, the state monopoly over education was strengthened, and all schools had to follow a common educational policy adopted by the department of education.

Many social "ills" practiced in India, such as *sati, thungi,* or *meriah* sacrifices, were absent from Sri Lankan society. Missionaries did not regard the prevailing social order as an impediment to evangelism. Except in Tamil-speaking areas of the country, missionaries in Sri Lanka were content to adopt a more gradual approach to social reform than were missionaries in India. Although the scale of missionary intervention in social reform was small, it influenced many local voluntary associations and social movements.[190]

Temperance was one of the main sites of missionary intervention among non-Christian native leaders who sought to launch a mass movement. Missionaries and Buddhists both participated in temperance work, although their approaches differed. Buddhists attacked alcohol consumption as "a western vice supported by the foreign government."[191] Temperance allowed a previously "quiescent if not inarticulate social class [to make] their presence felt as an indispensable link between the rural masses and the leadership of the movement."[192] The movement also provided opportunities for elites to enter the public sphere.

The elite Karava caste monopolized the liquor trade and other elites advocated temperance as part of a larger power struggle. "Above all, wealthy English-educated Buddhists appear to have attempted to establish themselves [...] as elites by taking a leadership role in the movement." It was a case, as one scholar put it, of "nobodies trying to become somebodies."[193] Temperance flourished briefly between 1903 and 1905, and culminated in "the first political confrontation between Sinhalese nationalists and the British in 1915."[194] Linking rural villages with urban areas, it reached the status of a mass movement by 1914 with the formation of the Total Abstinence Central Union.[195] Although short-lived, it helped to create the conditions for Sinhalese participation in national politics.

In the wake of the violent suppression of Buddhist activism by the British, missionaries withdrew from temperance activities and Buddhist elites began to question colonial rule. Meanwhile, Muslim leaders in Ceylon went the other direction, becoming "more conservative and supportive of the British [...] at a time when Muslims worldwide were critical of the British rulers for their treatment of Islam in the collapse of the Ottoman Empire."[196] Temperance ultimately brought the production and consumption of alcohol under the control of the government and only those who could afford steep licensing fees were able to thrive in the liquor industry. In the end, license fees and liquor taxes became two of the main sources of government revenue, with consequences that will be described below.

In 1854, Anglican missionaries, under the bishop of Madras, started the Tamil Coolie Mission among the plantation workers. It was entirely dependent on the financial support of the planters and its objectives were defined in narrowly spiritual terms.[197] However, missionaries used the media in Calcutta and Ceylon to draw the company's attention to public issues (such as drunkenness) affecting Indian immigrant bonded laborers in the plantation sector. The *Bengal Harakuru* in Calcutta and the *Sunday Observer* in Sri Lanka demanded a halt to emigration until social conditions on plantations improved.[198] Missionaries did not, however, press for reforms on controversial issues such as this. Their disinterest was due to several factors. Sri Lankan immigrant labor did not attract public attention in England because large-scale immigration to Sri Lanka took place after the abolition of slavery.[199] Criticism of plantation working conditions would have alienated the colonial government and the social elites whose economic power depended upon the colonial economy. And the attitude of missionaries towards plantations reinforced popular stereotypes of plantation workers as highly stigmatized second-class citizens.

Prior to colonial rule, Buddhist authority was scattered and limited, and Buddhists did not proselytize on any significant scale. However, in the wake of the expanded Christian missionary effort, Buddhist monks saw the need for a different and more aggressive way of articulating their relationship with the state and the society. Eventually, they began to see their project in much broader terms. Although the monks had begun contesting Christian missionary enterprises through government petitions as early as 1815, systematic and organized efforts began only after 1850. Mohottivatte Gunananda (1823–90) established the Society for the Propagation of Buddhism in 1862 using as his model the Christian Society for the Propagation of the Gospel, established in Ceylon in 1850. The Buddhist Society even acquired a printing press from the Church Missionary Society.[200]

Monks also created new educational opportunities for the laity. Between 1869 and 1880, there was a rapid increase in the number of schools started by non-Christians. Their progress was limited despite government support in the form of financial aid. Students were not attracted to *pansala* (Buddhist temple) schools, despite their high scholastic standards and long-established tradition of monkish scholarship, and strongly preferred secular education, which was crucial for upward social mobility.

Monks lacked the organizational competence of the missionaries and so the leadership of some schools was, consequently, assumed by lay persons.[201] The sangha were not enthusiastic about the rise of lay leadership in education. In 1904, it was proclaimed in a "Memorial of the Sangha of Ceylon to King Edward VII": "By laws of Buddha the laity form no part of religion." Among the signatories of the document was the president of the monastic branch of the Buddhist Theosophical Society, Reverend Hikkaduwe Sumangala, who was a leading opponent of the missionaries.[202] In his opinion, laity assumed leadership only in "extreme Protestant Buddhism." In other words, laity were "anti-clerical, holding that the clergy's corruption is so deep as to be irremediable and their function was hence palpably obsolete."[203] This attitude inspired the 1941 founding of the *Vinayavardana Samitiya* (Association for the Improvement of Buddhist Discipline) by a group of laymen who challenged monks to "public debate and attempted to belittle both their knowledge of canonical doctrine and their purity of conduct."[204]

Traditionally, the king had arranged for the obligatory labor needed to support temples and religious activities. However, after the demise of the *rajakariya* system, and in the face of the state's failure to support religious activities, local elite groups assumed responsibility for well-organized voluntary associations and maintained tenant services that were no longer managed by a centralized authority.[205] Differences among Buddhists due to caste and locality "stood as real or potential barriers to initiating programs to further the interests of Buddhism at the national level."[206] The problems were further exacerbated by the absence of any tradition of public financial contribution to support such programs and organizations. For example, the organizers of the first Buddhist press found it difficult to collect contributions, because, as Malalgoda notes: "Not many Buddhists were convinced of the 'merits' (*anisamsa*) of helping to establish a Buddhist printing press."[207] Contributions were not part of Buddhist custom and such projects fell outside the traditional activities of the laity as well. In 1873, when the Vidyodaya Oriental College was finally established, it was largely funded by the school's Committee of Managers (*Vidyadhara Sabha*). That changed abruptly in 1877, however, when the government began providing annual grants.[208]

The situation shifted once again when Colonel Henry Steel Olcott and Madame Helena Petrovna Blavatsky established the

Theosophical Society in 1880. They traveled throughout the country and began urging people to adopt a more aggressive attitude and organized approach to the propagation of Buddhism:

> If we ask how we should organize our forces, I point you to our great enemy, Christianity, and bid you look at their large and wealthy Bible, tract, Sunday Schools, and Missionary Societies—the tremendous agencies they support to keep alive and spread their religion. We must form similar Societies, and make our most practical and honest men of Business their managers. Nothing can be done without money. The Christians spend millions to destroy Buddhism, we must spend to defend and propagate it. We must not wait for some few rich men to give capital: we must call upon the whole nation.[209]

In 1882, the National Educational Fund for the promotion of Buddhist schools was established. This, and the many associations that followed it, adopted the organizational norms and practices of Protestant Christianity and increased lay involvement in displacing sangha from some of their traditional practices.[210]

The Buddhist Theosophical Society (BTS) was divided into two groups, a clerical and a lay division, each with its own local subdivisions. The objective of the former was to unite the monks of different fraternities of Buddhist clergy, while the latter aimed to create unity among the segment of the laity that was at least marginally involved in religious activities. Before the BTS, lay persons participated in secular activities under the guidance of monks. However, in the BTS, monks acted as advisors while the laity took on more organizational power and authority. Monks had no prominent role either as teachers or administrators, leaving them in the "background of the Buddhist movement."[211] Perhaps because of the monks' traditional disdain, the laity showed more enthusiasm in collaborating with foreigners than with monks.

In response to changing relations between religious institutions and the state, monks in the maritime province extended their reach by establishing new associations and broadening temple activities. According to Malalgoda, the monastic fraternity became "an institution commanding much esteem within the society; hence intrusion of the criteria of esteem that prevailed in the wider society followed into the monastic order as an almost inevitable consequence."[212] The Ven. Hinatiyana Dhammaloka Nayaka Thero's Rural Construction Movement saw the establishment of Rural Reconstruction Units (*Gramapratisamskarana Sabha*), orphanages, and homes for the elderly under the leadership of the monks.[213] These activities introduced a new element to the sangha, opening a new way for them to relate to the general public.

In the mid 1800s, conflicts developed among the leading monks, the laity, and the Theosophists. The monks considered the ideas of the latter to be alien to Buddhism. By the turn of the century, theosophical ideas were associated with Hinduism, especially after Annie Besant assumed a higher position in the Theosophist movement. The leading Buddhist revivalist and Sinhala nationalist, Anagarika Dharmapala, parted company with the Theosophists. Hikkaduwe Sri Sumangala, who was associated with the movement for 20 years, followed him, partly because he opposed the Theosophists' close association with Hinduism.[214]In 1891, he formed the Mahabodhi Society to regain the lost position of Buddhism. Anagarika Dharmapala's revival activities, carried out through numerous organizations, initially failed to generate local funding or widespread support from the traditional religious leaders. Dharmapala travelled extensively in the West to raise funds for the Mahabodhi society's activities. Mary Foster, a daughter of a wealthy ship builder in Hawaii, not only gave financial support from her family wealth, but also sent $50,000 worth of US government freedom bonds. Dharmapala's anti-Western activism was primarily a means by which local elites could monopolize the benefits of the Western project of modernity, and at the same time legitimize their claims to be "indigenous leaders." This particular form of elite hypocrisy evolved as a potent ideological force in shaping the relations between NGOs and the state.

Michael Roberts's study claims that the primary cause of the rivalry between the BTS and the Mahabodhi Society was not doctrinal differences, but tension between Goigama and non-Goigama, the two dominant caste groups competing for economic and political power. The Mahabodhi Society was associated with the Goigama caste, and the Salagama caste maintained a dominant position in the BTS.[215] Initially, Buddhist revivalism and activism were dominated by upcountry elites. Subsequently, the religious revivalism of Dharmapala took on extreme communal forms, acting against the interests of the Hindus, Malays, Christians, Muslims, and Burghers.[216] However, according to Gananath Obeyesekere, the orientation of Dharmapala's reformist activities was Protestant: "[Dharmapala] involvement was a Protestant model: the Anagarika is the modern Sinhala analogue of an early Calvinist type reformism with its increasingly this-worldly asceticism."[217] In other words, its "capitalist values entered the low country Sinhala bourgeoisie via creeping Christianity and the Buddhists recoiled against it [Christianity]."[218]

Native elites and the conservative monastic organizational alliances were challenged by changes in the social and political orientations of the Buddhist clergy. After higher education opened to monks from diverse social backgrounds, a "subculture" of Buddhist monks appeared who envisioned social change along radical paths and aligned themselves with mainstream political parties. In the 1920s, when the trade union movement was not yet tainted by communalism, Buddhist monks were active in the strikes organized by the unions.[219] Among these monks were Udukandewela Sri Saranakara, Balangoda Ananda Maitreya, Narivlia Dharmarathana, and Dumbara Palitha, all members of Marxist political parties. They studied at Shanthi Nikethan, in Calcutta, where they encountered the Tagore and Bengal communists. In particular, Udukandewela Sri Dhamarathana was a leader of the student union while he was at Calcutta City College. He later became vice president of the Communist Party (CP). At the same time that they were members of radical political parties, these monks also pioneered many rural associations concerned with social welfare, and they were more closely connected to the militant labor movement during that period than to the voluntary associations started by the same middle class. That middle class, which benefited from the colonial economy, despised these monks.

In 1946, the Young Turks formed a group called Lanka Eksath Bhikkhu Mandalaya (LEBM) in the face of protests from the ACBC, which had been formed by monks and lay persons who objected to monks participating in politics. These young monks were from the low country and were supported by wealthy, high-caste families. By the 1947 elections, all political parties had monks campaigning in support of their campaigns. The LEBM monks campaigned against the right-wing United National Party (UNP). In their political manifesto, the LEBM claimed that their aim was the amelioration of the economic conditions of the masses and the defeat of the capitalist parties. They vowed to defeat the "imperialist political parties" who did not work toward national independence.[220] As Tambiah notes, being associated with both the LSSP and the CP, they could not withstand the opposition's charge that Buddhism should be saved "from the flames of Marxism."[221] After the UNP won the general elections, the LEBM became defunct.

The emergence and diversification of public associations along ethnic, religious, and communal lines was influenced by the specific nature of capitalist development in Sri Lanka. Snodgrass explains that the colonial economy imposed on Sri Lanka an "estate revolution" which transformed the traditional paddy-based subsistence economy into an export-oriented, plantation-based economy integrated with the world market. The traditional subsistence economy was not entirely destroyed; rather, the colonial government created the conditions necessary for it to coexist with the plantation economy and to contain it within the economic and legal institutions of the colonial government. Taxation and agricultural development met the survival needs of the local population, and the traditional economy was integrated with a regime of accumulation, thereby subjecting the local economy to the vicissitudes of the global markets. Key institutions, such as a land market, wage labor, and credit, were gradually introduced and contributed to the emergence of landowning elites.

The mercantilist and monopolistic practices of the Dutch had made accumulation difficult for local entrepreneurs, but, after 1830, opportunities became available for local capital. The most lucrative form of capital accumulation during this period was selling liquor to plantation and urban workers. Profits from the liquor trade were then invested in coffee, tea, rubber, and the coconut industry, as well as in English-language education, from which the modern middle class emerged. The British infusion of cash was welcomed by politicians such as James Peries, who claimed in 1908 that "British planters deserve the credit for having brought capital into the country and shown us the path along which we may all win prosperity. [...] The interests of the Ceylonese planters are identical with those of the European planters."[222]

The Sinhala Buddhist revival was aided by Sinhalese support for the consolidation of capital. The Sinhalese middle class financially supported the voluntary associations, which in turn supported business ventures owned by the petty bourgeois intelligentsia. News agencies and reform associations attacked foreign merchants and called upon the natives to boycott the products of minority industry and businesses. Dharmapala praised Sinhalese merchants and asked them to support patriotic causes while denouncing "merchants from Bombay and Peddlers from South India who dominated the trade of the Island."[223] The new Sinhalese middle class was drawn from the traditional elite group, referred to as *palantiya* by Gananath Obeyesekere,[224] which derived status and power from land-wealth and officialdom. The palantiya were a diverse group, consisting of landowners, government administrative officers, lawyers, teachers, scholars, professionals, planters, merchants, and even clergymen, who had a symbiotic relationship with the elite classes. They shared an English-language education, but as a class they were fragmented along the lines of caste, community, territory, and religion.[225]

During the latter part of the nineteenth century, voluntary associations mushroomed among palantiya. Since 1854, the *Ferguson Directories on Sri Lanka* have provided details of associations from every social, political, ethnic, religious, and professional area. Most were concentrated in urban areas and served only their own membership. They lacked the interventionist character of the associations started by aspiring politicians, and the majority of them did not survive for long. Membership and influence fluctuated with the fortunes of the colonial economy and the migration of the population between Sri Lanka and other countries. Despite their instability, these associations were also at the center of the struggle among elites for consolidation of their economic base along the lines of caste and territorial affinities. The Corea brothers, who made their fortunes from the coconut industry, established the Chilaw Association with the objective of agitating for railways in the "coconut triangle." In 1882, the Ceylon Agricultural Association was formed under the leadership of C.H. de Soysa, one of the wealthiest among the Karava. It was intended to safeguard the plantations of their non-Goyigama members. The Ceylon Agricultural Association subsequently changed its name to the Ceylon National Congress (CNC) and styled itself after the Indian National Congress. As Patrick Peebles noted, this association was "essentially an organization of new elites other than the goyigama mudaliyars."[226] However, in contrast to its Indian counterparts, CNC was not even marginally successful in either initiating a dialogue or mobilizing large numbers towards independence.

At the same time, merchants, traders, writers, academics, and religious communities also formed associations, and their diversity demonstrated the cosmopolitan character of the elites in Colombo. Diversity was the norm until the 1950s, when broader religious, nationalist, and communalist agendas turned the associations into platforms for mainstream political parties which then began to dominate the institutional culture of the country. As Kumari Jayawardena noted, the leaders of these associations not only came from the influential classes, they "adopted the prevalent British view that charity had to be regulated as it often tempted people to adopt a vagrant way of life and resulted in dissipation and drunkenness."[227]

The activities of these associations provide evidence not only of competition within the middle class for economic opportunities, "cleavage between the various groups among the middle class was its widest on issues as poverty and working class agitation." They all agreed that poverty could be tackled by private charitable organizations, but on issues of trade union activism "the attitude of the wealthy Ceylonese and the British bureaucrats was almost identical and reflected the official thinking in Britain in the early days of industrialization, when trade unions were considered to be illegal combinations in restraint of trade."[228] (As we shall see in the next chapter, the same attitude is typical of NGOs after independence: they are isolated from labor unions, and do not focus their activities on class-based issues.)

Distribution of middle-class associations also had a spatial dynamic and closely corresponded to variations in revenue sources (plantation, trade, and professional middle class), and was associated with caste and religious affiliation. The majority of the philanthropic and charitable associations were concentrated in the maritime provinces, where the leadership of Karava and Salagama castes was more prominent than that of Goyigama. These associations concentrated on providing medical facilities for the destitute, and establishing orphanages and homes for the elderly. Their activities were an important part of ideological legitimization of the leadership of elite groups. Michael Roberts noted that these philanthropic activities were "infused by paternalistic and patriotic concerns," and "elites did not appear to be interested in drastic changes among the poor within their caste ranks."[229] The caste identities of these associations also overlapped with ethnic identities, and with political and economic tensions between their leaders. Out of this tension arose Tamil-Saiva and Sinhala Buddhist national consciousness, shaping the politics of the postcolonial state. The same leadership formed "village committees" to take control over economic and political affairs in the villages. One can find a good example of this in the politics of the Vivekananda Society (established in 1931), led by Ponambalam Ramanathan Saiva Mahasabha, and the Kataragama Protection Society and Preservation of Buddhagaya, started by A.P. de Zoyza in 1935. These led to the Kataragama-Buddhagya dispute between elite politicians of Tamil and Sinhala descent. Subsequently, even radical leaders who professed an interest in labor adopted communalist attitudes and succumbed to the influences of the religious nationalists. A.E. Gunasinghe, a pioneering leader of trade unions, "was not only influenced by the Dharmapala, but also received funding from him and several Buddhist monks for his trade union activities."[230] The fact that the leaders of both village committees and urban voluntary associations were of similar social and economic backgrounds reproduced the village/city split and, in turn, enabled these leaders to monopolize the benefits of tradition as well as of modernity. The village organizations of the postcolonial period became the partner agencies of NGOs started by the urban middle class.

The proliferation of communal associations had begun in 1833, when a legislative council consisting of British citizens and natives was formed and a communal representation system was introduced. This resulted in the development of associations along caste, ethnic, religious, and territorial lines. Those associations, in turn, became the platforms for new elite groups, such as Kandyans, Malays, Moors, Burghers, Ceylon Tamils, Indian Tamils, Sinhalese, Parsis, and so on. The associations emphasized the distinctiveness of their respective communities and expressed discontent with colonial government policy. They also began to enter the political arena where they voiced "the claims of the emerging political elites which aspired to a share of the political game commensurate with the economic power they have acquired, as well as in the administration which was still dominated by the British civil servants."[231]

Associations in areas populated by the Tamils were more active and showed more vitality than those in areas populated by the Sinhalese, since the latter were more inclined to accept the status quo. Elites generally did not show much interest in forming associations to foster "national identity" or demand independence. Interest in independence was first expressed by Tamil youth organizations. In 1914, at the Congress of Literary Associations, Nevins Selvadurai spoke of becoming "one united people—the Ceylonese."[232] In 1924, the Ceylon Youth Congress was formed by Tamil youth who were dissatisfied with the Tamil Mahajana Sabha. Its agenda differed from the All Ceylon Tamil League, and it condemned all communally minded politicians, issuing a manifesto calling for a "national culture, economic prosperity, social unity and self-government."[233] Commenting on the political activism of Tamil elites, K.M. de Silva wrote: "None of the Sinhala representatives during this period could match the intellectual dynamism, independent outlook and political maturity of Tamil leaders."[234]

Tamil youth associations were vitalized by a number of factors. Long-term concentration of missionary activities in Tamil areas had fostered education among the lower castes, and this made social reform more of an issue there than in other parts of the country. In addition, Indian associations had influenced the Tamils long before they had influenced the Sinhalese. Tamil associational activities were concentrated in the Northern Province, which was the center for Tamil cultural revivalism. The All Ceylon Tamil League and the All Ceylon Tamil Conference were both formed in order to secure from the British government rights for Tamil conservative elites, with the intention of maintaining dominance over the Tamil population. Their conservatism was apparent in their opposition to equality between castes, and their opposition to women's participation in public life, as described above.

In 1930, the Depressed Tamil Service League was formed with the assistance of the Jaffna Youth Congress (JYC). Both groups were politically at odds with the All Ceylon Tamil League and the Jaffna Association, and responded to the needs of the non-Vellala groups. A member of the JYC complained:

> The Jaffna Association was in a moribund state with a membership consisting of the turbaned heads who represent only the aristocracy of Jaffna, who go about echoing and reechoing with redoubled force the sentiments of the uneducated populace concerning communalism in the constitution.[235]

When Ponambalam Arunachalam called for a "boycott" of the constitution in 1918, Sinhalese leaders, whom Jane Russell refers to as "Constitutionalists," dissociated themselves by branding the boycott "disloyal" and condemning the "revolutionary" tactics of the Indian National Congress.[236]

Upper-caste Vellalas reacted by burning down the schools of the lower castes, and the JYC, under the influence of movements protesting the treatment of Harijans (the lowest caste) in India, started their own campaigns. Conservative associations like the Ceylon Tamil-Hindu Society were opposed to enfranchising women. In 1927, they urged the people of Jaffna "to see during next elections that they did not take their women to the polls. I would ask not even to register women as their electors. They should ask their women to mind their business in their homes." Neither the JYC nor the other native associations gave priority to women. Women's rights were not even a matter of serious debate in Sri Lanka, as they had been in India.

After Sarojini Naidu and Kamaladevi Chatopadyaya attended a meeting organized by the JYC, the *Swaraj* (self-rule) campaign began. The JYC had a broad base of support across all social classes in the Tamil community. It had repeatedly requested support in its boycott of the state council and its call for immediate Swaraj. However, these requests were either rejected or given only token support by both Tamil and Sinhalese elite associations, which kept away from campaigns against colonial rule because they were preoccupied with debates over communal representation in the government.

JYC organized a conference in 1932, and both Sinhalese and Tamil leaders gathered together to call for youth to support the independence movement. C. Balasingham, the president of JYC, attacked the communalists. In 1933, a "conference of Tamils was formed in order to oust the Youth Congress and sabotage the call for Swaraj. The Youth Congress which attempted to create a Ceylonese nation was publicly discredited by Tamil politicians."[237]

A number of new associations emerged to focus exclusively on the rights of low-caste groups, including the Depressed Tamil Social Service League, the North Ceylon Workmen's Union, the North Ceylon Vehiclemen's Union, the Jaffna Diocesan Association, and the Jaffna Free Library Associations. But even the North Ceylon National League, a Catholic political organization which had initially supported the JYC, opposed its boycott: "The Tamils in Jaffna have already had cause to regret the boycotting of the Council and trying to create a 'Ceylonese nation.'"[238] Disillusioned JYC members attacked the Vellala Tamils by publicly writing to the newspapers. One of the Colombo Tamil correspondents wrote to the *Ceylon Daily News* complaining of "[t]he bigoted mentality of the Jaffna man." Another said to the Depressed Tamil Service League of the Tamils: "It is not easy to persuade them [i.e., the upper castes] to adopt new methods. They like the methods of their ancestors."[239] After 1933, the JYC succumbed to communalist pressures from the upper-class Tamils and Sinhalese elites competing for dominance.

Tamil nationalism peaked earlier than Sinhala nationalism due to the heightened literary and cultural activities of numerous cultural and literary associations (e.g. Saiva Paripalan Sabai) in Tamil Nadu and Jaffna. Argumuga Narvalar (1822–1879), champion of the nationalist revival, was a generation senior to Anagarika Dharmapala, the Sinhala revivalist. Narvalar's anti-Christian revivalism was a response to threats to the Sudra caste (lower than the Brahmin caste) by members of lower castes. The threats resulted from the anti-caste education provided by missionary organizations to low-caste groups, and were a means of establishing the superiority of the Sudras (Vellalas) caste over lower castes. Charan noted that "Navalar was not a social reformer but someone who wanted to preserve the dominance of the upper caste and upper class Vellalas."[240] Sinhala and Tamil reform associations that evolved during this period were primarily aimed at preserving upper-elite dominance within their respective communities and exploiting the economic opportunities provided by the colonial system.

As an anti-imperialist, secular, and nationalist organization, the Jaffna Youth Congress sought to create an island-wide movement for national independence in collaboration with its Sinhala counterparts. J.E. Jayasuriya noted: "At a time when Sinhalese were prepared to do without Sinhala, the battle for Sinhala and Tamil was fought by the Tamil Leaders."[241] Notably, the ideology of the JYC did not include anyone who espoused the ideals of the Dravidian separatist movement (led by the Self Respective movement of Preiyar E.V. Ramaswami Naicker). The Jaffna Youth Congress's radicalism was suppressed by the Tamil elite and withered away due to this opposition and the rise of the explicitly anti-minority nationalist movement led by Anagarika Dharmapala.

The aspirations of the JYC to organize anticolonial struggle based on a Ceylonese identity were thwarted by both Tamil and Sinhalese elites in their quest to preserve their privilege. Tamil and Kandyan leaders broke away from the Ceylon National Congress and formed their own associations, which later demanded political autonomy for their respective regions. The Ceylon National Congress failed to develop a nationalist movement similar to that of the Indian National Congress.[242] Dharmapala's ideas were carried forwarded by the Sinhala Mahasabha, formed in 1935, which subsequently led to the formation of the Sri Lankan Freedom Party (SLFP). Thereafter, we see the intensified politicization of two competing nationalisms in Sri Lanka: Sinhala and Tamil. Sinhala nationalism came to be identified as Sinhala Buddhist nationalism, while Tamil nationalism remained chiefly linguistic because it incorporated Tamil-speaking Christians as well.

As we shall see, the nationalism of the elite classes, produced in and by the activities of numerous associations and the political parties aligned with them, did not go unchallenged. Janatha Vimukthi Peramuna (JVP), a self-proclaimed Marxist-Leninist political party that emerged in the late 1960s, challenged the elites of its community, as did numerous Tamil youth militant groups from the mid 1970s. Despite its alleged Marxist orientation, the JVP had specific caste biases and opposed the presence in Sri Lanka of the plantation Tamils. Neither the JYC nor the JVP developed inter-ethnic alliances, and both succumbed to reactionary ethnonationalisms espoused by elites. Subsequently, their militant activities were directed against the traditional elites of their respective communities as well as the other communities, leading to 20 years of war. While the Liberation Tigers of Tamil Eelam (LTTE) succeeded in virtually eliminating most of the traditional Tamil leadership, the JVP survived by becoming a leading proponent of majoritarian nationalism and opposed devolution of power to the Tamil minority, refusing to form coalitions with the mainstream political parties. As we shall see later, the tensions between NGOs and the state have intensified strongly since the beginning of the civil war in the 1990s, and were partly a response to the JVP's metamorphosis from Marxist-Leninist roots to an ethnoreligious nationalism, and to its competition with Jathika Hela Urumaya, an extremist Sinhala Buddhist Nationalist party.

The Great Depression, the radicalization of plantation and urban workers through unions, and the decline of commodity prices all helped to render unsustainable the colonial mode of accumulation. The declining economy disproportionately affected the Tamil middle classes, who depended on the colonial economy for employment. Both the economic crisis and cultural revivalism brought nationalism to the center of associational debates. Tamils feared losing power to the Sinhalese, and the Sinhalese were apprehensive that Tamils would be disproportionately employed in the colonial economy and civil service. The Youth Congress's campaign for an inclusive Ceylonese national identity had been subverted by the communalism and elitism of upper-class Sinhalese and Tamils. Subsequently, by the 1930s, even previously noncommunalist leaders like A.E. Gunasinghe were forced to take a communalist stand. At that time, the Youth Congress began searching for a specifically Tamil identity and political strategy, laying the foundation for the separatist movements of the late 1970s.

Another reason for the decline in the Sinhalese and Tamil radical associations towards the end of the colonial period was the expansion of the trade union movement and the growth of left political parties, which not only reduced the space for such associations but also absorbed their leadership. The convergence of the interests of unions, parties, and voluntary associations allowed them to emerge as a powerful force in opposition to the state, but the fact that they sought to realize their demands through state reform provided yet another opportunity for the state to expand its sphere of influence.

Cultural revivalism accompanied the spread of communalism. From 1920 onwards, associations shifted their emphasis to the revitalization of culture and religion. The Jaffna Oriental Studies Society and Jaffna Oriental Music Society were founded in that decade. The *Morning Star* of December 12, 1930, promoted the "[p]ure music of India as opposed to Hindustani music which, akin to the music of the Sinhalese, had been very much influenced by Persian musical forms."[243] Within the Sinhalese community many new organizations emerged, including the Sri Sasandhara Society (Society for the Protection of Buddhism), the Sri Saddharama Sevaka Society (Society for Promoting the Dhamma of Buddha), the Sri Lankadhara Society (Society for Preserving Lanka), the Buddha Gaya Defense League, and the All Ceylon Buddhist Congress.

In 1935, the Saiva Maha Sabha and the Kataragama Protection Society claimed that it was necessary to preserve the "Hindu Purity of Kataragama." These two societies were formed in reaction to the upsurge of Sinhalese Buddhist organizations, such as the Society for the Preservation of Buddhagaya, and to the spread of the religious revivalism of the Theosophical Society. Later, these associations debated the balance of political power between the two communities. A.J. Fraser, explaining the impact of the controversy, wrote: "The surface of society is cracked and seamed, sapped and mined with rents, fissures and yawning crevasses opened up by the disintegrating influence of religious dissension."[244] For several years, despite the attempt of Sinhalese associations to take full control over temple management, it became a ritual for those aspiring to political power to make an annual pilgrimage to Buddhagaya. Thus, a religious conflict was politicized.

In 1936, the Sinhala Maha Sabha was formed by a heterogeneous collection of Sinhalese politicians, literati, and religious and cultural revivalists. According to its founders, it was the counterpart to the Swadeshiya Mahasabha of India, and it was created to introduce Gandhian philosophy to Ceylon. R.S. Gunawardana said: "When the Sinhala Maha Sabhawas started, I was one of those who deplored the name of that Sabha. I feared that much might be made of that name and our work would be hindered and hampered by it."[245] The Jaffna Youth Congress also reacted to the Sabha:

The formation of a political organization by the Sinhalese, purely on a communal basis, is an evil pretext. If policies are a matter of race, caste and creed, then the Sinhala Maha Sabha supplies the best justification for the Ceylon Tamil demand for 50-50. I am proud of my race and culture; I shall let no man trample on them.[246]

In the face of opposition to the name Sinhala Sabha by several prominent Sinhalese leaders, S.W.R.D. Bandaranaike wanted to change its name to Swadeshiya Maha Sabha (The Greater Congress of the Indigenous People), but the change was opposed by some members. Subsequently, the *sabha* became the center of Sinhalese Buddhist nationalism and an important resource for Sinhalese politicians.

While there were Tamils, such as Dr. Saravanamuttu, who warned against Tamil militancy in reaction to the formation of the sabha, that militancy seemed all but inevitable. Bandaranaike made speeches with communal overtones at Sinhala Maha Sabha meetings, invoking the superiority of the Sinhalese race. Yet there were also Sinhalese leaders such as R.C. Kannangara who reproved the communalists.[247] The communal divide was so strong that, in October 1934, the Federated Communities Progressive Association was formed by C.S. Rajaratnam, a former organizer of the YMCA and a temperance activist who worked with Sinhalese leaders. His idea was that Sri Lanka should be divided into three states, comprised of Northern and Eastern provinces for Tamils; Central, Sabaragamuwa and Uva Provinces for Kandyans; and Southern and Southwestern provinces for low-country Sinhalese. All states, moreover, were to be united on a federal basis by a Central Council.

Attempts to achieve pan-Sinhala unity based on religious and cultural nationalism were thwarted by conflicts among elite Sinhalese groups. In 1927 the Kandyan National Assembly was founded, and it demanded a federal state for the Kandyan Sinhalese in opposition to the Ceylon National Congress. Specifically, they argued that "the Kandyan race [must] be separately represented in the Council, and that our country as a separate and distinct community be recognized and maintained."[248] As the demand for the federation grew, both Kandyans and Ceylon Tamils saw themselves as allies against the low-country Sinhalese, citing historical examples of the relationship between the two communities. According to T.B. Panabokke, "In matters of religion or interests they are united, and in most manners and customs there are many things common between the Tamils and Kandyan communities."[249]

Demands for federation by R.C. Rajaratnam and the Kandyan groups were opposed by Catholic and low-country associations in Jaffna.[250] By the time of independence, intracommunal differences had subsided and given way to broader ethnic interests. Associations advocating more pluralistic solutions to political identity were either crushed or absorbed into political parties. Paradoxically, S.W.R.D. Bandaranaike was critical of rivals who exploited these associations for political purposes. Bandaranaike noted that "any association with which they were connected [provided] a semblance of public opinion to their own wishes and opinions. Members of Congress, who did not come within the magic circle, were cold shouldered at every turn."[251] These associations provided the basis of the political parties as the public used them for projecting their demands onto the state.

Village Committees and Village Councils formed by the Tamil Mahajana Sabai and the Sinhala Mahajana Sabha spread throughout the country in the 1930s, and they provided the voter base for mainstream political parties led by conservative elites. Radical associations such as the Youth Congress and various left political parties concentrated their activities in the urban areas, and, as a result, could not develop a significant social base. Their agendas were effectively undermined and subsumed by their opposition. By the time of independence, there was hardly a village institution that had not been colonized by mainstream political parties.

It is important to examine the expanding role of the state in revitalizing traditional organizations and voluntary associations throughout the colonial and postcolonial periods. The British government inherited a broad spectrum of welfare institutions from its Dutch and Portuguese predecessors, including the Poor Fund, the Fund for Widows of Company Officials, the Military Fund for Company Soldiers and Sailors, the Sinhalese Poor Fund, and the Sunday Fish Rent for the Poor. Dutch charitable institutions had emphasized self-reliance as a means of avoiding parasitic dependence on charitable associations. For example, orphans were taught tailoring, and spinning wheels were given to widows to foster self-employment. The British adopted a more liberal policy toward welfare institutions and brought them under the supervision of the state. At the same time, the state reduced financial support as it strove to maintain a policy of religious neutrality.

Colonial administrators, however, held the view that the Sri Lankan villages were "little agricultural republics."[252] The *gamsabhava* was believed to be effective in carrying out local administration because it was guided by local consensus and led by "natural leaders of the community."[253] This imagery was extremely helpful in shaping the British government's policy on local government and rural development. From 1871 onward, the government took measures to revive traditional institutions as a means of mobilizing rural participation and resources. The goals of reaching the poorest of the poor, mobilizing the people's participation and local resources, encouraging self-help, and decentralizing the decision-making powers of the region steered these organizations away from central government and toward the local arena. Because they depended exclusively on the government for financial assistance, however, they were unlikely to pursue policies unacceptable to the authorities.

A powerful example of state-initiated voluntary sector development during the 1930s is the sporadic emergence of the voluntary associations known in official circles as anti-crime societies. These societies took local initiatives to prevent antisocial conduct. At first, colonial government officials were reluctant to intervene because they feared residents would resent external interference in local affairs. Officials were also hesitant to give these organizations complete autonomy because they feared it might undermine the legal authority of the state. In 1939, a police officer experimentally expanded the role of these organizations, and, as a result, village welfare societies were instituted in "backward" areas to deal with "crime, immorality or poverty." The state saw this as a program of "practical rural reconstruction." It settled land disputes and provided employment and a volunteer rural patrol service to prevent crime throughout the country.[254] These institutions closely involved the police in village welfare activities.[255]

Initially, the government thought that these revived traditional organizations could also be used to counter the anti-British propaganda of the *samasamajists* (left-wing political groups) and other subversives. The organizations gathered information about village activities for government administrative purposes. However, the government's attitude toward welfare organizations was ambivalent and contradictory. On the one hand, officials were concerned that, if they became directly involved in these organizations' activities, the associations would lose their capacity to mobilize local resources and participation that gave legitimacy to the colonial administration. On the other hand, the government understood that these organizations might eventually become involved in the struggle for political power. So, the police furnished guidelines for the operation of these organizations, and local police officers were instructed to screen all those who sought to participate.[256] These organizations preceded the rural development movement initiated by the government. In 1947, when it became clear that police officers were unable to manage organizational affairs, the Department of Rural Development (DRD) was created, and its officials were designated as Rural Development Officers.[257] In the process, the government broadened and increased its scope and influence in the political arena.

In the wake of government initiatives to promote the voluntary sector, the number of existing organizations mushroomed. *Shramadana* (donation of voluntary labor) was introduced and implemented extensively by the DRD. A branch was formed that initiated special programs for the backward outcasts, such as Veddhas and Rodiya. The Sarvodaya Shramadana Movement came into being after the Backward Communities Branch of the DRD sponsored a group of senior students from the Nalanda College of Colombo to participate in a shramadana camp.[258]

In 1946, the Social Service Commission recommended legislation for the establishment of the Department of Social Services (DSS) and the Central Council of Social Services (CCSS). The former would be in charge of all state welfare functions, while the latter would coordinate all voluntary service organizations. One of the reasons for the state's concern about the coordination and regulation of voluntary associations was the possibility that an organization might "overstep the limits that they have to observe."[259]

By the end of the 1970s, all areas of development came under the jurisdiction of either a rural development officer or the Gramasevaka Division (the lowest level of local government administrative unit). As a result, every Gramasevaka Division administered at least eleven different types of societies, such as funeral assistance, rural development, community centers and sports, religious, food production, school development, thrift and cooperatives, women, and Gramodaya Mandalayas. Each village contained cooperative societies, rural development societies, cultivation committees, an agricultural productivity committee, village councils, and NGOs. Despite their prevalence, it was widely noted that these groups "[n]otoriously failed to stimulate local enthusiasm."[260] They were more concerned with welfare than with actively participating in the project of decentralization.[261]

The average villager held memberships in at least ten different types of organizations. Membership in these associations enabled villagers to maintain a patron–client relationship with political leaders, which could be difficult given the political sensitivity of resource allocation. Although there was no official remuneration for office holders, membership in these associations served as a springboard for a political career, and it also provided "potential collateral sources of income and prestige."[262] The government's interest in revitalizing the local voluntary sector continued into the post-independence period, but studies demonstrated that the "desire of the government was not matched by an enthusiasm and a willingness on the part of the people to make use of the opportunity afforded to them."[263] Instead, they continued to look to the government as a provider.

As with the voluntary organizations, there was vertical development within government departments and line ministries. One of their objectives was to coordinate the diverse efforts of voluntary organizations in order to "create conditions of social and economic progress for the whole community with the active participation and with the fullest possible reliance on the community."[264] In keeping with the spirit of participatory development, specialized government departments were compelled to incorporate village-level organizations into their programs. At the same time, elected political representatives, who had control over the local associations, functioned directly under the political leadership. The interests of the politicians often conflicted with those of the technocrats. Consequently, the programs of specialized departments were caught between political imperatives and technical feasibility. Political structures played a significant role in issues that should have been resolved by administrators and technicians. Because voluntary organizations mostly functioned in collaboration with government ministries, they became appendages of the state and a means of distributing state patronage. The relative ease with which these organizations mobilized people for collective action remains unsurpassed by NGOs in comparable situations.[265]

British policy in Sri Lanka was not entirely based on the notion of "divide and rule." It might be better characterized as "ruling the divided," where such divisions were articulated with the mediation of numerous public associations. The contradictions and crises which emerged from the colonial regime of accumulation were effectively channeled into, and resolved within, voluntary organizations. These associations were the means through which different elite groups secured benefits from the colonial state and asserted popular legitimacy. The associations did not seek radical changes in the dominant mode of production, but facilitated its reproduction and managed resulting contradictions and crises by invoking primordial identities, which, in turn, became instruments in the ongoing contest for state power. Discord among public associations articulated along the lines of primordial identities was the major factor in the absence of an independence struggle in Sri Lanka during this period.

Before achieving independence, Bangladesh and Sri Lanka both had vibrant civil societies in which nongovernmental organizations played various roles. These organizations or associations provided fora for debates over the relations between elite classes and the colonial state. They were transnational in terms of their outlooks, sources of funding, and agendas. They were sustained by the colonial economy, and, in turn, the colonial state depended on them to negotiate its foreignness and domesticity, as some precolonial kings and empires once did. For native elites, these associations were instrumental in simultaneously alienating the masses from the class realities of the colonial regime and, at the same time, consolidating the benefits of the latter. Both elites and colonial officials could distinguish themselves from the masses and maintain control over them. Sanjay Joshi's analysis of the middle class in Lucknow sums up the functions of these public associations. He writes:

> It was through defining their distinction from other social groups, through their activities in the public sphere, that a group of educated men, and later women, were able to define themselves as middle class. Distinction here worked in both senses of the word; not only did cultural projects of the middle class distinguish it from other social groups, the Indian middle class also contended that the norms and values it was seeking to propagate were superior to those of the existing aristocratic elites, lower classes, and ultimately, to those of the British rulers. Empowerment— both against established social and political elites and *over* other subordinated sections of society—was at the heart of the projects constituting the middle class.[266]

Associations in Bangladesh and Sri Lanka embodied a class compromise between native elites rooted in the spatial diversity of global capitalist relations. These associations simultaneously became sites for the mobilization of protest against the colonial state and for the consolidation of native elite control over the postcolonial state. The divisions among associations in Sri Lanka were far more pronounced than they were in Bengal. Significantly, associational activities did not lead to an independence struggle in Sri Lanka as they did in India. When Bengal was divided between Pakistan and India and East Bengal became a colony of Pakistan, the formal and informal associations in East Bengal played a crucial role in the independence struggle against the Pakistani government. By the time of independence, NGOs in Bangladesh already held a significant share of responsibility for the country's social and economic development, and subsequently they established themselves as almost a parallel state. But in Sri Lanka, state welfare policies did not leave much room for NGOs, and the state incorporated the organizations as extensions of its own programs. Since the independence of Bangladesh and Sri Lanka, the ideals of secularism and pluralism have lost ground to religion, ethnicity, and nationalism, and the latter have come to determine the form of the state and shape its relationship with NGOs. Ethnonationalist revisions of social history and the origins of pre-independence NGOs have a greater influence on the NGO–state relationship in Sri Lanka than in Bangladesh, particularly since the early 1980s when Sri Lankan sovereignty came under challenge by the Tamil militant movements.

# 2
# Welfare State to National Security State: Post-Independence NGO–State Relations in Sri Lanka, 1948–2010

"Neither the shape of the state, nor oppositional cultures, can be properly understood without the context of the mutually formative (and continuing) struggle between them: in other words, historically."

Philip Corrigan and Derek Sayer[1]

This chapter explores NGO–state relations since Sri Lanka's independence in 1948. It clarifies the processes by which religion and ethnicity are utilized by political parties in their competition for state power, in response to the myriad of historically specific legitimacy crises of the state. It demonstrates how the evolution of NGO–state relations has shaped Sri Lanka's transition from welfare state to national security state. The complicity of NGOs in this process reflects that their economic and political paradigms are not radically different from those of the state. Although their relations have become increasingly antagonistic, NGOs and the state also rely on each other in many ways.

Since the earliest demands by Tamil militants for a separate state and the start of civil war between the government and the Liberation Tigers of Tamil Eelam (LLTE), both local and foreign NGOs have been accused of endangering the country's sovereignty and security. They are variously portrayed as foreign invaders, colonialists, Christian proselytizers, and imperialists by those who argue that the country's glorious past (according to the ideals of King Asoka of India) cannot be restored unless NGO activities conform to national interests. Unfriendly NGO–state relations are not entirely due to the activities of NGOs. Anti-NGOism as a populist ideology— deriving its power from revisionist histories, negative memories of colonialism and Western imperialism, national security imperatives, and popular criticisms of the internal practices of the NGOs—has been used to successfully mask the state's attempts to legitimize its authority in response to crises generated by capitalist development.

Particularly since 1977, the impact on state formation in Sri Lanka of NGOism as an ideology, more than actual NGO activities, has been far greater than in Bangladesh, where NGOs appear to present significant challenges to state power. In order to reveal the continuities and discontinuities of state–NGOs relations, the following analysis is organized chronologically.

## ECONOMIC AND ETHNORELIGIOUS NATIONALISM, 1948–1977

Since 1948, when Sri Lanka gained independence from Britain, political parties have embraced state-centered and ethnoreligious nationalisms as their main means of legitimizing competing claims; the evolutionary trajectory of NGOs in Sri Lanka has been shaped by these two types of nationalism. The state's project constitutes a large-scale class compromise that serves to both further capitalist development and mitigate the radicalism of the political left, in an attempt to manage the ongoing accumulation and legitimization crises of capitalism.

Until 1977, state-centered or economic nationalism involved massive state investments of export revenues from the plantation economy, and achieved extraordinarily high levels of development of physical infrastructure, education, and health care. Such welfare policies effectively prevented the radicalization of left-wing political parties. The political agenda of the left during that period is best understood as reformist, agitating only for state intervention in social development. Left reformism, the heterogeneous nature of the ruling block, the success of state welfare policies, and the clientelist state patronage of the local "bourgeoisie" limited the prospects of the "proletarian" revolution. According to Amita Shastri, economic nationalism was "an articulation and conflagration of social differences along primordial lines,"[2] with a bias towards the language, religion, and ethnicity of the majority Sinhalese community. At the same time, the spread of agrarian capitalism continued to attenuate differentiation among the peasantry, resulting in broad government-mandated agrarian reforms, failing to foster either agricultural or industrial development of the kind needed to sustain economic growth and employment.[3]

The industrial sector, in particular, has yet to provide consistent employment to educated young professionals. Nor did the local bourgeoisie pursue the type of entrepreneurship required for effective industrialization. Both the state and the bourgeoisie were content under the regime of the plantation system, and the local economy provided some limited opportunities for expanding the industrial sector and agricultural reforms. Since the colonial period, caste, religion, and race relations were important areas of competition in commercial culture and society. The complacency of the left, along with the welfare-oriented economic nationalism of the state, prevented the formation of meaningful class-based dissent among the subordinate strata.

In the 1950s, economic nationalism was met by a resurgence of campaigning among monks who demanded that the government protect Buddhism and Buddhist institutions, bringing religious activism, particularly among vernacular Buddhist monks, to the forefront of politics.[4] In the 1956 elections, monks formed the Eksath Bhikkhu Peramuna (United Front of Monks/EBP), which combined three associations: the Samathalanka Bhikkhu Peramuna (SLBP), the All Ceylon Buddhist Congress (ACBC), and the Sri Lanka Mahasangha Sabha (SLMS).[5] These organizations differed in terms of geography, caste, and political party. The most active were based in urban areas; for example, the EBP was based in Colombo, and its membership was drawn from the Amarapura and Ramanna sects which emerged during the nineteenth century under the patronage of the new Sinhala Buddhist middle class. Monks from the Siam Nikaya, the prominent Sri Lankan Buddhist Chapter in the Kandyan province, were underrepresented in these associations and their engagement in politics was relatively limited. Furthermore, they were divided between the two major parties, the United National Party and the Sri Lankan Freedom Party (SLFP). The EBP was anti-Catholic, anti-West, and anti-UNP. (One of its slogans was "A vote for the UNP is a vote for the Catholics; a vote for the MEP is a vote for the Buddhists.")

According to Phadnis, the EBP's success lies in "its role in the support and mobilization of Buddhist monks and providing countrywide Bhikkhu cadres to a party [the MEP] with very little organization and projecting its image as the party of the common man."[6] These religious organizations were directly aligned with the numerous voluntary associations at the center of Buddhist religious reforms during the colonial period. Elites seeking state patronage and social status were simultaneously members of both temples and voluntary associations. Some of these temples were themselves important centers for capital accumulation in the system that Hans Dieter Evers has described as "monastic capitalism."[7] The aspiring local bourgeoisie during this period took measures to represent Buddhism as a "rationalistic" religion that "incorporates the basic ideas of modern science, and is apt to solve the problems of a modernizing society."[8] The patronage of religious institutions is in many ways indispensable for the accumulation practices of a local bourgeoisie. With few exceptions, left-wing political parties advocated ethnoreligious nationalism.

Since independence, voluntary associations have been important resources for politicians and local elites in their attempts to represent themselves as guardians of the nation's economy and religion. For example, S.W.R.D. Bandaranaike broke away from the United National Party and formed the Mahajana Eksath Peramuna (MEP) in 1954. Bandaranaike, an Anglican, effectively invoked religion, language, and nationalism to form a broad social base that allowed him to capture state power. In the same year, the government appointed a Buddhist council, Lanka Buddha Balamandalaya (LBM). Since 1954, ethnoreligious and nationalist imagery and symbols have appeared prominently in official state propaganda.

The relationship between the state and religious reform associations has always been ambivalent. Politically active monks were themselves divided into right and left parties. State officials were cynical about the sangha and sought to confine their role to spiritual matters, thereby preserving the boundaries between religion and the state. As former President J.R. Jayewardene noted:

> It was to help humanity that the Buddha founded the Order. He intended it to be a voluntary association of dedicated persons, devoting themselves to the task of making the process of walking through life easier for their fellow beings who were weak, helpless and poverty stricken. It is another matter that the order never quite became what it was meant to be. The Bhikkhus (homeless ones) very soon became priests, living in temples built like palaces, maintaining its place in the society, not by tending to the sick, the poor and the helpless, but by placing a Messianic halo above the Buddha-myth, and by chanting Pali gathas to the cold, fruitless moon.[9]

On the other hand, there was intense competition among political leaders to represent themselves as the "true" protectors of Buddhism. They not only assumed leadership positions in all major religious associations, but also sought ideological legitimacy for social development programs by representing them as a means of revitalizing ancient Sinhalese Buddhist civilization. The mission of these ethnonationalist politicians would simultaneously establish their own popular legitimacy and undermine left-wing radicalism. One of the first campaign slogans of the UNP in 1947 was: "Don't give your vote to the Marxist because if you do, your religion, whatever it is, will be destroyed."[10] The first prime minister, D.S. Senanayake, told a delegation of Buddhists who requested special state protection, "Buddha has pointed out the path of development and no State aid can take man there."[11]

The monks were aware of the ambivalent relationship between the state and Buddhism, but their associations did not present a united front. Instead, they competed for economic and political power like everyone else. But the religious establishment's broad consensus regarding the ethnoreligious identity of the state brought Buddhists into conflict with the state's modernization project. By then, religious nationalism had crystallized as an important force in the country's political process, causing a political crisis precipitated by an economic crisis, and re-articulated through the invocation of religious nationalism, culminating in Bandaranaike's capture of state power in 1956. All subsequent governments have sought to balance religious nationalism and the social, economic, and political challenges it generates.

An inevitable consequence of institutionalizing ethnoreligious nationalism was the reactivation of voluntary associations along the lines of ethnicity, religion, family groupings, and caste. Associations in the south maintained a low political profile, while those in the Tamil-speaking northern and eastern parts of the country paved the way for the rise of Tamil nationalism. The prospect of the right to self-determination and self-rule dominated discussions in these associations, but the rise of Tamil nationalism was not only a response to Sinhala Buddhist nationalism in the south. It was also fostered by divisions within the Tamil community along the lines of caste and territorial and political affiliation.

In 1956, the Federal Party proclaimed its intention to establish an "autonomous Tamil Linguistic State within a Federal Union of Ceylon," which led to a pact between S.W.R.D. Bandaranaike and S.J.V. Chelvanayagam. As soon as the pact was announced, several organizations, including EBP and Sri Lanka Sangha Sabha, protested it. Another primarily Kandyan organization called Tri-Sinhala Peramuna (TSP) called for the UNP to oppose the pact. President Jayewardene led the chorus, calling the pact a "betrayal of the Sinhalese." Although the protest was soon discontinued, a religious ceremony was later held in the temples in Kandy to "persuade the gods to destroy the package."[12] As Jayewardene reflected, "The first cycle in a pattern has recurred as a central and poisonous feature of the political process at critical junctures. The party in power strives to foster communal accommodation. The major party in opposition manipulates Sinhalese parochialism to wreck that attempt."[13]

These policies encouraged the "tendency towards a 'pattern of amalgamation' of the interests of the lower middle class with state capitalism."[14] The political articulation of social antagonisms arising from the regime of accumulation continued the post-independence trend of reconciling the state's commitment to equality, "with an advocacy of the interest of a section of the indigenous capitalist class, namely its Sinhala Buddhist Section"[15] until economic nationalism took the shape of Sinhala-Buddhist nationalism. From the constitution of 1972: "The Republic of Sri Lanka shall give foremost place to Buddhism and accordingly it shall be the duty of the State to protect and foster Buddhism while assuring all religions the rights granted by Section 18(1)(d) of the Constitution." It continued:

[The] official language of Sri Lanka shall be Sinhala as provided by the Official Language Act of 1956 [and] all laws shall be made or enacted in Sinhala [...] the language of the courts and tribunals shall be in Sinhala throughout Sri Lanka and accordingly, their reports, pleading, proceedings, judgments, orders and so on shall be in Sinhala.[16]

Differences between the Sinhalese and Tamil communities sharpened, and Tamil militant movements subsequently emerged.[17] In 1972, the Federal Party, the Tamil Congress, and the Ceylon Workers' Congress (CWC) formed the Tamil United Front (TU). Their demands included equal status for the Tamil language, the adoption of a secular state policy in Sri Lanka, the protection by the constitution of the fundamental rights of minorities, the abolition of the caste system, and the provision of citizenship to all who seek it. Tamil and Sinhala nationalism each suppressed the internal contradictions within their respective communities, and each defended itself against the other.

The failure of both economic and ethnoreligious nationalism led to the radicalization of youth in both communities. Young Tamils, dissatisfied with their own political parties, formed associations to contemplate the possibility of achieving their goals through militant struggle. Thousands of Sinhala youth joined Janatha Vimukthi Peramuna (JVP), a radical Marxist-Leninist political organization, in an oppositional movement that culminated in the 1971 insurrection. The state, with the help of India, the United States, the Soviet Union, and China, suppressed the insurrection, which resulted in nearly 20,000 youth casualties.

The ideology of the JVP excluded Tamil plantation laborers, who constituted the majority of the "proletarian" class in the country, because the JVP considered them an extension of Indian expansionism. Some also charged that the JVP's politics were driven by non-Goyigama caste ideology, and that the JVP was not seriously concerned about the grievances of the Tamils.[18] Political divisions were intense and debates among students failed to result in a common front. The JVP regrouped around a re-entrenched ethnonationalist campaign in the mid 1980s, and staged another confrontation with the state. Militancy among Tamil youth grew with their demand for a separate state, which would be known as Tamil Eelam. The result was nearly 25 years of civil war.

Following the state's suppression of the JVP rebellion, political refugees who escaped death and imprisonment joined new associations and paved the way for contemporary progressive NGO movements. Many of these organizations were part of a global movement started by liberation theologists and Christian clergymen who offered a "preferential option" for the poor and searched for alternatives to state- and market-based economic development models. The ideological orientation of these associations was ecumenical and their memberships were open to anyone concerned with social justice. (Quite a few current anti-NGO lobbyists were once important members of these associations.) While the state did not directly suppress these, it kept a close watch over them, for their activities generated intense criticism of state-led liberal economic reforms.

The state sought ideological legitimacy through ethnoreligious nationalism while confronting a number of problems. For example, in 1959, minister of agriculture Philip Gunawardena enacted the Paddy Lands Act, which sought to secure the rights of tenants and fix the amount of rent paid to landowners who had customarily appropriated half of the produce. Both the Viharadhipathi and Trustee Association and the EBM protested against the Act. They demanded that temple lands be exempt and that Bhikkhus be exempt from fines and imprisonment for contravening the Act. Monks who did not own much land, particularly those from the low-country temples, proposed state redistribution of the land of the major temples of the Asgiriya and Malwatta Chapters. Protests continued until 1971, when the government, led by Mrs. Bandaranaike, finally exempted the Buddhist Temporalities from the Act.[19] Differences of opinion on the land issue among Buddhist monks reflected socioeconomic competition among elites. The combined force of both economic and ethnoreligious nationalism allowed the state to consolidate its control over economic development, and to present itself as guardian of the nation's civil and religious institutions.

There was little room left for NGO activity. Until 1977, the inward-looking economic development strategies of the state had focused primarily on local nongovernmental institutions with the object of promoting local participation and self-reliance. The District Development Councils (DDC) claimed they would "be the main link between the network of the government agency on the one hand and the local community and its representative institutions on the other." Their functions included "the formulation of development projects and the preparation of development programs for their areas," and they participated in "the co-ordination of development activity and the review of plan implementation."[20] Voluntary and self-help organizations, cooperatives, and NGOs were mostly funded by the state, and the state's interventions were generally similar to those of contemporary NGOs. The government thus inspired the voluntarism that led to the Sarvodaya Shramadana Movement (SSM), which became the nation's largest and most controversial NGO. State-centered development incorporated these local institutions as appendages of government departments and ministries, and the polity polarized from the local to the national level as parties incorporated these institutions into their strategies to gain political power. The officers of associations were elected through political patronage and their programs were then identified with the ruling parties. In effect, devolution meant the incorporation of local institutions into the party organizations that wielded state power.[21]

The results of SLFP economic policies were disappointing. Public sector GDP increased from 5.7 million rupees in 1961 to 12.2 million rupees in 1974.[22] The average growth rate in 1960 was 4.5 percent, while the average increase in per capita income was 21.1 percent. Unemployment in the mid-1970s totaled 14 million, or 20 percent of the total labor force. Inflation during the 1950s and 1970s was below 2 percent. It then increased to 25 percent in 1976.[23] The bias of local private capital towards real estate investments rather than industrial production, and the reliance of capitalists on the state, slowed the development of capitalism. Private investments in the industrial sector were heavily subsidized by the state, but the regime failed to generate sustainable growth.

By 1970, the very forces that had supported state-led capitalist development—import-substitution and state-aided industrialization—had become an obstacle to growth. Sluggish economic development and the state's inability to sustain its social welfare policy package led to rising unemployment and food shortages.[24] By 1976, the regime was so unpopular that it was forced to introduce emergency powers to control political parties, unions, and organizations. But the left had been brutally suppressed in the 1971 insurrection, and the 1971–72 coalition government between left political parties and the SLFP posed no threat to the existing mode of accumulation. The left lost its mass appeal when it failed to provide an effective response to the multiple problems faced by Sri Lanka.

Although the SLFP succeeded in suppressing the JVP insurgency, it failed to contain popular discontent. The closed economy and the import substitution policies of the SLFP regime did not meet public expectations. Restrictions on imports constrained accumulation by the local bourgeoisie who prospered only via state patronage. By the late 1970s, international support for such policies worldwide gave way to policies of export promotion. The constitutional changes introduced by the government, with the approval of the Sri Lankan Communist Party, led to the further entrenchment of ethnoreligious nationalism, frustrating Tamil youth who believed that economic and social parity between Sinhalese and Tamils would not be achieved under the UNP or the SLFP. Traditional Tamil political leadership, dominated by the Tamil United Liberation Front (TULF), exploited the Tamil institutional memory of poor relations with the government since independence—an important source of legitimacy for the "true" leaders of the community.

Under the SLFP regime, the space for NGOs increased, as it pursued social development programs which attempted to reconcile the excesses of socialism and capitalism according to the twin ideologies of economic and ethnoreligious nationalism. NGO self-help programs eased the suffering caused by economic losses. NGOs functioned as fora for reconciliation among a broad spectrum of social classes disenchanted with the bankrupt practices of the state. When the government extended both emergency regulations and its term in office beyond the period stipulated in the constitution, the resulting crisis of popular legitimacy stimulated activism among human rights NGOs, and many activists and opposition party politicians participated in their meetings. NGO efforts to mobilize public opinion helped to undermine the popular legitimacy of the SLFP and aided the transfer of power to the UNP.

## ECONOMIC LIBERALIZATION AND POLITICAL CENTRALIZATION

The converging interests of domestic and international capital brought the UNP to power in 1977, when an economic crisis was once again interpreted as a political crisis requiring state intervention. By then, counterhegemonic anti-capitalist activity had been effectively crushed on a global scale. Even those convinced of capitalism's inability to respond to the needs of marginalized groups were forced to search for alternative models of social change. The reforms of 1977 lifted restrictions on NGOs and gave them permission to operate anywhere in the country, as their programs, policies, and donor bases were consistent with those of the state. The number of NGOs boomed since the state lacked any restrictions or a regulatory framework, and they were only accountable to their international donors. A noteworthy feature of many of the NGOs that emerged during this period was their lack of interest in labor and alienation from the labor unions.

The 1977 elections intensified the polarization of Sri Lankan society along ethnic lines. The economic and ethnoreligious nationalism of the mainstream political parties had a great impact on many in the Tamil community in the northern and eastern parts of the country, who felt that they were economically marginalized. They put pressure on elite Tamil political parties based in Colombo, demanding an effective response that would not risk the benefits derived from state capitalism. The Tamil United Liberation Front (TULF) emerged as the main opposition party on the basis of its promise to call for political autonomy for the Tamil-speaking population. While it is unclear what proportion of the Tamil population shared the desire for political autonomy, the articulation of their grievances along ethnic lines was a response to the economic nationalism of the "ruling bloc" of the Tamil and Sinhalese bourgeoisie.

During this period, Tamil youth began to challenge the dominant political regimes of the northern and eastern elites. The Tamil community and the TULF argued that Tamil economic grievances stemmed primarily from the increasing influence of Sinhala Buddhist nationalism, rather than from class antagonisms resulting from capitalist development. Tamils voted for the TULF to increase their political autonomy by bifurcating state power along ethnic-territorial lines. The election of the UNP was followed by an acute economic crisis and the threat of secession by Tamil militants.

The UNP election marked a watershed in the country's economic development. UNP economic and constitutional reforms departed significantly from post-independence political traditions. Under executive presidential rule, Sri Lanka was transformed from a welfare state to a neoliberal state. For the first time, a single party secured a two-thirds majority in parliament, and the SLFP lost its position as the major opposition party. Instead, TULF, which campaigned for a separate Tamil state in the northern and eastern parts of the country, emerged and secured its place as the main opposition party. Also, for the first time, the two main Marxist political parties—the Communist Party and the Lanka Sama Samaja Party—failed to secure a single seat in parliament. Upon assuming power, the UNP immediately began dismantling the existing state machinery and adopting policies that favored economic privatization.

The government's role in direct investment activities became increasingly important between 1978 and 1984. In 1987, total government investments exceeded total private investments. Massive public sector investment programs were introduced to offset cuts in social-sector subsidies. The Accelerated Mahaveli Development Program accounted for 45 percent of international donor funding. Public-sector investments, which accounted for 8 percent of GDP in 1970, almost doubled to 15 percent of GDP between 1978 and 1983. Despite increasing privatization, the state sector continued to dominate the economy. For example, from 1978 to 1983, 25 percent of the annual budget went to public enterprise transfers. The comparable figure for the period between 1970 and 1976 was 10 percent. Foreign aid transfers also increased. External debt payments increased from 70 million SDR (Special Drawing Rights) in 1970 to 137 million SDR in 1980, and then to 353.5 million SDR in 1991. These public investment programs were supported by an inflow of foreign capital rather than surpluses generated from domestic capital accumulation or savings.[25]

The UNP introduced a number of reforms that developed agriculture in industrial capitalist directions, investing in large-scale irrigation and infrastructure development projects to modernize agricultural production using massive infusions of foreign capital. Multinational corporations were encouraged to invest in the agricultural sector through financial incentives such as the restructuring of tenurial relations in 1979 under Act No. 58, removing protection for farmers. In 1978, central bank guarantees were withdrawn from agricultural credit, causing commercial banks to adopt stricter lending standards, and making it difficult for small farmers to get credit. A water tax was introduced and the fertilizer subsidy was drastically reduced.

The reduction of budget deficits required drastic cuts to funding for basic services including food provision, health care, education, water, and sanitation. Total social welfare expenditure declined from 30.4 percent in 1977 to 8 percent in 1985.[26] The economic growth rate declined from 8.2 percent in 1978 to 6.3 percent in 1979, and continued to decline to 5.8 percent in 1980, stabilizing at an average growth of 3.6 percent between 1980 and 1990.[27] Much-needed government investments in public-sector projects then increased the budget deficit. Public investments as a percentage of total investments increased by 60 percent[28] yet there were no major shifts in agriculture and manufacturing's share of GDP, except for a marginal increase in construction, trade, and services. Domestic inflation increased costs, decreased savings, and led to a spending freeze across the board. Domestic supply-and-demand imbalances had a negative impact on price levels, as well as on the balance of payments and the external value of domestic currency. With the availability of Special Drawing Rights (SDRs), imports trebled, but exports increased slowly. The current account deficit increased, despite a depreciation of the Sri Lankan rupee's value (15.97 to an Indian rupee in 1977; 26.27 to one in 1984). Prices on agricultural products increased, as did input prices. Rural wages and the cost of production also increased, and the income gap grew substantially.[29]

The ideological legitimacy of the state's economic project was based on the assertion that it had not abandoned the post-independence government's commitment to socialism. The country was renamed the Democratic Socialist Republic of Sri Lanka, although "socialism" was rehabilitated within the imperatives of the market economy.[30] The state did not entirely abandon its commitment to social welfare. In response to the JVP's increasingly vocal calls for distributive justice, the UNP introduced a number of large-scale populist programs specifically targeting the poor. A million-dollar housing program for the homeless initially accounted for 7 percent of the state's overall capital expenditure. Janasaviya poverty alleviation programs provided funds for those adversely affected by structural adjustments and stabilization policies. A land redistribution program was introduced under the Mahawali development scheme, and Swarnabomi programs provided legal entitlement to land for qualified applicants. Mahapola higher education programs gave university students a monthly stipend. A national free textbook program for high school students was also implemented.

The regime deployed ethno-populist nationalism to authorize its agenda. Aid-dependent modernization programs, populist poverty alleviation programs, and the suppression of democratic freedoms were part of an ongoing attempt to revitalize Sinhala Buddhist civilization. Heads of state portrayed themselves as Buddhist leaders motivated by the righteousness of King Asoka. The aid-dependent Mahavali scheme was described as an attempt to bring back the ancient symbiotic relationship between the temple, the paddy field, and the water tanks.[31] State patronage of Buddhism was, first and foremost, a means of increasing state control over religion by suppressing interest groups that might otherwise have sided with the religious establishment against the state. Jayewardene's conception of Buddhism as a faith of individual responsibility justified both his use of religion and his desire to remove Buddhist monks from political life and secular vocations.[32]

Liberal market policies were implemented under the state's extreme vigilance. Its development program was entirely dependent on foreign aid, and it was the government's responsibility to create the institutional conditions necessary for a free-market economy. At the same time, the state needed to maintain its popular legitimacy by satisfying the interests of a broad social base. That was difficult in the face of growing social inequality and drastic cuts in social-sector expenditure, combined with poor overall economic performance. The economy was at the mercy of international donors and the turns of the global economy, and the regime had limited ability to respond to domestic conditions.

By the early 1980s, the legitimacy of the UNP regime was again challenged by the JVP, student unions, trade unions, professional associations, Tamil political parties, and separatist movements, leading to further centralization of power in the executive president and party members.[33] When UNP ignored the riots of 1977, it fed the Tamil militant demand for Eelam. The despair and frustration that Tamil youth felt about their own leaders and the policies of the Sinhala-dominated government[34] were directly linked to the national economic crises generated by the neoliberal economic reforms supported by the ruling party.

Eelam advocates believed that the "political autonomy" of the north and east was a prerequisite for regional economic development.

They saw that the material bases of development were undermined in Tamil areas by the extension of state-sponsored colonization schemes to expand agriculture-based accumulation along ethnic and racial lines. Safeguarding these bases was essential since Tamil youth employment in the south and state investments in the Tamil-speaking north rapidly declined under Sinhala-dominated government. Tamil youth resorted to militancy in part because Sinhala and Tamil political elites were attempting to expand and safeguard their own power bases through the militarization of communal politics. Yet this militancy failed to liberate politics from communalism; rather, they encouraged communalism or undermined the class based mobilization of social dissent. Similarly, the NGOs and State constrained their responses to militancy to narrow confines of ethnicity and counter-terrorisms respectively, and all stakeholders contributed to defensive nationalism as opposed to critical engagement with it.

The Eelam movement was not initially homogeneous.[35] In its early days, it consisted of many different militant groups with different ideological perspectives and different political strategies. Marxist groups agreed that political autonomy would foster growth throughout Sri Lanka in the wake of the economic liberalization that had rescued "the failing economy in 1977, but [...] also brought exacerbated differences between various economic classes."[36] However, the LTTE soon emerged as the dominant group by physically eliminating all other militant groups, including dissenting Marxists, Tamil politicians, intellectuals, and civil servants who did not support its uncompromising demands. EPRLF (Eelam People's Revolutionary Liberation Front), a militant group with pro-Marxist political sympathies that did not want to join LTTE, was forced into exile. Soon internal NGO opposition to the LTTE in the northern and eastern parts of the country ceased to exist, owing to the repeated failure of the government and the LTTE to find a political solution combined with the suppression of democratic freedoms by the LTTE. NGOs did little to address the growing public perception that they were contributing to the separatist agenda of the LTTE. Part of the reason is that the NGOs were financially and politically comfortable as they received the financial and political support of the international actors and social and political elites of the country.

From its inception the LTTE demonstrated signs of a movement that does not permit dissent. The expulsion of Muslims from the Jaffna peninsula and the massacre of hundreds of Sinhalese in northern villages were evidence of LTTE's exclusivist ideology, which was promoted and exploited by many Tamil political parties to suppress internal contradictions within Tamil society, particularly among the lower castes. The class basis of the state was preserved as exclusivist Sinhala and Tamil nationalisms effectively silenced anyone invested in multi-ethnic unity. NGOs critical of the state found it prudent to ignore or downplay class tensions and kept their distance from left-wing political parties, hence contributed to the polarization of the country along ethnic lines and institutionalization of ethnic conflict as a distinct area of intervention.

In response, the JVP became more militant in the 1980s. It retained its Marxist-Leninist underpinnings but adopted the language of ethno-populism, becoming known as Jaathika Chinthanaya, or National Thought, and adopting the slogan "Motherland First" to oppose the UNP and the presence of south Indian workers on tea and rubber plantations. JVP not only opposed the ruling party, it attacked the UNP and its allies. Its fierce opposition to the 1987 Peace Accord between Sri Lanka and India brought an Indian peacekeeping force to the country. The institutional culprits of the Peace Accord were NGOs.

By the early 1990s, the government's administrative machinery in the north and east had weakened, and the strongest links between the north and south were maintained through NGOs. The state suppressed all other opposition groups, confining Tamil political parties to Colombo. When the UNP regime lost power in 1992, the LTTE had already established strongholds in the north and east. The civil war slowed economic growth and increased unemployment. Internationally, the government lost popularity as it failed to resolve the ethnic crisis or prevent human rights abuses. The UNP regime ended in May 1993 with the assassination of President Premadasa, and the mobilization of ethnoreligious nationalism to extend capitalist accumulation continued, causing further economic and political instability and culminating in a bloody civil war.

Following Premadasa's assassination, the state admitted foreign NGOs to Sri Lanka and permitted local NGOs to accept foreign resources. The new regime gave NGOs greater freedom to experiment with a diverse array of social development interventions. The immediate surge in NGO activity was enabled entirely by international donor assistance. A leading Sri Lankan NGO officer explained:

> Within a short span of time, our people have also mastered the language and art of forming NGOs, so it was not difficult for anybody to form an organization. As soon as there were funds available, a new organization was a matter of identifying "projects," taking pictures, and forming a local group.[37]

NGOs became a source of full-time employment, leading to the emergence of a new class of NGO professionals. Although they were a heterogeneous group in some ways, the leaders of these organizations came from the urban middle classes, and they didn't want to function directly through political parties and trade unions. Some even came from the JVP. Their new associations were mainly funded by international donor agencies and both their survival and their bargaining power were contingent on their ability to exert pressure on the state.

The government failed to provide relief and rehabilitation for victims as the war escalated. Sensational accounts of Tamil suffering in the northern and eastern provinces sparked outrage in the West, leading NGOs to offer help in war-torn areas. NGOs obtained resources with ease, but their activities were controversial. They were the only means by which the government could maintain its ties to the northern and eastern parts of the country, but they were also seen as supporting LTTE separatism. Virtually everyone—media, local organizations, the Buddhist clergy, and the JVP—saw NGOs as a threat to national interests, claiming that they assisted terrorists, divided the country, and aligned themselves with Christians. Oppositional organizations sought to mobilize public opinion against both Tamil separatism and a negotiated settlement that would violate the Sinhala Buddhist identity and post-independence territorial integrity of the country.

During this period, The Sarvodaya Shramadana Movement (SSM) was active in over 8000 villages and was assisted by over 35 international donors; it was the NGO most trusted by the government and a major implementer of government programs. SSM's ideas and programs were virtually identical to those introduced by President Premadasa.[38] In the 1960s, SSM had received most of its resources from the government, but, late in that decade, it negotiated for aid with several international donors, including FAO, UNICEF, WHO, Oxfam UK, the Canadian International Development Agency (CIDA), the Alton Jones Foundation, the Ford Foundation, and the American World Jewish Organization. An influx of international funds led to SSM's rapid expansion—at one point its annual budget was larger than that of the Department of Rural Development. SSM promised to bring about a new social order based on "a system capable of organizing human society free from the exploitation of man by man."[39] Despite its increasing dependence on foreign aid, SSM offered a critique of "Western development," socialist and capitalist alike. As an alternative, SSM offered a paradigm ostensibly based on indigenous values and dedicated to the achievement of total human development, beginning with the individual and radiating outward to the family, village, nation, and global community. In many respects, SSM's ideology matched state-centered ethno-populism, except that the state sought legitimacy from popular Sinhala Buddhist nationalism and the SSM did not. Very few Buddhist monks were directly involved in SSM activities, and most participated only in its occasional religious functions.

International donors were concerned about a lack of SSM transparency, efficiency, and accountability. There were accusations of improper evaluation, fraudulent record-keeping, corruption, and mismanagement. Eventually, administrative problems at the executive level became visible to donors and the public. At the same time, international donors were themselves facing funding cuts from their own constituencies and governments. Increasingly, they demanded detailed program evaluations in order to monitor the results of their aid.

In 1986, a donor consortium was established as a collaborative project between SSM, CIDA, and NOVIB. When the evaluation process began, donors requested past evaluations but SSM could not satisfactorily comply. According to SSM, they had such evaluations, but they were written in the vernacular and were not accessible to international donors. When donors complained, SSM argued that the evaluation standards and criteria of international donors were inappropriate to SSM development projects, which were rooted in native Sri Lankan values that could not be quantified or measured in Western terms. All of the evidence suggests that SSM did not have any systematic plan for allocating funds or measuring progress. A long-term SSM employee stated:

> [I]n those days we informed about the plan and we got the money. We did not have to go through all the bureaucracy and red tape imposed by people who have nothing to do with the activities at the village level. We could directly get the funds from the "Loku Sir" [i.e., the Senior Office]. In fact, foreigners and Head Office staff wrote all the evaluations, and neither the villagers nor we had anything to do with them.[40]

The former head of NOVIB, Dr. Sjef Thenuis, asked the organization to be sensitive to the unique nature of SSM's philosophy and practices but the new NOVIB management responded: "We are not interested in philosophy. For NOVIB, development is a business. There is nothing idealistic about it. [SSM] should conform to a business relationship with NOVIB."[41] It had become increasingly difficult for SSM to mobilize voluntary participation unless monetary rewards were given to the villagers, and NGO donors and partners had an interest in establishing enterprises modeled on commercial counterparts and introducing income-generating activities at the village level. Poverty could not be addressed through volunteer work alone. However, SSM felt that donor insistence on business-like partnerships impeded progress.

Donor consortium evaluations and conflicts with SSM led to drastic funding cuts and retrenchment of SSM activities. As Dr. Jehan Perera explained, this led to a collapse of all development programs in the northern and eastern areas where Tamil militants were openly critical of SSM. Even some of the more moderate groups were cynical about SSM's ideology and practices. In Perera's words, "It was a classic example of an uneven confrontation between the dominant materialistic value-system of the Northern development paradigms and the humanistic and holistic approach to development of the south."[42] These pronouncements were not substantiated by systematic studies, and tended to reflect popular nationalist sentiments more than fact-based criticism. Popular opinion favored bottom-up as opposed to top-down development, but SSM programs collapsed after donor funds were reduced, indicating that, after a decade of work, the organization had failed to become self-reliant. Sarvodaya's critique of Western values and traditions served both to protect it from international criticism and to advance its ethnoreligious nationalist agenda.

The relationship between SSM and the government began to deteriorate after the election of Premadasa as president in 1989. SSM had been the government's most favored NGO since the 1950s, and Premadasa was a strong supporter.[43] But by 1990, SSM leader A.T. Ariyarathna had become President Premadasa's chief rival. Dr. Stephen Nef of the International Commission of Jurists (ICJ), who was on a mission to study the NGO Commission (see below), called Ariyarathna "a charismatic figure of national stature who could, consequently, be either an invaluable ally or a formidable foe of any ambitious politician."[44] A few weeks after Premadasa was sworn in, the chief of the National Intelligence Bureau interrogated Ariyarathna. Subsequently, SSM's radio program, which had been aired by the Sri Lanka Broadcasting Corporation (SLBC), was canceled, and the customs department confiscated its printing equipment. Thereafter, the media printed news stories detailing allegations of SSM misconduct.

A brief history of the Presidential Commission on NGOs demonstrates the government's fear that SSM would challenge the political power of President Premadasa. In December 1990, Premadasa appointed a Presidential Commission of Inquiry (which not all NGOs opposed) to examine all aspects of NGO activity in Sri Lanka. This was a response to the findings of an earlier commission appointed by the ministry of planning. The former commission had tallied about 3000 NGOs, but provided no legal framework for monitoring their funding or activities. Before the new commission began public hearings on March 25, 1990, 40 international donor representatives met with its chairman.[45] Ideological differences among NGOs were evident in the reports they presented.

The commission appeared to be guided by the government's interest in certain NGOs, and specifically targeted Christian and well-funded organizations. SSM was singled out and subjected to harassment by intelligence services.[46] Human rights NGOs worried that they were investigated last only because they were more likely to be "vigorously" scrutinized.[47] The sensationalist approach taken by the newspapers contributed to widespread anti-NGO sentiment. On several occasions, the press distorted the commission's proceedings by giving particular attention to misappropriation of funds and the funneling of money to Tamil militant groups. For example, the *Dinamina* carried a front-page article with the headline: "Funds from Dutch Agency Fall into Tiger Hill: Astonishing Evidence of First Witness." Two days later, State Counsel Nihal Jayasinghe issued a correction.[48]

The commission conducted its activities in a politically charged environment and some called it a "witch hunt." Judge Joseph Anthony Soza, a member of the commission, claimed that it had "no control over the general context in which [it] operated. Most notably, it had no control over the general high degree of attention the press was devoting to its activities, or to distortions which occurred in the reporting of the conduct of the Commission's sessions ... [The] donor community shared many of the same concerns and misgivings that the NGOs themselves did, concerning the NGO Commission."[49] Donors were more concerned about the implications of the regulatory framework that would result from the undertaking. The report noted, "The attitude of the donor community might best be characterized as watchful and concerned, rather than alarmist," because the "NGO situation in the country was somewhat chaotic or anarchic and abuses and misconduct were certainly not absent from the NGO realm."[50] USAID, however, pointed out that it was unnecessary for the Sri Lankan government to police NGO funds because USAID had rigorous internal mechanisms to do so itself.[51]

The commission's final report was not made available to the public, but the government passed a new law to regulate NGO activities, using its emergency powers to bypass the legislative process. The new Act made registration compulsory for NGOs with annual budgets exceeding Rs 50,000 and required that all receipts of NGOs with budgets exceeding Rs 100,000 were to be monitored by the government. NGOs were required to disclose to the government the names of aid recipients and the accounts and copies of all statements submitted to the Directorate of Social Services. Those disclosures were then to be made available to the general public for a nominal fee. The government also proposed establishing an NGO secretariat. A member of the civil rights movement, in a press release, demanded the release of the commission report, pointing out that these measures were a "serious interference with the free functioning of organizations with the freedom of association and expression."[52]

During the 1990s, Ariyarathna had been openly critical of the Premadasa government. He advocated change in the existing political and economic system, claiming that improvements would require the "present power-pyramid [to] collapse."[53] The government had become increasingly unpopular because of its treatment of SSM and other NGOs. SSM blamed the government for its slow progress[54] and successfully mobilized considerable international support. During a meeting held in the Sarvodaya Training Complex on September 1, 1992, Ariyarathna openly declared his intentions to enter mainstream politics.[55] Some Sarvodaya workers believed that Ariyarathna's campaign marked a positive turning point in the history of SSM. However, most donors felt that Ariyarathna was likely to destroy a decade of good work.[56]

Despite the ambiguities of SSM's articulation of the relationship between religion and politics, the government feared that SSM would emerge as a political force.[57] Those fears seemed to be realized when, in 1992, SSM joined Buddhist and Christian clergymen to protest the erecting of a massive luxury hotel close to an ancient temple in Dambulla. SSM demanded unequivocally that the project be canceled. Government supporters staged a counter-demonstration, focusing on the project's expected economic benefits. The media suggested that SSM leaders and clergymen had ulterior motives and denounced the organizers for having "desecrated a Buddhist environment by allowing other religions to display a cross in the precincts of the Dambulla Rajamaha Vihara."[58] The *Observer*, in an editorial titled "Political Pastors," attacked two protest leaders for not choosing "the path of meditation, prayer and a commitment to serve his fellowmen through his own personal (not political or organized) action."[59]

The SSM donor consortium demanded significant restructuring of financial and management systems[60] and made future aid commitments dependent upon this. Donors took a strong stand, arguing that their future relationship with Sarvodaya would be judged by its accomplishments.[61] Based on external reports, NOVIB and CIDA reduced their funding to Sarvodaya by almost Rs 35 million for failing to comply with donor demands.[62] At the same time, the Dutch government reduced NOVIB funding because of public outrage at home. Several Dutch-based NGOs entirely withdrew their support and membership.[63] Donors were unhappy with SSM's decision to accept large new grants, particularly from the government Joint Task Force (JTF), without prior approval of the consortium.[64]

In response, SSM drastically restructured and reorganized, closing down several unprofitable programs and reducing its staff. Other NGOs did the same. Staffing cuts led to labor crises. SSM, World Vision International, and Marga Institute workers staged public demonstrations and appealed to trade unions to safeguard their interests. SSM demanded "undated resignation letters" from its workers, requiring that they state their willingness to resign voluntarily. Workers were forced to comply or forgo compensation.[65] Lawsuits were filed and protests were held outside NGO premises, demanding worker compensation and alleging mismanagement. SSM workers who lost jobs formed an association after meeting with the Sri Lankan Trade Union Federation which declared the staffing cuts illegal.[66] During the same period, SSM faced internal crises provoked by the May 1, 1992, resignation of Harsha Navarathna, Dr. A.T. Ariyarathna's nephew and national chairman of the Elders Committee. Navarathna formed a new NGO in collaboration with the government, and subsequently became SSM's main critic. Thereafter, Sarvodaya progressively abandoned most of its social development programs in favor of commercial ventures, and lost its prominent place within the NGOs community.

Although President Premadasa succeeded in defeating SSM, two significant challenges remained. He had to deflect criticism from the JVP-led youth and the national and international civil society organizations, and he had to contend with Tamil militancy and the presence of Indian peacekeeping forces in the country. He adopted a multifaceted approach, encouraging ethnonationalist forces, rhetorically committing to a political settlement of the ethnic conflict, suppressing democratic freedoms and civil rights, and investing in social development programs. From its inception the ideological and rural development activities of Sarvodaya were grounded in the same ethnonationalist and economic ideology of the state. In fact, in many places Sarvodaya activities led to patronizing political elites by incorporating them as leaders of its village development programs. Especially, since the 1971 JVP uprising Sarvodaya ideology was instrumental in defusing forces that are critical of the state practices. Yet it failed to prevent another uprising of the JVP in 1980 that was more ethno-nationalist than Marxist in its ideological orientation. As the ethnic conflict began to take a central place in the political debates, the NGOs entered into the arena of ethnicity, conflict resolution, and peace building. Their preoccupations in these areas made them less concerned with the economic issues and their relationship with the ethnic conflict. Subsequently, the role NGOs played in the institutionalization of the ethnic conflict became the main source of anti-NGOism and the shaping of NGO-state relations.

NGOs had been involved since the mid-1980s in debates on the devolution of power to Tamil-speaking communities. Many state actors relied on these organizations for knowledge and advice for dealing with the ethnic conflict. Several NGOs, such as the Movement for Inter-Racial Justice (MIRJ), INFORM, the Center for Society and Religion, the International Center For Ethnic Studies (ICES), SSM, and the Social Scientists' Association, advocated devolution to the northern and eastern parts of the country. The political settlement favored by those institutions was determined by their position that Sri Lanka should remain a unitary state, a view shared by the majority of the country's citizens and by many other multi-ethnic nations. Only a handful of NGOs, mostly springing from a base of urban intellectuals, actually took part in this discussion. Most preferred to keep their distance from the devolution debate either for ideological reasons or because they feared that such intervention would marginalize them. Politicians from all political parties participated in NGO-organized debates on ethnic conflict and asked for NGO feedback on proposed devolution policies.

A notable step towards strengthening NGO bargaining power vis-à-vis the government was the establishment of the NGO Forum in 1990, at the request of NGOs in Sri Lanka and Amsterdam. The objectives of the Forum were to create conditions for peace, justice, and poverty alleviation, and to increase the institutional capacities of Sri Lankan and foreign NGOs to deal with these issues. Immediately after the Amsterdam conference, another meeting was held in Bangkok, under the heading "World Solidarity: Forum on Sri Lanka for Justice and Peace." The initiative was again taken by Sri Lankan NGOs that wanted to establish an international solidarity network. One of the unintended outcomes of the Bangkok meeting was the stipulation that the Forum would not issue any statement on behalf of Sri Lankan NGOs, since the drafting of such a statement was critical to the success of the latter.

While the Forum was being established, the JVP faced a country in political turmoil due to insurrection. The activities of the JVP, along with government suppression, constrained the ability of NGOs to offer opinions both locally and internationally. During this period, there were sharp divisions among NGOs, their supporters, and their detractors. The JVP joined NGOs in protest against the Indian Peace Keeping Force (IPKF) and the political settlement proposed by the government. Counterinsurgency efforts escalated against the JVP, and the JVP targeted all persons opposed to the regime. The truce between the Tamil militants and the government ended and the regime faced multiple crises.

The Forum's initial objectives were to represent the concerns of local NGOs at the UN Commission on Human Rights, develop a strategy on behalf of Sri Lanka's poor, work in collaboration with the peace lobby, assist refugees, and develop civil society. The government, however, encouraged local organizations to aid victims of the war in collaboration with NGOs. In 1991, it set up an NGO Coordinating Committee to enable NGOs more effectively to assist security forces. A memo stated: "Many NGOs could and should boost the morale of service personnel in the battle zone, and minister to their needs."[67] The Sinhala Women's Association for the Welfare and Advancement of Women responded by proposing a radio program to establish communication links between security force personnel and the general public.

## CIVIL WAR AND NGOs IN PEACEBUILDING AND HUMANITARIAN WORK

By mid-1993, the government's administrative machinery in the northern provinces and, to a lesser extent, in the eastern and Vanni regions had collapsed, and the war between government security forces and Tamil militants created new opportunities for

NGO intervention in the areas of relief and rehabilitation, human rights, peacemaking, ethnic conflict management, and the debate over devolution of powers. The LTTE had already established a stronghold and SSM was forced to terminate its programs in the Northern Province after its leader was assassinated in Jaffna. SSM also found it increasingly difficult to function in the eastern province. The majority of NGOs active in other parts of the country were not interested in working in war-torn areas, for ideological as well as safety reasons. In particular, they feared that their intervention in programs related to the situation in the north would be construed by both the public and the government as providing assistance to the militants. Only foreign and church-based NGOs were able to effectively continue their activities in areas controlled by the LTTE.

The LTTE in the north did not tolerate internal criticism of its conduct. Opponents were either assassinated or forced to operate from exile. With few exceptions, there was little dialogue among NGOs based in the southern, northern, and eastern parts of the country. Until the defeat of the LTTE, NGOs functioned in two different administrative regions and were the link between war-torn areas and rest of the country. The growing presence of NGOs in conflict zones presented a dilemma for the government. NGOs provided indispensable services and a means of exerting political influence over Northern and Eastern provinces. At the same time, it was impossible for NGOs to carry out programs to which Tamil militant groups were opposed, because those groups controlled the administrative infrastructure which the organizations needed to function.

Both the government and the LTTE exploited the claims and programs of NGOs, and each blamed humanitarian crises and human rights abuses on the other. NGOs in the north and east ignited local and international criticism of government policies when they reported news of human suffering in war-affected areas. The anti-NGO lobby argued that they were spreading false information, damaging national interests, and aiding the militants, but this did not prevent the international community from criticizing human rights violations by the government. Meanwhile international forces pressured the government to negotiate a settlement with the Tamil community.

NGOs opposed to the devolution of power supported a military solution to the ethnic crisis. Those sympathetic to the cause of Tamil militants pointed out contradictions in NGO rhetoric. The public and the government were equally suspicious of the motives of NGOs in the south. SSN leader Ariayarathna, while claiming to be "one belonging to Sinhala Buddhist ancestry and not having [a single] unBuddhist blood relative,"[68] had continuously advocated a negotiated peaceful political settlement that would promote unity among all races and religions. But his negative view of the Tamils' demand for a separate state was embedded in the dominant discourse of Sinhalese nationalism and he believed the "Sinhala Buddhist should take the difficult responsibility of rebuilding the nation."[69]

Several local NGOs not only challenged government peace efforts but also engaged in a nationwide campaign to demonstrate the futility of LTTE demands. NGOs that supported the government's efforts towards a negotiated political settlement were accused of being foreign agents, proselytizers, and pro-LTTE. Chintana Parshadaya, an organization at the forefront of the ideological campaigns against NGOs, opposed the Norway meetings and an alleged plan to bring United Nations peacekeepers to Sri Lanka, arguing that such measures would lead to imperialist control over the country. This and similar campaigns were primarily directed against those who advocated political devolution as a solution to the ethnic crisis. These organizations were nationalist and anti-Marxist. They agreed with the JVP, yet preferred to state their own case. Nalin de Silva, who saw links between world imperialism, Tamil separatism, and the NGOs, distinguished his group from the left:

> At this juncture, Marxism indeed played a subversive role along with the non-national forces [i.e., NGOs]. The non-national forces do not mean foreign forces but the forces opposed to the nationality of this country. [...] The Marxists can justify their existence only by attacking national identity. When their economic models are collapsing the only way to retain their intellectual glory is by promoting internationalism as against nationality. Today there are no differences between liberals and Marxists. With regard to economic policies they try to live as distinguished citizens of the so-called global village. Presently Marxism has turned out to be the obedient servant of world imperialists.[70]

Views like this isolated the traditional left and human rights NGOs, and gave credibility to JVP's economic nationalism. The protest against NGOs had finally reached a wider audience. NGO activities were conducted primarily in English for a small minority, while their opponents conducted their business in the vernacular and disseminated their ideas through the mass media. Anti-NGO groups presented the war and pro-devolution NGOs as the main obstacles to economic modernization, yet no one criticized neoliberal economic policies. Everyone maintained that the ethnic conflict and the economic crisis were two separate issues. The public was not aware that the state utilized ethnicity and the economic crisis to facilitate the conditions of capitalist expansion.

As international funding for conflict resolution poured in, NGOs in the peace movement launched a nationwide educational service to assist government peace initiatives. Some were aggressive in their support of Tamil political independence; others supported autonomy within the context of a united Sri Lanka. Although NGOs frequently opposed each other, in this case their interests were not dissimilar. The peace program included grassroots education, meditation, religious ceremonies, and public processions. Peace was conceptualized in abstract terms as a prerequisite for progress. NGOs did not attempt to challenge fundamentally ethno-populist assumptions; for most Sri Lankans, peace was the absence of war, nothing more.

The government's position on devolution remained ambivalent and contradictory. It feared that the NGO campaign would adversely affect public opinion and bring intense international pressure. At the same time, the NGO campaign allowed for a possible political settlement and continued relations with the Tamil population. Government policies towards NGOs were politically expedient, and NGO success in influencing government policy was contingent on their ability to mobilize international public opinion.

President Premadasa's "people-ization" social welfare policies practically bankrupted the economy as he attempted to garner popular support. For the masses, people-ization simply meant pauperization. Although Premadasa succeeded in suppressing the JVP, he failed to contain the civil war and mass protests. His skillful, opportunistic negotiations with the LTTE and the ethnoreligious nationalist forces in the south were not enough to contain their increased influence over the state, and only resulted in the further suppression of democratic freedoms. The activities of human rights and advocacy NGOs further isolated the government from local and international communities.

In December 1992, Premadasa was assassinated and NGOs played an influential role in bringing the People's Alliance (PA) under Chandrika Kumaratunga into power in 1995, marking the end of the longest period of one-party rule in Sri Lanka since independence. The transition period was dominated by NGOs' activities. Ideological divisions over solutions to the ethnic conflict continued to expand, and there was no emphasis on the relationship between human rights abuses, the civil war, and neoliberal policies in NGO agendas.

The PA promised to restore democracy. During the election campaign the PA had been accused of human rights abuses, particularly regarding the conduct of the security forces and the paramilitaries during the JVP uprising. Election issues also included the conduct of the military and the UNP in the Northern and Eastern provinces, and promises of a negotiated settlement of the ethnic crisis. The PA did not depart from the UNP's economic policies and underscored its commitment to "building a strong national economy within a market framework" and strengthening its partnership with the private sector. In addition, the PA promised to increase resources to develop private-sector infrastructure and to reduce war expenditures. There had been serious pressure from the IMF, and, in 1994, Sri Lanka's Aid Group withheld the last installment of a $490-million grant, pending a review of government progress on fiscal policy reforms. International aid agencies protested against the PA proposal to extend food subsidies.[71]

Unlike its predecessors, the PA publicly acknowledged that the failures of the post-independence political system were responsible for the ethnic crisis, marking a radical change from the rhetoric of its predecessor which had maintained that problems were caused by a "terrorist crisis." The PA expressed an interest in transforming the existing administrative system into "a union of regions," providing greater autonomy to the Northern and Eastern provinces. Prominent NGOs such as the MIRJ and Social Scientists' Association played a role in the PA victory and were included in the government's "kitchen cabinet" as policy advisors. Later, two NGO members were included in the first round of negotiations that took place between the LTTE and the government, giving further credibility to the claim of anti-NGO lobbyists that NGOs were part of a foreign-funded conspiracy against the Sri Lankan nation.

Negotiations between the government and the militants ended after the first round of talks, and civil war broke out again. By this time, international opinion favored government efforts to end the war and condemned the LTTE. The government justified the war on the grounds that the LTTE had failed to continue with negotiations, despite its promises. State-sponsored media represented the objective of the war as the "liberation" of the Tamils from the terror of the LTTE in order to facilitate a negotiated settlement. The government initiated a mass publicity campaign to mobilize the international community against the LTTE. Government forces increased control over northern and eastern Sri Lanka, silencing human rights NGOs.

Against this backdrop, anti-settlement NGOs mounted a media campaign against pro-settlement NGOs, branding them as Western imperialist agents and accusing them of conspiring against the government and the Sri Lankan people, attempting to form a parallel government, endangering national security, and collaborating with the LTTE.[72] The latter was the most serious charge, since it implied that pro-settlement NGOs were aiding terrorists in the guise of humanitarianism. Seventeen organizations, mostly Buddhist (including the Young Men's Buddhist Association, the Mahabodhi Society, the All Ceylon Buddhist Association, the Dharma Vijaya Foundation, the All Ceylon Buddhist Women's Association, the Buddhist Theosophical Society, the World Fellowship of Buddhists, the Sasana Sevaka Samithiya, the Success Colombo, the Chinthana Parshadaya, the Lanka Patriotic Movement, the Sinhala Lawyers' Association, the Buddhist Medical Association, the Deshapremi Bhikshu Peramuna, and the Ekeeya Sanividanya) called upon the government to monitor the activities of all foreign NGOs in Sri Lanka. NGOs pointed out numerous contradictions and misrepresentations in these arguments. The very NGOs that claimed to oppose foreign aid were themselves recipients of foreign aid. Accusations that NGOs were foreign agents emerged from an "ideology of xenophobia propagated by sections of Sri Lankans who made such accusations despite their own links with the foreign organizations."[73] Jayadeva Uyangoda, in his defense of NGOs, argued:

> We are in a very specific historical phase where capital and economy, politics and governance, culture and ideas are becoming increasingly internationalized. NGOs are not islands to themselves: they are human associations with international linkages in a global world. What is actually "unnatural" is not an individual or group having international linkages, but not having and testing foreign connections.[74]

NGOs explained that "'notions of security' and 'sovereignty' have no contemporary relevance if the democratic and human rights of the communities are excluded from the sphere of their application."[75] Moreover, they emphasized the need for "democratic ethnic relations" and argued that the "security of the people was no less important than the security of the State."[76] Uyangoda observed:

NGOs have come to stay in modern democracies. They represent the pith and substance of participatory democracy. Because of the very nature of their activities, some of them may cross the path of politicians, State officials and those who fetishize the State.[77]

NGOs campaigned for the PA after it won the Southern Provincial Council elections in 1994. When talks between the LTTE and the government broke down, the government adopted a policy of direct censorship, sparking protests by the Free Media Movement, which were silenced without serious incident. Less than a year after the election, tensions surfaced between the PA and NGOs because the latter persisted in criticizing government policies. The government, lacking sufficient parliamentary support, progressively succumbed to the imperatives of partisan politics, and some NGO leaders who had been rewarded by the PA with influential positions were forced to relinquish their government portfolios.

The international community exerted very little pressure on the PA government to address media censorship and human rights violations. The Ministers of Foreign and Constitutional Affairs successfully convinced the international community of the sincerity of the government's commitment to peace and democracy, possibly because the PA capably implemented privatization policies and World Bank development plans. At the same time, the US and several European countries became uneasy about "terrorism." In a departure from Cold War politics, Western nations were now reluctant to intervene in the internal affairs of developing countries, since those countries rarely challenged their hegemonic interests. The Sri Lankan government's language of anti-terrorism further weakened the impact of NGO advocacy at the international level.

The National Peace Council was formed at a conference in February 1995 with the participation of 85 representatives from different organizations. The NPC was an extension of the Peace Task Force formed in 1994. The initiative for the NPC came from the Catholic NGO SEDEC and it received international funding. It organized seminars and advocacy programs and sponsored foreign tours for national politicians so that they could study peace processes in Ireland, Mindanao (Philippines), and the Chittagong Hill Tract in Bangladesh. Among the associations participating in the peace initiatives were the Association of Relatives of Servicemen Missing in Action and the Association For Disabled Ex-Service Personal (ADEP), which stressed the futility of the war as a solution to the ethnic crisis and promoted the slogan "Peace is Life, War is Death." The peace front was ecumenical in its membership and used as a slogan for its 2001 peace campaign: "Let the tranquility and coolness of dharma (Buddha's teaching) douse the fire of the war." The Anti-War Front was formed in 2002 and the People's Peace Front in 1999.[78]

The National Peace Alliance was formed in 1998, with 300 members representing 140 organizations. The NPC was roundly criticized by ethnonationalist organizations like the National Movement Against Terrorism and the JVP for accepting foreign funds and for associating with Western Christians.[79] Voicing the views of the anti-peace lobby, the editor of the national daily paper, *The Island*, wrote: "The NGO and their allied peace brigade are the foot-soldiers engaged in uttering efforts to manufacture consent for Tamil Eelam. Their anti-war advertisements are calculated to discourage recruitment to the Security Forces."[80] Susantha Gunathilaka, a staunch critic of NGOs, asserted: "The National Peace Council is very plainly a psychological War Council aimed at Sri Lanka Sovereignty."[81] But many of the organizations involved in the peace movement did not receive international funding and are probably better understood as ad hoc anti-war groups. The anti-peace lobby silenced virtually all dissent and quashed the possibility of a settlement. Subsequently, anti-NGO sentiment was mobilized by President Rajapaksa and used to justify his abrogation of the Ceasefire Agreement between the government and LTTE.

The Kumaratunga government supported the peace movement through its own outfit, the National Integration Program Affairs Unit (NIPU) of the Ministry of Justice, Ethnic Affairs, and National Integration. NIPU was funded by Norad, the Norwegian Development Agency. The state's responses to peace initiatives continued to be driven by political expediency. NIPU positioned the state to co-opt peace interventions and to restore its international legitimacy as the guardian of peace. The peace movement, however, was internally divided, because of the scarcity of international funding and state patronage, and because of ideological differences. They promoted ethnic harmony while also accepting ethnoreligious nationalism. Trapped in contradiction, they could not alter the ways in which religion and race shaped the conflict. Ultimately the peace movement was both superficial and a colossal waste of resources, failing primarily because it did not engage with the deeper structural issues underlying the ethnic conflict.

In 1994, the Forum coalition of NGOs shifted its emphasis from peace towards the study of poverty and development, and the impact of international aid and World Bank development policies. The Forum represented the Economic Conference of Sri Lankan NGOs and debated whether or not to reject or adopt World Bank policies after commissioning a number of studies of poverty in Sri Lanka. They were expected to facilitate a strategy and create an alliance against the adverse impact of World Bank policies on Sri Lanka, but they did not do this. Though the Forum's concerns were shared by a number of NGOs in Sri Lanka, they lacked the institutional capacity to take an effective course of action, perhaps because Sri Lankan NGOs were under pressure from the government and international donors, both of whom favored neoliberal policies, to accept World Bank initiatives.

The government kept a watchful eye on the activities of the Forum, since aid from the World Bank was essential to the war economy. Dissension within GONGOS (Government Organized Non-Governmental Organizations) and the Forum might have been due to external factors, particularly the fear that NGOs could lose international funding. The government was uneasy about the Forum's attempt, particularly in the northern and eastern parts of the country, to link human rights violations with economic development, since that might have interrupted the flow of international funds. The Forum's lobbying efforts at the Paris Donor Consortium were generally unproductive, although they did induce Denmark and Canada to provide material support for protests against government policies.

In 1994, the Forum campaigned against the repatriation of Sri Lankan refugees from Europe. It also initiated strategies to address the human rights abuses of the LTTE, hoping to make them comply with international humanitarian standards, following similar initiatives undertaken by Amnesty International. In the media, the Forum was accused of being pro-LTTE for not giving equal emphasis to human rights abuses on both sides. Negative publicity further jeopardized the activities of the Forum and local human rights groups. A meeting organized by the Program on International Conflict Analysis and Resolution at Harvard University was canceled. Meanwhile, more NGOs distanced themselves from the Forum.

The Forum organized its annual consultation of NGOs in 1995. Local groups objected to the meeting on the grounds that it was against national interests. After addressing this misconception with the foreign ministry, the Forum held the meeting. On November 14, daily newspapers around the country published stories claiming that it was urging the government to halt "Operation Rivirasa," aimed at taking control of LTTE-controlled Jaffna.[82] The SLBC claimed that the meeting was organized by the British Refugee Council, and that it was designed to pressure the government to halt its military offensive.[83] Demonstrators rallied outside the meeting, demanding its adjournment, when hotel administrators and police were informed that the situation was beyond their control. A political correspondent of *The Sunday Times* implicated PA politicians in these protests.[84] The editor of *Yukthiya*, a newspaper controlled by a leading member NGO of the Forum, was assaulted.

On November 15, the meeting was relocated to the premises of Kamkaru Sevena, another NGO. Police visited the premises and asked Mr. Charles Abeysekera, a leading personality of the NGO movement in Sri Lanka, and Mr. Wolf, the secretary of the Forum, to clarify the purpose of the meeting. The police pointed out that, under the emergency regulations, special permission was needed to hold public meetings. There was a question of security for the participants of the meeting, as some groups were likely to disrupt it. Before the meeting was adjourned, 25 to 30 protesters carrying anti-NGO placards tried to invade the premises. A privately run radio station reported the incident and gave out the names and addresses of participants, along with the hotels where they were lodged. Immediately afterward, two government ministers visited to convey their regrets and one of the ministers arranged a reception for Forum members. The prime minister sent a personal representative, Mr. Vasudeva Nanayakkara, to convey her apologies. On November 17, he invited Forum members to lunch with him in the parliament.[85]

Meanwhile, pro-devolution NGOs shifted their attention to peacemaking programs that explained the benefits of the government's constitutional reforms. Eventually, NGO peace initiatives were taken over entirely by the government. The credibility of the Forum's claim to represent the interests of Sri Lankan NGOs in the international arena was then called into question. The divisions were made clear when the GONGOS organized its own forum in Sri Lanka, and the Forum organized its "international consultation" in London. Another attempt to coordinate NGOs thus came to an end, reflecting sharp and long-standing ideological divisions.

During this period, government ministers adopted the language of NGOs, forcing NGOs to use greater caution in articulating opposition against the state in the international arena. Repeated promises to achieve peace, the international community's campaign to end terrorism, and multiple human rights abuses by the LTTE all helped the government to deflect international criticism. But by the beginning of 1999, the PA had failed to stimulate new economic growth. The GDP growth rate contracted from 5.8 percent during the first half of 1998 to 2.7 percent in the first half of 1999. The fiscal deficit increased from 79 percent of GDP in 1997 to 97 percent in 1998. Export growth fell from 13 percent in 1997 to 2 percent in 1998. The agricultural sector grew by 2.5 percent in 1998, compared to 3 percent in 1997. The Colombo Consumer Price Index increased by 9.3 percent in 1998.[86] Sluggish growth, an increasing budget deficit, and rising cost of living were attributed both to adverse conditions in the world economy and to the civil war. Ultimately, the PA failed to generate political consensus for any of its promised reforms. It also lacked a majority vote in parliament and lost control over economic and political processes, incapable of providing stability or negotiating a political settlement of the ethnic problem.

From the time of her election as prime minister in 1999, and then as president, Chandrika Kumaratunga's attempts to facilitate peace negotiations consistently failed. During this time NGOs were under intense scrutiny by both the government and the LTTE. Kumaratunga's inability to manage the economic crisis and her coalition government's general instability left her without a strong incentive to negotiate in earnest with the LTTE. The anti-negotiation lobby gained greater support in the south as the LTTE continued to assassinate anti-LTTE Sinhala and Tamil intellectuals.

The UNP came to power in 2001, and signed the Ceasefire Agreement (CFA) on February 22, 2002. Nationalist parties and a large segment of Kumaratunga's party opposed the CFA, arguing that it was an international NGO-led conspiracy to undermine national sovereignty. Following the 9/11 attack, international criticism of the LTTE rose sharply, due to the focus on LTTE terrorist activities and its continuing recruitment of child soldiers. The anti-NGO lobby did not recognize those NGOs that were in the forefront of campaigning against the child soldiers by the LTTE. Instead these NGOs were accused of either ignoring or aiding the child soldier issue. With few exceptions, a majority of NGOs of the Tamil diaspora remained silent or indifferent to the recruitment of children by the LTTE. The government in turn used the anti-NGO claims about soldiers to enhance its international credibility vis-à-vis the LTTE. The child soldier issue was no longer about the rights and well-being of children, it was an ideological and territorial battle between the government and the LTTE. The government effectively managed to claim the moral high ground, while NGOs failed to create conditions for a non-military solution to the ethnic crisis.

Government ministers and the anti-NGO lobby accused journalists of collaborating with anti-national and pro-LTTE forces. Journalists thus faced some of the same difficulties that NGOs had faced and were similarly denied access to war-torn areas. Contact with anyone in those areas was viewed as pro-terrorist if it led to criticism of the government. Under the Prevention of Terrorism Act, criticism of the government could even be considered criminal if it was seen as "inciting communal disharmony." Fear of prosecution limited media and NGO efforts in development and humanitarian activities. At this point, INGO activities became the specific target of state criticism. Rajiva Wijesinha, a former member of the Liberal Party of Sri Lanka and later the secretary of SCOPP and the Minister of Human Rights, was the government's main apologist for its position on peace, human rights, and humanitarian assistance. He described INGOs as the extension of a suspicious Western influence that was likely to be detrimental to the country.[87] Along these lines, the anti-NGO lobby presented the Sri Lankan government as more qualified to deliver humanitarian services and improve human rights conditions than foreign governments. INGOs were associated with the UN, and there were suggestions that the former were using the weaknesses of the government as an excuse to advance their agenda in developing countries.[88] The anti-NGO lobby consistently reiterated: "The Human Rights Watch is not really concerned about facts or human suffering, as compared with its heavily financed agenda of trying to embarrass the Sri Lankan government. It is not alone in this practice."[89] The lobby ignored the ways in which INGOs had helped to weaken support for the LTTE in the international community.

Samir Kumar Das describes the fragile February 2002 ceasefire, brokered by the Norwegians, as the result of "a general war-weariness among the general population, economic debilitation, and the threat of the US led war against terrorism" which "put pressure on the conflicting parties to compromise and resolve their disputes through political negotiations."[90] This initiated the "longest sustained stretch without active warfare in Sri Lanka for twenty years."[91] In October 2003, the LTTE officially handed over a proposal for an Interim Self-Governing Authority (ISGA) as a framework for addressing the urgent humanitarian, resettlement, and reconstruction needs of people in the north and the east. The proposal received widespread support from the UNP and international governments, including the European Union, Japan and the US.

Fearing a political coup, after the ISGA proposal was submitted Kumaratunga sacked three key ministers of the UNP government and brought all of the government ministries under her close supervision. The ISGA plan was not authored solely by the LTTE, for it included input from pro-settlement NGOs. However, it was represented as a pro-LTTE, NGO-mediated agreement to divide the country. In February 2004, Kumaratunga dissolved the democratically elected parliament under the leadership of Ranil Wickramasinghe, thereby effectively preventing the UNP government from renewing talks with the LTTE. Then she called for a new election in April, repeating an important historical pattern in post-independence Sri Lankan politics: the government in power proposes a settlement to the ethnic conflict, the opposition party meets its demise, and other political parties then steer policy to serve their interests.

In the 2004 general elections, Mahinda Rajapaksa of the United People's Freedom Alliance (UPFA), facing stiff competition from Wickramasinghe, agreed to form a coalition government with the SLFP and the JVP. The agreement explicitly denied the notion of an "exclusive Tamil homeland," the core demand of the LTTE. It also promised to revise the ceasefire agreement, which, according to the Rajapaksa campaign, was a secret agreement between the UNP and the LTTE, mediated by NGOs. Rajapaksa promised a negotiated political settlement, but the JVP, the JHU, and several members of his own party denied the existence of an ethnic problem. Instead, they argued that the LTTE was a terrorist organization and should be treated as such. Rajapaksa neither acknowledged nor condemned anti-NGO beliefs because he desperately needed anti-UNP support, and he simultaneously exploited and remained detached from ethnoreligious nationalism. Moderate left-wing political parties promised support for Rajapaksa, since they could not support the neoliberal policies of the UNP. They, too, refrained from addressing the links between ethnonationalism and neoliberal economic reforms.

Against popular expectations, the LTTE forced Tamil voters to boycott the elections, contending that Tamils could not trust either candidate. Rajapaksa proceeded to earn a victory over Wickramasinghe by a narrow margin of 50.3 percent to 48.4 percent of the vote. His victory was clearly a result of the boycott and he immediately offered to open negotiations with the LTTE, but the government had no real incentive to negotiate a political settlement.

Meanwhile, the LTTE was less interested in negotiations and more interested in advancing its military campaign. Suicide bombings of civilians continued, leading people in the south to believe that the LTTE was preparing to escalate the violence. At this point, even some "progressive" NGOs silently accepted defeating the LTTE became an essential precondition for any political solution.

## TSUNAMI, HUMANITARIANISM, AND PEACEBUILDING

Just a few months after the election, on December 26, 2004, when Sri Lanka "was still in a no war/no peace situation,"[92] a tsunami hit its shores. Nearly 38,000 people lost their lives and property damage was estimated to be in excess of $1.5 billion. Neither the government nor the LTTE were prepared to meet the humanitarian needs of the populations under their respective jurisdictions. In the first three days, hundreds of local NGOs and thousands of individuals offered assistance. Two weeks later, nearly 100 international NGOs had arrived in the affected areas. The government lacked both the leadership and the infrastructure to coordinate the rescue mission and NGOs were allowed unrestricted access to virtually all areas of the country, including those controlled by the LTTE. However, the government soon appointed a three-member committee and formed the Reconstruction and Development Authority (RADA) to oversee and coordinate tsunami assistance.

Thereafter, government restrictions and an influx of well-funded international NGOs led to the decline of spontaneous efforts by individuals, small local organizations, and the military. Local political actors from all parties forced NGOs to strike a balance between political and humanitarian imperatives. In several locations, political actors commandeered NGO relief supplies and packaged them with their own flags and emblems. NGOs competed for territory and formed alliances with local elites. National and local authorities became uneasy when larger NGOs used powerful donors and diplomatic support to pressure the government to remove restrictions; NGOs interpreted the government's demands for accountability as attempts at co-optation. Victims expected large NGOs to provide more assistance than could small local organizations, resulting in a further decline in local NGO activity.

The state and private businesses attempted to relocate tsunami victims, but failed due to resistance from citizens and politicians who feared that the government would not compensate them adequately for their property, and that relocation would shift electoral demographics. The ethnic minority Malay community in the Hambantota area feared that the government was resettling them because it wanted to build a harbor on their land. Under the pretext of securing the area against future natural disasters, the tourism industry sought to ensure cleaner and safer beaches by evicting affected populations from the coast. Poor coastal residents were evicted from their homes of decades when they could not provide legal title to their land and property. Accepting government relocation "offers" was often a precondition for receiving aid, and NGOs refused to aid those whom the government didn't approve. At the same time, local politicians exploited national propaganda, urging Sri Lankans to keep a watchful eye on NGOs so that the tsunami would not be used to further their agendas or otherwise undermine national sovereignty and security. NGOs had limited success in coordinating their aid disbursement, and were often inefficient. Their credibility was seriously undermined by their egregious misappropriation and mismanagement of resources.

Fishermen in the tsunami-affected areas claimed that the distribution of NGO aid benefitted local politicians, who then allowed NGOs to evade government bureaucracy. They protested their relocation to areas where they could not fish. Subsequent discussions of their resettlement and rehabilitation ignored the largest obstacles to improving their situation: the increasing cost of fishing due to the privatization of services; the use of large trawlers by government politicians and their family members, who not only harvested fish in large quantities but also destroyed fragile ocean habitats; the failure of the government to prevent the influx of hundreds of Indian fishing boats into national territorial waters; and nearly 20 years of restrictions on fishing imposed by the military due to security considerations. The consensus among small-scale fishermen:

> Our problems are privatization of services available to us, private sector and the government control of our space, and the exploitation of the tsunami to relocate us to areas that are not conducive to fishing. These problems predate the tsunami, and we know that the tsunami reconstruction will only worsen them.[93]

A few local NGOs attempted to address these grievances, but they were either ignored or suppressed by the government and the donors. Individualized relief and resettlement projects by NGOs distanced affected populations from the government and became a means by which their livelihoods could be reorganized according to neoliberal rationality. Tsunami aid provided by NGOs legitimated the shrinking of the government's role in social welfare provisions, and integrated the poor into the neoliberal economy.

Many NGO attempts to coordinate their own activities failed due to competition between them for territory and influence. To address this, in December 2006 some international NGOs and their donors, with support from Norwegian mediators, drafted a Memorandum of Understanding (MOU) on Post-Tsunami Operational Management Structure (P-TOMS), subsequently signed by both the government and the LTTE. Its main objective was to provide the institutional environment necessary for the coordination of relief and rehabilitation activities. The Jathika Hela Urumaya (JHU) and the JVP staged countrywide protests against P-TOMS.

While both the government and the LTTE saw powerful opportunities in P-TOMS, they also had reasons to be apprehensive about it. Government officials feared that P-TOMS would weaken the already fragile coalition. The LTTE objected because P-TOMS had such a well-coordinated approach to tsunami recovery that it could conceivably hobble the struggle for Eelam and limit the LTTE's control over the territory. Virtually everyone overestimated the capacity of P-TOMS to respond to the crisis. Amarasiri points out:

> The attempt by the GoSL [government of Sri Lanka] to establish P-TOMS is viewed here as the product of a misreading of the emerging cooperation among divergent civil society groups and local political organizations following the materialization of a burgeoning partnership between the GoSL and the LTTE.[94]

P-TOMS was ultimately ineffective because NGOs competed for territory and donor funds, and progress was derailed by conflicts between different ethnic groups, particularly Muslims and Tamils in the eastern provinces. Ethnicity had become the organizing principle for restructuring post-tsunami power relations in the district.

As representatives from 42 civil society organizations, leftist parties, and trade unions held demonstrations in support of the P-TOMS, the protests against it turned into a protest against NGOs. Rajapaksa made a campaign promise to abolish the P-TOMS. Popular support mounted for the resumption of war against the LTTE. The JVP and the JHU, supporting Rajapaksa, promised to end the ceasefire. The LTTE, too, became increasingly suspicious of the activities of the NGOs, especially those which brought with them international criticism of the LTTE agendas. Following the verdict of the supreme court, P-TOMS was abolished. Thereafter, NGOs functioned only under the government and the LTTE administrations. Ultimately, there was very little incentive for the LTTE or the government to use the tsunami as a platform for a political settlement to the crisis.

Following the collapse of the P-TOMS, pro-war sentiment grew at an alarming rate. Defeating the LTTE militarily became, once again, an essential precondition for any political solution. The government coalition consisted mainly of members who believed that the LTTE should be crushed by force. The global war against terrorism following the attacks on the US on September 11, 2001, favored the Sri Lankan government. Contrary to the claims of anti-NGO groups, NGO protests against the LTTE's numerous human rights violations and practice of conscripting child soldiers had strengthened the government's position. Meanwhile, the LTTE was uninterested in negotiations. Local and international conditions were in place for the third phase of the war against Tamil militants.

The Kumaratunga regime saw the end of the two-party system as it became nearly impossible for traditional mainstream parties to form a single-party government without the support of a coalition including smaller parties such as the JVP and JHU. Although these smaller parties did not command a political constituency sufficient to capture a parliamentary majority, and although mainstream parties were cautious about their motives, the JVP and JHU carefully exploited their ethnoreligious nationalist ideological framework in order to interpret the economic and political crises, and to shape their relations with the general public. For JVP and JHU, NGOs were the living examples of colonialism, imperialism, and negative aspects of Western and Christian civilization. JVP and JHU carried out extensive propaganda against the NGOs as a way of legitimizing their respective political agendas as well as building broader political alliances to increase their stakes in state power.

Initially, Chandrika Kumaratunga's regime closely collaborated with NGOs, and at the same time maintained a distance from them in response to growing anti-NGO sentiment within the parties. Kumaratunga provided even greater space for transnational capital and its local counterparts to control the economy under highly corrupt state patronage. The private interests of individual politicians, rather than the economic and environmental interests of the country, determined the distribution of patronage among businesses. Eventually, the president sidelined the NGOs who helped her to get elected and became an ally of the forces she had condemned during her campaign. Some of these NGOs in turn became the front-running critics of the state.

Kumaratunga's failure to stabilize her power base within the coalition resulted in the escalation of the war and the rapid decline of the economy, making her reign one of the most economically and politically chaotic periods in the country's post-independence history. As the economic and political crises escalated, ethnoreligious nationalism appeared to be the only means of competing for state power. Kumaratunga's regime plunged deeper into a legitimacy crisis and her political opponents used the situation to dislodge her. Some of those opponents later became the leaders of the anti-NGO lobby and elected members of the UPF government. Anti-NGOism targeted organizations that were opposed to the war and in favor of political devolution, and it continued to grow as an influential ideology in the political processes of the country.

## WAR AGAINST TERRORISM, HUMAN RIGHTS, AND PEACE

Unlike its predecessors, the UPFA had no interest in halting the war until the LTTE laid down its arms or was militarily defeated. It initiated a sophisticated, multi-pronged strategy to generate and maintain local and international support for the war, and appointed closely allied diplomats and intellectuals to its key international missions aimed at countering LTTE propaganda. Their mandate was to present the LTTE as a terrorist movement oppressing Tamils as well as Sinhalese. The propaganda strategies of these government representatives closely emulated those of the Western countries' ambassadors of the war against terrorism. They positioned Sri Lanka as an important ally in the global war against terrorism, and whenever terrorist attacks took place anywhere in the world, spokespersons for the state suggested the potential involvement of the LTTE. The LTTE was increasingly unable to convince the international community that its struggle was mainly political and directed at restoring the fundamental rights of the Tamils. The government also did not hesitate to suggest that LTTE-friendly international governments were being misled, and occasionally accused the international community of hypocrisy and inconsistency when it demanded that the Sri Lankan government agree to a ceasefire. UPFA saw humanitarian NGOs as obstacles to its own war on terror.

But international pressure from foreign donors and NGOs, along with the deterioration of human rights conditions, led the government to establish Sri Lanka's Secretariat for Co-ordinating the Peace Process (SCOPP) and a new Ministry of Human Rights and Disaster Management. SCOPP was to "act as the cutting edge of the Government of Sri Lanka to consolidate and strengthen the peace process on behalf of all Sri Lankan citizens, whilst promoting a negotiated settlement to the current conflict." [95] In practice, the Peace Secretariat was supposed to defend the government against allegations of wrongdoing, and it neither challenged nor initiated dialogue with opponents of the devolution of power. Nor did the state or SCOPP counter claims made by influential members of the government that "Sinhalese are the original and organic people of the country and the rest are foreigners"[96] who "can live in this country with us. But they must not try to, under the pretext of being a minority, demand undue things."[97] The PTA ignored intimidating and inflammatory remarks such as this.

NGOs did not cooperate with SCOPP. Instead, SCOPP appropriated the peace and human rights activities of NGOs and became the frontline agency for defending the government against NGOs' allegations. SCOPP's lack of neutrality became increasingly obvious and many Sri Lankan intellectuals and activists who favored a political settlement resigned from the organization, questioning "whether it may not be more appropriate to rename it rather, as the 'Secretariat for Coordinating the War Process.'"[98]

The Ministry of Human Rights and Disaster Management had two stated objectives: "To facilitate harmony, prosperity and dignity of human life through effective prevention and mitigation of natural and man-made disasters, while promoting and protecting human rights in Sri Lanka." It was expected to provide the framework within which humanitarian and human rights organizations could function. The flexibility of that framework was constrained by the government's national security parameters, and the Ministry of Defense would not allow the humanitarian and human rights concerns of NGOs to undermine the government's bargaining power. All criticism was construed as unpatriotic. So the Ministry of Defense controlled NGOs, while SCOPP and the Ministry of Human Rights and Disaster Management countered international criticism of the government.

Due to ideological differences, a number of civil society representatives resigned from SCOPP and it was turned into another government ministry. SCOPP and the ministry were successful in limiting the international community's pressure on the government to rhetorical announcements of concern for humanitarian conditions and human rights in the country, and NGOs were pushed to the margins. Peace rallies and many civil society organizations were brought to an abrupt end by threats and physical assaults by unidentified groups. Meanwhile, divisions within the LTTE led to an exodus of military commanders and hundreds of cadres from the Eastern province, who subsequently collaborated with government military cadres. Two former military commanders entered mainstream politics as supporters of the ruling party. By granting political concessions to former LTTE commanders, the government demonstrated its willingness to devolve powers under the thirteenth amendment to the constitution, providing legitimacy to its claim that the LTTE was not the sole representative of the Tamils, and showing that it was prepared to work with Tamil militants who laid down their arms.

Many international state actors remained ambivalent. The US, India, China, and many other countries provided the government with military support and did not contest its position that terrorism should be defeated as the precondition for a political settlement. They also underlined the necessity of a political settlement, but this dual approach enabled the government to continue the war. Despite making rhetorical protests, international donors did not significantly reduce economic and military aid or trade concessions. The few restrictions imposed by European donors and the World Bank did not threaten the government, since it could borrow funds and purchase weapons from countries such as Iran, Israel, and China, and obtain military support from the US and India. The government continued to increase the prices of basic necessities and to print money, despite the fact that inflation was reaching a historical high of 20 percent per year. The public did not protest against economic difficulties because the pro-war lobby successfully argued that sacrifices were necessary to protect the motherland and any organized protest was to be viewed as a threat to national security.

## CRISIS OF HUMANITARIANISM, NATIONAL SECURITY, AND SUPPRESSION OF POLITICAL DISSENT

For the past 25 years assistance for development and humanitarian work among the Tamils has been channeled primarily through NGOs which have no choice but to work within the administrative structures of the LTTE. As an example, in 1989 members of

University Teachers for Human Rights, a local NGO managed by a group of Tamil scholars, were forced into hiding following the assassination of one of their colleagues, Dr. Rajani Thiranagama, a feminist and human rights activist who lectured in the medical faculty of the University of Jaffna. The LTTE has consistently accused NGOs of treacherously providing information to the government.

As the position took hold that military victory was a precondition for peace, the government pursued a policy of zero tolerance for negative publicity, sending the message that certain freedoms simply had to be sacrificed until the country was free from terrorism. Journalists were detained and charged with aiding and abetting terrorism under the PTA. With the suspension of civil rights, a confession became sufficient evidence for conviction, whether or not it was forced. To date, at least 34 journalists have been threatened, deported, abducted, or murdered. Despite protests and government promises, and continuing demands from the Free Media Movement, Reporters Without Borders, the International Federation of Journalists, and Human Rights Watch, none of the persons responsible for these attacks have been identified or brought to justice.

During this period, international donors funded several independent media projects including the outreach website started by J.S. Tissainayagam. NGOs also hired freelance journalists. On several occasions the government accused both journalists and the NGOs that hired them of collaborating with terrorists. In response to arguments in favor of freedom of expression, the secretary of defense stated: "Everyone, the media included, should understand that there is no meaning to any freedom if we don't have a country in which we can exercise that freedom."[99] Journalists and some members of the NGO community, not surprisingly, disagreed. Tamil activists, in turn, asserted that "States that want to oppress a people do so by breaking their political will to resist injustice.... It is easier to enslave a people who have lost their ability to understand the nature of their oppression."[100] Jayathilaka, a former member of the EPRLF, condemned the assassination of W.D. Sivaram, a journalist whose writings significantly influenced both NGOs and national governments concerned with human rights and humanitarian work in Sri Lanka.[101]

The government's increased awareness of the role of NGOs in influencing international criticism of its policies has led it to more closely monitor their activities. In view of the high-profile confrontations between the state and the media, NGOs have put greater pressure on the government to secure freedom of expression. Local media organizations derived much of their credibility through their international network, which included Reporters Without Borders, Human Rights Watch, Amnesty International, and International Federation of Journalists. The government has routinely ignored these organizations' demands for freedom of expression. In March 2009, Sunanada Desapriya, the convener of the Free Media movement, was sacked by the Center for Policy Alternatives for misappropriation of funds, adding to anti-NGO criticism. In response, NGOs never seem to be voluntarily interested in systems of accountability and transparency, except when pushed by their international donors, further legitimizing negative claims about NGOs and the state's suppression of legitimate NGO criticism of the state.

## NATIONALISM, HUMAN RIGHTS, AND NGOs

Anti-NGO critics present NGOs as self-serving and unaccountable:

> In a "war against terror" situation, no country in the world has so far reported to have maintained the so-called human rights or humanitarian levels set by these INGO groups. All these groups do is to write something and issue communiqués regularly to satisfy their funding agencies for their own survival and to mislead the world.[102]

Some went so far as to propose that NGOs be banned from Sri Lanka.

The JVP and the National Patriotic Movement (PNM) protested vehemently against the devolution of power, presenting it as an NGO attempt to Westernize and Christianize the country.[103] Dr. Dasarath Jayasoriya, the president of the Society for Peace, Unity, and Human Rights in Sri Lanka (SPUR), in opposition to Interim Self-Governing Authority (IGSA), stated:

> We also take this opportunity to remind the Government that a peace proposition that has been fashioned by an inner core of Government "modernists" and treacherous NGOs wedded to the alien concept of Federalism for Sri Lanka will only be acceptable to the terrorist friendly Norwegian peace facilitators and the LTTE.[104]

SPUR demanded that the government extricate itself from the deceitful web woven by the LTTE and its covert supporters, including the Norwegian Government and NGOs: "It must not fall in to the 'Venus Trap' set by the LTTE under the guise of helping people in the North and the East affected by the tsunami."[105]

Since 2009, the number of anti-government activist groups and media organizations has dramatically increased, and NGOs and journalists have been accused by the government of patronizing them. Tamilnet, the main news source of the Tamil diaspora, was eventually banned in Sri Lanka because of its anti-government views. Both the government and the LTTE have taken measures to counter the growing phenomenon of web-based activism with web sites of their own. Lankadissent.com, another web-based news organization, closed down following the assassination of the editor of the *Sunday Leader*, Lasantha Wicramathunga. It observed in its farewell:

> This compassionate Sinhala Buddhist land does not tolerate "dissent". Those who would not want to learn that living would have to learn that in death. We, who live, would come back when "dissent" comes back as a democratic right, accepted and enjoyed in a modern land of compassion.[106]

The government appointed a special parliamentary committee in 2006 to investigate NGO activities. All NGOs were brought under the control of the NGO Secretariat, which wielded unprecedented powers. The Ministry of Defense gained further powers to regulate NGO activities by reducing visa durations and numbers. Registration fees and bureaucratic controls were increased to the point that many NGOs were forced to restructure. A number of international NGOs were expelled, and between 2004 and 2009 nearly 40 humanitarian NGO workers belonging to Action International, International Committee of the Red Cross (ICRC), and CARE were killed.[107] The government and the LTTE accused each other of the murders.

As the number of internally displaced persons (IDPs) increased, international NGOs lobbied their governments to pressure Sri Lanka to grant access to media and humanitarian workers. This backfired, however, increasing government hostility toward NGOs. A deadline was given to NGOs to withdraw from LTTE-held areas of northern Sri Lanka, and the Sri Lankan government refused to guarantee the safety of humanitarian workers remaining in rebel territory. The LTTE followed with a deadline for NGO workers to vacate the Mullaitivu area of Sri Lanka's Northern province. Defense secretary Gotabhaya Rajapaksa insisted that "denying LTTE access to INGO and NGO material" is a critical element in Sri Lanka's efforts to destroy the group. In an interview with the *English Daily*, he referred to concerns about the "use of heavy vehicles belonging to the Norwegian People's Aid (NPA) by the LTTE for terror activities."[108]

In 2009, INGOs were once again at the forefront in exposing the government's human rights abuses and censorship of the press. Because so many civilians were trapped by the fighting, and because the internally displaced population, civilian injuries, and deaths escalated, the government was once again under intense pressure from the international community to call for a ceasefire and to allow NGOs to enter war zones and provide humanitarian aid. However, only the ICRC, a politically neutral NGO, was allowed to work in government-controlled areas. Between 230,000 and 300,000 displaced persons were trapped, and the LTTE refused to allow them to move to government territory. Human Rights Watch, in its international campaign, highlighted the responsibility of the LTTE for the suffering of the civilian population. Apologists for the LTTE countered that fear of arrest and detention prevented civilians from moving. Amid increasing government restrictions on NGOs, the ICRC temporarily withdrew.

The government did not permit independent media or human rights NGOs to report on humanitarian issues in the war-torn areas. The available information about the conditions of the IDPs has come from LTTE-sponsored sources alleging that the government is engaged in genocide, and from government-sponsored sources claiming that the LTTE has been using civilians as human shields. Both the government and the LTTE have primarily been concerned about international views of the war rather than domestic opinion. Currently the Sri Lankan government is more concerned about its relationship with India, China, Russia, and Iran than about its relationships with Western nations. These Eastern states provide both protection from Western criticism and much-needed financial and military assistance, which in turn strengthens the hold of Eastern nations over the Sri Lankan government and economy. India, in particular, has provided aid to both Tamil militants and to the government, while the anti-NGO lobby conveniently ignores the irony inherent in such duplicity.

The government's criticism and even its acts of oppression do not mean that it intends to completely suppress NGO activities in war-affected areas. Complaints have largely been rhetorical. One reader of the *Island* warned that the public

> should not forget the services of people [who] had the courage and conviction to take on the "arm chair" critics of the war effort. In doing so, they were also able to bring to light the nefarious activities that most of the INGOs and NGOs were engaged in. They exposed the "hollowness" of foreigners who are demanding the Government go for a ceasefire, when their Governments act differently in Iraq, Afghanistan and Pakistan. Mother Lanka is indeed proud to have such sons.[109]

Telling the public that it did not "surrender to the pressures of the foreigners" has helped to boost the government's domestic credibility.

Despite international requests, the LTTE rejected the conditional ceasefire and promised to continue the war. The government also rejected calls for a humanitarian ceasefire, which has left NGOs with only two options: work within the framework provided by the government, or continue to campaign internationally for access to conflict areas. Yet other states have shown little sympathy to NGOs, and there is plenty of economic and military aid available from non-Western countries and private sources without humanitarian strings attached. When the LTTE was on the verge of defeat it called for an international campaign to pressure the government for a ceasefire but at that point there was absolutely no political incentive for the government to agree.

There has been a significant rise in religious violence, particularly against Christians. Churches have been vandalized and two clergymen have been murdered. These attacks have neither been condemned nor seriously investigated. Anti-religious violence is not random, but is part of a "campaign of hysteria against conversion to Christianity" portraying "the Christian minorities as a source of immediate threat to the Buddhists." Sri Lanka's anti-Christian violence can be compared with the anti-minority violence of the Hindu right in India: in both places, monks were deliberately employed to lead rallies, "mobilizing thousands before moving into action."[110] Several local NGOs, influenced by urban professionals and businesses and the ideology of the JHU, emerged to monitor the activities of churches and Christian NGOs. Collectively, their efforts led to the introduction of two bills, one against "unethical conversions" and one against the slaughter of cows, both of which are pending parliamentary approval.

## NATIONAL SECURITY, NATIONALISM, AND THE CONSOLIDATION OF STATE POWER

Since the beginning of civil war, the government and the LTTE intensified their accusations that NGOs are unpatriotic institutions run by Westernized elites with Western financial support, and increasingly viewed NGO activities as detrimental to their respective national projects. The anti-NGO lobby and a group that identified itself as Sri Lankan Patriots of New Zealand accused the NGO Eradicating Sexual Child Abuse, Prostitution and Exploitation (ESCAPE) of tarnishing the image of Sri Lanka by discussing child abuse, and of giving international interviews for the sole purpose of raising funds. An email containing these allegations was widely circulated and promoted by international ethnonationalist organizations to counter LTTE propaganda. The director of ESCAPE, a Tamil Christian doctor, was questioned by the Central Intelligence Department (CID). Although the government did not take any action and treated the doctor fairly, the event was exploited by those who criticized NGOs.

Similarly, the critics of a report by the Jaffna Teachers Association (UTHUR) pointed out that, although it correctly described the violence of the LTTE, it provided less analysis of the transformations and social forces that shape violence. Nor were their writings grounded in other literature of Tamil nationalism. Of course, UTHUR was not a Marxist organization, but a humanist one that provided a valuable moral critique of the contradictions and fascist tendencies of the LTTE. Both the LTTE and the state appropriated UTHUR criticism in different ways in order to justify their respective claims. The LTTE used the report to suppress Tamil critics; LTTE propaganda focused more on the social conditions that led to its militancy because that was more resonant with the Tamil masses. Some critics' argument that the Tamils are less critical of the activities of the LTTE is partly due to their failure to read literature in Tamil by LTTE proponents. As Charan points out, there is plenty of material critical of the LTTE by ex-militants regrouped against LTTE in Europe and Canada.[111]

One cannot underestimate the impact of Sri Lankan feminist organizations on policy reforms relating to the safeguarding of women's interests. In 1993, owing to NGO advocacy work, the

Sri Lankan government signed the United Nations Declaration on the Elimination of Violence Against Women, adopted the women's charter, and created a national committee on women to monitor the charter. Many feminists are disappointed that sole responsibility for implementing the charter is assumed by the state, because state reforms have been ad hoc rather than holistic and comprehensive. In her remarks on the rape and murder of Krishanti Kumaraswami, Lisa Kois noted that "as happened here human rights pressures may have a tendency to legitimize a flawed national legal system and/or exacerbate its flaws."[112]

The Mothers' Front consisted of many grassroots organizations active in protesting against disappearances and other injustices allegedly committed by the government and the LTTE. These organizations did not welcome the women's NGOs based in Colombo, despite their common ideas and struggles. In popular parlance these NGOs were believed to be managed by Colombo-based elite women, lesbians, and unpatriotic women acting in collaboration with foreign agents who supported the LTTE. Organizations in the northern and eastern parts of the country such as the Poorani Women's Home and Women's Study Circle of Jaffna University were critical voices weighing in on human rights conditions within the Tamil community. Some of these organizations saw women's involvement in Tamil militancy as a form of empowerment, opening spaces for women's potential liberation. However, some scholars and feminists influential in Colombo-based NGOs point to the ambivalent agency of women in LTTE (for example, suicide cadres and front line infantry fighters), since their choices and their sexuality were heavily controlled by the LTTE. Unlike Periyar of the Self Respect Movement, these feminists did not base their claims about women's oppression within the institution of private property or economic realities, but in narrow postmodern identity politics that jettisoned class in favor of other identities. Their claims about women's agency under the LTTE were isolated from the history and transformations of Tamil militancy in particular, and the corresponding changes in the relations between state and society in general. Ideological differences and competition for donor funding between these NGOs did not enable them to become a coherent counterhegemonic movement in collaboration with other NGOs or progressive elements in the society. Society as a whole (Cheran, 2009) was ill prepared to accept radical feminist ideals. Consequently, ideologues of the LTTE and the critics of NGOs in the global South dismissed these feminists as Westernized women with abnormal sexual orientations, engaged in foreign-funded projects that are counterproductive to the respective nationalist projects of the LTTE and the government. The activities of these organizations are critical and timely from the perspective of human rights, and particularly for their impact on the lives of women during a time of war and militarization. But the government's claims about these organizations, couched in the language of ethnonationalism and counterterrorism, had strong public appeal and further contributed to prevailing anti-NGO sentiments in the country and the strengthening of highly gendered state power.

While the government was fighting terrorism and the threat of secession, economic sovereignty rapidly eroded as multinational corporations made inroads across the country's major industries, including agriculture, hospitality, mining, telecommunications, and health care. The majority of these ventures came from India, but it would be misleading to identify them as Indian since they are part and parcel of transnational capital. India's involvement in the Sri Lankan conflict has been much more intrusive of Sri Lanka's sovereignty controversial than that of Western countries. The political parties, the government and the ant-NGO lobby downplayed India's role because during the war the anti-Western claims locally popular and politically safer means of legitimizing the government agenda. The government has foisted the blame for the war upon the West by associating Western nations with NGOs. This, in turn, has enabled transnational and regional capital to secure their interests in Sri Lanka.

Throughout the war, the government's economic policies were guided by the political and security imperatives of the state rather than by those of free markets. The government continues to cite the war as the chief reason for its failure to fully implement neoliberal economic policies. While the JHP and the National Liberation Front (NLF) do not command enough support to gain power through seats in parliament, their position on the war and ethnic conflict has proven to be sufficient for suppressing class opposition to neoliberal economic reforms. JHU and the NLF are supported by middle-class professionals and businesses. They not only embrace ethnoreligious nationalist explanations of the war and ethnic conflict, they also exploit religion and nationalism to leverage their influence over the economy and society by characterizing class struggle as ethnic conflict. NGO activism has enabled ethnoreligious nationalism to emerge as the dominant shaper of state–society relations, precisely because NGOs have failed to explore the relationship between ethnoreligious nationalism and the reproduction of capitalist social, political, and economic relations. This has contributed to two important political trends. First, it has encouraged Sri Lankan ethnic groups to protest against social, economic, and political inequities and injustices along ethnic rather than class lines. Secondly, it has aligned Sri Lanka with non-Western countries, and with anti-Western and anti-NGO forces in general.

This realignment has enabled the state to secure economic and military aid without human rights or humanitarian conditions attached. This has also helped substantiate the state's claim that Western countries and NGOs are allies of terrorism. China, Iran, India, and Pakistan are now providing loans and military aid to Sri Lanka without the conditions generally attached by the World Bank, IMF, or Western governments. The Sri Lankan government continues to involve the private sector but has also given itself greater flexibility in procuring arms, making Sri Lanka part of the global military industrial complex. The penetration of Chinese, Indian, and Iranian capital into Sri Lanka is an integral aspect of global capital's expansion, and that process is critical to capitalist development in Western countries as well. Critics of Western aid and imperialism often ignore the links between Western and non-Western capital.

Jayatilleka's version of political realism addresses everyone, including liberals, neoliberals, imperialists, postcolonialists, Marxists, anti-imperialists, and ethnoreligious nationalists:

> In this struggle, we need the support of our neighbors, particularly the support of Asia's rising super-powers: India and China.
>
> China is a reliable and long standing friend and shares our views on state sovereignty and secessionism. However, we also need the support of our closest neighbor—Asia's other rising power—India. A laissez-faire policy on her part would enable the LTTE to operate relatively freely from or through Southern India. Given the simple realities of geography—India is a vast and very near neighbor—we will not be safe if India turns against us, or simply turns away from us.
>
> For its part, the West has demonstrated that it is not averse to the fragmentation of existing states and the proliferation of new ones. The recent recognition of Kosovo by Western countries is a clear example of this. Moreover, other powerful phenomena, such as transnational capital, neo-liberal economic policies, international NGOs, the influential Tamil Diaspora, and the Sinhala and Tamil "federalists" also give the West both incentives and instruments for undermining this nation's sovereignty.[113]

This rhetorical eclecticism encourages the international community to reinforce the position of the Sri Lankan state vis-à-vis the LTTE. Jayatilleka's main objective, as a government diplomat, is to bolster the powers of the state by shielding it from international criticism and countering LTTE propaganda. He maintained that the war against the LTTE was a "surgical" approach to terrorism and that Western countries and NGOs have no right to intervene in the government's attempts to eliminate terrorism. Such intervention does more harm than good, so the story goes, because it undermines national sovereignty. At the same time, he also advocated a responsible political settlement to the ethnic conflict. Jayatilleka's preoccupation with political realism blinds him to the fact that sovereignty is a sociological concept, and that the current conflict is a result of the framing of Sri Lankan sovereignty along the lines of the ethnoreligious nationalist ideology embraced by both Sinhala and Tamils. More important, he seems unaware of the fact that the establishment of unified nation-states and their subsequent fragmentation, particularly in the post-Cold War era, can favor both imperialism and anti-imperialism.

In his deliberations at the United Nations, Jayatilleka correctly pointed out the double standards and hypocrisy of Western countries in dealing with terrorism. But he conveniently overlooked the same hypocrisy in the emerging regional and global powers such as India, Russia, and China. Instead, he solicited their support. Despite his Marxist rhetoric, his political realist approach considers imperialism a purely Western, purely political phenomenon, rather than a historical economic phenomenon in which China and India are implicated along with Western countries. He has ignored the ways in which the collaborations between emerging powers and transnational capital have undermined both the economic and political sovereignty of the country. The cultural relativist political realism of Jayathilaka effectively exploited the existing divisions between international states to safeguard the Sri Lankan government from international criticism of the it's conduct of war, and in the process provided legitimacy for anti-NGO criticisms.

The distinction that the Sri Lankan government draws between "unfriendly" Western countries and "friendly" India seems superficial, if not simply an ideological construct. For example, in an interview on June 14, 2010, Robert Blake, the US Assistant Secretary of State, said to rediff.com: "The US and India have a very similar view of the situation in Sri Lanka and the steps that need to be taken." He went on to acknowledge, "We have worked very closely throughout the last several years on the situation in Sri Lanka, and again we have a real convergence of view on how that situation has evolved." While anti-Western sentiments are a popular source of legitimacy for the state in Sri Lanka, and may even attract external funding from non-Western sources, Western countries are unlikely to antagonize India or China over Sri Lanka. The West has more to gain by letting India adopt whatever policy it wishes towards Sri Lanka: it is far cheaper for the West to exert capitalist control over Sri Lanka through India, and less likely to lead to direct confrontation. Under these circumstances, Western international NGOs cannot succeed in using international states to exert pressure on the Sri Lankan state, mainly because for these states their economic and political interests always take precedence over human rights. Put differently, intervention for human rights is a first step towards geopolitical control of human welfare.

This critique of Western governments grossly oversimplifies global capitalism and imperialism by viewing them as national discourses instead of as diverse networks and relations *between* nation-states. Eastern and Far Eastern nations now exercise more control over the economic and political destiny of Sri Lanka than do Western nations. Today the penetration of international capital into Sri Lanka is facilitated almost entirely by non-Western countries. It is no accident that, in Sri Lanka, the rise of ethnoreligious nationalism coincided with the consolidation of capitalism, because the former allows the state, with the help of NGOs and their critics, to manage more effectively the accumulation and legitimization crises of capital.

The dominance of the state over NGOs was again demonstrated in February 2007 when Ramu Mani, director of the International Center for Ethnic Studies, had her visa revoked for encouraging external interference in Sri Lanka. Mani had allegedly written a concept paper in which she attempted to gain support for international interference in Sri Lanka by emphasizing the need to implement the United Nations' doctrine of Responsibility to Protect (R2P). The government canceled her visa because her paper questioned the state's sovereignty. Mani's treatment sparked a flurry of controversy in the press, revealing the government's growing anxiety about the extent of NGO influence over the war.

In 2007, Jayathilaka wrote:

> Sri Lanka cannot make the mistakes of Gorbachev (in the latter years) and Yeltsin, be tranquilized, have its sovereignty penetrated, be weakened and dismantled ... Sri Lanka cannot be oblivious to

the use of the slogan of "humanitarian crisis" to dismantle the former Yugoslavia. Today the West stands ready to ignore the UN resolution that reiterates that Kosovo is a part of Serbia, and to recognize Kosovo as an independent state. The anti-Sri Lanka campaign will accelerate next year as Sri Lanka makes headway in the struggle to overcome the Tigers. The West, preceded by the Western-dominated media, will howl about a "humanitarian crisis," and brandish the policy of R2P ("Responsibility to Protect") at us as we close in on Prabhakaran's bunker.[114]

Wijesinha was equally outraged by Mani's call to implement R2P.[115] The call was evidence, according to the government, that NGOs were supporting the secessionist demands of the LTTE and undermining the sovereignty of the country. The government responded by increasing its surveillance of NGOs. When Bradman Weerakoon tried to defend Mani, Wijesinha accused him of being "openly associated with the opposition UNP, which has been seeking to undermine the government ever since it lost the last election."[116]

The popular depiction of tensions between the International Center for Ethnic Studies and the government overshadowed the conflict between the ICES branches in Kandy and Colombo. These clashes often highlighted ideological and personality differences between branch leaders, and their struggles to gain control over each other in their respective organizations. The government's criticisms of the ICES were to a large extent aided by individuals within the latter who were unhappy with existing leadership and institutional structures. At the politicized ICES board meeting held in Colombo on March 27, 2007, many original members were replaced by a group of prominent and internationally known intellectuals and corporate executives.

Whatever the truth of the allegations against ICES, they were exploited by the anti-NGO and pro-war lobby, which put pressure on the government to regulate NGOs. The allegations reinforced and legitimized the government position on the ethnic conflict and the war against terrorism. A narrow understanding of imperialism has blinded critics like Dayan Jayathilaka and Wijesinha to the ways in which global capitalism immunizes the state to international criticism at the *expense* of Sri Lankan national sovereignty. Their efforts to protect the country's sovereignty by defending the government's position on war and international charges of human rights abuses has enhanced the government's popular legitimacy and given credibility to its anti-NGO activities. Their criticism of the West has increased Sri Lanka's vulnerability to the geopolitical and economic influences of China and India. Moreover, they have created even more space for transnational capital and regional powers to colonize the country, and in the process helped reduce Sri Lanka's bargaining power vis-à-vis transnational capital. (A few weeks after the government's victory over the LTTE, Jayathilaka, who was a consistent supporter of the thirteenth amendment to the constitution as a means of devolving political powers to the Tamil minority, was abruptly relieved of his duties as the Sri Lankan ambassador to the United Nations.)

Throughout the conflict, the government and NGOs have selectively called for international intervention. In the process, the state, the anti-NGO lobby, and NGOs themselves have contributed to the erosion of Sri Lanka's economic and political sovereignty. The erosion was not caused by Western imperialism, but by the collaborative efforts of local and foreign elites who patronized extremist ethnoreligious nationalist political parties, bowed to the anti-NGO lobby, and sought state patronage to advance their own agendas. In the final analysis, ethnoreligious nationalism is a class project. In as much as it defines the specific nature of capitalist development in Sri Lanka, it also determines the form and the nature of the Sri Lankan state. Future historians may find that the Sri Lankan government was willing to give everything away to foreigners, but not an inch to the Tamils. Sri Lanka might have minimized the loss of economic and political sovereignty if the LTTE and the government had been able to reach a political settlement.

All international calls for a ceasefire and requests that NGOs be allowed to enter affected regions failed. The state and pro-war lobby interpreted these as part of an international conspiracy instigated by the NGOs against Sri Lanka. Indeed, in the areas of human rights, humanitarian assistance, and conflict resolution, NGOs have recorded more failures than successes. In that respect, the record of NGOs in Sri Lanka is no different from that of their counterparts in Rwanda, Bosnia, and Kosovo.

The Sri Lankan government has succeeded in gaining complete control over the activities of NGOs, particularly those involved in humanitarian assistance, human rights, and conflict resolution. It has consistently denied NGOs any flexibility in these areas primarily by imposing a strict regulatory environment. It has been remarkably successful in creating strong anti-NGO sentiment among the general public. It selectively holds local and provincial elections, the timing of which coincides with government claims that its military has made significant territorial gains. Today, the majority of Sri Lankans accept the largely unfounded allegations that NGOs contributed to the popularity and military strength of the LTTE and tarnish Sri Lanka's international image.

On May 18, 2009, the civil war officially came to an end. The next day, in his address to the nation, Rajapaksa reiterated the familiar political position that "war is not the answer."[117] He promised to rebuild the nation and facilitate a speedy resettlement of the thousands of IDPs. Following his speech, Russia, China, Pakistan, Libya, and the US congratulated the government for its military triumph, and the US, India, and European countries also continued to urge the government to implement a political settlement and permit access by humanitarian workers. Ban Ki-moon, the Secretary General of the United Nations, who had failed to secure a ceasefire and gain flexible access to the IDPs during the war, visited Sri Lanka. He underscored the need for speedy reconstruction and the swift rehabilitation of IDPs. The IMF, the World Bank, and other international donors opened discussions about releasing aid that had been forfeited during the war. On May 26, 2009, the European Union (EU), which many times failed to secure a ceasefire from the government and the LTTE, also decided to extend a general preferential tariff treatment (GSP, or Generalized System of Preferences) to the Sri Lankan export textile industry. NGO campaigns against human rights violations during the war played an influential role in the EU's decision to withhold the extension of the GSP facility up to that point.

## DIASPORA AND THE INTERNATIONALIZATION OF NGOs

Among Tamils and Sinhalese in Australia, New Zealand, the US, and Western Europe, NGO activism has gained momentum. Satellite communication technology and the internet make it impossible for the government to control the flow of information between Sri Lankans and exiles in Western countries. However, newspapers in Sri Lanka do not offer comprehensive coverage of the activities of diasporic NGOs, nor do they accurately portray the complexity of the Sri Lankan government's international dealings. Instead, government-controlled media provide extensive criticism of international NGOs, and the journalists and local organizations that collaborate with them. Only a very small segment of the population has access to the internet, and international opinion has little impact on government policy.

The ideologies and strategies of the two Sri Lankan diaspora communities are sharply divided. The organizations of the Sinhala diaspora exposed what they characterized as the terrorist activities of the LTTE, and condemned the LTTE for using the Tamils as human shields. In contrast, the Tamil diaspora accused the government of ignoring the human rights concerns of Tamil civilians. The protest language of some of these Sinhala NGOs is identical to the language of the war against terrorism in Western countries. Their intention has also been the same, namely to mobilize international support for the government's war and to shield the government from international criticism. Tamil diaspora organizations sensationalize civilian suffering in government-controlled refugee camps by depicting them as modern "concentration camps." Among the Tamil diaspora community, some celebrate the heroism of the LTTE, while others are critical of its humanitarian failures and human rights abuses. Pro-LTTE organizations that celebrate its heroism and sacrifices have further isolated themselves from the international community, lending credibility to the accusations of the Sri Lankan government.

Even Tamil diaspora organizations critical of the LTTE continue to worry that, now that the LTTE has been militarily defeated, there will be no incentive for the government to fulfill its promise of finding a political settlement to the ethnic crisis. Couching their respective claims in the language of humanitarianism, the war against terrorism, and human rights allows these organizations to obscure their ethnoreligious nationalist ideological content. Paradoxically, the distinction drawn in the international community between the war against terrorism and the ethnic conflict enables ethnoreligious nationalism to remain a dominant political force. Today, diaspora NGOs have internationalized the conflict to the extent that protests are now staged in Western nations such as Australia, as well as in Eastern nations such as India. Three Tamil youths immolated themselves, others staged fasts, and violence erupted between Sinhala and Tamil groups in Western capitals. As the government scored military victories, the international community intensified its criticism of the LTTE and its affiliated organizations.

In 2009, Tamils Against Genocide (TAG), a US-based organization, filed genocide charges against the Sri Lankan secretary of defense and the commander of the Sri Lankan army. It also filed a complaint against the secretary of the US Treasury, Timothy Geithner, and the US executive director of the IMF, Meg Lundsager, seeking to obtain a "declaratory judgment that a failure of the United States to oppose Sri Lanka's pending $1.9 billion IMF loan application would constitute a violation of 22 U.S.C. 262d."[118] US-based NGO activism led to the first US Senate hearing on the humanitarian crisis in Sri Lanka on February 24, 2009.[119] Among those who testified were representatives of Human Rights Watch and the Committee to Protect Journalists. US Secretary of State Hillary Clinton collaborated with the governments of India and European countries in taking initiative to respond to the ongoing war.[120] Tamil and Sinhala organizations continue to raise international awareness of the Sri Lankan issue. In many countries, the Tamil diaspora is no longer a passive minority, but an important political constituency.

The European Union threatened to withdraw the GSP Plus facility unless Sri Lanka complied with basic human rights conventions. The Sri Lankan government adopted a multi-pronged approach to secure the GSP Plus concession, arguing that the withdrawal of GSP ignored their success in defeating terrorism and presented a major obstacle to postwar peace and economic development. They made the case that the loss of GSP would cost nearly 250,000 jobs in the textile sector, which had already begun to suffer due to a global economic crisis, the availability of cheaper labor in East Asian countries, and domestic political instability. The imposition of humanitarian conditions on aid would arguably jeopardize the rapid resettlement of IDPs, leading to further political instability and possibly even halting the peace process.

The government dispatched its diplomats and politicians to secure the continuity of GSP, maintaining that Sri Lanka would not permit the EU or any other foreign power to investigate its human rights record. They argued that the threat of GSP withdrawal was part of a conspiracy against the country, spearheaded by NGOs and traitors in opposition parties. Meanwhile, some UK businesses cautioned European governments that depriving the Sri Lankan government of GSP would be counterproductive. The EU has delayed a final decision on the GSP as its members continue to air contradictory opinions in their various dialogues with the Sri Lankan government. In the final analysis, the government's handling of the GSP crisis serves to boost its domestic image as the only institution capable of securing economic concessions from Western countries without bowing to their demands. At the same time, it has given foreign governments even more influence over Sri Lanka's economic and political affairs.

The positions of international state actors on their relations with Sri Lanka remain contradictory and unclear. Demands for the release of the IDPs and the admission of NGOs have, once again, gained momentum. The UN, the EU, and Human Rights Watch and other NGOs continue to argue that the government's claims are empty and that the progress of resettlement is unsatisfactory. Among these protesters, Jean Lambert of the European Parliament noted that the "indiscriminate detention of IDPs is a clear violation of international law." Her remark suggests that the apprehensions of the House are widely shared, and there is a broad feeling that government impunity, as well as the harassment of journalists, must come to an end. Although the government continues to resist such demands, it is cautiously beginning to relax restrictions.

Critics argue that the government keeps IDPs in camps to engineer social, economic, and political developments in the region according to its own political and economic priorities. The government has total control over the flow of foreign aid to humanitarian workers and over the resettlement process in general. It solicits private contractors to disburse aid. Both the EU and the US have backtracked on their initial positions, giving the Sri Lankan state ample time to respond. Closed-door meetings were regularly held to restructure relations between the Sri Lankan government and the international community.

Although NGO-mediated international protests against the Sri Lankan state appear to be the only source of criticism of the government's handling of the IDPs, international opinion lacks not only popular legitimacy in Sri Lanka, but also consistency and persistence. In fact, international pressure enhanced the legitimacy of claims made by the government and anti-NGO lobby. More important, the protests are shaped by specific economic and geopolitical concerns rather than the humanitarian issues faced by the IDPs: "The US and European powers certainly have vested interests in Sri Lanka, but this has nothing to do with reviving the LTTE, or defending the democratic rights of the Tamil minority."[121] Noam Chomsky, referring to the policies and noble rhetoric of Western countries towards Sri Lanka, pointed out that the West doesn't protect people unless it is in its own interest to do so, and the plight of Tamils doesn't meet this criterion. Of China's engagement with Sri Lanka, Chomsky said that China doesn't "gain anything by supporting the Tamil refugees in concentration camps, so why should they do it?"[122]

The government, while complying somewhat with humanitarian demands, also sought to highlight the inconsistencies and contradictions in Western policies. Its position was strengthened by its eventual success in securing the IMF loan, and by its ability to raise funds from India, Iran, Japan, and China without accepting problematic human rights conditions. International NGO perspectives on human rights issues often do not take into account the links between those issues and the economic and geopolitical interests of powerful states. Even when they do take these into account, NGOs are not only inconsistent but also hypocritical, which, in turn, undermines their popular legitimacy and strengthens the government.

Recently, contentious relations between the Sri Lankan government and NGOs were spurred by the detention and subsequent conviction of Tamil journalist J.S. Tissainayagam. In addition to writing for mainstream newspapers, Tissainayagam published a journal and managed a multilingual, multicultural website. Some of these activities were supported by the same foreign organizations that provided funds to the government. Tissainayagam worked for several human rights NGOs and earned a reputation for being a journalist advocate of human rights. He was ultimately sentenced to 20 years in prison for collecting funds and publishing articles that generated "ethnic disharmony." NGOs said that the conviction was unjust and an assault against the ideal of freedom of expression.

NGOs maintained that the Sri Lankan justice system lacks consistency and equal treatment. Tissainayagam was convicted under the Prevention of Terrorism Act (PTA) for inciting ethnic disharmony, while, at the same time, racially inflammatory statements were regularly being made by higher ranking military officers and politicians. Former military commanders of the LTTE who were responsible for killing hundreds of unarmed civilians were freed and rewarded with prestigious ministerial positions, while Tissainayagam was arrested. Indeed, the only evidence against him was his own confession, given under duress while he was in detention. Subsequently, Global Media Forum and the US branch of Reporters Without Borders recognized Tissainayagam by awarding him the first Peter Meckler Award for Courageous and Ethical Journalism.

Many international fora concerned with aid and trade relations in Sri Lanka cite his conviction as evidence of the country's violations of human rights and freedom of speech. In response to requests for a pardon, the government maintains that Tissainayagam was given access to due legal process and that he has been permitted to appeal. In response to NGO activities, the editorial of the *Lakbimanews*, known for its critical perspectives on NGOs and Western countries, defended the sentence as technically inevitable: "If he connived with terrorists and took money from them—as the state alleges—he deserves some form of punishment." But it still did not agree that the sentence was necessarily fair under the circumstances. A later editorial noted:

> In the Tissainayagam case, the government may have been convinced that he is a terrorist, but should not have prosecuted him with such a vengeance, if the only evidence the prosecution had was a confession of his having used a not very substantial amount of money given by the LTTE.[123]

The editorial suggested that NGOs would be effective only if they could solicit the support of the state, and faulted international human rights and media organizations for exaggerating the truth about Tissainayagam and giving him awards for bravery in journalism.

Such perspectives are popular in the mainstream Sri Lankan press. They reinforce anti-NGO and anti-Western sentiments, strengthen xenophobia, and shield the government from international scrutiny. They also provide more opportunities for international actors to gain a foothold in Sri Lanka. There exists a serious dilemma for human rights and humanitarian NGOs. On the one hand, their effectiveness is based on their ability to solicit support from the international state system—support that is unlikely to materialize if they interfere with the economic and geopolitical affairs of the country. On the other hand, their international credibility is contingent on protecting the human rights of marginalized populations without respect to particular economic and political concerns. Despite the fact that human rights and humanitarian assistance are invariably politicized, NGOs need to maintain their neutrality and impartiality if they are to be successful. Failure to maintain this balancing act invariably undermines their ability to meet the needs of their would-be beneficiaries.

Western countries have historically exhibited double standards in the application of human rights at home and abroad. Human rights theoretically transcend the political practices of particular states. It is not the affected populations that oppose Western interference in Sri Lanka, but the government. NGOs have argued that, in situations of ethnic conflict such as that in Sri Lanka, they are the only means by which marginalized groups can voice their opinions. The majority of Sri Lankans believe that the government's actions are justifiable in so far as they are consistent with those of governments in similar situations in other parts of the world.

The government's continued refusal to allow third parties to study the state of affairs further cements the national consensus. The government thus protects the political interests of the majority Sinhalese community that supported the war, at the expense of the nation's interests taken as a whole.

A number of Sinhalese readers pointed to newspaper stories about influential military and political personnel who shared the view that Sri Lanka is a country of original people among whom the rest live as foreigners.[124] The Sinhalese majority, they believe, should rule the country. These observers were critical of the government's human rights violations and policy contradictions, but they did not see those as a reason to prevent the government from supporting NGOs involved in safeguarding human rights in other countries. They believe that Sri Lankans are part of the global community, interested in protecting the rights of marginalized groups. They see no justifiable historical reason to rely on states alone to ensure human rights. Sinhalese readers indicated that citizens of all countries have a responsibility to ensure the accountability of states. Ultimately, NGOs do not represent the needs and interests of states, but rather the needs and interests of their own constituencies.

## ANTI-NGOISM AND THE CONSOLIDATION OF STATE POWER

The course of the war and the increasing influence of the anti-NGO lobby over state policies sidelined NGOs in the peace movement. In their place, the Center for Policy Alternatives, the Sri Lankan Branch of Transparency International, and Corruption Watch have emerged as the main critics of government policies. Their interventions were instrumental in many of the decisions against the government by the Sri Lankan Supreme Court in cases involving corruption and human rights violations. Some of these NGOs were criticized in various ways by the anti-NGO lobby. Some were even subjected to attacks by unidentified groups. (On September 8, 2008, one such group threw a grenade into the home of the chief executive officer of Transparency International. Another group, an underground organization known as Mahason Balakaya, continued to threaten the lawyers prosecuting the human rights cases filed by those detained under the Prevention of Terrorism Act.) Charges that NGOs were foreign conspirators and unaccountable were directed specifically toward those NGOs that question government practices. There was no incentive for the government to respect these NGOs, as long as it could mobilize international aid without "good governance" conditions.

Meanwhile, Tamil diaspora NGOs continued to pressure international agencies and the government to either stop aid to Sri Lanka or attach human rights conditions. By May 2009, a consensus among international actors seemed to have emerged that further aid to Sri Lanka should be stopped until the civilians were freed and the fighting brought to an end. This decision was followed by the UN Security Council's decision to discuss Sri Lankan issues after months of protests by some of its members. On March 15, 2009, US Secretary of State Hillary Clinton announced: "We have also raised questions about the IMF loan at this time. We think that it is not an appropriate time to consider that [loan] until there is a resolution of the conflict." Despite US opposition, the loan was approved. The Sri Lankan government interpreted this as a vindication of its policies.

NGO financial investments were seen as indispensable by the bankrupt government and corrupt politicians. The public will soon forget anti-NGO criticism as the organizations adapt themselves to suit postwar conditions. However, with international opinion increasingly shifting in favor of the government, it seems unlikely that the NGO lobby will successfully influence the terms of international government aid, for several reasons. The surplus is used by transnational capital to exploit opportunities for investments, particularly in natural resources, tourism, and commodity production. The overwhelming military presence in the northeast and the government's success in suppressing political dissent will also provide extremely secure conditions for international investment. Furthermore, the sheer magnitude of the humanitarian crisis of the IDPs will make it impossible for the international community to withhold aid on the basis of the Sri Lankan government's alleged noncompliance with international laws.

For various reasons, many of which have nothing to do with Sri Lanka, several non-Western countries such as India, China, Russia, and Malaysia will block the UN's attempts to attach human rights conditions to aid. Despite intense lobbying by NGOs, the Sri Lankan government, in collaboration with a few non-Western countries, recently defeated a Western-sponsored UN resolution to begin inquiries into possible war crimes. Not surprisingly, the minister of foreign affairs in Sri Lanka interpreted the rejection of the resolution as an endorsement by the international community of the Sri Lankan government's policies. The victory bolstered anti-INGO and anti-Western prejudices.

Access to the IDPs and information about them is still restricted by the government. Tensions between the government and NGOs demanding access to war-ravaged communities continues to grow.[125] Relations between NGOs, the military, and the state are likely to remain unstable, especially in light of the charges of genocide and war crimes against the government, and repeated calls for investigations by international organizations. In response to these charges, the government has pointed out the duplicity of Western countries regarding their own wars against terrorism. Faced with requests that access be granted to humanitarian workers, the minister of human rights and disaster management stated:

> Our position is that we welcome anyone who wants to complement the troops of the government but they have to work within a national framework. And as long as they work within that national framework we would facilitate them to the maximum.[126]

Security forces have temporarily relocated nearly 200,000 IDPs at a site known as Menik Farm. A few NGOs, such as Lanka Evangelical Alliance Development Services (LEADS), World Vision, and Sarvodaya, are now permitted to conduct humanitarian operations there, and the government is gradually easing restrictions for others as well. However, NGOs are not permitted to enter "uncleared" areas or provide information to the media. Local NGOs are permitted to provide only basic material assistance under the strict supervision of the government, while international NGOs continue to advocate for human rights safeguards for the IDPs. After the establishment of the National Confidential Information Investigation Unit (in charge of human rights and media security), the government refused to extend visas for five officers of nonviolent peace NGOs.[127] NGOs also find it difficult to carry out programs relating to gender and violence in the north and east. The government claims that such activities would undermine national security imperatives. This leaves a huge institutional void for dealing with issues pertaining to extremely gendered postwar reconstruction and development efforts, under the strict regulatory framework imposed by the government, the military, and transnational capital. After the United Nations established an advisory panel to investigate war crimes in Sri Lanka, the government founded the Lessons Learned and the Reconciliation Commission, further diminishing the space for NGOs. The "discourse of truth" that emerged from the proceedings of the commission further legitimates the government's pre-war claims about the ceasefire. Yet the LLRC provided some democratic space for the expression of diverse opinions, including those of people living in the northern and eastern parts of the country. The decision of Human Rights Watch to boycott the government's invitation to make submissions to the Commission has further reinforced popular suspicions about the human rights agendas of NGOs.

More comprehensive postwar humanitarian reconstruction and development work in the north and east is already underway with the help of transnational capital, particularly from non-Western nations such as India, China, and several Middle Eastern countries. Some of these areas have been closed to transnational capital due to the war and to protests by Tamils who fear that it might lead to further colonization. This has placed Sri Lanka in the middle of geopolitical competition between India, China, and Western countries. Ethnoreligious nationalism and the ideology of national security will continue to serve as means of managing the crises arising from transnational capital's penetration into these areas.

Immediately after the government declared an end to the war against the LTTE in 2009, both the popular press and the government likened President Mahinda Rajapaksa to the Sinhalese King Dutugemunu, who saved the country from Tamil tribes in ancient times—the first successful struggle for independence. In the midst of the euphoria, the Most Venerable Mahanayakas of Malwatta and Asgiriya Chapters conferred upon Rajapaksa at a magnificent royal ceremony the honorary title "Vishva Keerthi Sri Thri Sinhaladheeshwara," the highest honor ever awarded to a civilian leader. The metaphor of the victorious king carries over into the postwar discourse of nationalism, especially as it concerns NGOs. Both local and foreign NGOs are compared to the enemies vanquished by King Dutugemunu, and are accused of endangering the sovereignty and security of the country. The importance to Sri Lankan history of ethnoreligious nationalist interpretations of the government's victory in the civil war, and their implications for larger political and economic processes in the postwar period, should not be underestimated. Ethnoreligious nationalism in all communities will continue to inform how Sri Lankans come to terms with life after the war. The resurgence of popular nationalist histories is evident in the symbolism seen in the victory celebrations and the festivals honoring war heroes, and it is also evident in the popular equation of Rajapaksa with the revered Dutugemunu, who eventually defeated the Tamil King Elara. Following that ancient war, religious authorities consoled Dutugemunu, who was remorseful about the slaughter and destruction, and the king then built a number of magnificent Buddhist monuments (*stupas*) and patronized charitable and development activities.

Dutugemunu's war against Elara was the result of territorial conflict between kings, and it had nothing to do with ethnicity.[128] Nor did Dutugemunu rebuild his kingdom with transnational capital. After consolidating power, he ruled according to the dharma of Buddha, not according to the ideological imperatives of ethnoreligious nationalism. This nuanced and cosmopolitan version of national history is not widely disseminated. Postwar political rhetoric underwrites the ethnoreligious nationalist narrative. Competing accounts of national history reflect the underlying tension in NGO–state relations since independence. After the defeat of the LTTE, the narrative of the majority community has evolved as the dominant narrative in terms of shaping the country's development, the resettlement of the internally displaced population, and the restructuring of the country's social, political, and cultural landscape. The parochialism inherent in these narratives is no different to one advanced by a visible Sinhala and Tamil diaspora. NGO engagement with the competing narratives is limited and has no influence on the majority of the country's population.

The end of the war did not lessen the state's restrictions on, and surveillance of, NGOs. In the popular imagination they continued to be held responsible for international criticism of the Sri Lankan state. Few anti-NGO critics bother attempting to substantiate their accusations. Nevertheless, they constitute an ideological force to the extent that their supporters associate NGOs with negative historical memories of colonialism and the West. At stake, then, is Sri Lanka's national imagination.[129] As in the case of the international campaigns against terrorism, anti-NGOism reveals the ethnoreligious nationalist ideological content of the wars. Ethnoreligious nationalism is a class project that enables elites to both compete for power and represent themselves as indigenous leaders. This is why anti-NGOism receives the warmest welcome in countries where most citizens either do not or cannot critically examine competing historical accounts of their national past.

The delay of aid to Sri Lanka by the IMF and the EU had less to do with the country's failure to comply with human rights norms, and more to do with its failure to comply with neoliberal economic reforms. NGOs played an important role in this. Donor conditions included reducing the size of the public sector and further liberalizing the economy. During the Rajapaksa regime, private-sector investments by transnational capital in education, health care, and natural resources continued to increase. They have reached into areas in the northeast that were previously impenetrable due to the war and resistance by Tamil groups. The government continues to comply with the dictates of international capital, creating favorable investment conditions for Indian and Chinese industries, especially those who produce for Western markets. The foreign exchange reserves of the country have grown, mainly due to commercial borrowing from Iran, India, and China. The reduction in social welfare, increase in unemployment, and acceleration of debt-driven inflation have increased protests by labor unions and political parties. The government's interest in introducing stricter NGO regulation has taken a back seat, although NGOism as an ideology continues to be a dominant force. NGOs themselves fuel anti-NGO sentiment by their failure to question popular nationalist historiography and neoliberal policies.

The end of the war did not necessarily create political stability as expected by the Rajapaksa regime. The public protests against the economic crises, suppressed during the war, have resurfaced. The government rapidly ceased to be the sole beneficiary of the victory over the LTTE. General Sarath Fonseka, who led the war against the LTTE, became the leading candidate of the opposition alliance. He was seen as an upholder of majoritarian interests and apparently had the best chance of depriving Rajapaksa of electoral victory. The discourse of the opposition alliance, however, does not focus on the failure of the ruling party to solve the ethnic crisis politically. Although the government was successful in jettisoning a political settlement to the intercommunal conflict and gaining territorial control over the northern and eastern areas, its inability to resolve the economic and political crises isolates it from the very local and international forces that underwrite it. The state is finding it increasingly difficult to contain the NGO sector, which is becoming more and more technologically savvy. Meanwhile, the government, while exploiting religion, patriotism, and national security policies to prevent a military coup or potential defeat in the next presidential election, seeks to appease transnational capitalist interests. During the elections the campaign of the ruling party portrayed Fonseka as a traitor who betrayed the country's armed forces. Fonseka's entry into politics has sharply divided both the Sri Lankan polity and the religious establishment. The charges of corruption and abuse levied against each other by the Fonseka and Rajapaksa camps were the same ones that they had denied during the war against the LTTE, and the same allegations levied by NGOs against the government.

The ruling coalition led by President Rajapaksa won a landslide victory in the presidential elections of January 2010. The triumph demonstrated the extent to which the masses are alienated from the influence of NGOs, and the irrelevance of NGO activities to the country's political processes. After the elections General Fonseka was arrested and imprisoned on charges of conspiracy, corruption, and mismanagement. The anti-NGO lobby characterized Fonseka as part of an international conspiracy against the state, carried out in collaboration with the international NGOs. During his Independence Day celebrations on February 4, President Rajapaksa, while denying self-rule to Tamils, declared: "Hereafter, we will not entertain narrow divisions based on race, religion, language and political ideology in terms of regions. There is no one called a minority in this country, all those who love the country are children of mother Lanka." Many Tamil groups interpreted such universal claims as the further consolidation of Sinhala nationalism, and a demonstration of lack of interest in finding a political solution to the ethnic conflict.

Following the elections, the state embarked on elaborate programs to "develop" the northern and eastern parts of the country. NGOs were invited to assist in these programs in collaboration with the state. NGOs of the Tamil diaspora and local organizations alike view the current development projects in the north and east, the proposal to reform customary laws governing property ownership in the north, and other symbolic gestures by the state as further extensions of Sinhala colonization. The referenda organized by diaspora NGOs gave overwhelming approval for a separate Tamil state in Sri Lanka. The government views the growing politicization of these NGOs as evidence of the continuing threat of LTTE terrorism, and as justification for stronger counterterrorism measures. Under these circumstances, national security and ethnoreligious nationalism will further militarize Sri Lankan society, particularly when the government finds it difficult to implement neoliberal economic reforms.

The crisis of the NGO–state relationship is a crisis of historical consciousness; the underlying force of the crisis is a battle between different ethnic groups over competing histories of the country. The notion of NGO foreignness provides legitimacy to the majoritarian history, and strength to the state's claim to be that history's heir and guardian. The claims and counter-claims of NGOs and their opponents have political meaning largely among elites, because they ignore the class dimensions of social and political problems. The organizations and their critics do not explicitly engage in debates about how religion and ethnicity are exploited by members of their own classes, across all ethnic communities and political parties.

On April 30, 2010, the government announced that it was bringing the NGO secretariat, the Urban Development Authority, and the Land Reclamation and Development Corporation under the umbrella of the Ministry of Defense (MOD), which in the war's aftermath has emerged as the most important agency framing the state and transnational capital's reconstruction of the country's economic, political, and cultural landscape. NGOs, in particular the international NGOs, need to register with the MOD and request clearance to work in the northern and eastern parts of the country.

Since January 2011, any NGO or INGO working in the North has to register their projects with the Presidential Task Force (PTF) and work within the master plan supervised by Minister Basil Rajapaksha who is the Chairman of the PTF. Since then, contrary to the government's earlier position on limiting INGO operation in the country, INGOs and NGOs were invited to play an active role in the reconstruction and development work in the North and East. The leadership of the TRO, an NGO blacklisted allegedly for it's for pro-LTTE bias, was placed under former strongmen Kumaran Pathmanathan (alias KP). The Central Intelligence Department stared criminal investigations the National Peace Council on the allegation that it continued to be funded by foreign donors despite the end of the war and claiming that it is serving the interests of their funding partners. On 24th March 2010, ICRC closed its office in Vavuniya in response to government's request to carry out its operations from Colombo. The government initiated a program in collaboration with the SSM and commercial banks to rehabilitate the ex-LTTE combatants by turning them from crusaders for Eelam to entrepreneurs.

The subsumption of urban development under the Ministry of Defense and the oversight of the military of reconstruction and resettlement in the war-affected area should not be viewed simply as a matter of national security. This securitization of development is also an attempt to overcome cultural, economic and social barriers to the expansion of capital—the same barriers that once shaped capitalist development, and provided legitimacy to the state. The National Security state is in part about disciplining the legal and substantive sovereignty according to the demands of capital.

On September 12, the Sri Lankan parliament approved the Eighteenth Amendment to the constitution and removed the two-term limit on the presidency. The Center for Policy Alternatives noted:

The Eighteenth Amendment to the Constitution Bill represents nothing less than an assault on constitutional democracy in the service of partisan advantage, and a consolidation of authoritarianism it would be too late to rue when its potential consequences begin to take effect.[130]

The government defended the executive presidency as necessary for economic development and the defeat of terrorism, promoting the new amendment as a national security and economic imperative. In the same week, the World Bank approved a $60-billion loan to the government, and the International Monetary Fund recently extended a $2.6-billion standby loan facility as well. The flow of international aid by those organizations further increased the confidence of the government to carry out reforms that would consolidate its drive towards concentration of power. The government has successfully established popular consensus that development under the imperatives of national security is a priority, and has begun to adopt aggressive policies of economic reform in order to attract private investment. NGO resistance against these political developments is extremely limited and inconsequential, as NGOs have lost popular legitimacy and failed to evolve as a coherent force. We can also observe the increasing competition between them for international funding, state patronage, and territory.

Public euphoria over the government's victory is dissipating, the conduct of public officials during the war is coming under increased scrutiny, competition for state power is on the rise, the economy has stalled, and the government is losing its hold on the new spaces of activism emerging through the country. The religious establishment that unanimously supported the state is now being polarized, and some are organizing in opposition to the state. As we have seen since 1977, the very instruments mobilized to fight terrorism get deployed to combat any opposition to the state. One-time patriots easily become enemies of the state if the state sees them as threats. One-time enemies of the nation and of the state become its allies. The state eventually exhausts its ability to manage economic and social crises by appealing primarily to national identity, and must resort to militarism as the only promising means of maintaining the state's "autonomy" and disciplining the social order according to, not always compatible, interests of political elites and transnational capital.

As the state continues to search for an ideology for legitimizing its activities, militarism (i.e. extension of military involvement in civilian affairs) will masquerade as national security, which in turn becomes an essential prerequisite for "peace" and "development." The attempt to legitimize militarization by appealing to generalized identity and loyalty increasingly produces apathy among citizens and fear of state practices. As long as the "perception of the threat of terrorism" persists the impacts of militarization continue to be unevenly distributed along the lines of race, ethnicity, religion, and gender, often with visible geospatial specificity. The NGO activities in the north and east are subject to far greater surveillance by the state, and no NGO can function in those parts of the country without the oversight of the military.

While NGO activism in Sri Lanka is severely constrained and brought under the control of the government by the national security imperatives of the Ministry of Defense, the activism of international NGOs and the pressure they place on the government to improve human rights conditions continue to escalate. Yet, the internationalization of NGO activism, along with the formation of the Transnational Government of Tamil Eelam, continues to enhance the legitimacy of the state when these protests are branded as exclusively organized by the diaspora and NGOs sympathetic to the LTTE, especially when some of these protests openly display the LTTE flag—a symbol of terror and genocide for a majority of the Sri Lankan population. The legal attempts by Tamils Against Genocide (TAG) to hold Sri Lankan politicians accountable for "war crimes" further enhance the local popularity of these politicians and anti-NGO sentiments.

The government's continuing appeal to the diaspora for contributions to development efforts in the north-east and their lack of positive responses enhances its local and international legitimacy by making it appear as if it is driven by humanitarian interest for the Tamil population, as opposed to the diaspora which is primarily interested in a separate state. Many observers of the diaspora that funded the LTTE are less enthusiastic about doing the same for the development activities of many grassroots NGOs struggling to respond to the needy population in the northern and eastern part of the country.

The relative freedom of mobility of people in the country has earned the government a great deal of social capital and enhanced the legitimacy of the state. The belief among the majority of the population that they need to forget the past and quickly develop the country (which they think is the road to peace) has further marginalized NGOs and diaspora demands for investigations into human rights abuses and for a political solution to the ethnic conflict. International states are unlikely to heed these demands because the

Rajapaksa regime has successfully allowed international actors with diverse economic and political interests to have significant economic and political stakes in the country. Rather than exerting pressure on the government, international actors are busy trying to establish their respective credibility with the government, further diminishing the influence of NGOs who cannot be an effective force without the help of the international government. Moreover, the activism of the diaspora and the international NGOs hardly have an impact on the flow of transnational capital into the country or effectively mobilize substantive pressures on the Sri Lankan state.

The government is likely to face a serious legitimacy crisis in response to rising food prices and debt, as well as over major economic activities that are increasingly under the control of transnational corporations and international governments. The presence of international actors with conflicting economic and political interests could increase the local and international vulnerability of the state. In response to new spaces of dissent emerging throughout the country the government will be forced to deflect this dissent away from transnational capitalist institutions and donors to "elsewhere." Even if the government consolidates its electoral power, it is extremely unlikely that the importance of the "war on terror" national security apparatus ethnicity, nationalism, territoriality for the legitimacy of the state will diminish. Historically unprecedented concentration of power in the hand of state apparatus has increased the flexibility for the transnational capital to colonize country's resources economy. A few NGOs occasionally questioned the political, rather than economic aspects of such concentration of power. Questioning the activities of transnational capital runs the risk of undermining the ideological and material bases of the NGO or being accused of undermining the economic progress now an integral part of country's security. The postwar economic crisis and the government's loss of control over the economy to transnational capitalist institutions will only bolster the political influence of these forces, since they offer the most promising means of facilitating capitalist control over the economy, and the public lacks an ideology and political leadership that could serve as an alternative to primordialism and capitalism. The NGOs do not show signs of evolving as a counter-hegemonic force. Instead, the territorial battles between them have intensified and their survival depends on building closer partnerships with the state itself. Unless a more equitable and democratic social contract between the government and the population emerges, the inevitable social and economic crisis will lead to more securitization and militarization, further constraining the space for NGO activism.

# 3
# Secularism, Religion, and Parallel States: Post-Independence NGO–State Relations in Bangladesh, 1971–2010

"Religious distress is at the same time the expression of real distress and the protest against real distress. Religion is the sigh of the oppressed creature, the heart of a heartless world, just as it is the spirit of a spiritless situation. It is the opium of the people."

Karl Marx[1]

Bangladesh is a predominantly Islamic country, founded on the ideals of secularism and language-based identity. Independent Bangladesh was devastated by war, and international NGOs gained control over the economic and political affairs of the country before the government did. At the time of independence, economic nationalism was the driver of protectionist economic policies, but these would soon undergo crisis and give way to a neoliberal agenda. Since then, NGOs and the government have been evolving as two parallel regimes, and the interdependencies and tensions between them have created the conditions for the transformation of society according to the imperatives of transnational capital, all within a precarious geopolitical context shaped by Indian and Chinese interests. Capitalist institutions in Bangladesh use large NGOs as models for co-opting and disciplining the poor and marginalized, especially women. At the same time, the failures of NGOs and governments to address economic and political crises are construed as state failures. In attempting to manage these crises, governments cautiously mobilize ideals of national sovereignty and security tempered with ethnoreligious nationalism, a process in which the state's relations with NGOs play a critical role. While NGOs are vocal in denouncing the excesses of ethnoreligious nationalism, the majority of them are in fact either complicit with it, or their activities produce the social and political conditions for its evolution as a powerful political force. The absence of politically significant ethnic and religious minorities, and the fiscal limitations of the state, could limit religious nationalism's impact on political stability in Bangladesh. The potential for religion to become a potent force for social mobilization against economic inequalities in Bangladesh is far greater than in Sri Lanka. Such possibilities are considerably undermined by the complicity with neoliberalism of NGOs and the state.

In 1971, Sheikh Mujibur Rahman and other exiles formed the dominant ruling bloc and gained control over the first government of Bangladesh. From the beginning, the regime was plagued by factionalism, making political consolidation and legitimization more urgent than long-term social development. To appease diverse social groups, "Mujibism," as the state's official agenda was called, sought to combine the principles of socialism, secularism, democracy, and nationalism. The new constitution prevented Islamic political parties from contesting elections by prohibiting the use of religion for political purposes. But rather than disassociating itself from Islam, the state redefined religion.

Mujib declared that he was proud to be a Muslim and insisted that secularism could be preserved even in a religious environment.[2] He instituted prayers in the parliament and declared Bangladesh the largest Muslim country in the world. He also increased funding for Islamic institutions and took a leading role in international Islamic fora. Mujib's version of secularism was embedded in the ethnoreligious nationalist ideology of the predominantly Muslim Bengali-speaking population. This marginalized non-Bengali speaking ethnic minority groups, who opposed Mujib's brand of nationalism.

At the time of independence, Bangladesh inherited a bankrupt economy with a vast resource deficit, worsened by war and famine. The incapacity to internally generate a surplus for investment was prolonged by fragmentation in the agricultural sector and the absence of a strong capitalist class. From 1972 on, Bangladesh was vulnerable to the vicissitudes of the world economy and the dictates of international donors. Ever since the establishment of the new country, ideas about development have been shifting from state to market paradigms. External aid also fostered the emergence of an indigenous bourgeoisie whose fortunes would remain dependent upon access to foreign resources through state patronage.

Entrusted with the responsibility of formulating a program of reconstruction, a Planning Commission preferred a mixed economy in which the state played a leading role. But it could not resist enormous donor pressure to accept the debt previously incurred by the Pakistani government as a condition for future aid. In early 1972, the commission rejected the proposal for a Western donor-sponsored aid consortium for Bangladesh, with the World Bank as coordinator. Concerned about national sovereignty, Bangladeshi think tanks and prominent politicians advocated an anti-World Bank economic agenda. The bank, in turn, complained about the lack of opportunities for private enterprise and criticized the commission's goals and notions of self-reliance.[3] Mujibism lacked a coherent plan for social and economic reforms.[4]

Mujibism's primary opposition came from the military and the bureaucracy, the two institutions most affected by Mujib's interventions into the economic and political process. He had responded to the deepening crisis by using coercion to strengthen his personal power. When he failed to secure his position, he was ousted in a political coup on August 15, 1975.[5] The new socialist Awami League government, which held power for a short time before Mujib died in 1978, did not succeed in creating a new alliance despite repeated attempts to dislodge the military bureaucracy.

NGOs in Bangladesh began to grow in importance as early as 1971, since the government did not have the capacity to respond to pressing developmental needs. Many organizations evolved from pre-existing Christian organizations. After independence, expatriate professionals returned to the country and formed associations with the aim of nation building. Former members of radical political parties, disenchanted with revolutionary politics, sought alternative ways of meeting basic human needs and their search led them to NGOs. A few Holy Cross Catholic missionaries from the United States, sympathetic to liberation theology, played an influential role in the ideological synthesis of capitalism and socialism within the organizational structures of NGOs.

Most NGOs came to Bangladesh for relief and rehabilitation work, and later branched out into other areas of development. It was less the specific needs of Bangladeshi society and more its secular ethos and welcoming nature that gave NGOs the freedom to enter and experiment with developmental models. It was argued that NGO involvement in Bangladesh was justified because the country was a "basket case" and among the poorest countries of the world, but international donors also had an interest in controlling the country's economic and political affairs because of its geopolitical importance.

The financial resources and organizational structures of NGOs allowed them to intervene in social development more effectively than could government ministries. They established themselves as a kind of parallel government and engaged in relief, development, and activist work. A number of peasant social movement leaders joined NGOs as well. The institutionalization of these social movements within the organizational structures of NGOs brought them under the legal purview of the government and the supervision of international donors, and provided the newly independent state with a convenient means of controlling political dissent.

Most NGO leaders belonged to the urban, English speaking middle class, and had close links to Western agencies. During this early period, NGOs in Bangladesh did not usually invoke religion or tradition in articulating their agendas. Their views were shaped by debates about dominant development models and the popular alternatives of the day. Mainstream NGOs in Bangladesh shared the general opinion that improving conditions for the country's rural poor depended on transforming the oppressive social and economic relationships that caused landlessness and deprivation. They debated approaches to changing societal power relations through raising awareness and mobilizing oppressed groups.[6] NGOs were flexible, collaborating with individuals and organizations with diverse religious and political views. They pursued a middle path between capitalism and socialism, implementing their programs independently, and were not perceived by either the public or the government as significant actors in the social development of Bangladesh.

In October 1973, the first meeting of the voluntary associations was held at Notre Dame College in Dhaka. It was organized by the Christian Organizations for Relief and Rehabilitation (CORR) and the Mennonite Central Committee, and resulted in the formation of the Association of Voluntary Organizations in Bangladesh (AVAB). This was the first time NGOs were represented as a unified group. Dr. Windburn Thomas, a retired missionary who had worked in Japan and Indonesia, and Father R.W. Timm were elected the first director and chairman of the Association's executive committee, respectively.[7] The AVAB functioned as a forum for dialogue between organizations on development matters, and undertook the coordination of specific programs.

In 1976, the AVAB limited its focus to agricultural development, changing its name to the Agricultural Development Associations of Bangladesh (ADAB). During this period, ADAB members conducted long discussions on whether they should constitute a representative body for policy negotiations with the government. Most of them ultimately rejected the idea since they already "had direct contacts with the government which they preferred to maintain."[8] Although ADAB took initiative in the coordination of collaboration between the government and NGOs, many NGOs still preferred to engage directly with the government. Since independence, NGOs had been lightly regulated, obliged only to register with the Ministry of Social Welfare. This leniency was due, in part, to the administration's inability to implement strong regulations following liberation.

The government invited NGOs to participate in fora bringing together researchers, government departments, and international donors. Amid turbulent political conditions, NGOs provided a neutral institutional space and a seemingly stable path to social development. The paralyzed administrative system and ineffective ruling class opened a large space for NGOs, which organized to meet the massive needs created by floods and famines. A widespread belief in the comparative advantage of NGOs vis-à-vis the state in social development, the power of the NGO-friendly neoliberal political economy, and a flood of foreign aid paved the way for NGO expansion.

After consolidating power in 1975, Ziaur Rahman had seemed more willing than his predecessor to introduce neoliberal economic policies. He abrogated socialism and replaced its rhetoric with that of social justice and "fidelity to the spirit of Islam."[9] Although he offered incentives to the private sector toward the end of his term, industry contributed only 8 percent of GDP compared with 19 percent in countries of similar standing. "Industrialists without industry" (lumpen capitalists),[10] who, through state patronage, gained control over foreign aid, national resources, and state power, benefited most from government policy.[11] But businessmen and international donors were not convinced of the government's institutional capacity to facilitate private-sector reforms.[12] A drastic move toward the privatization of state-owned industry and state-subsidized services would have faced strong opposition from both wage workers and the salaried middle classes. Zia failed to gain the international donor assistance needed to carry out his three-phase revolutionary agenda, which promised to achieve self-sufficiency in three years, full literacy in five years, and the reduction of the population growth rate by half in seven years.

Agrarian reforms led to the withdrawal of the fertilizer subsidy and an increase in rent on tube wells. Rising agricultural input prices, coupled with the government's restrictive credit policies, had an adverse effect on small- and medium-scale farmers, many of whom were forced into mortgage foreclosure and driven to seek employment in other sectors. Reduced competition enhanced the power of "surplus farmers," who had strengthened their power base and made inroads into the political arena since the Basic Democracies regime in the 1960s, leading to increased socioeconomic differentiation among the agrarian classes.

Local government administrative reforms were introduced to decentralize planning and facilitate the implementation of social development programs. But the government was not genuinely interested in any devolution that would disturb the existing power structure, nor were rural elites willing to provide space for such a change. Decentralization was intended to extend the power base of the ruling party by making local government institutions crucial to the distribution of state patronage, as it had been during Basic Democracies. In 1978, the National Democratic Party (JAGODAL) was established to consolidate Zia's position. Under the pretext of broadening participatory democracy, Zia's supporters sought to compete with established political groups in urban areas. Once the elections were over, JAGODAL was scrapped and replaced by the Bangladesh National Party (BNP).

By the 1980s, it was clear that the economic plan had failed to produce the anticipated results. Global economic conditions led to a drop in foreign aid, while rising oil prices and the world recession in 1980–81 reduced Bangladesh's foreign currency reserves from $337.3 million in March 1981 to just $89.3 million in October of the same year. In July 1981, the IMF asked President Abdus Sattar's BNP government to impose stringent policy measures including restrictions on bank credit, reductions in nonproductive spending, reduced import expenditures, and increased exports. The IMF pressured the government to withdraw rice and fertilizer subsidies, transfer control over the distribution of agricultural inputs to the private sector, raise the prices of petroleum, gas, electricity, and water services, and devalue the taka (Tk), the Bangladeshi currency, by 30 percent.[13] But the Sattar government was facing impending presidential elections in November 1981, and did not implement those measures because they would have been unpopular.

After a July 1981 review, the IMF stopped disbursements from its three-year $912-million Extended Facility Fund after only two quarterly payments, on the grounds that Bangladesh had not complied with aid conditions. The state plunged into a legitimacy crisis and protests arose from students, unions, and NGOs concerned with human rights. Development and rehabilitation organizations remained silent. The protests did not lead to a democratic change of government because no political party was able to consolidate enough support to resist government suppression. Eventually, the regime was toppled by a group of officers in a military coup.

In contrast to Mujib's regime, Zia's had been fairly successful in pacifying the military and the government bureaucracy, as well as in broadening its power base in rural areas. The sources of the challenges Zia faced were widespread and complex, as the agrarian classes began to articulate their demands through the newly emerging political parties. Increased dependence on foreign aid had restricted his flexibility in shaping economic policies, so he embraced the tactic of substituting "Bengali" nationalism for "Bangladeshi" nationalism. New impetus was given to state-sponsored Islamization, first by amending the constitution to omit the word "secularism" in its preamble, Article 6, and Article 8, and replacing it with references to Islamic principles and values. The new document read: "In the name of Allah, the Beneficent, the Merciful, the states shall endeavor to consolidate, preserve and strengthen fraternal relations among Muslim countries on Islamic solidarity." Ghulam Azam, a prominent collaborator with the Pakistani government, was allowed to return from exile in Pakistan. He subsequently became the leader of the Jamaat-I-Islami, which had been banned after liberation, revitalizing political activism by Islamic groups. It is unlikely that the state intended to encourage or collaborate with these groups; rather, it sought to make the state the champion of Islam and thus to preempt the use of religion by other groups competing with it for power.

Saudi Arabia and other Islamic countries, which had refused to recognize Bangladesh until the assassination of Mujib, now made aid available to madrasas, Islamic NGOs, and educational institutions in order to spread Islamic values. Against this backdrop, new Islamic NGOs emerged, such as Chattragram-al-Jamiya-Islamia, Jamaat-al-Sabah, Rabit-al-Islam, Islam Prochar Samity, Masjid Samaj, and Dakheli Complex. Existing Islamic organizations again became active and expanded their influence, supporting mobile clinics, medical services, and charities aimed at "well-organized proselytization and welfare work."[14] In tribal areas such as Chittagong, Bandarban, Rangamati, Rajshi and Mymensingh, preaching and vocational training centers, charitable dispensaries, hostels, and self-employment schemes were established. Local funds were mobilized via local contributions through *zakat* (charitable giving), the sale of books, and other local donations, although international donors still constituted a major source of funding.

This period also saw increased efforts in education and research aimed at fostering Islamic intellectual leadership, through organizations like the Islamic Research Bureau. Islamic foundations allocated increasingly large budgets to training imams in health care management, agricultural extension, scholarships, and youth vocational training. In 1980, the Saudi Arabian ambassador was the guest of honor at an Islamic conference on economics held in Bangladesh.[15] The ideological orientation of the conference participants strongly diverged from that of the progressive, secular, and liberal intellectuals who held prominent leadership positions. Islamic conference proceedings were critical of the rhetoric and ideology of mainstream development organizations, and condemned "Western" development programs outright. Participants denounced the Western notion of equality between the sexes, and decried the attention given to women by "so-called progressive intellectuals." They believed that equality of the sexes would lead to the collapse of the moral fabric of society.[16]

Despite the availability of state patronage and foreign funds, the growth of Islamic NGOs was slow and practically insignificant. Programs lacked continuity and management expertise, financial assistance from Islamic countries was irregular, and Islamic donors did not show much interest in NGO development. Most Western donors and their local counterparts neither provided assistance to Islamic NGO programs nor advocated categorizing them as NGOs. However, at the local and national levels, Islamic NGOs were far more successful than others in utilizing existing social institutions such as mosques, Samaj, and philanthropic practices to develop their programs. Despite their low levels of resources and organizational development, Islamic NGOs developed social networks that enabled them to emerge as a powerful constituency with which both the state and other NGOs would eventually have to reckon.

The state's response to the increasing activity of Islamic groups was inconsistent. It encouraged Islamic institutions and bowed to their pressures, curtailing women's education by excluding them from madrasas, the Islamic Center for Vocational Training, and the Islamic University. On the other hand, the state implicitly endorsed the "women in development" (WID) concept promulgated by NGOs and the secular international donor community by providing greater opportunities for women in its programs and modifying its policies to encourage women's involvement in previously restricted areas of the public sector.[17]

NGO interest in human rights grew, partly due to initiatives taken by church-based organizations in the 1970s. On June 12, 1974, the Catholic Bishops Conference (CBCB) established a national commission in Bangladesh, also known as the Bangladesh Commission of Human Rights (BCHR). BCHR, in turn, created the Bangladesh Inter-Religious Council for Peace and Justice (BICPJ) and the Commission for Peace and Justice (CPJ). Over 35 NGOs became members of BCHR, and Father Timm was appointed as its convener. BICPJ was formed to promote dialogue between Christians and Muslims. It sought to address human rights issues through "non-violent reconciliation."

Inspired by new ideas of the church's role in social change, the commission developed a comprehensive framework for NGO intervention focusing on the relationship between human rights, freedom, and economic inequalities. Particular emphasis was given to land reform, peasant grievances, and human rights violations in the tribal communities in Bangladesh. After three years of meetings and organization by the BCHR and Caritas, the Coordinating Council of Human Rights in Bangladesh (CCHRB) was established in 1986. It registered as an official organization with the Department of Social Welfare in 1989, becoming a crucial national forum for groups to advocate for rights that had hitherto been pursued by individuals, student associations, and political parties. Amnesty International's Bangladesh chapter, the Institute for Democratic Rights, and several other groups began to consult with each other. Initially, the commission functioned under the umbrella of the Bangladesh Society for the Enforcement of Human Rights (BSEHR), founded by the barrister Sigma Huda. CCHRB differed from the BSEHR in terms of its integrated approach to human rights, its concern with economic, political, and social equality, and its more active intervention in the arena of human rights for tribal and minority groups. Through CCHRB, Bangladeshi human rights groups became more active participants in international fora.

During the political crisis under the Ershad government, NGOs documented human rights violations by the government and monitored elections. Human rights work became politically sensitive, however, especially since some activists coming forward were women. For example, Kazi Montu, the brother of state minister Kazi Feroz Rashid, allegedly used his private army (known as the "U.S. Army" or Upazila Special Army) for rape, arson, looting, forced collection of funds, and attacks against Awami League supporters, minority Christians, and Hindus. CCHRB conducted detailed surveys, and their advocacy efforts led to a detention order against Kazi Montu, who fled to India. Another debate over the relationship between politics and human rights activism centered on Nazmul Huda, the secretary general of the BSEHR, and Zafrullah Chowdhury, then chairman of the ADAB, who was linked with the Ershad government. The infiltration of NGOs by mainstream political parties was evident when Chowdhury was expelled from the ADAB. His expulsion was a politically motivated act by NGO leaders who used their organizations to make alliances with political parties. Several NGOs and the leaders of human rights groups objected to the use of human rights advocacy as a political instrument, but NGOs could not prevent their criticisms of incumbent political parties from being used by opposition parties.

On December 12, 1978, the government enacted the Foreign Donations (Voluntary Activities) Act. Its stated purpose was to control the flow of foreign funds into the country. NGOs were expected to register with an authority and submit a declaration showing the amount and sources of funding and the purposes for which funds were intended. Some NGOs claimed that the Act was intended to prevent funds from getting into the hands of groups aiming to destabilize the regime. Others argued that the bureaucracy had pressured the government to give them greater control over NGO activities. NGOs involved in legal aid programs pointed out that they were being protested against by union chairmen who were unfairly administering the Enemy Property Law of 1965, "applying it indiscriminately against all minorities, whether religious or ethnic,"[18] and who had a vested political interest in shutting them down.

On December 24, 1982, General Ershad seized power, dismissed the president, suspended the constitution and declared martial law. Ershad, too, inherited a stagnant economy and faced a reduced flow of external resources due to donor dissatisfaction with the mismanagement of the economy. However, as a result of Zia's efforts, the potential opposition to the regime from the military and the bureaucracy had subsided and many of the institutional prerequisites for the consolidation of Ershad's power bases were already in place, and he soon established a military government.[19] Ershad had no qualms about supporting Islamization and market-oriented economic reforms, partly because Zia had already created favorable conditions for them. Initially, his policies received the broad endorsement of the World Bank and bilateral donors. In June 1982, the New Economic Policy (NEP) was introduced, calling for broad-based privatization and limiting the public sector to six strategic industries.

The business elite and the World Bank liked the policies, but they met opposition from students, middle-class intellectuals, unions, and powerful members of the bureaucracy.[20] Although protests were muted under martial law, the government was forced to move cautiously with privatization and introduced a series of populist programs to appease the masses. By 1985, the momentum of the NEP had declined, and in 1986 the government negotiated the Revised Industrial Policy (RIP) with the World Bank. This allowed the government to retain 49 percent of the shares in the public sector in order to placate the unions, while 15 percent were allocated to employers. Despite these efforts, RIP failed to create a favorable environment for economic reforms. Marginal improvements in the garment industry, in shrimp cultivation, and in chemical fertilizer production were made, but the overall economy failed to produce the projected results.

Administration at the district level underpinned the state apparatus in both British India and United Pakistan. In November 1982, an administrative reform changed the names of the 460 districts and subdivisions from *thanas* to upazilas. The people were allowed to elect the chairmen of the upazilas and the members of *parishads* (council of upazilas), removing these powerful positions from the unelected civil servants who had previously held them.[21] Conflicts of interest made it difficult for the government to implement its programs, and the increasing power of elected representatives politicized the allocation of state resources, extending political parties' control over rural populations.[22] Competition for resources and power at the local level undermined the ability of any central authority to exert direct control over local affairs through local intermediaries.

Ershad's intention was to present himself as the sole champion of Islam, and thereby to isolate Islamic political parties and interest groups who might have threatened his power. When Jamaat-I-Islami joined a seven-party alliance opposing the regime, Ershad accused them of misinterpreting the Quran to suit their own purposes, claiming they were acting against the interests of Bangladesh and Islam.[23] In a 1983 meeting of Islamic scholars, Ershad declared: "The place of Islam as a religion will be maintained above all in the Constitution of the country. Our struggle is to fight against all enemies of Islam and turn Bangladesh into an Islamic state."[24] This was followed by a proposal to read the Quran at Martyrs' Day celebrations. Both proposals drew widespread opposition from students, civil rights groups, and lawyers, but the opposition eventually withdrew. There is no evidence that the ADAB or mainstream NGOs, with the exception of some organizations concerned with women's issues, took part in the protests.

By 1987, the regime was not only internally fragmented but also growing isolated from the military and the bureaucracy. Under new pressure to resign, Ershad set out to please the military and international donors, speeding up the privatization process and in 1987 introducing the National Investigation and Coordination Agency Bill in the *Sangsad* (parliament) in order to broaden the military's constitutional role in the administration. The bill was withdrawn in the face of opposition from members of parliament, but another was passed instead giving military officers non-voting membership in the parishads and entrusting officers with considerable administrative authority. The government accelerated its efforts to transfer the functions of distribution and the sale of agricultural products from the Bangladesh Agriculture Development Corporation (BADC) to the private sector. It passed a budget for the 1987–88 fiscal year including unusually high taxes, proposed withdrawing all subsidies from agricultural products, doubled tuition fees for public educational institutions, and introduced fees for outdoor patients at the *upazila*-level hospitals. It even attempted to transfer the distribution authority of *Khas* (government land) to NGOs.

In 1988, Ershad resigned in the face of mounting pressure but he was re-elected for a second term in the elections that established a civilian government. Immediately afterwards, he introduced the Eighth Amendment to the constitution, declaring Islam the state religion while adding the caveat that "other religions may be practiced in peace and harmony in the Republic." Although it was a signatory of the World Action Plan of the Declaration of Women, the Bangladesh government refused to ratify certain clauses relating to the inheritance, marriage, and divorce of Muslim women on the grounds that they conflicted with Islamic law.[25] At the same time, the state used the WID language in its public declarations, promising increased opportunities for women's participation in social development, and refrained from condemning women's participation in NGO programs. In 1978, mandatory women's wings were created in every government department, although they were subcommittees in various ministries rather than "pressure groups on party decision-making bodies."[26] In 1983, the Union

Parishad (UP) stipulated that Unionist councils would consist of nine elected members, including three nominated female members.[27]

Along with the participation of women in NGO programs, the number of women employed in the garment industry also increased significantly. Local factory owners who were closely associated with the regime were supportive of Islamization policies. Others without direct party affiliation expected the government to create the institutional conditions necessary for uninterrupted manufacturing. Women were recruited from rural as well as urban areas. Rural recruitment was assisted by intermediaries who often maintained close relations with local authorities, and the process was highly politicized. Local authorities did not appear to prevent women from migrating to the cities for employment, nor was there organized protest from Islamic fundamentalist parties against women's participation in the garment industry. The difficulties encountered by women and children in the garment factories did not receive significant attention from mainstream NGOs. Some, despite requests by donors from Scandinavia, refused to intervene, confining themselves to reporting conditions to donors. Ershad had been encouraged to incorporate women in the economic and political spheres by the state's dependence on foreign aid, the emergence of the garment sector, and the influence and pressure of international organizations, but when garment factory owners emerged as an important social class with influential transnational networks, neither the government nor NGOs were inclined to act against their interests.

Ershad's regime authored the New Drug Policy (NDP) in 1982 and the New Health Policy (NHP) in 1990. The NDP reduced the number of essential drugs that could be manufactured, sold, or imported, and specified new standards for dosage levels and prescriptions. It was intended to address problems in "the patterns of pharmaceutical consumption," including improper prescription and information, poor labeling, conflicts of interest due to connections between physicians and pharmacies, as well as drug costs and distribution problems. Dr. Zafrullah Chowdhury, chief executive of Gonoshasthaya Pharmaceuticals (GPL), head of the NGO Health for All, and chairman of ADAB, played an important role in formulating the NDP and ensuring that the order applied World Health Organization (WHO) guidelines. One of the NDP's prime targets was the Bangladesh Shilpa Samity (BASS), which represented the interests of eight multinational companies and at least three larger local producers. The NDP was supported by NGOs and health activists in Europe, India, Canada, and the US, as well as organizations such as WHO, Oxfam, Health Action International, War on Want, and the Public Citizens' Health Research Group, which argued that the plan would address the needs of the poor. NGOs played an important role in mobilizing support for Ershad's NDP, and Ershad received an international award for his contribution to population policies in Bangladesh.

Though it was popular internationally, the NDP sparked strong resistance from the Bangladeshi manufacturers who dominated the industry.[28] Both domestic and international pharmaceutical firms argued that NDP "would discourage foreign investors," and claimed it would end pharmaceutical production in Bangladesh.[29] Multinational corporations exerted pressure on foreign governments—American, German, and British—to intervene while pressuring Bangladesh to abandon the NHP. The ambassadors of these countries applied enough pressure to force Ershad into consultation with the drug industry. Though the NDP was not withdrawn, the government soon made concessions, including "bringing some banned products back on the market, extending the time periods for implementation, introducing an appeals process, and altering the list of allowed products."[30] Commenting on US policy toward Bangladesh, the American public health activist Sydney Wolf said:

Imagine the outrage of the U.S. public if a foreign government asked us to delay implementing a health protecting decision by our Food and Drug Administration or Environmental Protection Agency. Moreover, it is rather naive to ignore that Bangladesh is a U.S. aid recipient and that a hope expressed by our State is perceived as a threat, veiled or unexpressed though it may be.[31]

Ershad's health policy reforms continued to draw loud protests from the Bangladesh Medical Association (BMA) which had previously opposed the NDP. The BMA presented the NHP as "anti-people," claiming that it would lead a flourishing industry "toward extinction."[32] Local media called the NHP a "neo-colonial plot hatched by the GPL, Oxfam, foreign NGOs, and the Christian churches."[33] Industry representatives criticized a small group of pro-NHP reform doctors as "anti-capitalist and anti-multinational" and claimed that Chowdhury received foreign funds to promote his company and sabotage the rest of the industry.[34] Violent protests were staged against the GPL, and Shamsul Alam Khan Milon, the joint secretary of the BMA, was killed. Ultimately, the pressures placed on Ershad as a result of his health reform policies contributed to the downfall of his government, and one of the first acts of the interim government was to overturn the NHP.

Initial attempts to wholly sabotage the 1982 drug policy failed because Ershad received massive international support, its opponents failed to build a strong base at either the local or international level, and the response of most local doctors was ambivalent. Some aspects of the NDP were implemented, and the debate surrounding it continued through the early 1990s. In 1991, a review committee comprised exclusively of industry personnel was formed to investigate the allegations made against the Gonosasthaya Kendray (GK), the GPL, and the Bangladesh Association of Voluntary Sterilization. Meanwhile, Chowdhury's memberships in the Drug Control Committee and the Drug Pricing Committee were canceled. Kochenek describes this crucial drug debate as a battle between multinationals and a new force—international NGOs— each with its own coalition of supporters and agendas.[35]

When Ershad came to power, the economic growth rate was 3.5 percent. It increased to 4.2 percent in 1986, and dropped to 2.5 percent in 1989. Employment in the formal sector dropped from 39.7 percent in 1984–1985 and then to 9.6 percent in 1989–1990. During the same period, informal sector employment increased from 60.3 percent to 90.4 percent. The population living below the poverty line shrank marginally from 67.3 percent in 1981–1982 to 51.3 percent in 1988–1989. The agricultural real hourly wage rate dropped from 3.60 Tk in 1987 to 3.29 Tk in 1990, while total unemployment increased from 11.09 million in 1978–1980 to 11.75 million in 1989–1990. Against this backdrop, the government became increasingly unpopular and authoritarian, despite establishing populist programs. The majority of NGOs, especially those who were prominent members of ADAB, collaborated with the government, which used them both as subcontractors and as direct agents of government-sponsored schemes.[36] In 1990, the Palli Karma-Sahayak Foundation was established with government assistance to provide financial resources for NGOs, particularly those involved in microcredit programs, but Ershad was also Islamizing state–society relations and Islamic groups were increasingly adopting an adversarial position towards NGOs.

Ershad resigned for the last time on December 6, 1990, and Chief Justice Shahabuddin Ahmed of the Bangladesh Supreme Court was appointed as interim leader. The BNP government was elected in

1991, led by Begum Kaleda Zia, widow of Sheikh Mujibur Rahman. The debate over NGOs grew heated, and their liberal agendas raised questions. What should be their level of political involvement? After Ershad was ousted, political parties and NGOs met to discuss the matter. In 1991, NGOs undertook a project commissioned by the caretaker government to research the ways in which political processes could be articulated in service of national interests, leading to the formation of the Bangladesh Mukto Nirbacon Andalon (BAMNA), a Dhaka-based NGO consortium charged with monitoring elections. Joe Devine commented, "Although there was an inevitable sense of envy that NGOs had organized such a significant constituency, it was the fact that these constituencies could be deployed or mobilized in different areas which worried most political parties."[37]

In the Union Parishad (local) elections in 1992, a number of NGOs, such as Gono Shahajo Sanstha (GSS), presented members as candidates. Members of the Grameen Bank followed suit without the knowledge of the organization's leaders. Local elites did not welcome this development. GSS members were attacked and their buildings destroyed. Local government officials endorsed the repressive measures: "When the poor get uppity and want to sit on the head of the rich, when they want to dominate, that cannot be allowed."[38] Such events were not widespread since most NGOs tried to avoid direct involvement in politics, but their activities inevitably exacerbated political tensions.

The microcredit groups organized by NGOs were similarly divided along party lines, and political pressure was effectively used in allocating credit and enforcing repayments. At the village level, partly in response to increasing pressure to repay loans, credit-based NGOs were identified as BNP. Those that gave credit on easier terms were known as allies of the Awami League (AL). No systematic evaluation of the relationship between NGOs and political parties emerged, and divisions sharpened within the NGO community. As a result, smaller NGOs and their donors withdrew from direct interventions in the political process which might have jeopardized their members and activities.

During this period, NGOs grew both in numbers and in scope. New strategies and the availability of international funds led to greater diversification of their activities. In the process, larger NGOs, such as BRAC, PROSHIKA, and Grameen, expanded to develop "miniature governments" where they established a "cell," "department," or "unit" to cover areas like sustainable development, civil society, women and development, and children's rights. Those who left an NGO because of ideological differences simply established new NGOs. Reorganization was encouraged and supported by international donors. According to one observer, over 35 BRAC employees established new NGOs.[39] Ideological differences and personality conflicts crystallized within new organizations in proportion to the availability of international aid, which often increases divisions among NGOs, lessening their bargaining power with the government and diminishing their credibility. The tendency towards thematic and organizational diversification was countered by increasing homogenization through the adoption of common professional and organizational standards dictated by donors along lines similar to those structuring the private sector. Organizations that could not adopt international standards were left out of the competition.

NGOs that focused exclusively on women's interests now moved from the margins to the center.[40] These organizations were started by the urban middle-class intelligentsia as part of the international network of women's organizations. Their programs brought women's issues, such as male violence, dowry, polygamy, inheritance laws, and land rights, into the national and international spotlight. The attention put international pressure on the Bangladeshi government to take action. Women's organizations were at the forefront of protests against state policies that supported the interests of fundamentalist groups. For example, Naripokko, Rupantro, and Nari Shonghoti were opposed to the state's attempts to mix religion and politics in ways that strengthened the interests of fundamentalists by authorizing them to police women's behavior.[41] In 1987, Oikobaddho Nari Samaj, a coalition of 14 like-minded NGOs, demanded a 17-point program to implement policies promoting equal rights for women.[42] Women's activism did not, however, draw the support of most mainstream NGOs, although they, too, were negatively affected by fundamentalism. Instead, support for the anti-fundamentalist crusade was offered by university students, lawyers, and citizen watch groups which were not active members of ADAB.

After 1983, ADAB was a unified representative body responding to pressure from international donors. The growing presence of transnational NGO networks and their increasing participation in national and international fora once dominated by the state required the formation of a new network linking the government and NGOs. Tensions rose as smaller NGOs grew suspicious of the ADAB coalition, viewing it as an attempt by larger NGOs to dominate the entire NGO community.[43] The director of ADAB, Dr. Samsul Huda, anonymously published a booklet criticizing smaller NGOs, leading to a censure motion being passed by ADAB. Smaller NGOs pointed out that an autonomous ADAB could lead to more government control over NGO activities, since the leadership of ADAB was not politically neutral.

Donors were dissatisfied with the government's handling of relief aid for flood victims in 1987 and 1988, and insisted that NGOs implement relief programs. In February 1988, high-level representatives, including the American ambassador and the Canadian and British high commissioners, met with President Ershad to express their concern about "the deteriorating state of response to NGOs, [and] the negative effects this was having on donor governments' views of Bangladesh."[44] Pressured by international donors, the president held two meetings with NGOs to discuss their problems, attended by bureaucrats, NGOs, and donor representatives. He listened carefully, indicating that bureaucrats failed to inform him about the problems faced by NGOs: "I must admit that your initiatives are immensely commendable ... My efforts alone are not adequate. Hence, I want you to stand beside me. I promise to you, steps would be taken."[45]

In 1989, ADAB elected its executive committee, which included Chowdhury as its chairman and Dr. Azizur Rhaman, Minister of Health and Family Planning, as a member. In the same year, a group of NGOs approached international donors requesting the relaxation of government oversight over their projects. (Out of 109 proposed projects that year, 91 remained unapproved after 75 days, and six remained unapproved for over a year.[46]) In 1990, the NGO Affairs Bureau was established after NGOs and donors requested a separate agency outside the Ministry of Social Welfare (pre-1978), the External Resource Division (pre-1988), and the Cabinet Division (pre-1990). Among the concessions to NGOs was approval of relief projects within 24 hours.[47] Segments of the bureaucracy and the Department of Social Welfare, under which all the voluntary agencies were registered prior to the NGO Affairs Bureau, expressed disapproval.

During Ershad's rule, NGOs began drawing criticism from the public, Islamic interest groups, academics, and the media.[48] Even NGO sympathizers, such as Atiur Rahman, of the Bangladesh Institute for Development Studies, saw that, despite evidence of some success, NGOs had not employed an alternative development model, but were entirely dependent upon foreign funds.[49] The state was equally successful in areas where NGOs claimed to have an advantage, and NGOs were criticized as being mere government appendages.[50]

Left-wing intellectuals and political parties argued that, despite NGO advocacy for people's participation in democratic politics as a necessary condition for social transformation, they failed to directly advocate an agenda for political change through mass movements or to encourage their members to align with political parties.[51] Instead, by appropriating the language of "radicalism," they reduced participation in radical political activities.[52] Most critics contended that NGOs aided the interests of the ruling party, since NGOs and the state were supported by the same donors.

By the late 1980s, when democratic movements against Ershad gained momentum and violent protests became widespread, NGOs were high-profile targets. Protesters attacked the Dhaka office of Gonoshasthaya Pharmaceutical and vandalized 16 vehicles belonging to CARE and the BRAC office in Mahakhali. The democratic movement regarded NGOs as Ershad's allies, and ADAB feared isolation and public rejection. On December 3, 1990, ADAB called a private meeting to discuss matters. Chowdhury, the chairman, was not invited. (He believed that he had been excluded because he was too closely allied with the government.) A statement in support of democracy was drafted at this meeting, and a follow-up was scheduled for that evening, attended by Qazi Faruque Ahmed (Proshika), Dr. Huda (ADAB), Ms. Sandra Kabeer of the Bangladesh Women's Coalition, Mr. Atiur Rahman of Gono Unnyan Procheshta, Jeffery Pereira (Caritas), and Shushanto Adhikari (CCDB). Chowdhury was presented with the statement signed by just seven members on behalf of 58 NGOs, and he refused to sign the document without revisions. After his signature was added, the document was released to the press. According to Chowdhury, the ADAB committee was "well aware of the opposition party's assessment of them as imperialist agents keeping the Ershad government going. This fear, in combination with political ambitions of others, promoted the eleventh hour move in declaring support for the movement."[53]

On December 6, the *Morning Sun* reported that all donor agencies in Bangladesh had suspended their work until the restoration of normalcy. ADAB set up a fund to help victims of the campaign to oust Ershad, and some members contributed a day's salary.[54] On December 13, ADAB met to discuss disciplinary action against Chowdhury, who was advised not to attend by the members of the executive committee due to a possible assassination attempt. The ADAB office was surrounded by student protesters who gathered to prevent Chowdhury's arrival. Following hours of deliberation, both Chowdhury and Rahman were expelled from ADAB. The event was widely publicized in the newspapers. On December 8, the headline in the *Morning Sun* read: "ADAB to take action against Ershad lackeys." The *Bangladeshi Observer* wrote that the ADAB has passed a "no-confidence motion against Chowdhury for his 'anti-people role'."[55]

These events brought some NGOs abruptly into the political arena. Thereafter they received constant public attention. ADAB was increasingly considered a political entity rather than an organization serving the interests of its members, which heightened tensions between ADAB and other NGOs. Some members withdrew from ADAB, while others ceased to play an active role, pointing out that ADAB's identification with Ershad's regime and its poor public image would jeopardize their ability to maintain good relations with the new government.[56]

Although the ousting of Chowdhury was an isolated incident, it exposed a part of the NGO world that had been hidden from the public eye. The leaders of mainstream NGOs generally maintained close relations with the government and political parties. Yet, when their political allies ran into a legitimacy crisis, they tried to distance themselves. The expulsion of Chowdhury and the entry of NGOs into the "popular movement" against Ershad marked a convergence of interests between donors, multinational corporations, and NGOs, all of whom were opposed to Ershad. Popular movements were successful not because NGO constituencies mobilized, but because Ershad's government was discredited internationally. Neither the democratic movement nor NGO-led protests against the Ershad regime resulted in the election of a more NGO-friendly government. Despite the rhetoric of democracy, the BNP, which came into power in 1991 under the leadership of Begum Khaleda Zia, adopted more restrictive policies towards NGOs than its predecessor.

Zia's 1991 BNP election campaign called for democracy, nationalism, Islam, and social justice. People supported her for different reasons. Owners and managers in the garment industry tended to believe that democracy meant less government restriction and more government investment in infrastructure, such as roads and communications. They firmly believed that Bangladesh was an Islamic country and needed to be protected from non-Islamic influences. All of them categorically disliked the Jamaat-I-Islami and regarded them as Pakistani collaborators, but they did not take the organization seriously because it had no power in Bangladesh. At the village level, both landlords and peasants wanted the government to increase subsidies for food, health, fertilizers, and other agricultural inputs. The urban salaried middle classes objected to Ershad's government mainly because it cut subsidies and increased prices. Public-sector workers felt that the BNP would not try to privatize government industries. Everyone at the village level hoped that peace would follow Ershad's removal from power. Neither peasants nor landlords brought up Islam or nationalism as an important consideration in their preference for the BNP.

The BNP government turned out to be the longest-lasting civilian regime since independence, with the broadest scope for democratic politics, showing even greater commitment than Ershad in adhering to the economic policies recommended by the World Bank and IMF. Although the BNP met some of the targets set by international donors, it failed to produce the anticipated macroeconomic performance. Under the BNP, the growth rate of the economy declined from 6.6 percent in 1989–90 to 4.6 percent in 1993–94. The agricultural sector also showed no appreciable improvement, and there was an absolute decline in crop production of 2 percent. Rice production stagnated at a growth rate of around 37 percent per annum, partly due to the slowdown in the use of chemical fertilizers, irrigation expansion, and the reduction of farmer incentives. Agricultural daily wages declined steadily from 21.19 Tk in 1980 to 17.44 in 1994, which correlated with an increase in rural poverty in 1993–94. Between 1988 and 1995, the landless increased from 46 percent to 49.6 percent of the total population, with a growth rate of 3.8 percent.[57]

The small-scale and cottage segment of the manufacturing sector, which accounted for the greatest share of employment, also stagnated. Expansion of employment in the non-agricultural sector declined to 0.3 percent in 1994 compared to agriculture's 3.3 percent in 1989. The participation of men in the labor force decreased from 86 percent to 82 percent (women's share increased from 7.4 percent to 11.2 percent). Government's poverty alleviation efforts declined. Total food grains distributed dropped from 789,000 metric tons in 1991 to 706,000 in 1994, while, during the same period, the number of beneficiaries of these programs declined from 600,000 to 400,000.

Only the export-oriented textile and garment sectors showed reasonable improvement, and became the leading exporters and sources of domestic income. Those involved benefited from open economic policies and brought a new dynamism to the political equation. The immediate interests of this class were different from those of the bureaucrats, the military, and politicians. Nonetheless, they were dependent on the bureaucracy to find solutions to their particular problems, and thus became major players in the political arena, influencing the economic policies of the state and patronizing its political parties. They emerged as new and powerful patrons in the religious, social, cultural, and political spheres.

Approximately $60 million was donated yearly by individuals and businesses to local charitable and philanthropic activities, mostly in the form of zakat. The government established the Zakat Fund in 1982, under the Zakat Ordinance, which allocates the largest percentage of funds to the Prime Minister's Relief Fund and smaller amounts to local charities. Allocations are managed directly by donors. Only in exceptional situations, like the Aga Khan Foundation's financial contributions to BRAC, have NGOs been able to mobilize resources from the corporate sector. Private donors are generally interested in receiving credit for donations directly rather than through intermediary agencies. Interviews with representatives of over 20 donor companies indicated that they are concerned with NGO transparency and accountability, and prefer to maintain their autonomy while avoiding association with the "politics" of NGOs. Within the corporate sector, it is commonly believed that NGO staff are "'fat cats': they get too much money, have too high overheads and too high lifestyles."[58]

The BNP did not introduce new policies to promote Islamization, but it also did not roll back the advances made by Islam under the previous regime. It complied with the demands of Islamic parties and used religious symbolism as its chief means of political mobilization. During the parliamentary elections of February 1991, one observer noted that the election was perhaps unique in that all contesting political parties used "religious symbols, sentiments or apparels to win over voters."[59] In the 1986 elections, Jamaat-I-Islami had won only ten seats, but by 1991 it held 18. Following a negotiation with the BNP, it was given two of the 30 seats allocated to women. These two seats became crucial for forming the government and both the BNP and the opposition sought Jamaat's support. On December 1991, Jamaat announced the appointment of Ghulam Azam as *Amir* (chief) of the party. The violence that followed the increase of communal tensions was mainly attributed to Jamaat and the Islamic Shashantantrik Andolon (Islamic Constitutional Movement). There were many *fatwas,* religious edicts that allegedly gave permission for Muslims to commit acts otherwise illegal under Islamic law, like murder, and calls for restrictions on women's participation in the public sphere.

An important development under BNP rule was the increasing influence of the "new business" elites who were the products of government liberal economic reforms. The Federation of the Bangladesh Chamber of Commerce and Industry (FBCCI) represented their interests. During the BNP regime, the FBCCI was openly critical of the government's inability to improve conditions for the private sector, and attributed slow growth in industry to poor government planning and decision making. When the BNP attempted to end political instability in 1996, the business community and the FBCCI directly intervened to bring about a settlement, leading to a controversy in which business leaders were accused of "attempting to become the king makers of Bangladesh politics."[60] Although the first attempt by the FBCCI to bring a political settlement failed, the Bangladesh Garment and Export Manufacturers Association issued ultimatums, and the FBCCI called for the formation of a citizens' committee and a public rally. A broad segment of dissident groups supported them, leading the BNP to hold elections on June 12, 1996. Several prominent NGOs made public statements against the ruling party and even openly supported the Awami League, as they had during the collapse of the Ershad regime. However, the majority of the NGOs refrained from participating in political protests.

Microcredit became the central focus of the majority of NGOs in the 1990s, and their activities often strengthened rather than destabilized existing power relations. The emphasis on credit led to an ideological rift within NGOs, although even those belonging to the "anti-credit" group have been forced to compromise. The Palli Karma-Sahayak Foundation (PKSF), funded by government grants amounting to 750 million Tk, emerged as the main local donor to NGOs. Between 1990 and 1995, it lent 663 million Tk to 133 NGOs. Some donors have proposed that NGOs should establish their own banks, but, except for BRAC, they have not tried to do this, and the government of Bangladesh has not yet approved BRAC's proposal. NGOs initiated large-scale commercial ventures in printing, garments, cellular telephones, and private education, both as a means of creating employment and of reducing dependence on foreign aid.

By 1993, 3.28 million rural households had been granted credit. Of the estimated 7.9 million landless households, NGOs provided credit for 41.5 percent of them. The number of borrowers increased from 1.45 million in 1990–91 to 3.26 million in 1993–94, representing a 126 percent increase. Five NGOs accounted for 95 percent of them; 64 percent were members of the Grameen Bank. NGO lending was concentrated in the non-crop area, which accounted for 76 percent of the credit provided to the rural sector. The unit value of loans has increased, as the rate of growth in credit disbursement is higher than the number of borrowers.[61]

Consortiums developed consisting of bilateral and multilateral donors, for the purpose of regulating funding and monitoring NGOs. They pledged funds for three- to five-year periods, and introduced sophisticated and stringent criteria to manage and evaluate programs. Substantial funds were allocated to improving professional standards of NGOs, with the assistance of international experts and consultants who emphasized quantitative evaluation methods. In 1992, of the total official development aid allocated to Bangladesh, the NGO share was 8 percent or $120 million. Of aid allocated to NGOs, the 30 largest NGOs claimed $96 million (80 percent of the total), while the eight largest together claimed $69 million.[62] In 1993–94, ten leading NGOs controlled about 68 percent of total foreign funds released by the NGO Affairs Bureau (NGOAB). From the donor perspective, large NGOs have the institutional capacity to properly manage loans, and this led to a reduction in the number of smaller organizations.

Smaller NGOs grew apprehensive about donors' preference for larger NGOs,[63] and believed that their own effectiveness was undermined by the competitive approach used by larger NGOs in "selling" their programs to people.[64] These trends increased the financial difficulties for smaller organizations. In Sarkhiria, in the Kulna district, as many as 500 NGOs closed due to lack of funds.[65] In Mudhupur Thana, in the Tangail district, 23 small organizations closed, including clubs and youth organizations. The majority of these were membership organizations relying on local resources and leadership.

International donors began to focus on issues of institutional development, accountability, and transparency. The World Bank and the Asian Development Bank (ADB), once primary targets of NGO criticism, seem to have reconciled their differences with mainstream NGOs, for they now conduct studies on NGO–government relations.[66] The World Bank Report now argues that the roles of NGOs and the government are complementary. It even calls for the reorientation of their respective policies toward each other. The report proposed a task force with representation by ADAB and other NGO networks. It includes a fiscal policy that would provide tax rebates and other incentives to encourage private investments. It also advocates public lotteries for fundraising and recommends that the government consider a "National Development Plan" to fund NGOs.[67]

In 1992, the ADB awarded a subcontract to the Institute for Development Services (IDS) in Melbourne, Australia, to assess the role of NGOs in Bangladesh. A project agreement was signed between the government of Bangladesh and the ADB in order to foster increased involvement from NGOs in the design and implementation of government development projects by improving the institutional environment in which both sectors collaborate.[68] Neither the government nor NGOs were initially enthusiastic about ADB intervention in NGO–government affairs. However, they become more enthusiastic once the Government–NGO Consultative Committee (GNCC) was established on October 17, 1996.[69] A secretariat was also established within the NGOAB. The nature of the relationship between existing donor consortiums and the GNCC remains to be clarified. What is clear is that the same individuals are involved in all consortiums.

The objectives of World Bank–NGO–donor collaboration can be inferred from the attempts of international donors to regulate NGO practices. These are, namely, to ensure that NGOs operate according to a neoliberal economic agenda,[70] a goal that was realized in 1996 when the Bank mobilized Bangladeshi NGOs as its defenders at the microcredit summit. Smaller donors who were likely to have ideological differences with the Bank over development policy were marginalized, and smaller NGOs feared that World Bank efforts would result in the government consolidating control over NGO activities.

The professionalization and systematization of organizational behavior was accomplished in various ways, one of which was the Bangladesh Learning Group on the Participation of NGOs, comprised of academics, researchers, donors, and NGO representatives.[71] A salient feature of such fora was that they were all attended by the same members of the larger NGOs. Smaller NGOs did not take part, and outcomes were not conveyed to them, further reinforcing their hostility and suspicion towards larger NGOs and donors. In 1994, there were approximately 250 consultants in Bangladesh, most of whom were foreign, but the practice of employing local academics drawn from universities and government-sponsored research institutions as consultants and advisors expanded after 1990. Consulting was a lucrative source of income, as locals were paid the same as foreign consultants—an average of $100–300 per day. The majority worked part-time and retained their day jobs. As consultants established relationships with donors, they tended to resign and establish private firms.

The market for consultants is highly competitive and growing due to the professionalization and privatization of knowledge about NGOs. Most academics consulting for NGOs have developed long-term relationships with favorite clients, and the academy has become polarized by ideological and political differences in the NGO world. Academics argue in favor of "their" NGOs, providing local legitimacy to the agendas of international donors. Knowledge produced by local consultants tends to be invoked as evidence of indigenous participation in development projects.

Islamic fundamentalists branded NGOs in general as Christian, Jewish, anti-Islamic, and, therefore, anti-Bangladeshi. Jamaat-I-Islami and Jamiatul Moderesin, in particular, made such claims. A group led by Maulana Mannan sought to ban all NGOs from Bangladesh. Fundamentalists were particularly upset by the increasing economic power of women, viewing NGO programs as a conspiracy to break up the family by undermining *purdah* (the traditional seclusion of women), an institution which forms the basis of patriarchy.[72] They argued that NGOs undermined the dominant role of men in society, and questioned NGO investments in women. Why, for example, did NGOs not provide similar assistance to millions of unemployed men?[73]

In some areas, Islamic groups used fatwas to prevent women from participating in NGO activities. In 1992, there was a series of attacks on the BRAC schools, which offered informal education to women. By then, BRAC had expanded its primary-level schools to approximately 20,000 students, with 80 percent female teachers and 70 percent female students.[74] Out of the nearly 1000 NGOs receiving assistance from foreign donors, only BRAC and the Grameen Bank were made targets of fundamentalist groups. The groups vandalized schools, harassed officers, and destroyed newly planted trees. There were no reports of attacks on Christian NGOs or schools, with the exception of a few isolated incidents that occurred during the 1991 Gulf War. Fundamentalist attacks did not spread throughout the country, and were not sustained. Damaged and burned schools were repaired and rebuilt, and no similar incidents were reported afterward. Meanwhile, women's participation in NGO programs continued to grow.

The United Action Council (UAC), a coalition of 13 Islamic groups, held a rally demanding the enactment of an anti-blasphemy law and government control over NGOs.[75] The government's response was cautious. Officials condemned attacks on NGOs and promised to take action against their perpetrators, but did not explicitly associate them with Islamic political parties. It continued to emphasize its commitment to the improvement of the social, economic, and political status of women both in national and international fora. The *Review of Bangladesh Development* noted in 1995 that more than 325 NGOs were involved in the Non-Formal Primary Education Program. The government included BRAC and 13 other NGOs working in 2,143 centers which gave preference to women learners and teachers.[76]

The debate in the media over fundamentalism was not initiated by NGOs, nor did it emerge as a response to fundamentalist attacks on them. Anti-fundamentalist mainstream newspapers offered limited coverage of antagonism toward NGOs by "objectively explaining the role of NGOs in the development of Bangladesh." Local newspapers brought NGOs to the public's attention in their general coverage on fatwas and other related issues. They covered the revitalization of Jamaat-I-Islami in the political arena, and the opposition to it by professional groups, students, and individual citizens. Mainstream NGOs were on the sidelines of this controversy. Their protests against fundamentalism were limited to program-evaluation reports submitted to donors and the international media, highlighting fundamentalist threats as a major impediment to NGO progress.

As one among many observers noted: "the pro-fundamentalist camp was more organized and motivated in their coverage of NGOs and took a critical position." In contrast, "we rarely found any newspapers which can be categorized as pro-NGO or NGO sympathetic."[77] At the same time, there is little evidence of conflict between Islamic political parties, mullahs, NGOs, or their members. To the contrary, family members of two mullahs were members of Christian NGOs in Madhupur and some family members of NGO workers were members of Jamaat-I-Islami. NGO-assisted micro-enterprises were implemented within the context of existing social and religious networks, which NGOs did not challenge.

With few exceptions, such as GSS and Nijira Kori, NGOs neither directly participated in politics nor provided explicit support to social movements or interest groups advocating land reform, tribal rights, and increased wages, despite their claims to be engaged in social transformation by improving the conditions of the poor. NGOs had no clear policy for interacting with other forms of political mobilization. Microcredit forced NGOs to favor radical oppositional politics in one form or another, or to retreat and adopt a more passive approach to social change. For example, BRAC and Proshika decided in 1992 to neither support nor oppose their members running for public office, some of whom were elected into the Union Parishads.

GSS strategy mobilized rural people into autonomous "village committees," which were then amalgamated into a confederation supporting a people's movement, and GSS has sought to influence the policies of UPs. In the 1992 elections, about 400 GSS members ran for positions in the UP, and over 250 were elected. Nine were elected chairmen. In some cases, elites allied with GSS members who were typically landless and poor. According to Kristen Westergaard, this indicates that powerful elites are trying to reckon with the emergence of the poor as a political force. In some cases, elected GSS members were harassed, and when the GSS chairman refused to offer bribes, he was unable to get wheat from storage for the Food for Work Program. When the GSS threatened to suspend its programs, the government threatened to withdraw its registration. Even when GSS members were elected, they were stymied by lack of cooperation from the administration.

In the 1992 UP elections, Nijira Kori groups put up candidates who formed an alliance with the union chairman and the middle peasants, and some of them won. The reason for the alliance was that the middle peasants and the Nijira Kori members were against the cultivation of shrimp. However, in some cases, NGO members were attacked by local elites. The NGOs responded by suspending their activities in the area. Subsequently, the NGO Affairs Bureau asked the NGOs to resume their programs. The fear of losing members compelled the NGOs to continue the programs.

NGOs faced difficulties due to conflicting donor interests. The World Bank provided credit to private shrimp cultivators through local banks, and the local banks, with the assistance of Caritas, organized shrimp farmers to keep absentee farmers away. A Dutch development agency opposed shrimp cultivation and provided funds for Nijira Kori programs in the same area. In 1990, landless groups organized by Nijira Kori protested shrimp cultivation, and during one of these protests a woman was killed and several others were injured.[78] There was no evidence of negotiations between Caritas and Nijira Kori or between the respective donors on this issue. In such instances, the question of how NGOs and donors respond to new political constituencies is ignored. Donor ambivalence may play a central role in the conflicts between political parties and NGOs.[79]

The Ford Foundation, one of Bangladesh's main donors, provides funding for a wide range of activities. It is also a major donor to Proshika Manobik Unnayan Kendra, which emphasizes advocacy and empowerment in its programs. Although Proshika was clearly directly involved in Bangladesh's political processes, the Ford Foundation explicitly denied this. An inter-office memo from the Ford Foundation's Dhaka office to its New York office stated: "Proshika does not carry on propaganda or otherwise attempt to influence legislation."[80] Political participation poses dilemmas for NGOs, donors and the state. Existing laws give the state leverage in preventing NGOs from engaging in such participation. Most NGOs take the position that involvement in electoral politics creates tensions in their communities. International donors share that view.

Minorities in Bangladesh consist of Hindus, tribals, Bengali Christians and Biharies. Both secular and Islamic versions of Bangladeshi nationalism are based on a notion of a "greater Bengali community." Arguments for citizenship based on non-Bengali identities are typically rejected, impeding the formation and political mobilization of ethnic and religious minority identities. Although it claims to be secular, the government does not acknowledge the presence of *advasis* (indigenous) people in Bangladesh. The Chakma tribals are viewed as traitors and the Garos, indigenous tribals living in the forests of the Mymensingh and Tangail districts, are viewed as Indian immigrants.

The forest is both an economic asset and the home of the Garos people. Protection of the forest is considered to be crucial for the cohesion of their community and their long-term survival. The government, declaring the forest a "national" park, brought it under the control of the Forest Department. Since then, the Garos have lost land due to forced eviction, government land and forestry policies, poverty, and intrusion by Bengalis. At the national level, NGOs are reluctant to get involved in issues concerning tribal and ethnic minorities, primarily because the needs of these groups involve land rights, rights of self-determination, and issues of national identity. The tribal groups, in turn, are extremely suspicious of NGOs, which they perceive as intrusive agents of the government and of the larger Bengali community.

Missionary organizations have been at work in these communities since the seventeenth century. Caritas and CORR began their activities among the Garos before independence. Those organizations are all deeply invested in indigenous education and in raising awareness of the legal rights of tribal communities. As a result of their work, the literacy rate of the Garos is more than twice that of the Bengalis. The Garos' most crucial need is legal aid to settle their land disputes. Ironically, they have been forced to sell much of their land to meet legal costs. In 1979, Caritas established legal aid programs in the Dinajpur, Rajshi, Mymensingh, Jamalpur and Sylhet districts with the objectives of educating people about land values and legal documents, and providing legal assistance in settling land disputes. The program included not only tribal communities but also poor Bengali families. After three years, 228 cases in the Mymensingh district resulted in 1092 families recovering their land. The legal aid program was scheduled to run from 1979 to 1984, but the government stopped it in 1982 without giving any reason. Since then, no NGOs working in the area have initiated any legal aid programs.[81] On a few occasions, the government of Bangladesh responded positively to Garos demands, giving assurances that their land rights and security were guaranteed. However, those guarantees were little more than executive orders, since the government could not "impose its fiat in rural areas dominated by one or two powerful individuals."[82]

The Chakmas are the largest tribe in Bangladesh. They live in the Chittagong Hill Tracts which cover 10 percent of the total land area of the country. The area is located along the borders of Burma and India, and is classified as strategic and closed to foreigners. It is noted for having the highest incidence of human rights violations by the military and by Bengali settlers.[83] The most serious violations in this area are thought to have occurred after the Shanti Bahani began to clash with government forces. NGOs organized a hotline to disseminate information about human rights violations to national authorities and to the international community. Father Timm was honored with the Magsaysay Award for his human rights work with the Catholic church among the Chakma tribal community. He investigated violations against tribal minorities caused by thoughtlessly executed development projects. However, the government, in response to local criticism of Timm's role in the NGO movement, permitted a Filipino scout to enter the country only after the Magsaysay Foundation threatened to cut aid to Bangladesh. Subsequently, the government peacefully ended the conflict.

Organizations such as Proshika have attempted to create social development programs under the rubric of "sustainable development" and "re-forestation," but tribal communities view these programs with suspicion, fearing that they are simply tactics used by the state and non-tribal groups to take control of tribal land. Tribal minorities generally receive positive government attention only when NGOs are successful in generating international pressure. The Bengalization of the church and church-based NGOs has undermined the bargaining power of tribes, and drawn tribal communities into the orbit of the greater Bangladeshi state. Minority Christians are now far less likely to take radical approaches to solving the problems faced by non-Bengali Christians. Church leaders of Bengali origin have also adopted a conformist approach. With the retirement of radical foreign missionaries, such as Father Timm and Father Homrick, tribal communities have found it harder than ever to make their voices heard by the international community. The increasing colonization of traditional tribal land by the Bangladeshi state and the search for employment outside tribal territories further weaken the capacity of NGOs to address the specific needs of the endangered tribal communities.

To understand the tensions between NGO agendas and neoliberal policies, it will be useful to look back on Chowdhury's involvement in ADAB in the early 1990s. At that time, ADAB's association with the Ershad regime drew so much criticism that the NGO coordinating body was forced to dismiss Chowdhury. ADAB's financial management and its capacity to fulfill its promises came into question, following the resignation of six senior staff members and a director who had held his post for twelve years. Program cells were closed, and chapter members were unhappy about the centralized decision-making process. The financial collapse of the ADAB was averted by the PRIP/PACT, a USAID-funded NGO which provided a bridge grant.

In the summer of 1992, tensions peaked between the NGO Affairs Bureau and the ADAB. That was just after the United Nations Conference on Environment and Development in Brazil, a conference which was attended both by representatives from the Bangladeshi government and by NGOs. On July 30, 1992, the Bureau issued a "showcase" letter threatening ADAB with the revocation of its registration for publishing two articles in violation of the Foreign Donations Registration Act of 1978. The NGO

Affairs Bureau submitted a detailed report to the prime minister describing "irregularities" and "corruption" in NGOs and calling them "anti-state and dangerous."[84] The Bureau pointed out that a few NGOs had become dominant under the pretext of representing the entire NGO community and suggested that it was "time to reduce the size of some of the larger NGOs and thereby make more money available to their smaller counterparts."[85] The report incorporated charges made by Islamic groups and the public in general.[86]

In the early 1990s, a "cold war" erupted between the government and NGOs. On August 20, 1992, the NGO Affairs Bureau issued an order canceling the ADAB's license, but the Prime Minister's Secretary canceled the order later that same day. The director of the Bureau was subsequently removed from his post. The government's decision was influenced by pressure from donors: "Strong support for the NGOs was a mixed blessing with some seeing this as further evidence in support of the criticisms."[87] A Ford Foundation memorandum pointed out three reasons for the hostility toward the NGOs. The Bureau had become hostile and "jealous of the leading NGOs' funding, prestige, limelight and perquisites." Secondly, Islamic fundamentalists who were against the more progressive NGOs had joined with the BNP. Third, there was deep antagonism within the NGO community. Against this backdrop, the previously ousted Chowdhury "made a common cause with certain officials and [was] stoking anti-ADAB fires."[88]

In March 1993, the Bureau issued new rules and regulations barring NGOs from engaging in any form of political activity and extending an earlier prohibition that excluded NGOs from entering into political alliances with parties. These new rules increased the power of government officials, solidified control over the NGOs, and prohibited programs that might upset local religious sentiment. The issue was raised by donors at the Paris Donor Consortium, forcing the government to make significant changes in its development policies.[89] On July 27, 1993, the Prime Minister's Secretary issued an amendment to the circular, entitled "Working procedures for foreigners engaged in Bangladesh and foreign aided Bangladeshi Organizations (NGOs)."[90]

An eleven-member committee, headed by the Secretary to the Ministry of Finance, drafted the Bangladesh Voluntary Activities (Regulation) Act in 1993. The Ministry of Social Welfare was actively involved, as were officials of the Directorate of Social Welfare, which oversees voluntary organizations. The latter had recently seen its powers undermined by the NGO Affairs Bureau.

The Act was introduced in order to "consolidate and clarify the provisions of law relating to registration, legal status, operations, function, rights, duties, accountability, and dissolubility of voluntary societies under the provisions of this Act." It identified the laws under which NGOs had operated,[91] and made the Directorate of Social Welfare responsible for registration and regulation.

ADAB opposed the bill, pointing out that it restricted the democratic space for NGOs, decreased democratic pluralism, and increased bureaucratic control, making NGOs vulnerable to "politically motivated officials interfering in the NGO affairs."[92] An urgent memorandum submitted by the ADAB insisted: "Deregulation of bureaucratic control is accepted universally as a principle means of democratization of society and to bring more efficiency and productivity and to lessen opportunity for corruption."[93] The memo continued by asserting that:

NGOs are to be firmly recognized as part of the private sector in development, in this case the non-profit private sector. The arguments in favor of the need for deregulation in the private sector in business and industry should be similarly applicable to the NGO sector.[94]

It rejected the notion that the nonprofit status of NGOs "compromises their private independent status."[95] ADAB chairperson Kushi Faber claimed that greater efforts should be made to "deregulate and liberalize State control" and to create an "enabling environment" so that organizations in civil society could "play a greater role in promoting sustainable development."[96]

As in the past, international donors exerted pressure on the government on behalf of NGOs. The Chargé d'Affaires of the European delegation of the European Commission warned: "Agitation against the activities of the Non-governmental Organizations (NGOs) across the country by the fundamentalist forces might scare the investors, affecting the flow of foreign investments."[97] On April 7, 1994, the government published the draft law in a *Gazette* notification. Several weeks later, the government announced that the publication had been a mistake. A two-member committee was appointed to investigate how it had been released to the press without the approval of the ministry or the parliament. The Act was never adopted, mainly due to donor pressure and other initiatives that shaped relations between the government and NGOs.

In June 1994, an ad hoc coalition was formed by Islamic organizations (including Gambit Islam, Nauseam Islam and Islami Oykojote) and independent intellectuals to "combat NGO atheism and immorality." On July 29, 1994, a march of 100,000 protesters called on the government to reprimand Taslima Nasrin and other "anti-Islamic" writers by passing an anti-blasphemy law. The coalition demanded that NGOs refrain from anti-Islamic activities, that the Qadiani (Ahmadiyya) sect be declared non-Muslim in Bangladesh, and that no foreigners should be allowed to intervene in the internal affairs of the country. Afterwards, there were several protests around the country demanding stricter regulations on NGO activities. The protests were organized largely by religious extremist groups.

In March 1995, a group of NGOs under the umbrella of ADAB planned to organize a rally of landless women. NGO field workers pointed out that neither they nor the people were ready for such an action. They believed that it would have led only to unnecessary conflicts between them and the local authorities. The rally appeared to be the result of decisions taken by a small group of NGOs after the World Summit for Social Development in Copenhagen in 1994. The timing was crucial because NGO donors had criticized organizations for not undertaking follow-up activities after international conferences. The protests were organized to demand the implementation of promises made at the World Summit for Sustainable Development conference to work for poverty alleviation, including promises to provide *kash* (wet and sandy) land to the landless poor and fund the maintenance of forests, water, credit, and healthcare facilities.[98] Despite the NGOs' appeals, the government withheld permission for the rally. Some officials accused NGOs of trying to "fish in troubled waters" at a time when the government was faced with a serious legitimacy crisis caused by rising food prices and fertilizer shortages.[99] Extremist religious groups and right-wing political parties held a rally against NGOs in the same location where the ADAB demonstration took place. Speakers criticized the NGOs for their programs for women, and also criticized BNP MP Farida Rahman for pushing a bill against polygamy and supporting equal inheritance rights for women.[100]

Several salient points should be made about the relationship between NGOs and Islamic groups. The NGOs challenging Islamic institutional authority were not mainstream organizations, nor did they receive assistance from foreign sources, with the exception of a few conservative NGOs that were concerned exclusively with women's issues. According to NGO field workers, the chief reason for the slow progress of NGO activities was a lack of funding for social development programs and increasing pressure, especially on those involved in microcredit, to become financially independent. They also pointed out that the lack of participation among women and children in education programs was not due to fundamentalist protests but to a lack of resources and the unwillingness of international donors to invest in such programs. Nor have NGOs developed an effective strategy for addressing conflicts with Islamic groups.

During the 1996 elections, NGOs and the business community entered political debates actively, playing a role historically taken up by student organizations and those directly patronized by political parties.[101] On March 16, 1996, NGOs and the FBCCI led a citizens' rally which gave a 24-hour ultimatum to the government, demanding that it hand over power to a caretaker government. The rally included groups from different parts of the country, compelled to join the protests by NGO leaders. When asked what they expected to gain, the protesters answered: "If the Awami League comes to power, then the NGOs supporting them will be able to get more money from foreign donors as the BNP government does not release the funds allocated to them by the foreign donors."[102] In other words, the protestors expected to gain more assistance from NGOs.

The BNP responded to a non-cooperation movement of students, professional associations, and political parties by arresting and detaining opposition leaders under the Special Powers Act. The spread of violence and international donor pressure forced the government to cede to the demands of the protesters. Although the NGO community has claimed credit for the collapse of the government, the number of NGOs that participated in the movement was insignificant compared to their overall numbers. The impact of participating NGOs was due mainly to their success in mobilizing the support of the international community. Both the opposition political parties and the NGOs benefited from the government's collapse. The former were able to capture state power, and the latter increased their credibility among international donors as the true defenders of civil society.

Among the ten advisors who were appointed to the caretaker government, two represented NGOs: Dr. Muhammad Yunus and Dr. Najma Chowdhury, both of whom were associated with the Grameen Bank. On March 16, another citizens' rally was organized by Grameen, and it was officially convened by Kazi Faruque and

Salman F. Rahman, of the ADAB and FBCCI respectively. The day after the rally, the press published a letter by F.H. Abed, then executive director of BRAC, to Kazi Faruque, the chairperson of ADAB, arguing that NGOs did not have a legitimate role to play in a political rally. The debate that followed in the press was divided between those who were in favor of NGO participation in politics and those who were opposed to it. The latter argued that NGO members were traitors and CIA agents who squandered funds designated for helping the poor. As a result, divisions between mainstream NGOs widened. Smaller NGOs sought to distance themselves from ADAB.

Another issue on which NGOs were divided was voter education. NGOs who opposed voter education programs argued that such programs treated the entire population as a homogeneous whole, obscuring the gross social and economic inequalities against which NGOs were fighting. Voter education material provided by the ADAB promoted the idea that democracy and good governance would eliminate economic inequalities, but different material was provided by the Multidisciplinary Action Resource Center and Election Commission. The circulation of those materials sparked protest rallies sponsored by the Proshika and Trinamul grassroots movement. The voter education efforts of these groups utilized over 50,000 members of different organizations who formed a human chain. According to Joe Devine, their rallies demonstrated NGO unity regarding NGO participation in politics. As even Abed was forced to concede, "sometimes in the history of a country there arises the occasion when they [NGOs] have to take a political line."[103] If NGOs were to participate in social mobilization, involvement in the political process seemed to be inevitable.

In so far as NGOs are legally regarded as nonparty institutional formations, their efforts will invariably be influenced by political parties. Information provided to voters was clearly biased when it specified criteria for the election of candidates, instructing people not to vote for "terrorists" who were "involved in bribery and corruption," and condemning those who did not fully support the independence struggle. The latter instruction effectively ruled out voting for candidates other than those put forward by the Awami League and Jamaat-I-Islami. The Awami League rewarded members of NGOs involved in voter education with government positions and greater access to state resources.

On September 25, 1996, Rasheda Choudhury, director of the ADAB, resigned in protest. The deputy director, internal auditor, and administrative officer were all subsequently expelled from the executive committee. The main reason for Choudhury's resignation was her belief that the association misunderstood the difference between "advocacy" and "power brokery." She claimed: "ADAB has been involved lately in certain areas of 'power brokery' that may be explosive enough to push the Association into a backward slide."[104] Oxfam also resigned from the ADAB executive committee because of the politicization of ADAB and its exclusion from the decision-making process.

After Sheikh Hasina Wazed was elected to power in 2000, many NGO personnel were given positions in the government. Shamsul Huda, a former banker and bureaucrat in the government's external resource division, was appointed as the director general of the NGOAB. Kushi Kabir, former chairperson of the ADAB and director of Nijira Kori, was appointed as a member of the governing body of the government-owned Sonali Bank. Proshika gained lucrative contracts from the government, which further isolated it from other NGOs. By then, the few "like-minded" people who pioneered NGOs in Bangladesh were sharply divided along the lines of their allegiance with political parties and their views on the role of NGOs in broader political processes. As one observer noted, "in the eyes of the public the larger NGOs have always been political. They survive with the help of the politicians and bureaucrats, however much they criticize them in public."

Throughout the 1990s, the entire political left was absorbed by the NGO sector. Progressives abandoned class-based politics in favor of "empowerment," in which class relations are only one among many oppressive relationships. The advocacy and social mobilizations led by NGOs did not demand redistribution or protest neoliberal reforms. They lacked a coherent ideology or a program to challenge capitalism. Some NGOs relied on mainstream political parties to achieve their goals, and NGOs financed and provided leadership in the competition for state power. That led to the indoctrination of the poor in neoliberal rationality. Ironically, the government undermined the credibility of NGOs by appointing their leaders to influential positions.

The claim that NGOs are facilitating structural change in power relations is seriously misleading. By 2000, most NGOs had moved away from direct investment in empowerment projects, perhaps because they recognized that such projects in fact pay "little or no attention to the oppressive power structures or to the promotion of political participation of the poor."[105] The organizational cultures of NGOs and for-profit organizations remain amorphous. The empowerment projects facilitate individualism, entrepreneurship, and self-reliance to create the necessary conditions for market-led economic reforms. They provide legitimacy for the withdrawal of the state from social development.[106] In the process, these NGOs have contributed to a depoliticization of poverty elimination,[107] and they have shifted the focus of oppositional politics away from neoliberal economic policies. Many expect changes in power relations to have a "trickle-down" effect on commercial enterprises, such as nonprofit businesses, microfinance, and small businesses. The relationship between NGOs, the state, and donors may be best described as antagonistic corporation, and perhaps even "mythic,"[108] as these relationships are "organized through family ties, contracting relationships, and an often overlapping dependence on foreign donors."[109] "NGOs are careful not to challenge the state directly, or especially the strong role of foreign capital in the country."[110] The public in Bangladesh is anxious about the excessive power of NGOs, power which is acquired with the help of foreign donors.[111] Such power in the hands of NGOs generally strengthens the power of corrupt bureaucrats and politicians.

International donor policies facilitate the structural changes necessary for capitalist development, changes that cannot be enacted through state policies. At the same time, they do not diminish the state's capacity to suppress social discontent. The anti-poverty mass social movements[112] organized by NGOs have been sporadic and unfocused. Both the participants and NGOs have failed clearly to define either the target or the ultimate goal of their protests. NGOs brought thousands of poor into the city for protest marches, and microcredit groups and local politicians pressured many to attend them. These movements replaced class-based movements focused on redistribution with a myriad of organizations focused on safeguarding the rights and privileges of their members.[113] When they formed a united front, they lacked a clear political agenda. The only visible outcome of these movements is the transfer of state power from one political party to another. They legitimize competitiveness in international donor markets by discrediting the state's role in social development. Tensions between NGOs and the rest of civil society are not indicative of a radical social mobilization agenda, but are due to competition between NGOs and the government.

International donors have become less receptive to radical social mobilization. In response to the Bangladeshi government's anxiety over the radicalization of mass social movements, international donors instructed Nijira Kori and GSS, two of the largest radical NGOs, to "set aside their radical messages."[114] The GSS was almost driven into bankruptcy by donors concerned with its "radical activities."[115]

The BNP came into power in 2001 as a coalition government with the support of radical Islamic political parties, at a time when everyone was extremely anxious about NGO involvement in anti-government political activities, particularly those associated with ADAB. Despite the assistance given their campaigns by NGOs, party members accused ADAB, which, along with other large NGOs, had directly identified with the Awami League, of malfeasance. Other NGOs had given indirect support to the BNP. The attacks focused on financial irregularities in the NGO sector. Although NGO accountability seems to be a very legitimate concern, it can also be used to rein in NGOs when they are perceived as threatening to state power. Relationships between the government and NGOs can change according to the balance of power between them at any given moment.

The government introduced the Foreign Donations (Voluntary Activities) Regulation (Amendment) Act in 2004. ADAB nearly dissolved because of government backlash, and the government also attempted to restrict funding to Proshika, detaining some of its staff, including its executive director Kazi Faruque. Fear of further restrictions caused NGOs to call a National Convention which resulted in the establishment of the Federation of NGOs in Bangladesh (FNB).[116] FNB was open to influence by any and all political parties, as ADAB had been, depending on the power struggles among its leadership. Suppression of NGO activity continued, and in January 2007, soon after the proclamation of the state of emergency and enforced curfew, the Rapid Action Battalion (RAB) arrested two prominent NGO leaders: Mohamad Abdul Kashem, the principle program coordinator of Proshika, and Mohamad Aminual Islam, the director of ADAB. The high court, however, ordered their immediate release on February 26.[117]

The BNP completed its term on October 28, 2006, amid violent protests. The AL rejected the BNP nominee for the post of Chief Advisor of the caretaker government, and called for a strike to press for an alternate and for electoral reforms. The constitutional mechanism of the Neutral Caretaker Government (NCG) was introduced to monitor, conduct, and supervise elections in a free and fair manner. Agitating political parties, led by the AL, the

BNP, and the Jamaat-I-Islami, issued a joint declaration stating that "the head of the interim caretaker government must be a non-partisan neutral person."[118] The NGO community was divided between the specific positions of the AL and the BNP. The caretaker government was backed by the military. During this period, the activities of radical Islamic NGOs subsided as they came under closer government scrutiny.

Islamic NGOs make use of their education and development programs to promote the view that the fundamental reason for the repeated failures of BNP, AL, and the caretaker government is the moral weakness of politicians who deviate from Islamic principles. The fiscally bankrupt Bangladeshi government simply cannot afford to refuse the resources brought in by Islamic NGOs or to antagonize oil-rich Islamic countries offering employment and financial aid. While Islamic NGO candidates have failed to gain a significant number of seats in parliament, they have successfully reinforced and legitimized Islamic perspectives in the popular mind. Critics of Islamic NGOs have been unable to offer a compelling explanation of the economic and political crises that people face. The ideologies of Islamic groups are thus extraordinarily attractive to a disaffected Bangladeshi public. The widespread failures, corruption, and lack of accountability of NGOs lend credibility to the claims of religious extremists. The same individuals accepting microfinance and NGO assistance interpret the hardships they face according to the anti-NGO rhetoric of Islamic organizations. This is the cultural context in which microfinance programs and NGOs are embedded. Virtually no one defends NGOs against attacks by religious extremists in Bangladesh.

In 1999, intelligence agencies tracked Suffering Humanity International, an NGO with strong links to fascist Islamic elements in Bangladesh. Intelligence reports also recommended banning the Kuwait-based Revival of the Islamic Heritage Society (RIHS), and taking action against other Middle Eastern organizations linked to Islamist extremists.[119] In 2002, the US Department of State blacklisted some RIHS offices, citing their support for Osama bin Laden and Al-Qaeda. On February 17, 2005, Jamaat-ul-Mujahiden (JMB) claimed responsibility for 500 serial bombings in 63 out of 64 districts of Bangladesh. Bangladesh was a logistical hub for transnational groups such as Akrakan Rohingya National Organizations and Rohingya Solidarity Organization, who claimed to be fighting for an Islamic state in Myanmar. Radical groups based in Pakistan and parts of Kashmir, like Lashkar-e-Taiba, had established bases in Bangladesh. In 2005, JMB and Jagrata Muslim Janata Bangladesh (JMJB) were suspected of the attacks, bombings, and vandalism of BRAC and Caritas in Dinajpur and the Grameen Bank branch at Nabagram in the Sirajganj district.[120]

As Muhammad Hussain explained: "The government, including many misguided secular intellectuals of respectability, blamed the opposition Awami League Party or foreign intelligence agencies—CIA, Mossad and RAW (India)—for these attacks." The sheer magnitude of the violence and the pressure from international donors forced the FNB to take action because the violence threatened to escalate beyond national boundaries. Hussain continued: "Hundreds of terrorist cadres were apprehended by the *authorities*; they were all connected to Islamist organizations, including JMJB and Harkat-ul-Jihad; no RAW, MOSAD, CIA and opposition party agents were amongst them."[121] The government banned both JMB and JMJB in February 2005.[122]

A US security delegation comprised of a congressman and military veterans visited Bangladesh in April 2007 to develop the framework for a major conference on homeland security issues, to be held in the country in 2009.[123] The caretaker government was sensitive to the rise in the activities of Islamic NGOs. Its finance minister, A.M.A. Muhith, stated: "There is an international network against terror financing. Bangladesh has not completely become a part of that network." He alleged that most of the NGOs, now under the close scrutiny of government agencies and the Bangladesh Bank, arose during Khaleda Zia's tenure (2001–06), when she shared power with Jamaat-I-Islami and other Islamists. Bangladesh Bank Governor Salehuddin Ahmed said the central bank had intensified monitoring at commercial banks to determine whether or not there was any link between suspicious transactions and militants.[124] The caretaker government was backed by the military, and the military was equally intolerant of both Islamic and human rights NGOs.

While taking steps to restore law and order, the government also curtailed freedom of expression and human rights activism. On February 2, 2007, the military used the Special Powers Act to arrest and detain Mr. Shahidul Islam, executive director of the development NGO Uttaran and a leading human rights defender.[125] On February 23, the government arrested Rang Lai, a member of the Maro tribal community who was also an elected chairperson of the Bandarban District Local Council and the president of the Maro Social Council. Lai was sentenced to 17 years in prison for the possession of illegal arms. Following his arrest, in March 2007 the army announced that

400 indigenous families from Rang Lai's Maro region would have to leave their land for extension gardens.[126] On August 1, 2007, under the supervision of security forces, the caretaker government resumed its raids on the plantations of the Garos, a non-Muslim ethnic minority, in the Modhupur forests, resulting in the destruction of the banana gardens there. NGO advocacy played an important role in defending the rights and improving the social and economic standing of the tribal communities in Bangladesh. At the same time, their interventions also facilitated the penetration of the state's authority into the ancestral territories of the tribal groups and increased its control over their property.

On August 20, 2007, student protests erupted at Dhaka University. They were directed against the military personnel based there. Jahangir Alam Akash, a journalist and human rights activist, was arrested on October 24, 2007, by the paramilitary Rapid Action Battalion. The resulting culture of fear forced NGO activists to retreat from public fora, and the civilian leaders who controlled the caretaker government became extremely impatient in searching for a peaceful and quick way out of the situation. University students and unions had played a far greater role than NGOs in protesting against the actions of the military government.

The largely peaceful general election of December 29, 2008, resulted in an astonishing landslide victory for the AL, led by Sheikh Hasina, over the BNP, led by Begum Khaleda Zia, with a 70 percent voter turnout. Immediately after the election, the AL government moved to strengthen the powers of the NGO bureau. However, the strict oversight of the NGOAB did little to control the activities of larger NGOs which had enormous financial and donor influence. There were also long-standing personal and patron–client relations between NGOAB bureaucrats and the NGOs. In March 2009, Social Welfare Minister Enamul Haque Mostafa Shahid announced the government's intention to form a "National social commission to control the NGOs." The commission would withhold NGO registration pending police authorization. It would also cancel the registrations of any organizations it believed lacked accountability or threatened national security. Critics viewed the commission as no different from the NGOAB, since it was also managed by government officials who used bureaucratic mechanisms to further their particular interests.[127]

Over the past 25 years, Bangladesh has failed to foster efficient collaboration between the government and NGOs. NGOs compete with each other for territory and favors from the government, but are still a strong force because of their sheer financial and political power. Shelly Feldman commented:

> It is equally important to note that the kin networks and class positions that NGO leaders share with those in government and the industrial sector, particularly at the present juncture, give them access to political power in ways that can lead to lobbies for modest reforms that do not reflect the interests and needs of their constituencies.[128]

Feldman does not say that NGOs have also transformed the consciousness of their constituencies, changing their understanding of poverty, empowerment, and democratization to conform to neoliberal thought. NGO counterhegemonic consciousness-raising projects are often the unintended vehicles through which the state reinforces its dominance over society. Such projects prevent people from directly addressing the shortcomings of capitalist development and force them to seek solutions within a capitalist framework.

The number of NGOs in Bangladesh is greater than ever. Despite nearly 20 years of government and NGO attempts to coordinate and collect data, there is still no central source for reliable statistics, largely because registration and monitoring are heavily politicized. In 2009, there were over 78,000 NGOs registered in Bangladesh.[129] In the fiscal year 2007–08, according to NGOAB, a total of 2,235 local and foreign NGOs were receiving international aid. Over 90 percent of these organizations are directly or indirectly dependent on that aid. Total aid to NGOs in Bangladesh rose from an average of $232 million (0.7 percent of GDP) in 1990–95, to $326 million (0.7 percent) in 1996–2004, while total aid to Bangladesh fell from an annual average of $1.62 billion (4.9 percent of GDP) to $1.35 billion (2.9 percent) during this period. Since then, the share of aid to NGOs as a portion of total aid to Bangladesh has risen from 14.4 percent in the first half of the 1990s to 24.5 percent.[130]

NGOs continue to dominate all areas of social development, either independently or in partnership with the private sector and the government. They have started their own schools, universities colleges, and hospitals. These ventures are managed as both nonprofits and for-profit businesses, and the differences between the two are fast disappearing since the organizations are often interdependent. For example, as many as 1.5 million children, approximately 8 percent of all currently enrolled primary students, are in NGO primary schools. Of these, 1.2 million alone are enrolled in BRAC's network of 34,753 non-formal primary schools. Donors encourage NGOs to start private for-profit institutions, replacing government efforts and programs. This is attractive to donors because the privatization of state enterprises and programs by the state would lead to sudden political instability, and the transfer of ownership from the government to the private sector is unlikely to automatically improve its efficiency. BRAC, while still actively encouraging its members to become more politically active, has diverted a large fraction of its activities into so-called income-generating operations, namely nonprofit business, and runs the largest chain of retail shops in the country. NGOs have invested in dairy farms and fisheries, and countless looms and mills for the production of medium-quality garments.[131] Most of the larger NGOs charge fees for their services. "Use fees" represent the most important revenue source for NGOs.[132] The fair trade organizations organized by The Body Shop are struggling for survival. They cannot meet consumer standards and fair trade practices have failed to reconcile the tensions between commercial objectives and social or environmental ones.[133] NGO involvement in businesses has negatively affected their public image, since the shift to for-profit activities is perceived as illegitimate. Donors emphasize developing partnerships between the NGOs, the for-profit sector and the public sector within the context of neoliberal rationality.[134]

International donors also encourage the financing of NGOs through the government budget as a way of building a comprehensive fiscal framework and improving the quality of public policy choices. The government contracts NGOs in almost every area of social development, strengthening mutual interdependence. Subcontracting is also attractive to a bankrupt government, bureaucrats, and NGOs, for it enables them to exploit each other for collective and personal favors. As Lamia Kareem points out, "Through rallies and gatherings, the NGO speaks for the poor—but careful consideration will show that this voice is a voice of the patron—in a patron–client relationship."[135] The relationship is both constitutive of and constituted by the accumulation and legitimization crises of capitalism. NGOs and states are the means through which capitalism manages its crises. The tensions between them result from their mutual failure to provide a long-term solution.

Microfinance is also responsible for the growing presence of NGOs in Bangladesh, reaching as many as 37 percent of all Bangladeshi households and around 60 percent of poor households. The sector is dominated by the Grameen Bank, BRAC, ASA and

Proshika, who between them lend to 76 percent of all borrowers. Microfinance does not simply provide credit. It also provides a tool of empowerment and social mobilization. The popularity of microfinance has forced many organizations to use it as a means of achieving financial self-sufficiency, and the microfinance sector has transformed and subordinated other progressive NGOs. Economically empowering beneficiaries and reaching financial self-sufficiency are considered essential if NGOs are to effect long-lasting social, cultural, and political changes. But, as critics have pointed out, the success of microfinance is based on the very institutions that need to be changed or overthrown in order to empower the poor. Microfinance, in practice, has enabled international donors to resolve the problems of high transaction costs, moral hazard, and collateral issues typical of rural credit markets by removing the structural constraints against the expansion of capital into the rural economy. The techniques used to secure loan repayment and mobilize savings transform the assets of rural poor borrowers into cash and transfer them to wealthier segments of the population.

Just like commercial banks, microfinance agencies focus on financial sustainability. As the competition for the microfinance market continues to grow, the broader goals of reaching and empowering the poorest of the poor have taken a back seat. Microfinance forces the poor to absorb the costs of neoliberal economic reforms and to contribute to economic growth and reduce their reliance on the state for social welfare, education, and health. It also connects rural populations with global centers of capital and makes them vulnerable to changes in the volatile global economy. The Partnership between the Grameen Bank and multinational corporations has allowed the latter to bypass government regulations and penetrate into rural areas. In July 1998, Monsanto offered the Grameen Bank of Bangladesh $150,000 as capital loans for farmers to buy Monsanto's agriculture products and establish a Monsanto-Grameen Centre. Subsequently, Grameen by giving financial incentives, mobilized thousands of poor women to gather in Dhaka, the capital of Bangladesh, to participate in anti-poverty marches. A few years later Mohamad Yunus declared his intentions to run for the office of President of Bangladesh.

Microfinance can also be used to mobilize social movements against the state. However, such mobilizations cannot demand that the state redistribute wealth or invest in the social sector. At most, they can seek to undermine the legitimacy of the state's involvement in social development. Contrary to the empowerment rhetoric, NGO-led social movements are typically funded by international donors, who use NGOs to pressure the state to be responsive to market rationality, and effectively silence social protests against economic injustice. If there is massive default in microfinance programs, as is likely, a serious legitimacy and sustainability crisis for NGOs will ensue. NGOs will be caught between the plight of their borrowers and their own financial survival. In this event, the responsibility of filling the vacuum of social development left by NGOs and their donors will devolve to the state.

Reviewing the social history of NGOs in Bangladesh, we see several important patterns. NGOs did not initially articulate their social development programs along the lines of religion and tradition, nor were religion and tradition a threat to their activities until the state consolidated its power. In the early days of independence, they often adopted radical methods of social change, bordering on socialist policies, especially in the areas of land reform and rural–urban relations. Gradually, the pioneering bloc of NGOs in Bangladesh divided over ideological, personality, and political issues. At that point, they formed new associations and transformed NGOs into highly competitive semi-private organizations, thereby reducing their capacity to act as a unified sector. The radical edge of NGOs was thus blunted as these organizations sought increasingly to function according to the patron–client networks in society at large.

Two seemingly contradictory forces have shaped NGOs in Bangladesh: the tendency towards thematic and organizational diversity; and the homogenization of NGO activities due to the standardization of organizational practices in accordance with neoliberal rationality. The latter is the dominant factor, as NGOs, donors, and governments are increasingly functioning according to the neoliberal ideals of capitalism and democracy. NGO success is based more on the ability to mobilize international public opinion and less on the ability to mobilize local support. The extent to which governments concede to the demands of the international community is determined more by the amount of aid provided by donors and less by their fear of NGOs becoming a political threat. If not for the constant influx of tremendous sums of international assistance, NGOs simply could not survive. Ultimately, NGO capacity to mobilize local resources and voluntary participation has progressively declined even while their international profiles have risen.

NGOs have been successful in exposing the limitations of the government and in disciplining it to act according to certain international norms. They have also helped to provide the ideological justification for the government's withdrawal from the economy. The international donor community looks to NGOs for popular and non-partisan opinions. Yet NGOs *have not* filled the vacuum left by the government's withdrawal from the economy, and they *have* left the most vulnerable sections of the population in even more desperate straits. As the income gap widens, and as NGOs adopt more coercive measures for the collection of loans, they are likely to lose credibility with their constituencies. This may create new opportunities for alternative ideologies to flourish.

The political equalities for which NGOs fight are continually undermined by inequalities in the economic sphere. On that front, NGOs and the state alike have struggled to provide meaningful solutions. NGO participation in politics is a natural outcome of their agendas for human rights and social change, but as a non-party political formation they cannot directly compete for state power. Instead, they must cooperate with existing political parties. Were NGOs to articulate a political platform and form a party to advocate it, they would be violating widely shared expectations.

It would be a mistake to regard Islamic fundamentalist ideology as the main threat to NGOs. At the field level, NGO programs do not challenge rural power structures, despite their claims to the contrary. As was demonstrated in the case of microcredit, NGOs often strengthen existing power relations. Fundamentalist ideology is used by the ruling party as a tool to marginalize its opponents, but it does not yet command any significant social base in the overall political processes. If the NGO, donor, and state collaborative project does not resolve growing economic inequalities or provide a more politically meaningful ideology, fundamentalist ideals will inevitably have more influence over the country's politics. The diminishing differences between the political parties, and the absence of alternative forms of political mobilization for NGOs, result in a situation where political parties and NGOs alike rely on fundamentalism to emphasize their differences. Thus the socially transformative capacities of NGOs appear to be limited, in the last instance, by the same forces that repeatedly plunge the state into legitimacy crises.

Many observers argue that the rise of Islamic NGOs, funded by Muslim nations, foreshadows the formation of a parallel state in Bangladesh. Mainstream NGOs are deeply critical of the influence of Islamic NGOs on social policy and claim that they represent the forces which advocate the formation of an Islamic theocratic state in Bangladesh. This situation is the product of a historical exchange between religion and politics in a state that prides itself on its secular nature. A number of factors compel mainstream political parties to form alliances with the religious groups. Despite their avowed commitment to secularist ideals, both the BNP and AL have exploited religious interest groups and political parties, in large measure because without that support they find it difficult to win a parliamentary majority sufficient to capture state power. The differences between the two parties' economic policies have disappeared in the face of their efforts to cast themselves as defenders of Islam. Tribal communities, Hindus, Buddhists, and Christians in the region which now comprises Bangladesh have suffered the most from partition, first in 1947 and then again in 1971. Since independence, the rise of Islamic nationalism has resulted in increasing oppression for all ethnic and tribal communities.

The ruling party, mainstream NGOs, and Islamic NGOs operate as three parallel states in Bangladesh. While these entities are ideologically and operationally different, all of them are dependent on transnational capital. However, each absorbs capitalism's accumulation and legitimization crises in different ways. The basic roles of mainstream NGOs and their ethnoreligious nationalist critics are the same. Both provide interpretative frameworks through which capital can subordinate state and society. In the final analysis, Bangladeshi NGOs have failed both to replicate their local programs on a national scale and to respond to economic crises. People continue to look to the government as the primary guardian of their welfare, while NGOs blame the state for a myriad of social crises and at the same time expect it to resolve them. The failure of NGOs to overcome the state's limitations is not due to government bureaucracy, but to the fact that their programs are dependent on the relations and forces of capitalist production. Because of this, they will continue to reproduce inequality and social exclusion. Unless class-based social mobilization occurs, religious nationalism will remain a powerful paradigm for shaping both state–society and NGO–state relations.

In 2010, the state began to adopt even more stringent measures to control the activities of the NGOs. On January 27, 2010, Bangladeshi authorities shut down nearly all charities. Altogether, the government plans to immediately shut down 2,931 NGOs in 16 districts of the country, owing to what it considers their inactivity, absence of transparency in fund-related matters, faulty registration, and alleged involvement with militancy. The government also announced, as per Article 10 of the Voluntary Social Welfare Agencies (Registration and Control) Ordinance of 1961, that it plans to shut down nearly 20,000 charities altogether. Bangladesh has been seeking to crack down on groups bankrolled by donors in wealthy Muslim countries, claiming that their aid projects are used to spread radical Islamic ideas. The social welfare secretary announced that "Individuals or chiefs of NGOs have to be recommended by district commissioner now to get registered under the department."[136] Critics believe these shutdowns are inspired by growing challenges to state power by Islamic militants, public protest against exploitation by microfinance agencies, and the active participation of NGOs in political mobilization.

Those who claim NGOs have an anti-Islamic agenda are pleased by their suppression. Suppression also strengthens the public legitimacy of the state as a guardian of Islamic interests, and allows the state to move against Islamic and other NGOs in the parallel state. On April 9, 2010, the activist Salah Uddin Shoaib Choudhury suggested,

> Possibly the ruling party in Bangladesh dislikes any criticism from the opposition. They want a nation of sycophants, where no one would even think of uttering a single word against the rulers or even family members of the ruling leaders. In brief, the ruling party in Bangladesh has almost established extreme authoritarian rule under the garb of democracy. Freedom of speech and freedom of press is by now greatly screwed by the ruling elites in Bangladesh.[137]

The increasing role of religion in shaping the relationship between the state and the NGOs needs to be understood in the context of intense competition between a small minority of business elites, who thrive on state patronage to secure the limited economic opportunities in the country, and the ability of NGOs to mobilize international pressure on a state heavily dependent on international aid channeled through NGOs.

The optimism of Bangladeshi NGOs has faded. Despite the fact that Bangladesh has the world's largest NGOs, investing in development far more than the government does, the evidence of their positive impact on poverty alleviation remains inconclusive. Most of the recipients of NGO assistance continue to live below the poverty line and suffer from chronic food shortages. In fact, the commercialization of NGO interventions has not only worsened conditions among the poor, but has also made them even more vulnerable to the vicissitudes of the global economy. Under these circumstances, the continuing failure of NGOs to provide a coherent interpretative framework for social mobilizations will ensure that ethnoreligious nationalism and militarization continue to function as the dominant forces shaping NGO–state relations. The strategic geopolitical importance of Bangladesh for regional and international superpowers, especially in their "global war against Islamic terrorism," will continue to justify the government's use of national security ideology to suppress political dissent resulting from the economic crises.

# 4
# The NGO Industrial Complex: Modernizing Postmodernity

"The starting point of Marxist theory of politics and the state is its categorical rejection of this view of the state as the trustee, instrument, or agent of this 'society as a whole' ... In class societies, the 'concept of the society as a whole' and of the 'national interest' is clearly a mystification."

Ralph Miliband[1]

"It is clear that the arm of criticism cannot replace the criticism of arms. Material force can only be overthrown by material force; but theory itself becomes a material force when it has seized the masses."

Karl Marx[2]

NGOs are among the most basic institutions shaping the process of social change. This analysis of NGO activities provides us with a comprehensive understanding of the trajectories of social change, with the goal of assisting scholars and activists who seek to redirect those trajectories towards better ends. While NGOs have facilitated the process of capitalist state formation, they have also interrupted it by reinventing their activities in creative and influential ways. Although nation-states have prevailed, their identity vis-à-vis society has become more uncertain. The impact of NGOs on social change depends on their role in the state's struggle to maintain its capitalist nature. Under these circumstances, the potential of NGOs to realize their goals of social and environmental justice in the future depends on how they position themselves in relation to capitalism.

Below, I illustrate the impact of NGOs on state formation in two ways: in terms of their actual activities and in terms of the discourse of NGOs. (By the "discourse of NGOs," I mean the purposeful framing of the activities of the NGO sector in order to structure its relations with the state and society.)

Discourse is shaped by the relationship of NGOs to religion, ethnicity, nationalism, capitalism, and so on. One may refer to NGOs as a discursive formation when the regularities of their ideas and practices are configured as a coherent framework. While the reference points of NGO discourse are NGO activities, the interests of those who frame the discourse may be far removed from those activities. In those moments, the conversation about NGOs functions as an ideology, which I refer to as NGOism. NGOism conceals more than it reveals about NGOs and their impact on state formation. If we seek to improve NGO performance, we need to examine NGOism as well as NGO activities.

This chapter outlines a general theory of NGOs in social change, focusing specifically on their role in state formation in Bangladesh and Sri Lanka from the precolonial to the contemporary period. The engine of social change I have identified in this book is the historical development of capitalism, and the role of NGOs in creating and sustaining social change is best understood in terms of their relationships with the state. The fluctuations and variations in NGO–state relations directly correspond to the specific nature of accumulation and the legitimization crisis of capitalism, and illustrate how capitalism has historically incorporated NGOs and the state.

Though the bulk of the chapter focuses on the colonial and postcolonial periods, it is crucial that the analysis be grounded in precolonial history (the focus of Chapter 1). Contemporary readings and misreadings of the social histories of earlier associations continue to shape NGO–state relations today: the discourse of NGOs is a site of contestation over history, and the participants in this discourse use their particular versions of history to make sense of and legitimate their claims about the present and the future. NGOs are not only constitutive elements of that history; their agency is also shaped by it. First I provide a general theory of the role of NGOs in social change, followed by a detailed discussion of their impact on five historically specific forms of the state: 1) the precolonial state; 2) the colonial state; 3) the post-independence national state; 4) the neoliberal state; and 5) the national security state. My theoretical discussion moves in tandem with the historical examples offered, since each era presents us with an opportunity to analyze and theorize the influence of NGOs on the state's shifting forms as it realizes its capitalist nature.

## THE GENERAL THEORY

The social histories of Bangladesh and Sri Lanka since the nineteenth century offer a rich legacy of ideologically and operationally diverse organizations that share characteristics with contemporary NGOs.

These early organizations did not have a common origin; they have followed different evolutionary paths and most were eventually absorbed, isolated, marginalized, or forced into oblivion by larger organizations including the modern state. Nonetheless, they influenced the evolution of modern NGOs in the region, which have served as ideological tools and voter mobilization springboards for political leaders and social movements. The evolution of the modern state simply cannot be understood independent of the activities of these organizations. Today, because of their sheer number and growing influence, NGOs in Bangladesh and Sri Lanka are no longer a marginal opposition. They have become a significant force representing the interests of diverse social groups capable of challenging state actors. The impact of these organizations cannot be easily measured, but they have clearly raised awareness, challenged conventions, and developed new terminology to describe their humanitarian and social work.

Though NGOs are not a homogeneous category, they can be analyzed as a unified institutional category in terms of their relationship with the state. "Unity" identifies a relational attribute between NGOs and the state, established within the context of capitalism:

> The category of totality does not reduce its various elements to an undifferentiated uniformity, to identity. The apparent independence and autonomy which they possess in the capitalist system is an illusion only in so far as they are involved in a dynamic dialectical relationship with one another and can be thought of as the dynamic dialectical aspects of an equally dynamic and dialectical whole.[3]

The whole is dynamic, and constantly prone to crises, which are expressed in the ideologically and operationally diverse activities of NGOs, while their diversity is disciplined according to the logic of capitalist modernity. NGOs as an institutional totality are linked to patterns of "economic" accumulation, associated with given modes of production and the eruption of crises at specific times and places. Since its inception, capitalist accumulation's central historical problem has been the tension between "cultural het-erogenization" (i.e., the fragmentation of the social order) and "cultural homogenization" (i.e., the reconfiguration of national and transnational solidarities). This ongoing tension has resulted in highly complex, overlapping, and disjunctive social disorders or antagonisms. With that in mind, we can begin to see how NGO interventions attempt to target the opportunities created by these dynamics. In a sense, NGOs derive their identity and popular legitimacy by responding to the crises generated by these factors, as well as by holding the state accountable for them. At the same time, they do not possess the ideological and material flexibility to manage these crises beyond the parameters of capitalism, and instead discipline their own activities according to its imperatives.

The remarkable creativity and power of the capitalist system is evident throughout the whole history of NGO–state relations. Capitalism has incorporated NGO ideas and practices, even when they are voiced by opponents to its expansion and popular legitimacy. In the process, the activities of proto-NGOs and NGOs in the past 200 years have contributed to the conditions necessary for centralization (the extension and consolidation of state power in diverse spheres of society) and "domestication" (the legitimization through popular consensus of the state's role as the primary agent of social development) of state power within the context of capitalist modernity. In Bangladesh and Sri Lanka, the drive towards centralization predates colonization, although its means of expression have changed. Centralization and domestication of state power result from the state's efforts to maintain its capitalist nature through periodic changes in form. Historical differences in the form of the state are shaped by the accumulation and legitimization crises of capitalism, which, in turn, result from intrinsic contradictions in capitalism itself. These contradictions are often resolved through hegemonic projects that simultaneously and paradoxically assert any number of conflicting class interests. The success or failure of such projects must "depend on specific political and ideological activities that interpolate subjects, endow them with interests, and organize them in conjunctually specific ways."[4]

The tensions between the form and the nature of the state become most apparent when dominant social groups or institutions fail in some major political undertaking, ignore or even forcibly silence their constituencies, or confront real social unrest and political upheaval.[5] Gramsci described such occasions, in which societies yearn for new political conditions to emerge, as follows: "The old is dying and the new cannot be born; in this interregnum a great variety of morbid symptoms appear." He continued: "[N]either conservatives nor progressives have the strength for victory, and [...] even conservatives need a master."[6]

NGOs have initiated and even led debates over "troubled" practices and social relations. They are highly visible and often draw serious criticism from the state, society, and social theorists, especially during legitimacy crises. In many instances, the crises have been precipitated by NGO criticism of the state. NGOs, in turn, help to manage these crises, but once political climates stabilize and the state consolidates its power, interest in NGOs diminishes rapidly. More often than not, prominent NGOs simply disappear from the scene. Some toil on in obscurity, others disband, and still others are absorbed by larger organizations, such as the state, a political party, an international agency, or a political or social interest group. Particular NGOs may strive to maintain their relevance and autonomy, but they rarely succeed, and only a very small number outlive their original causes.[7] In Sri Lanka and Bangladesh, when the two-party system was established, NGO leaders were appointed to high government positions, thereby rendering the difference between NGOs and political parties virtually insignificant. In many instances, the state has championed NGO agendas by aligning them with its own. In the final analysis, the state maintains its status as the guardian of both public and private interests.

Crucially, the state's dominant status in the political economies of both countries is not presupposed by the logic of capital. Rather, it derives from the institutional separation of politics and economics which enables the state to define the legal parameters of NGO activities. Because NGOs are legally defined by the state as non-party political formations, their success is largely contingent on the state's political support. This need for state support does not contradict the claim that NGOs help to define the state; rather, this relationship embodies the tensions between the general and the particular interests which are manifested in the form–nature dialectic of the state. An analysis of that dialectic will enable us to better understand the role of NGOs in social change.

The ideologically and operationally diverse activities of NGOs and their critics since the colonial period have enabled the state to consolidate its capitalist nature by changing its form. I explain the evolution of the NGO–state relationship by reference to the form–nature dialectic of the state, in relation to changes in the mode of production. My argument rests upon eleven overlapping theses:

First, NGOs can function and be recognized as legal entities only within the institutional boundaries set by the state. NGOs enhance the capacity of the state to create the institutional conditions for capitalist development by investing in programs to address inequalities, vulnerabilities, and human suffering caused by capitalism, without undermining that system's ideological and material foundations. Capitalist development increases food insecurity; NGOs invest in projects that aim to free people from hunger by using microfinance. Neoliberal economic reforms have increased vulnerability of the poor after natural disasters and complex emergencies; humanitarian assistance provided by NGOs is an important means of facilitating reforms that would not have been possible under normal circumstances.

Social reforms introduced by NGOs can be replicated, institutionalized, and implemented on a national scale only with the recognition of the state and its various political parties. While NGOs have been more successful at introducing reforms that directly contribute to the expansion of markets, they are less successful at effecting reforms that require the changing of ethnoreligious ideologies or that challenge the power of political parties. The effectiveness of NGO programs in Bangladesh and Sri Lanka is almost entirely determined by their ability to mobilize international state donor support.

Second, although NGOs regularly claim to challenge the ways in which the state manages capital accumulation and legitimization crises, they do not typically advocate changes that would require a radical transformation of the nature of the capitalist state. In other words, the political economy of NGOs is perfectly compatible with capitalism. In fact, most NGO perspectives on social progress generally accept capitalism as one among many causes of social change. NGO interventions in good governance and empowerment projects frequently obscure, rather than reveal, the practices that spring from the state's commitment to neoliberal policies, thereby suppressing and disarticulating the development of a political consciousness capable of seriously challenging those policies. The good governance projects of NGOs are only concerned with "state failures" as opposed to NGO failures, or with holding NGOs accountable for the state's actions. The objective of good governance projects is to ensure that the state and NGOs function in a manner consistent with neoliberal policies.

Third, the alternative social development models advocated by most NGOs are underwritten by the very state institutions and practices they set out to challenge. Still, successful counterhegemonic models of development—which Anthony Bebbington refers to as "islands of sustainability"—are scattered throughout society.[8] But replicating them on a larger scale would threaten neoliberal hegemony, limiting their prospects to the extent that these projects rely on the state for both resources and permission to operate. NGOs do not have the legal mandate to solicit the support of political parties. Indeed, the attempts by a few NGOs in Bangladesh and Sri Lanka to become active in national politics have adversely impacted their credibility and even encouraged state suppression of the entire NGO sector.

Fourth, although NGOs are ideologically and operationally diverse, their relationships with the state all take place in the context of capitalist development and are embedded within neoliberal rationality. Humanitarian and development NGOs may be critical of the state, but their ideas or programs don't challenge its capitalist nature. Competition, collaboration, and collusion all play a role in NGO–state relationships, and in the final analysis these strategies help rather than hinder the capitalist system in its attempt to resolve its internal crises. NGOs do not question the relationship between capital and labor in ways that threaten capitalist development. Instead, their preoccupation with ethnic and religious identity politics, at the expense of class identity, has added to the marginalization of labor unions and class-based political movements and expanded the space for ethnoreligious nationalism to overdetermine the relationship between labor and capital. The state avoids NGO challenges to its antidemocratic practices by linking them with the colonial legacy, with neocolonialism and Western civilization, and it justifies militarism by claiming that NGOs, among other forces, are undermining its sovereignty. Stymied in their attempt to promote universal norms, NGOs find that individual states can always find allies within the hierarchically structured and already militarized international state system. In these situations states have successfully isolated NGOs from the general population by exploiting negative claims about them. States also take refuge in the fact that historically the United Nations and international donors have privileged state sovereignty over the demands of the NGOs.

Fifth, one can classify the post-independence forms of the state in Bangladesh and Sri Lanka as "neo-galactic" or "neo-segmentary,"[9] in which capital seeks to incorporate, preserve, reconfigure, and suppress diversity to advance its own reproductive logic. Such state forms give the illusions of decentralization of development, and of governance grounded in the cultural diversity of their respective societies. In practice, however, they continue to increase the concentration of state power, while also mystifying it. Diversity of social, religious, and political institutions can be a means by which the state achieves this concentration. The change in state forms since the precolonial period (when they were segmentary and galactic) is a shift in the degree of concentration of state power and in the means used to achieve it. During the precolonial era, segmentary and galactic states used a certain set of practices to maintain their control over diverse social units. While some of the same practices are evident today, we also find that ethnoreligious nationalism and neoliberal ideology have evolved as much stronger forces by which the state maintains its relations with other administrative units. NGOs are complicit in this process through their celebration of diverse and spatially fragmented projects and through their reciprocal relations with local and national governments.[10]

Thus NGO projects espousing cultural relativism and identity politics have not coalesced into counterhegemonic practices powerful enough to confront capitalism. Relativism eventually becomes universalism when it operates according to the expansionary imperatives of capitalism. Cultural relativism disempowers local populations when NGOs, through their transnational networks, become the only means available for voicing grievances and ensuring state accountability. Bangladesh and Sri Lanka are both "neo-galactic" or "neo-segmentary" states where capital seeks to incorporate, preserve, reconfigure, and suppress diversity to advance its own reproductive logic. In both states, the cultural relativism of NGOs masks the essentially political character of ethnoreligious nationalism and elides the class basis of local struggles.

Sixth, the discussion of NGOs constitutes a distinctive discursive formation, namely NGOism. The ideological (i.e., voluntarism, philanthropism, localism, globalism, and indigenism) more than the material thrust of NGOism seems to overdetermine both the role and the agency of NGOs. NGOism is a highly contentious relation of production that is dialectically linked with, although not entirely reducible to, the forces of a given mode of production. Since precolonial times, NGOism, as a relation of production, has served as a means through which different modes of production have managed their respective accumulation and legitimization crises. For the neoliberal phase of the capitalist mode of production, NGOism has become an even more important tool for disciplining and managing potentially counterhegemonic modes of production. The complex ideological functions of NGO discourse become more visible when we consider the ways in which the state-sanctioned charges of treason, extravagance, and unaccountability levied against NGOs obscure not only the partisan political and economic agendas of the state, but also the ideological content of the war against terrorism, and the complicity of NGOs in the culture of capitalism. Anti-NGOism often becomes a potent political force when the activities of NGOs are associated with institutional memories of colonialism, neocolonialism, and Christianization. Anti-NGOism is also an integral component of contests over the histories of the nation, particularly the attempts by dominant social groups to rewrite their national history.

Seventh, simple distinctions between NGOs and the state overlook the similarities between their arts of governance, their sources of funding, and their collaborations with each other. In their struggle for territory, NGOs collaborate with state actors, who, in turn, seek NGO assistance to carry out their projects. International donors can fuel tensions between NGOs and the government in order to discipline each of them, while the entire social order functions according to neoliberal rationality. Often neither NGOs nor state actors can claim the moral high ground when faced with charges of corruption, mismanagement, nepotism, human rights abuses, and poor outcomes of performance (either internal or external to their respective institutions). They may engage in such practices collaboratively, and the antagonism between them sometimes works as a means of legitimizing their respective agendas, obscuring their collaboration and their dependence on foreign funding, as both assist the capitalist system in overcoming obstacles to expansion. Both compete for international legitimacy for their respective actions, and both are used by transnational capital to discipline society so that it functions according to capital's interests. Yet state criticism of NGOs has great public appeal and commands the support of the international state system, not only because international capital still relies on the state as the primary agent responsible for its expansion and stability, but also because state claims are embedded in popularly held beliefs about ethnicity, religion, nationalism, and national security. In general, NGOs either avoid, or are reluctant to engage with, the fact that these realities shape relations between state and society. Often we find that criticisms of NGOs do not simply concern their activities, but also stem from the competition between different versions of national history and attempts to rewrite it. Here NGO discourse functions as an ideology: NGOism as revisionist history.

Eighth, NGO reforms concerning good governance, peacebuilding, and development target the state, rather than the nation. State and nation are not synonymous, though they have a symbiotic relationship. The sociological character of the state, including its anti-NGOism, is configured in the nation by appealing to patriotism, religion, history, culture, and so on. Nation is the space where social hierarchies—and thus forms of domination, including the masculinization and militarization of the social order—are made and legitimized, and where opposition against them is silenced. In the process, the class character of the state is produced and mystified. The sources of state legitimacy remain unchallenged; in fact, many NGOs help to reproduce these sources. This is also the fundamental weakness of the political left: the tensions between class and nationalism are resolved in favor of the parochial interests of the nation.

Ninth, we must not overlook the potential for NGOs to function as spaces in which to develop counterhegemonic ideas and practices. In many situations NGOs function as the only means by which social groups can organize their struggles towards democratization and demilitarization. Their success depends to a large extent on solidarity with their international counterparts. Particularly in the case of NGOs working on human rights issues, such solidarity is critical not only for the exertion of external pressure on the state, but in order to secure the safety of NGO workers themselves. But the search for solidarity invites suppression by the state, which fears international conspiracies that undermine its sovereignty. If NGOs are to deflect the array of charges that anti-NGO ethnonationalists and states levy against them, they must begin to examine the ways in which their projects—humanitarian assistance, peacebuilding and conflict resolution, good governance, resettlement and rehabilitation of displaced populations, development, empowerment of women, etc.—can become instruments of state power and serve ethno-nationalist interests, and thus increase the vulnerability of the very marginalized communities that NGOs attempt to serve.

Tenth, the limits to both the socially transformative agendas of NGOs and to the state constitute the limits to capitalist expansion. NGOs are grounded in the forces and relations of the capitalist mode of production. Programs that appear to be counterhegemonic almost invariably end up serving the very forces they seek to transform. NGOs cannot compete with the creativity of global capitalism or match its uncanny ability to exploit the language and practices of its antagonists. As agents of social change, NGOs and the state are two sides of the same coin; both ultimately operate according to capitalism's imperatives.

Eleventh, and finally, what I have written should not be interpreted as a claim that capitalism marks the end of history. It does not. Nor have NGOs exhausted their capacity to advance counterhegemonic ideas and radical political agendas. The accumulation and legitimization crises of capitalism will continue, and so will states' attempts to resolve them. The never-ending crises of capitalism continually open new spaces for NGO activism and reconfigure the role of NGOs as agents of social change. My position is thus that the ability of NGOs to develop a truly counterhegemonic form depends on their willingness to challenge capitalism.

With the above points in mind, the rest of this chapter examines the specific impact of NGOs on specific forms of the state in Bangladesh and Sri Lanka, from precolonial times to the present, with an emphasis on continuities and discontinuities.

## TRADITIONAL ASSOCIATIONS AND THE PRECOLONIAL STATE

As in other societies, social change in precolonial Bangladesh and Sri Lanka was shaped by a complex culture, in which associations engaged in collective activities. Traditional organizations were primarily concerned with maintaining rather than transforming the existing social order. They were mobilized to advance alternative interests, but were not concerned with extending their power beyond their immediate localities. Traditional associations were integral to the accumulation practices of the state, which, in turn, played an active role in patronizing them. At the same time, the state built up the autonomy of traditional associations by a conscious policy of encouraging local leadership and local practices in order to secure favorable conditions for the accumulation of capital. The contradictions arising from accumulation were localized, and there is little evidence of direct intervention by central authorities. These conditions were shaped by the particular form of the precolonial state, which was patrimonial rather than bureaucratic. Centralization was episodic, although the drive towards centralization was ever present. Precolonial state formation was largely segmented, giving local institutions a high degree of autonomy—a factor that permitted the state to maintain its popular legitimacy.[11]

During the colonial period, these organizations began to undergo changes in response to increased centralization and pressures arising from internal contradictions and crises. Instead of letting indigenous associations wither away or modernize, the colonial government and missionary organizations attempted to revitalize traditional associations in order to extend and legitimize their own spheres of influence and control. These indigenous organizations were first incorporated as appendages of government departments and ministries. Subsequently many of them became "partner agencies" of the NGOs. Thereafter, a complex tripartite relationship developed between indigenous organizations, government institutions, and NGOs, in a balance that shifts with evolving social relations in response to the imperatives of global capital. For the colonial state, this was a means by which it could domesticate its rule and acquire popular legitimacy. For native elites, traditional associations were important vehicles for mobilizing anti-state or anti-clerical sentiment, as well as a means of suppressing popular dissent as the masses began to question injustice and inequality. Traditional associations played an influential role in nationalist political discourse and social mobilization against the colonial government, but they also allowed elites to suppress popular dissent in the name of tradition and national independence. Post-Cold War claims that NGOs safeguard "indigenous culture" and "national independence" either wittingly or unwittingly ignored the double-edged nature of revived traditional associations.

Tradition-based social development models enable NGOs to advance criticism of conventional development policies and differentiate themselves from the state. The resulting practices provide ideological legitimacy for neoliberal claims that the state should play a limited role in social development, that the resources allocated to basic welfare services for marginalized groups should be reduced, and that such resources should be used instead to develop infrastructure that would attract foreign investment. Traditional organizations figured prominently in debates about the revitalization of tradition and later proved central to the development of nationalism and communalism, shaping relationships not only between the state and society but also between the state and NGOs.

Bangladeshi NGOs regard the traditional institutional order as a tremendous obstacle to improving conditions for marginalized social groups, so they often come into conflict with political and economic conservatives. In Sri Lanka, however, the history of NGOs has been written by those who believe that the colonial government and Christian organizations destroyed traditional institutions that were better suited to respond to social and economic crises. Even the most progressive Sri Lankan NGOs, with interests in environmental and social justice, do not challenge this nostalgic revisionism. In Sri Lanka, NGO investment in tradition has contributed to the rise of the very same religious nationalists that they now militate against. The dominance of ethnoreligious ideology shapes relations between state and society, creating an environment in which NGOs are unable to counter criticism that their activities denigrate tradition, religion, and the territorial integrity of the nation.

## MISSIONARIES, NATIVE ASSOCIATIONS, AND THE COLONIAL STATE

Long before the colonial period, religious organizations in Bangladesh and Sri Lanka played an influential role in the evolution of social organizations. Christian organizations are especially significant because they shaped the associational culture of NGOs in the colonial period, and have been increasingly visible players in NGO–state controversies. Christianity predates both modern colonialism and capitalism, and played a vital role in their interconnected social histories. The spread of Christianity to South Asia, then, cannot be described simply as a product of colonialism. Christian missionary organizations were a new addition to the existing culture of collective associations in Bangladesh and Sri Lanka. They both influenced and were influenced by traditional associations since the early sixteenth century.

Missionary organizations established the conditions for the evolution of NGO culture in Bangladesh and Sri Lanka. Among the characteristics and goals they transmitted were community development, empowerment of the poor through education, self-reliance, self-sufficiency, the mobilization and utilization of local resources, extension of suffrage to marginalized segments of the population, advocacy of social reforms, cooperative-style economic organizations, and the use of credit as a means of improving the economic status of the poor. Some missionaries engaged in these activities with the goal of evangelizing the natives, but other undertakings evolved as pragmatic responses to concrete problems that prevented missionaries from achieving other ends. Missionary agencies were a truly global phenomenon, spreading their discourses and practices across the world, coordinating at the transnational level. Like the NGOs that followed, they had a relationship of "antagonistic cooperation" with the state, a dialectical movement from conflict to compromise and then back to conflict. Missionaries sought to transform both state and society according to the imperatives of evangelism, but found themselves caught in a contradiction: on the one hand, Christian reforms challenged existing social relationships; on the other hand, missionary agencies played an important role in creating the social conditions and institutions necessary for legitimizing worldly power. Thus missionary organizations eventually found themselves challenged by native elites who called into question the mission of Christianity using the very same means developed by the missionaries themselves.

Although all missionary agencies shared the common goal of evangelism, they took different approaches to it. Some embraced the idea that radical social change should precede the conversion of the natives to Christianity. Others believed that commitment to the Christian worldview was an essential prerequisite for sustainable and meaningful social change. Still others believed that social change was an integral part of evangelism and that both objectives needed to be achieved simultaneously. Many agencies gradually moved into diverse areas of social reform and development, placing less emphasis on conversion. Their underlying assumption was that the eradication of social injustice and the creation of an enlightened community would result in the long-term expansion and survival of the church, and would ease tension between missionaries, natives, and the colonial state. Radical short-term change was considered counterproductive to the long-term survival of the church, especially if it predicated tensions between the state, the natives, and the missionaries. Differences among missionary agencies hinged on interpretations of scripture, as well as on ideological and organizational biases. The interests of particular denominations also often undermined the possibility of missionaries' emergence as a unified sector.

Missionary agencies were more active in social reform in the western parts of Bengal and in the northern and eastern parts of Sri Lanka. Eastern Bengal, where the majority of the population had converted to Islam before the arrival of Christianity, was entirely unreceptive to missionary activities. In general, missionaries were less aggressive when it came to social reforms in Sri Lanka and their influence was limited compared to that of missionaries in Calcutta and Bengal. They did not consider the "social evils" of Hinduism—caste, sati, and so forth—to be serious obstacles to evangelism in Sri Lanka or in eastern Bengal where Hindus were a small minority. Except in the north, which is inhabited mainly by Tamil-speaking people, missionaries in Sri Lanka took a gradual approach to social change. While anti-caste sentiment arose in both countries, the majority of missionaries either remained silent or fell in line with the state's policy on caste.

Sri Lankan social hierarchies were more ossified than in Bengal. Thus, in Sri Lanka, convincing the native middle classes and the rest of society to accept the demands of the colonial state was easier than in Bengal. In Sri Lanka, associations led by native elites were fragmented along lines of caste, ethnicity, and territory, and were concerned with maximizing benefits for the groups they represented through collaboration with the colonial regime. Caste, ethnic, and territorial divisions also helped define institutional life in Bengal, where such divisions were more sharply defined than in Sri Lanka. But native organizations in Bengal were more successful in transcending the differences among associations, and thus in facing the challenges presented by missionaries and the colonial system.

Collaboration is one explanation for the conspicuous silence of Christian missionaries about the social problems faced by the South Indian tea and rubber plantation workers, brought into Sri Lanka by the British in the late 1880s. Although the missionaries were concerned with improving conditions for native Sri Lankans, advocacy for improving those of Indian plantation workers would have resulted in serious conflicts with the state and native elites, including Christian converts, some of whom were important church members. The plantation sector formed the primary economic base of colonial and native power. Christian reforms would have antagonized native elites who considered South Indian workers to be social outcasts and non-citizens. Colonial planters did patronize reform attempts by a few missionary organizations, in the belief that some of the ethical values that the missionaries espoused, like temperance, were likely to increase worker productivity, but most of these efforts were short-lived. Church-led organizations did not become interested in human rights and social welfare in the plantation sector until the early 1970s.

From the beginning, the relationship between the colonial government and missionaries was contentious. The regime occasionally sanctioned missionary reforms. For example, during the indigo plantation crisis of 1883, the state supported missionary reformers because the missionaries had been able to mobilize the support of native associations. While some landlords were genuinely interested in alleviating hardships on the plantation, they also agreed with missionaries for other reasons. Native landlords took advantage of the reform movement to shift blame for poor working conditions from themselves to the Europeans who founded the plantations. If the colonial government had sided with European planters against the missionary reformers, it would have created unnecessary tension between the administration and native elites. Because the world demand for indigo had greatly decreased, the government also had little interest in opposing reforms.

In general, missionary organizations campaigned for active intervention by the state to improve conditions for disenfranchised and marginalized segments of the population. Their success mainly depended on the enactment of laws and regulations, and the state determined what kinds of protests and demands were "legal," extending its sphere of influence as the defender of the public good. Missionary organizations restricted themselves to agitating for reforms that eased the burden of marginalized groups, rather than seeking changes in institutions that fundamentally shaped the accumulation practices of the state. The colonial state was quite willing to suppress missionary activities whenever native groups accused state administrators of collaborating with the missionaries. As the state consolidated power with the help of native elites, it increased restrictions on missionary agencies, effectively marginalizing them. The success of the colonial state's drive toward centralization depended on its ability to "domesticate and nativize" its rule through partnerships with native elites.

Missionaries developed measures to cope with these challenges. Many began to promote local languages, traditions, and institutions. On several occasions, the state and the native middle class opposed indigenizing attempts by the missionaries because indigenization empowered otherwise marginalized groups and interfered with the creation of the elite social class necessary for administering the colonial regime. Native middle classes also protested the education of the masses, claiming that education should be offered in the official language of the state and then allowed to trickle down. Both feared the social upheaval that could be caused by educating the lower classes.

As missionaries indigenized, native mission agencies adopted a more ecumenical approach to social reforms, increasingly accommodating local customs, values, and traditions. Progressive missionaries began collaborating actively with native reformers. Gradually, social reform and conversion became interlocking goals. New types of Christian voluntary organizations emerged in the 1800s, such as the YMCA. These progressive church-based organizations were Christian, but evangelism was not their primary goal and membership was open to people of other faiths. They specialized in various aspects of social development and derived their financial resources from a broad constituency rather than from a single congregation. At the same time, they worked with national governments and native groups more closely and were less likely to antagonize them.

Although Christianity has been associated with the dark history of racism, slavery, and sexism, missionary organizations in Sri Lanka and Bangladesh also introduced the ideal of equal opportunity for all people, irrespective of social status. In this respect, missionary organizations facilitated the social upheavals that helped to establish both colonial hegemony and anticolonial struggles. The reason behind the paradoxical position of the missionary organization was its adherence to the idea that all human beings are created equal. Social inequalities could not be tolerated as they were neither natural nor authorized by God. Theologically, many also believed that individuals were not the private owners but rather the stewards of knowledge, property, and human relationships. Humans were believed capable of overcoming inequalities; society and the state were thought responsible for helping them to do so. All cultures contain within them good and evil; all cultures ought to be transformed. Such sentiments informed the worldviews of the missionaries, and their associations provided social fora for political pluralism. The embrace of vernacular languages and education by missionaries opened public spaces hitherto dominated by elites and the language of the state.

Missionary activities inevitably disrupted the social, political, and economic order and provided a means for people to question its inequalities. This also resulted in hostility against the native elites who benefited from services provided by the Christian associations. Those elites, in turn, started their own associations modeled after missionary organizations. They used these associations to advocate pluralism and equality, and, at the same time, to regain their power over the masses and the colonial state. Eventually, they suppressed and distorted a more comprehensive history of Christian missionary organizations, particularly their progressive contributions. Anti-Christian agitations helped the elites to distinguish themselves from the "foreigners" and indigenize their legitimacy, often revising institutional memory of the role of missionary organizations in social change. However, throughout the colonial period, missionaries and native elites alike solicited the state, albeit in different ways, to implement their demands for social change. Tensions between native and missionary organizations reflected the social conflicts in the colonized world that were to be resolved within the apparatus of the colonial state. Urban elites also suppressed the traditional

Islamic and Buddhist associations that aligned with radical political parties. Native elites benefited from the opportunities offered by the missionary organizations, criticized them for destroying the native religion and culture, and then claimed to be their defenders. The activities of, and tensions between, missionary and native associations provide a nuanced explanation of the formation of the class basis of the colonial state.

Most of the vernacular missionary schools were eventually nationalized, but the schools that remained in the hands of conservative missionary organizations continued to serve native elites, despite conflicting interests. These elites believed missionary schools provided the type of education that led to social mobility. The masses, on the other hand, were educated in state schools, with little likelihood of finding employment in the colonial economy. In this way, native elite protest against progressive, vernacular missionary education helped to reproduce the hegemony of the ruling classes, even as the state appeared to accept and promote the vernacular.

Missionary organizations traditionally placed great faith in the education and professionalization of elite social groups, believing that it would serve the interests of the church in the long run. However, some of these social groups eventually opposed the missionaries and collaborated with the state to impose more restrictions on missionary activities. Native elite opposition to missionary agencies had a number of contradictory and overlapping effects. The first was the alienation of missionaries from the local population, which prevented the missionaries from posing challenges to the established social order. Second, native elites demanded that the state restrict missionary activities, using its power to suppress challenges to elite interests from subordinate groups. The state did not hesitate to impose restrictions on missionaries because doing so reduced the potential for social tension and upheaval. Third, suppressing missionary activities helped the state to domesticate its rule. Native elites turned this to their advantage by using state suppression to justify the struggle for independence. By linking the colonial state with missionary organizations, native elites authorized their role as defenders of the nation.

Even a decade after independence, Christian organizations continued to play an important role in Sri Lanka and Bangladesh, despite increasing hostility toward their activities. On many occasions, these agencies were active in situations in which marginalized groups from all religious faiths lacked the institutional means to articulate their concerns. While there has been increasing pressure on the state to curb the activities of missionaries, governments still collaborate with them, especially in areas where state resources are lacking. On occasion, Christian agencies have even served as "neutral" mediators between state and society, particularly when the state's administrative machinery is weak.

Although Christian organizations work with different ethnic groups and generally maintain relative neutrality in intercommunal conflicts, the majority of their members tend to preserve their respective ethnic, territorial, and class interests. The hierarchical structure of the Christian church means that in general it does not favor radical social reforms. Generally, the church distances itself from such efforts, and on several occasions priests engaging in them have been reprimanded or even excommunicated. Despite the dramatic decline in the number of NGOs that are in one way or another linked with the church, anti-Christian rhetoric is still mobilized as a means of protest against NGOs in general, including those not even remotely linked with Christian activity. Anti-Christian arguments affect the form of the state and its relations with NGOs only to the extent that religious nationalism serves to legitimize state–society relations. Despite scattered incidents of violence against Christian organizations, church-based NGOs are not completely suppressed by the government, but the link between anti-Christian rhetoric and anti-NGO rhetoric has enabled the state to exploit ethnoreligious nationalism to its advantage. Ironically, even progressive NGOs which typically bear the brunt of state repression have not been critical of the roles of religion and religious nationalism in perpetuating the social, economic, and political crises that those organizations address. Many NGOs in Bangladesh have been relatively critical of the role of Islam, but Sri Lankan NGOs have tended to keep silent about religion altogether or to limit their efforts to mobilizing religion as a positive means of addressing social issues. Progressive NGOs do not evaluate anti-Christian attacks from the point of view of human rights, justice, and equality. Nor do they discuss the ways anti-Christian rhetoric is used by the state as a response to the social crises created by neoliberal reforms. This failure makes NGOs unwitting collaborators in the reproduction of state power, and tacit supporters of ethnoreligious nationalism.

In Sri Lanka and Bangladesh, critics who accuse Christian faith-based organizations of proselytizing and contributing to Westernization make some unsupported assumptions. It is not clear that those who converted to Christianity did so purely because of the material benefits they received from missionary organizations. There are other explanations. Christianity may actually have appealed to them. Conversion may have been a kind of social protest. Converts may even have seen material assistance as a manifestation of Christian spirituality; they may not have separated the material from the spiritual. It is important to keep in mind that Westernization happens not only through Christian faith-based organizations, but also through non-Christian faith-based organizations, and through entirely secular organizations like the state. Finally, Christian faith-based NGOs have often been critical of Western capitalist lifestyles and some have expressed strong preferences for indigenous lifestyles.

Criticism of Christian NGOs does not generally come from those who benefit from missionary or secular Christian organizational activities. Rather, it springs from urban interest groups whose political ideology may conform to the ethnoreligious nationalism of the state. For the most part, the condemnation of Christian NGOs is part of a larger political project which has less to do with NGOs themselves and more to do with practical questions of governance. Since the 1990s, there have been many scattered incidents of organized violence in Sri Lanka, particularly against smaller Christian churches and organizations, by groups adhering to ethnoreligious ideologies. Religious nationalists wield enormous power over the country's political consciousness. However, there is no evidence that the governments of Sri Lanka or Bangladesh have resolved to ban or suppress Christian faith-based NGOs, despite the demands of ethnoreligious nationalists. Since colonial times, state responses to critics of NGOs have been inconsistent and largely determined by the ideological exigencies of the moment.

## NATIVE ASSOCIATIONS

Precolonial traditional associations arose organically as a result of internal pressures. Membership was limited to local communities and members sought not to change existing power structures but to maintain them. Native associations were founded by members of the local middle class, often in association with colonial institutions and missionary organizations that emerged during the colonial period. Some of these associations played important roles in the nationalist struggle, especially in Bangladesh. Native associations are perhaps best understood as transformative. However, some of their interventions were intended to revitalize traditional institutions with the goal of strengthening the power of the colonial and postcolonial state. This tendency persists.

Native associations were an important means through which the landless middle class became part of the ruling class. This process may be called the "bourgeoisification of the nonproprietary class," since it results in the assimilation of the nonproprietary class into the proprietary class, making them more or less equal in terms of their influence over the society. As Marx and Engels observed:

> Property rules. Property enables the aristocracy to dominate the election of representatives from the rural areas and the small towns; property enables the merchants and factory owners to pick representatives from rural areas and the small towns; property enables both to increase their influence through bribery. And since influence through property is the essence of the middle class, since the aristocracy takes advantage of property in any election and, therefore, acts not as aristocracy but puts itself in par with the middle class, and since influence of the middle class is much stronger than that of the aristocracy, it is the middle class that really rules.[12]

This middle-class–merchant–landlord alliance had a number of effects. During the precolonial period, popular resistance, headed by tribal chiefs, religious reformers, lower castes, zamindars, moneylenders, peasants, artisans, princes, and kings, was scattered and localized, as were the ways in which such crises were managed. With the formation of native associations, the middle class assumed leadership of these popular struggles and eventually brought diverse forms of resistance under the control of the state, making the state the official arbiter of social conflict.

When missionaries began their activities, Bengal and Sri Lanka lacked a "public sphere." Conditions for the evolution of native associations were created more by external than internal forces. Native associations emulated the organizational model of missionary agencies, though their agendas were often competing. They served the interests of both the colonial state and of native social groups. In the beginning, landlords, European settlers, and merchants took a keen interest in promoting native associations. This was because they were an important means of transmitting knowledge, technologies, and practices useful for increasing the productivity of land, commerce, and industry. Subsequently, they became important centers of both cooperation and conflict between

Europeans and natives. On the one hand, administrators exerted pressure on the colonial state to organize its economy in a way that would not discriminate between natives and Europeans. On the other hand, Europeans and native elites competed for special privileges. Policies favoring Europeans were harshly condemned by native elites, but the withdrawal of such privileges precipitated sharp divisions within the associations. Occasionally, Europeans took over associations and expelled native members.

The colonial state's chief responsibility was to subordinate the local economy to the interests of the empire and the metropolis. Local elites, who did not share those interests, were essential to the colonial economy but also retained some of their traditional bases of power. The colonial state had to cooperate with native elites in order to maintain popular support. Native associations gave local elites influence over the evolution of capitalism's form but not its nature, so the forces enabling them ultimately prevented their success. Their victories were hollow, resulting in "the annihilation of the old Asiatic society, and the laying of the material foundations of Western society in Asia."[13]

The expansion of native associations during the nineteenth century was a result of the emergence of a middle class fractured along ideological, ethnic, religious, and professional lines. The colonial administration and the middle class depended on each other, but their alliance divided the native middle classes from the masses, whose support they needed to maintain power within the colonial regime. This was a conundrum, particularly for those who did not own property but derived their class status primarily from their association with the government. In this context, native associations became a means through which the middle class articulated its relationship with the state and society in light of the new challenges it faced.

The numerous middle-class associations that emerged during this period can be divided into three categories: conservative, moderate, and radical. Conservative associations sought to revitalize the traditional social order according to conventional religious and cultural orthodoxies, and opposed those who sought to bring about change through Western models. Moderate associations sought social reform through reinterpretation of traditional and religious texts in light of the challenges posed by missionaries and the colonial state. Radical associations opposed the interests of conservatives and moderates and were marginalized because of their inability to withstand the pressures of conservative and moderate associations.

Throughout this period, religion and tradition shaped the activities of associations, both limiting and enabling their impact on social change. According to Ranajith Guha, commenting on the pressure on Hindu associations in Bengal:

> Even when an initiative was clearly liberal in form and intent, such as setting up a village school, its rationale was sought in Dhamma, understood broadly as the quintessence of "virtue, the moral duty," which implied a social duty conforming to one's place in the caste hierarchy as well as the local power structure— that is, conforming to what Weber called the "organic" societal doctrine of Hinduism.[14]

Arubindo Ghosh asserts that "the aim of Hindu civilization and the original intent of caste"[15] was to provide the ideological basis of the landowning aristocracy's power in the postcolonial state. Sumit Sarkar notes that, although progressives correctly observed "the negative consequences of industrial capitalism, they refer to [the] petty-bourgeois conception of a cooperative society with a 'Brahmin aristocratic intellect on the top far away from the toiling masses.'"[16] Sivanath Sasthri, the founder of Sadharan Brahmo Samaj, C.H. Mukherjee of the radical faction of Brahmo Samaj, and members of the Fabian Society who took a working class approach to social change eventually espoused revivalist religious nationalism over Western socialism. Ghosh argued that socialism was "essentially an Asiatic and especially Indian" concept, and that "what is known as socialism in Europe is the old Asiatic attempt to effect a permanent socialism of old economic problems of society which will give man leisure and peace to develop an undisturbed higher self."[17]

Native associations influenced both state and social development in Bengal and Sri Lanka. Many factors made the development of associations in East Bengal slower than in West Bengal. The evolution of the Muslim middle class was not continuous in East Bengal as a result of political instability. Missionary involvement in the east was extremely limited, and the Muslim population was slow to take advantage of the colonial economy. Moreover, the proprietary class in the east was made up of Hindu landlords, and a majority of Muslims were farmers and wage laborers whose economy was controlled by the Hindu zamindars.

Violent popular uprisings erupted in East Bengal as confrontations between peasants and landlords. In West Bengal, such confrontations were shaped by the identity politics of the public associations involved. The activities in the eastern associations were more subversive than those in the west and were viewed with greater suspicion by the government. The stark differences between East and West Bengal suggest that the presence of robust native associations was an obstacle to the possible articulation and mobilization of social discontent between peasants and landlords along economic lines.

By the early twentieth century, native associations emerged within the Muslim community as the Muslim middle class consolidated its position. Most of these associations were centered in Calcutta because of its administrative and commercial importance, and Muslim participation in the Calcutta-based associations was limited. Muslims felt excluded from debates over Indian identity since India was widely regarded as part of a "greater Hindu community." As members of the Muslim middle class took leadership positions in native associations, the grievances of the subordinate classes, especially those of peasants against their landlords, were channeled through them. These grievances then took on communal form in part because so many large landowners happened to be Hindus. As a result, within a short period of time the Muslim associations became part of larger political movements concerned with the interests of a "greater Islamic community." Native associations thus became fora for discussions between the Hindu and the Muslim communities.

During the independence struggle in Bengal, native associations played a key role in social organization. Radical associations were marginalized in this process because liberating the state from colonial rule was considered an essential prerequisite for eradicating other forms of oppression. For example, female activists argued that national liberation went hand-in-hand with women's rights and called upon women to "play [a] full and legitimate role in national affairs; otherwise all other rights become illusory."[18] But, as Deniz Kandiyoti has noted, "Women who were also active participants in nationalist movements felt compelled to articulate their gender interests within the parameters of cultural nationalism, sometimes censoring or muting the radical potential of their demands."[19] The rhetoric of nationalism subsumed social mobilizations concerned with women's rights. It is worth noting that, although they were influenced by Enlightenment ideas, radical leaders unwittingly endorsed the practice of achieving emancipatory struggles within the boundaries of nationalist ideology.[20] As in the bourgeois revolutions of Western Europe, "this illusion of the common interests" worked rather well at first, for, as Marx observed, "in the beginning this illusion was true."[21]

The independence movement could not sustain a consensus among different organizations for very long. As Guha observed, "its claim to speak for all was being contested more and more vigorously along the major axes—that is, the communal and class axes—of Indian politics."[22] Communal divisions among associations influenced the emergence of Pakistan and Bangladesh as new nation-states. Subsequently, the demand for autonomy came from the Tamils in Sri Lanka and separatist tribal groups in Bangladesh. The most influential native associations of the later period were frontline organizations for political parties and other interest groups competing for state power. They were also the sites in which nationalist historiography emerged in opposition to colonial historiography, effectively concealing the continuity of power.

Many elites who assumed power in the postcolonial states were members of the native associations, and used them as a means to form political parties and to mobilize popular support for their respective agendas. Analysis of associational culture vis-à-vis the state during the colonial period reveals a comprehensive picture of pre-independence class realities. Colonial associations provided the ideological and social capital that allowed the state and the natives to domesticate and maintain control over the colonial regime of accumulation. That also explains why an export and subsistence economy emerged during the independence period. The notion of improvement, which subsequently became development, was itself part of the debate within these associations. The key terms were borrowed from the West in what Partha Chatterjee refers to as "derivative discourse."[23] Native elite criticisms of the colonial state and its allies were primarily a means to mobilize the masses and maintain power after independence. This approach facilitated the nationalization of class relations under the colonial government and the post-independence appropriation and consolidation of those relations by elites. The notions of representative government, improvement, and civil rights and liberties were the historical antecedents to those of good governance, development, human rights, freedom of expression, and humanitarian assistance. They were part of the political vocabulary of these associations, although "only as long as they were compatible with the rule of the law and with the kind of order which kept the poor in their place."[24] Later, they became the constituents of contemporary NGO discourse.

It is capitalism's effect of maintaining class dominance that continues to fuel nationalism, ethnicity, and religion, with all their chauvinistic connotations. Those ideologies provide the means of defining state–society relations and help to explain the failure of secularism worldwide. Today they continue to deny us "a necessarily democratic and inclusive alternative to the political economy of liberalism."[25] The activities of public associations during the colonial period demonstrate the complicity of the native classes in the universalization of capitalist modernity as a class compromise instead of as a Western phenomenon. The reproduction of the binary oppositions between "West" and "non-West," "citizens" and "foreigners" ensure the persistence of class relations. That, in turn, results in the continuing subjugation of economic and political sovereignty to "foreigners." That subjection of sovereignty has been reproduced in NGO discourse ever since independence. Such binaries simultaneously produce and are produced by the spatial variations of capitalist development. They give meaning to the forms of the state. Ironically, civil society's elites during this period were critical of Western modernity. The organizations associated with it were, in fact, at the forefront of anti-missionary activity. They sought to preserve traditional values, which at that time included left-leaning political formations.

During the independence struggle, the leaders of these associations argued that the masses should not be a primary concern until the state was liberated from the colonial governments. By concealing the class basis of state formation, these organizations were complicit with ethnoreligious nationalism. After independence, when the state assumed primary responsibility for social and economic development, the vitality of the native associations declined, even while the social forces that they helped to establish have survived. Colonialism in Sri Lanka, unlike in Bengal, did not inspire a sustained debate on native associations as frontline organizations for anti-state social mobilization. Perhaps this is another important reason why in Sri Lanka neither an independence struggle nor a secular ideal of the state has ever captivated the public mind. The marginalization and replacement of class-based politics with ethnoreligious nationalism in both Sri Lanka and Bangladesh shaped state–society relations in both countries as the newly independent states integrated into the global capitalist system.

Prior to independence, Bangladesh and Sri Lanka both had vibrant civil societies in which numerous associations operated. These associations were crucial spaces for debates on the relationship between the elite classes and the colonial state. Many of those associations were transnational in terms of their outlook, funding, networks, and agendas. They were sustained by the opportunities offered by the colonial economy. In turn, the colonial state and its local elite classes depended on voluntary associations to negotiate their foreignness and their domesticity within the country, as precolonial kings and empires had done. For native elites, these associations were instrumental both in alienating the masses from the class realities of the colonial regime and in consolidating its benefits. Both elites and the colonial state could preserve their distinctiveness from the masses and maintain control over them. Sanjay Joshi's analysis of the middle class in Lucknow sums up the functions of these public associations:

> It was through defining their distinction from other social groups, through their activities in the public sphere, that a group of educated men, and later women, were able to define themselves as middle class. Distinction here worked in both senses of the word; not only did cultural projects of the middle class distinguish it from other social groups, the Indian middle class also contended that the norms and values it was seeking to propagate were superior to those of the existing aristocratic elites, lower classes, and ultimately, to those of the British rulers. Empowerment— both against established social and political elites, and over other subordinated sections of society—was at the heart of the projects constituting the middle class.[26]

The history of these associations suggests capitalism, development, and imperialism are not simply Western phenomena. Associations in Bangladesh and Sri Lanka embodied a class compromise between native elites that was rooted in the spatial diversity of global capitalist relations. They became sites for the mobilization of protest against the colonial state and for the consolidation of native elite control over the postcolonial state. The state, meanwhile, drew on secularism and ethnoreligious nationalism alike as the source of its identity. In the process, the state's class character was suppressed. Divisions among the associations in Sri Lanka were far more pronounced than they were among the associations in Bengal. Their activities, moreover, did not lead to an independence struggle in Sri Lanka as they did in India. Associations in metropolitan Sinhalese Colombo were much less enthusiastic about joining the independence struggle than associations in the Tamil-dominated Jaffna peninsula. When Bengal was divided between Pakistan and India, and East Bengal became a colony of Pakistan, the formal and informal associations in East Bengal played a crucial role in the independence struggle against the Pakistan government. In East Bengal, associations tended to be secular. In contrast, associations in Pakistan tended to be religious. In Bangladesh and Sri Lanka, interest in secularism and pluralism rapidly gave away to religion, ethnicity, and nationalism, which quickly became the main means of distinguishing between the political parties in competition for state power.

## THE POST-INDEPENDENCE STATE

During the postcolonial period, national independence and development were the two main projects of the state and were aligned with capitalism. Variations in the form of the state during this time were determined by the state's responses to capitalism's accumulation and legitimization crises, with policies favoring either free-market or socialist ideals. Developmental variations in the two countries depended on how they responded to the crises, forming alliances with the bipolar power blocs of the Cold War political economy.

The state in these countries carried out numerous initiatives to promote voluntary organizations. It began modeling its own social development programs on NGO programs. State-led development programs not only used NGO models but also solicited their participation. Appropriation of the language and practices of NGOs by the state enabled it to contrast its identity and agendas with those of the colonial regimes. National development was presented as an attempt to revitalize the glories of "traditional civilization." State programs emulating the institutional and organizational characteristics of NGOs were grafted onto the dominant discourse of religious nationalism. Through this process, the state brought a broad spectrum of voluntary organizations under its control.

As political parties gained power in Sri Lanka, native associations lost their influence. Increasingly, the interests of their constituencies were represented in discursive arenas controlled by political parties. Economic problems were redefined in political terms which were more easily understood by state agencies. This "welfarist" ideology produced remarkable improvements in basic living standards for the majority of the population in the areas of health, education, and infrastructure. The results legitimized the state's role as the leading actor in social development. It also enabled people to participate in economic and political processes without much intervention by third-party intermediaries like NGOs.

Until Bangladesh gained independence from Pakistan, state investments in social development were limited. The government based in West Pakistan neglected social and economic development in the East, which was used as a resource base. The massive destruction of life and property and the dislocation of populations caused by the war of liberation, along with the low level of development of state agencies, made it difficult for the new state to assume sole responsibility for social development and governance. Moreover, from its inception Bangladesh was under enormous pressure from international donors to limit the scope of state intervention in the social sector. International development policies favored free-market liberalism over state interventionism. Without a well-developed economic base such as Sri Lanka's export-oriented plantation sector, Bangladesh and its patriotic intelligentsia could not withstand the pressure of international donors, although they were aware of the danger that their country might become a "foreign aid colony." NGOs thus had more space in Bangladesh than in Sri Lanka to establish themselves as important actors in the development process. In Sri Lanka, a new wave of NGOs emerged following the "failure" of state-led development programs, the state suppression of the JVP insurrection in 1971, and a rise in labor union activities. This new generation of NGOs rose to prominence as the only institutional avenues for organized protest against the state.

As they had in the nineteenth century, church-affiliated organizations played a crucial role in this process. Liberation theology and socialism provided much of the intellectual impetus for NGOs. As in the colonial period, most of the participants in these organizations were from diverse religious, ethnic, and racial backgrounds, and they focused on indigenous and bottom-up models in their search for progressive alternatives to socialism and capitalism. Although they were funded by international donors, these models grew increasingly inward-looking and focused on micro-level interventions that exploited local resources and institutions. They attracted intellectuals and activists, some of whom were members of radical revolutionary movements. Everyone involved was searching for alternative paths to progressive social development. This pursuit was extremely attractive to international scholars, and to donors who feared future insurgencies and were interested in replacing state-led development models. However, NGOs during this period were complicit with the economic nationalism of the state. In fact, many of them received financial assistance from the state as well as from international donors. Subsequently, these internationally funded NGOs were on the frontline of criticism of the social welfare state. International donors saw NGO protests against the state as the "voice of the masses," a voice in favor of their neoliberal economic agendas. The objective of international development during this period was to find creative ways of making neoliberal economic reforms acceptable to natives in order to localize the management of capitalism's crises. The promise of NGOs to provide institutional support for these donor demands made them appear as a "third sector" endowed with the capability to overcome the limitations of the state and markets. Since the late 1970s, when Sri Lanka and Bangladesh were flooded with foreign capital, the differences between mainstream political parties disappeared. The "radical" left parties suffered severe electoral defeats. Some of their members then joined the NGOs. Although newly elected political parties were willing to liberalize the economy, they were less inclined to democratize state control of democratic institutions or to interrupt the growing influence of ethnoreligious nationalism on state–society relations. These developments opened a wide space for NGOs to assert their influence vis-à-vis states and for-profit organizations.

## THE NEOLIBERAL STATE

When the Cold War ended, the political parties competing for state power concurred that the same neoliberal economic policies that had enabled their countries to adjust to the imperatives of the world economy offered the most viable path toward future economic development. The neoliberal program in Sri Lanka is expressed in ethnoreligious nationalist terms as an attempt to revitalize traditional civilization. In contrast, religiosity in Bangladesh was more subtle. During the early period of neoliberal economic reforms, relations between NGOs and the governments of Sri Lanka and Bangladesh were generally amicable. Lingering hostility toward NGOs among left-wing political parties was short-lived. Tensions between NGOs and the state began to grow only when free-market economic reforms failed to satisfy basic social and environmental requirements.

NGO criticism of the economic, political, and social failures of the state played a crucial role in providing ideological legitimacy for the state's neoliberal retreat. International donors quoted NGO opponents in an effort to limit the state's economic influence without fully acknowledging its positive impact on social development. The government of Bangladesh was simply not able to invest in social development to the same extent as the government of Sri Lanka.

The higher levels of economic and social development in Sri Lanka were due to the success of the country's welfare policies. The crises resulting from the transition to a market-driven economy did not lead the state to abandon its commitment to neoliberal economic reforms. The state simultaneously adopted two strategies to manage political dissent. One was to introduce constitutional reforms. The other was to use ethnoreligious nationalism to represent itself as the nation's guardian. During this period, NGO activities were ideologically and operationally diverse. However, at the same time, they adhered to the principles of neoliberal capitalism. Using David Harvey's analysis of the political economy of postmodernity, we can see that the celebration of NGO diversity has proven an effective means of eliding the similarity of their projects and their outcomes. It functions as a kind of

> masking and cover-up, [of] all the fetishisms of locality, place, or social grouping, while denying that kind of meta-theory which can grasp the political-economic processes (money flows, international division of labor, financial markets, and the like), that are becoming ever more universalizing in their depth, intensity, reach and power over daily lives.[27]

Although these organizations appear to open up prospects for radical social change by acknowledging the authenticity of marginalized voices, their practices have further marginalized minority social groups.[28] This is true of all NGO interventions concerned with empowerment, good governance, sustainable development, peacebuilding and conflict resolution, food security, and so on. The cultural relativism celebrated in NGO programs is among the most promising means of achieving the universal goals of capitalism, simultaneously increasing capitalism's authority and localizing opposition against it. For example, the argument that microcredit empowers women has served as a centerpiece for these programs. Empowerment discourse springs from the intertwined beliefs that economically empowering women is important and that women are likely to be effective agents of social development. Eventually even radical NGOs that once claimed to oppose capitalist institutions adopted microcredit as a central component of their programs. In the process, they became banks and the people they assisted became borrowers.

The microcredit movement brought commercial banks, international donor agencies, governments, and NGOs into a common sphere in which the broader ideological and institutional parameters for debate and action were provided by the neoliberal model of development. The new organizational and project management practices imposed on NGOs, often under the guise of accountability, transparency, and efficiency, further resulted in the standardization and homogenization of the "NGO world" according to the imperatives of the market. In response to these demands, NGO management has shifted from more radical, ideologically driven approaches to more technocratic approaches. Microcredit has been an effective means of integrating Third World communities into the market economy and disciplining their local economies to function according to the logic of capitalism. Microcredit was a response to the legitimization and accumulation crisis of capitalism. It permitted the expansion of credit markets by promising to resolve information asymmetries, reduce transaction costs, and obviate the moral hazards of conventional credit programs. Microfinance successfully incorporated countless informal-sector organizations into the diverse culture of neoliberal capitalism. Its promise of self-sufficiency, self-reliance, and self-empowerment for women provided ideological justification for the state to reduce investments in social sectors that are not necessary for the functioning of neoliberal institutions.

Microcredit promises to integrate complex cultural practices into a highly dynamic yet unstable economy geared toward sustaining the capitalist system. In this context, the significance of micro-enterprises cannot be underestimated. Micro-enterprises should not be

> seen as a matter of scientific knowledge, a body of theories and programs concerned with the achievement of true progress, but rather as a series of political technologies intended to manage and give shape to the reality of the Third World.[29]

Microfinance does not so much humanize capitalism as it capitalizes on humanism, increasing the market's control over the resources of the poor—and poor women in particular—by making them bear the economic and social costs of the neoliberal economy. It is the "feminization of capitalism"—i.e., the economic exploitation of social and political demands for gender equality—that has forced progressive NGOs to reorganize their activities according to the shifting parameters of neoliberalism. Microfinance involved a trickle-down economic approach at the grassroots level. Poor women were told that their overall well-being would flow out of the success of micro-enterprises.[30] Microfinance brings about perhaps the most subtle form of alienation under capitalism among those who do not directly participate in wage labor. In the final analysis, such alienation at the grassroots level needs to be understood as an integral part of the production of class relations on a national scale through the apparatus of the state. It essentially reproduces class relations in the ongoing struggle for gender equality.[31]

The euphoria over the success of microcredit, however, is rapidly fading. This signals an emerging crisis not only for NGOs but also for the state. There is little evidence that a high repayment rate signifies an overall improvement in the economy and the likelihood of widespread NGO-loan defaults is great. If such defaults occur, the state may be forced to bear the economic burden. If that happens, the state would be unlikely to mediate on behalf of NGOs. Similarly, it is unlikely that international capital will rely on NGOs to create the social, economic, and political stability needed to ensure its continuity. Both the successes and the failures of microcredit will bolster the credibility of the neoliberal state, not only by distancing the masses from direct engagement with capitalist forces, but also by encouraging the dominance of ethnoreligious nationalism in state–society relations as the state continues to fail to provide political and economic stability.

## WOMEN'S ORGANIZATIONS FROM MISSIONS TO NGOs

Missionary interventions in home science, health, and vocational education for women sparked local debates regarding the meaning and scope of female agency in colonial society. In the process, they also facilitated women's entry into the public sphere and the transformation of the household. Women were situated dialectically between anti-colonial nationalisms and international feminisms. This made them instrumental in the processes of state centralization (i.e., the control of the household through gendered division of labor) and domestication (i.e., the representation of the state as the mother).[32]

Kumari Jayawardena suggests that Christian missionaries were the first feminists on the subcontinent. She argues that they had a genuine empathy with indigenous women, and a wish to elevate their status, despite the fact that liberation from traditional hierarchies did not necessarily liberate women from the patriarchal structures of Christian families, or change the gendered nature of the colonial and postcolonial state. In her study of missionaries, social and political reformers in South Asia, Jayawardena points out that the female missionaries were aware of the problems of indigenous women.[33] She argues that the strong, independent, often single women who became important missionaries were feminists in their own way. It was the pious woman's "duty" to overcome her "natural diffidence" in order that she might better serve the mission.[34] While women were often in subordinate positions in the missionary hierarchy, the mission movement contributed significantly to the entrance of women into the public domain. Thus, domesticity was emphasized, while at the same time evangelism encouraged women to move away from the home and into the "world" because it was a practical religion that placed service and manners before doctrine. Evangelism stressed self-sacrifice and service to others—characteristics that were seen as naturally feminine—and thus encouraged women to leave the home sphere to do charity work in the "outside world." Most female reformers of the nineteenth century believed that the guarantor of social progress, the agent of civilization, was woman herself. However, the same women reformers put nationalist interests over feminist concerns because national liberation was considered an essential prerequisite for women's liberation, making the state an important agent of transformation of women's lives. Until the introduction of neoliberal economic reforms, women's associations tended to adopt a welfare approach and sought concessions from the state.

The failures of the state led to the growth of many women's organizations concerned with women's role in development. With the advent of neoliberal economic reforms, NGO activism centered on gender-related issues increased. Demands for women's equality in development soon turned into demands for broader changes, leading to the mainstreaming of gender in development, which subsequently promoted "empowerment" of women. Economic empowerment was considered an essential prerequisite for social, cultural, and political empowerment, and this drew women into the orbit of global capitalism, and transformed the NGO sector as a whole. At that moment, microcredit "colonized" many progressive women's organizations, leading them to compromise their radicalism. Microcredit lending also created divisions and competition between women's organizations. Internationally funded feminist NGOs never evolved into a coherent sector or a social movement because their focus on isolated projects fragmented them. They were driven by competition for international funding, wracked by the ideological differences between them, and unable to successfully manage their relationship with the state. Many of their projects jettisoned class politics, and the majority of women's NGOs remain distanced from grassroots organizations. The isolation of women's NGOs is encouraged by the propaganda of the anti-NGO lobby, and bolstered by state claims that NGOs are run by women who want to spread Western values and are involved in international conspiracies against the nation. The long history of attempts by women's organizations to challenge gender inequalities and the gendered nature of the state includes too few successes, and many of their efforts have had unintentionally counterproductive results because they were embedded in capitalist forces and relations of production. Like other NGOs, women's NGOs must confront and challenge capitalism as well as gender hierarchies.

## THE NGO-IZATION OF KNOWLEDGE PRODUCTION

As a result of the state's monopoly of the education industry, the vibrant culture of cosmopolitanism in voluntary associations has significantly declined. When the local economy opened to international markets, international development institutions and governments shifted the production of knowledge to civil society organizations. Since the 1970s, due to diminishing financial resources for public universities and the politicization of academia, many intellectuals have given up their positions as instructors to pursue careers in the NGO sector. Some of these intellectuals were Marxist-Leninist radicals and members of insurgencies and underground resistance movements.

In contrast to state-funded organizations, NGOs provide a higher degree of freedom and resources to those engaged in critical intellectual work. Activities that challenge state power only receive international donor assistance if they are conducted outside of state institutions. Yet the political economy of NGO knowledge production is the same as that of neoliberal institutions. Many NGO research projects are subcontracted by international donors interested in specific development issues and policies. While NGO knowledge systems are "progressive," they have systematically de-centered and marginalized class relations by characterizing it as one among many other social relations. The concepts of the proletariat and the bourgeoisie have all but disappeared from their social praxis, and been replaced with concepts such as multicultur-alism, relativism, and diversity, none of which commands a central place. These new intellectuals prefer ad hoc social movements to political parties and labor unions, and have severed their links with political parties, leaving them isolated from the general population.

NGO-ization has proven itself an effective method of managing knowledge-producing activities, including potentially counter-hegemonic ones, in conformance with neoliberal agendas. The purposefully cultivated native identity of these intellectuals, including those with postcolonial intellectual sympathies, lends the knowledge they produce an air of indigenous authenticity. Considering the difficulties of privatizing knowledge production in Sri Lanka and Bangladesh, where education is considered a public good and attempts to privatize it often lead to political instability, native intellectuals can also offer neoliberal institutions a degree of legitimacy.

Responding to increases in international funding in the late 1990s, academics in state universities started semi-independent research centers which played an extremely important role in transforming university curricula and learning cultures in accordance with the imperatives of the market economy. The knowledge systems of those intellectuals are not broad or comprehensive enough in scope or aim to undermine capitalism's ideological authority. Unfortunately, the limited explanatory power of this "progressive knowledge" obscures the "role of structuring structures" and the existence of "totalizing discourses" in the global economy. The influence of postmodernism in anthropology, for example, has been "less radicalizing than many of its exponents hoped."[35]

The disjunctures and disarticulations created by these knowledge production practices are often exploited by ethnonationalism, which provides a coherent narrative for people trying to make sense of a fragmented social order. This is ironic, as radical intellectuals are the most vocal critics of ethnoreligious nationalists. Ethnoreligious nationalists condemn radical knowledge production activities as foreign and unpatriotic, further limiting the expression and dissemination of truly counterhegemonic knowledge. Today in Sri Lanka and Bangladesh, the space available for critical knowledge production activities is highly restricted, and the prevailing culture of state-induced fear has sidelined most of the intellectuals who might otherwise have offered thoughtful critiques of state power. The concentration of knowledge production activities among NGOs has also led to tensions between state-appointed intellectuals and those who work exclusively for NGOs. Personality and ideological differences, as well as competition for donor funds and consulting projects, add to the tensions, which, in turn, are exploited by the state to justify its control over NGOs. NGOs and their critics have colonized knowledge production and in the process have jettisoned class from their respective analyses and actions, making them complicit with capitalist development.

## ETHNORELIGIOUS NATIONALISM AND THE NATIONAL SECURITY STATE

As the differences disappear between the economic policies of mainstream political parties, ethnoreligious nationalist groups (ERNGs) have emerged as the most prominent anti-NGO voices. ERNGs are not homogeneous. Most extremist groups want their countries to become exclusivist ethno-theocratic states, although some are willing to accommodate other religious groups in order to achieve specific political and economic ends. ERNGs represent a small minority of clergymen, professionals, politicians, and businessmen whose claims to political power are made possible by their collaboration with mainstream political parties.

The NGOs targeted by ERNGs are typically small and poorly funded. Ethnoreligious nationalist criticism is sometimes sparked by competition between NGOs and ethnoreligious nationalist groups for state resources. They may also evolve out of personal and ideological conflicts. To a large extent, NGOs, like other institutions, are interested in their own survival. In the struggle for territory and legitimacy, they enter into formal and informal partnerships with political actors who criticize them, just as politicians move from one party to another and switch alliances. Popular views of NGOs, whether positive or negative, should not blind us to the fact that such partnerships often involve bribes and the politicization of NGO investments.

Ethnoreligious nationalism pervades all the ethnic and religious groups of the region, but NGOs are often criticized for disproportionately accusing a specific community of ethnoreligious nationalist biases. The real differences among different ethnoreligious nationalist groups involve access to resources. Anti-NGO ERNGs acquire popular legitimacy because they associate NGOs with neocolonialism, imperialism, Westernization, and Christianization—forces that are widely thought to undermine the sovereignty of the country. Some ERNGs are, in fact, highly organized NGOs supported by international donor funds. At a basic level, ERNG criticism of NGOs seeks to establish the validity of one historical narrative over another. ERNG groups accuse NGOs of collaborating with "foreign powers" and denying the influence of colonialism on modern associations, ERNGs included. By describing mainstream NGOs as both foreign and Christian, ERNGs are helping the state to consolidate political power.

Here the public faces a dilemma. On the one hand, the ERNGs point to potential ways in which NGO activities could help the transnational economic and geopolitical interests that control the internal affairs of the country. On the other hand their claims also legitimize government allegations that those who demand political autonomy through militant struggle are simply "terrorists" manipulated by external actors. "Terrorism" necessitates a military solution, so the story goes. War has thus been proposed as the only real solution to ethnic conflict. This narrative, bolstered by popular condemnation of terrorism, suppresses the conflict's long political history. Terrorism is seen as an aberration in the country's history which can only be corrected through military victory. Secessionist groups also portray military victory as the only means of safeguarding the rights of minorities. Neither the government nor secessionist groups tolerate NGO criticism. Both simultaneously suppress NGOs and selectively exploit their services to advance their respective agendas. Anti-NGO criticism strikes the public as plausible because NGOs have lost legitimacy in the areas of humanitarian, human rights, and conflict resolution, where their policies have been contradictory and their actions far from transparent.

Terrorism is also blamed for the persistence of economic problems. It is described as a serious impediment to the country's progress towards economic and political modernity. In the absence of an alternative to capitalism, terrorism and economic stagnation are invariably viewed as two separate issues. The government contends that the masses must tolerate economic hardships and the high costs of war until terrorism is defeated. Conflict resolution, peacebuilding, and humanitarian interventions by NGOs, including the ones that are opposed by ERNGs, do not challenge the dominant nationalist paradigm. NGOs rarely question the sociological meanings of popular sovereignty. Those who do challenge those meanings represent a small minority of foreign-funded NGOs. Both the government and military use constitutional and extra-constitutional means to shut these critics down by branding them as traitors and terrorists.

Mainstream political parties, both secular and religious, refrain from directly challenging the ethnoreligious nationalist paradigm. Instead, they compete to become guardians of ethnoreligious nationalist interests. Politicians are extremely skilled at appropriating the rhetoric of ERNG groups while at the same time attempting to prevent those groups from becoming too powerful. Political parties exploit ERNG criticism of NGOs and use ERNGs to weaken any organizations that might threaten or embarrass the state. Ethnoreligious nationalism sanctions the state's efforts to institutionalize the national security paradigm.

The militarization of ethnoreligious nationalism drives competition among states, militants, and NGOs for access to and control over humanitarian spaces. In Sri Lanka, the United Nations and international donors alike have completely failed to get the government or the LTTE to open space for humanitarian interventions. The presence of humanitarian actors in war-torn areas tends to legitimize the claims and actions of one party over another. It threatens access to international financial, political, and moral support. International responses to humanitarian crises are shaped more by strategic economic and political interests than by human needs. Anti-NGO discourse is an outgrowth of the competition between the state and militants for international support for their respective agendas. Anti-NGO claims framed in the language of national security and the war against terrorism justify the government's monopoly over humanitarian activities during natural disasters and civil conflicts. The state exploits these situations to carry out its key objectives, such as acquiring property, resettling populations, and effecting market economic reforms. Such objectives would not be feasible under normal circumstances due to their high costs, their unpopularity, and their technical difficulty. The competition between political actors for the financial resources of NGOs also encourages them to court the organizations. The competition between NGOs for territory and access to beneficiaries forces them to seek political patronage. The rehabilitation and reconstruction programs of NGOs are also consistent with neoliberal rationality. Humanitarian assistance is exploited as a means of introducing market-based economic reforms that would not have been possible under normal circumstances.

The international community is hypocritical, often employing double standards in its dealings with underdeveloped countries. Western countries have become increasingly apathetic or "neutral" towards humanitarian and human rights issues, pursuing a dual policy of supporting the war against terrorism while at the same time promoting political solutions. The government of Sri Lanka and, to a lesser extent, the government of Bangladesh can ignore the demands of Western countries that human rights be a condition for receiving aid, since that aid is often available from non-Western countries with no strings attached. The international community does not question the regional, economic, political, or security interests of these newly emerging non-Western donors. They are important partners in extending the control of transnational capital to developing countries. The anti-Western, anti-NGO lobby is not critical of transnational capital's impact on the country's sovereignty. Instead, the lobby is at odds with groups critical of those effects.

The anti-NGO voices ignore the role of India in shaping the political conflict in Sri Lanka and Bangladesh. Anti-NGOism provides popular legitimacy for ethnoreligious nationalist and national security paradigms that in turn suppress freedom of expression, freedom of the press, and political dissent in general. This protects the state against critical analysis of its military, economic, and political transactions between the local elites and the international actors. Ethnicity and national security become the fundamental determinants in the competition for state patronage and economic resources. The masses are desensitized to the plunder of the economy and the undermining of national sovereignty. Forced to tolerate the human, material, and psychological costs of the war and the erosion of their economic and political stakes, they are led to believe that war is the basis of peace, security, and development.

Although most ethnoreligious nationalists claim to be concerned with national sovereignty, they are primarily concerned with the sovereignty of their respective ethnic groups. They don't protest the historically unprecedented economic, political, and military subjugation of the country to transnational capital in collaboration with local elites because the ethnoreligious nationalist project is a class project. NGOs and their critics ignore or suppress its class character. By vilifying ethnoreligious nationalists and reconfiguring the conflict in terms of ethnicity rather than class, NGOs, like their critics, legitimize neoliberal capitalist agendas. In the final analysis, ethnoreligious nationalism and national security paradigms serve as vital means of domesticating and managing the ongoing crisis of accumulation and legitimization, which is manifested in the continuing centralization of state power.

NGOs will be unable to carry out truly counterhegemonic interventions as long as their thinking and practices do not transcend the relations and forces of production. Without genuinely alternative thinking, neither NGOs nor their critics will be able to challenge what Rudolf Hilferding called "organized capitalism," a paradigm in which the state and giant corporations or FPOs manage the economy and in which individuals submit to state and corporate control.[36] Citizens thus become credulous spectators of media presentations and discourses which arbitrate public opinion and reduce audiences to consumers of news. NGOs limit the possibility of raising political awareness of current economic and political conditions. They fail to prevent the public consciousness from being colonized and subverted by ethnoreligious nationalism.

The problem is only exacerbated by the efforts of ethnic diasporas to mobilize international support for their respective communities back home. Civilians caught in conflict seek assistance from diaspora NGOs in expressing their grievances to the international community, seeing them as the last resort in their efforts to influence the state to end their suffering. Diaspora organizations often completely overlook humanitarian and human rights issues in favor of supporting the agendas of their respective constituencies. They, like the state and its antagonists, consider military victory an essential prerequisite to peace. The involvement of diaspora-supported NGOs invites even further state suppression of local and international NGOs, which are perceived to strengthen the influence of diaspora organizations against the state. Diaspora NGOs reinforce ethnonationalism and the security state as the defining paradigms of the conflict, thus further augmenting the power of the state. The state claims about NGOs' international links bolster its accusations that they undermine national sovereignty, and justify the state's increased regulation of their activities.

In engaging with the debates between NGOs and ERNGs, one should be careful not to fall into the trap of essentializing religions as fundamentally opposed to democracy in doctrine and/or in practice. The histories of Sri Lankan and Bangladeshi governments demonstrate that so called "secular" governments have suppressed democratic participation of its citizens more than the religious conservative governments. The role of religion should not be confused with ethnoreligious nationalism; religion should not be reduced to the political and economic institutions associated with it. Government and societal responses towards religion always depend on how religion is associated with projects that compete in the solicitation of state patronage. Here one finds that the arguments of so-called "progressive" NGOs who criticize the ethnoreligious nationalists and demand a neutral, secular state neglect two issues. First, what is a "neutral" state? If one takes "neutrality" to be the given characteristic of the state, then one would find it extremely difficult to explain the social inequalities that are structured in and through state practices. Secondly, as Vinoth Ramachandra suggests, we might explore the possibility that people embrace ethnoreligious nationalism because its religious component provides them with a moral basis for their being and action:

> Much of the discussion of democracy and secularism in political circles is hopelessly abstract and outdated, and less grounded. These discussions seem to move in a world devoid of nuclear missiles, of acid rain or tropical deforestation, of transnational corporations or financial deregulation. Whether these challenges can be tackled merely by an expanded notion of "human rights," "good governance," "corporate social responsibility," and the organization of more interregional and international conferences is highly dubious. The self regulating interests, in whatever guise it appears (and even the language of rights descends to self-interests when the theological roots of that language are forgotten), is an inadequate basis for moral action.[37]

Ethnoreligious nationalists' accusation that NGOs engage in "proselytization" should not simply be reduced to conversion from one religion to another. It should also be seen as a response to the search for a moral foundation that does not separate the "spiritual" from the "material" determinants of human life; the religious component is not always a derivative of the political projects associated with it. At the same time, in both Sri Lanka and Bangladesh, one must not overlook the possibility that linking NGOs with proselytization is also a means of exploiting ethnoreligious nationalism as a means of centralizing state power.

However, at some point it has to be channeled through an economic system that can only be maintained through the continuous reproduction of inequalities. This makes such moral bases vulnerable to exploitation. The charge of "unethical conversions" attributed to NGOs should also be understood as an instrument of the highly partisan political and economic projects of its proponents. Perhaps the most important characteristic of these projects is that they are only concerned with the "conversion" of those they identify as poor, i.e. "soft targets," but not the rich and the powerful.

The charge of proselytization preempts public criticism of political exploitation of religion. In contrast to the Sri Lankan case, NGOs, intellectuals, and political parties in Bangladesh have been more active in challenging such exploitation, but NGOs have failed to grapple with the complexity of the relationship between the state and religion. The state, far from being a neutral actor, derives its legitimacy, in the Hegelian sense, from its power to embody "true freedom" or "ethical totality" by appealing to the metanarratives, like religion, which provide a moral base for society. The states' choices of these metanarratives often do not provide formal and substantive equality to all under their jurisdiction. And even when they are inclusive, formal equalities in the political domain are always undermined by substantive inequalities endemic in the economic domain.

NGOs' demands for a neutral state do not address the influence of religion in state formation. This power is not derived through state practices but through faith, which provides an explanation for the existence of good and evil. The anti-NGO lobby always grounds its claims in a religious worldview embedded in historical consciousness, whereas "progressive" NGOs ground their claims in secular ideals which may seem naive and unrealistic. NGOism is a manifestation of evolutionary trajectories of state–society relations, embedded in symbiotic relations between competing accounts of religio-historical consciousness and the historical development of capital.

## THE POLITICS OF THE ANTI-POLITICS MACHINE

NGOs are involved in every aspect of social, economic, and political life. They have not left any area of policy untouched, and governments and international bodies pay a great deal of attention, both positive and negative, to their activities. The expansion of NGO activism is expressed in phrases such as "self-sufficiency," "self-reliance," "good governance," "empowerment," "conflict resolution," "peacebuilding," "sustainable development," and "livelihoods." We can imagine these organizations as "individual firms" in the "NGO-industrial complex" because their material and ideological projects function as another space within which capitalism resolves its accumulation crises. While their interventions are responses to crises generated by capitalism and its manifestations within the nation-state, NGOs ideologically and operationally fail to attribute problems to capitalism, just as they do not seek to transform society by challenging it. The firms in the NGO industrial complex simultaneously localize and internationalize the management of these crises. Just like the firms in capitalist industries, NGOs absorb the crises of capitalism, and in turn provide material and ideological resources to those affected by the crisis to resolve them within the parameters of capitalism. In effect, NGOs appear to fulfill the dream of neoclassical institutional economists by facilitating conditions to correct market and state failures, so that the capitalist economy can move toward the ideal of perfect competition—an ideal that promises to improve both producer and consumer efficiency. This suggests that the diverse activities of NGOs could be conceptualized as an "NGO mode of production": an auxiliary capitalist mode of production that facilitates the development of relations and forces of production which complement the capitalist mode of production. This is often achieved by the commodification of dissent that is potentially counterhegemonic and threatening to capitalist ideology and institutions.

However, like capitalist firms, NGOs have failed to achieve the ideal of perfect competition found in mainstream economics. Competition between NGOs for funding and operational territory forces them to control and manipulate information about their projects and to offer personal favors to politicians and businesses. That, in turn, results in increased state regulation of the entire NGO sector. In fact, the NGO industrial complex resembles an oligopoly. When NGO protests target states and corporations, they almost invariably ensure that the fundamental imperatives of capitalism do not become the object of their protest. Partnerships between the state, NGOs, and corporations or FPOs employ neoliberal governmentality to discipline the ideals and practices of these institutions, as each one of them absorbs the other's legitimacy crises and manages them according to the logic of capital. This is neoliberal governmentality masquerading as good governance.[38]

The NGO industrial complex derives legitimacy from its claim to be located in civil society. In Bangladesh and Sri Lanka, the organizations that are most influential in civil society are those funded by international donors. That, of course, excludes labor unions. Many of the formal equalities in these countries would not have been possible without the mediation of these organizations. However, their scope and aims are limited by their relationship with the state and their allegiance to capitalism. Civil society, then, is equally empowering and disempowering. It brings formal freedoms by liberating society from the state in political, legal, and market domains. Yet capitalism's universal drive toward self-realization via the accumulation of profit undermines the appearance of equality in the sphere of exchange by generating inequality in the sphere of production. This duality is sustained by the separation of politics and economics into two distinct spheres, in which the liberal capitalist State is [...] engaged in a continual process of upholding the principles of freedom and equality, while constantly modifying their application in practice, in order to overcome the contradictions continually created by the central contradictions at the heart of the relations of production.[39]

NGOs produce and sustain the civil society/state duality as the primary basis of alienation in modern society. In relation to the state, the individual is at once a citizen participating in the affairs of society and an object of political regulation.

As a member of civil society, despite or because of one's freedom to determine one's will, the individual is subject to those alien powers (economic laws) that determine his chances, impose interest structure onto his needs, and deny autonomy of social life.[40]

Thus, Marx wrote:

The basis of the State in antiquity was slavery; the basis of the modern State is civil society and the individual of the civil society, that is the independent individual, whose only link with other individuals is private interest and unconscious, natural necessity, the slave of wage labor, the selfish needs of himself and others; the modern State has recognized this, its natural foundation, in the universal rights of man.[41]

Marx, in his observations on civil society and the various intermediary associations representing it, pointed out that socially transformative capacities and limitations must be derived from the nature of the relationship to a given form of the state. As Marx argued,

the social stability attained through the institutionalization of voluntary associations as corporations requiring State recognition and representation of the State bureaucracy on their councils— that is, the closure achieved through group representation of civil society in the State via the estate system—fatally undermines the independence of civil society, whose principles are individuality, free association, and self determination.[42]

In this sense, civil society reproduces the ruling class. In "On the Jewish Question and The Holy Family," Marx noted that civil society was a communal movement because it concerned the emancipation of the bourgeoisie vis-à-vis the feudal order. The communal character is evident in the continuing reproduction of the hegemony of the ruling class through the associations of civil society, from colonial times to the present.

As capitalism matures, the philanthropic, voluntary, and corporative practices associated with civil society's organizations facilitate the production and contestation of class relations. Despite the fact that such organizations have the potential to become counterhegemonic forces, Marx noted in the "Inaugural Address":

> The corporative movement was already a "great fact," representing a preliminary victory for labour over that of property. It had already shown, and by deed rather than argument, that the masters were not necessary for large scale production. For this reason it acquired many false friends between 1848 and 1864, "philanthropic middle-class spouters" anxious to use it for their own quack purpose. This has to be resisted, as did any tendency towards localism and self-sufficiency. Corporation could never defeat monopoly unless it developed into national dimensions.[43]

NGOs are unlikely to inspire counter-hegemonic national movements. That would compromise their distinctiveness (e.g., diversity, localism, apoliticism) from the state and for-profit organizations. Even if they did inspire such a movement, that movement would be limited by the fact that it would be grounded in capitalist relations and forces of production. As individual organizations, NGOs would not be able to confront the monopoly powers of capital, as exercised through the apparatus of the state. Under capitalism, such associations, even in their most radical forms, "bear the husks of the old system as well as the seeds of the new."[44]

Despite their best intentions, NGOs contribute to the polarization of social crises along class lines because they have embraced a neoliberal agenda. This polarization of social relations through NGO activities underwrites capitalist class relations, as it is manifested in the spatially uneven development of global capitalism articulated within the boundaries of the nation-state. Both NGOs and the state are contributors to the "institutional configuration of power" that characterizes the "development regime" of the late colonial and postcolonial states,[45] where development is simply not the Western imposition Arturo Escobar said it was.[46] NGOs are less an "anti-politics machine" and more a neoliberal political machine.[47] In practice, the post-development school is complicit in the spatial division, fragmentation, and localization of social dissent. In that respect, it helps to perpetuate the type of governmentality that capitalism requires for its reproduction.

Throughout history, NGOs have been ideologically and operationally diverse. The very diversity of NGOs has given them a semblance of autonomy vis-à-vis the state, an illusion that ultimately serves the interests of "neoliberal governmentality". The spatial multiplicity of power relationships and the contestations associated with NGOs along the lines of class, race, gender, environment, and territorial identities are never consolidated into a functional counterhegemonic paradigm. The fragmentations of NGO projects along the lines of diversity and cultural relativism completely obscure and suppress public consciousness of the way diversity is coordinated and disciplined by the ever-universalizing class logic of capitalism. The historical relationship between state forms and NGOs shows the creativity of capitalism in appropriating and disciplining the ideas and practices of NGOs and their opponents. The disappearance of class from the ideas and practices of the NGO industrial complex makes that complex complicit with the hegemonic ethnoreligious nationalist and national security paradigms that shape relations among NGOs, the state, and society. It must be noted that the general public is not privy to the true character of interactions between NGOs and the state. The public may be aware of the anti-NGO claims filtered through the media, but the media is, in part, owned by the active patrons and beneficiaries of ethnoreligious nationalist organizations and the military industrial complex in general.

## A POST-NGO STATE FORMATION?

Today, several factors continue to restrict the space available to NGOs in general and human rights NGOs in particular. Among those factors are local and international conditions, favorable to the state, for mobilizing ethnoreligious nationalism and national security; the erosion of the public legitimacy of NGOs as defenders of the public good, due to their inconsistency, hypocrisy, and unaccountability; the colonization of NGO activities by market forces and the blurring of the boundaries between the two; and the ability of the state to shield NGOs from international scrutiny of their actions and practices. The state's power has grown beyond the expectations of both neoliberal thinkers and their critics. State power over NGOs is reinforced by competition for resources and operational territory and diversity in the NGO sector. The government's goal of restricting the available space for NGOs does not necessarily entail controlling their financial and developmental operations. However, such control is an important element of the state's overall economic, political, and security agenda. The UN is unable to make a difference because, as journalist J.S. Tissanayagam noted, it is nothing but a "club of states." As such, it lacks consistency, transparency, and accountability.[48]

Even if the threats to national security from local, regional, and international sources are brought under control, society will have to cope with the serious social, psychological, economic, and political consequences resulting from a highly militarized ethnoreligious nationalist social order. The prospects of improving the general economic well-being of the masses are grim. While the state may be successful in securing political sovereignty vis-à-vis its own minority populations, its national sovereignty has become far more subservient to regional actors, particularly to non-Western ones, such as India, China, and oil-rich Islamic countries. States have very little economic sovereignty.[49] The public's tolerance of economic difficulties in the name of national security and national independence is reaching its limit, as their anxiety about the future grows. The form of the state, and its relationship with NGOs, will be shaped by its choices in managing economic and political crises. It may either continue to embrace ethnoreligious nationalism and militarization, or nationalize social development and reestablish the state as the main provider of public goods. The state's choices will depend on its capacity to shield itself from international scrutiny and to avoid compliance with international treaties, as well as on its ability to suppress domestic political dissent. The international state system has tended to hide behind national sovereignty to avoid enforcing individual states' compliance with international treaties, particularly when recalcitrant states are important allies in the global war against terrorism. The two most glaring consequences of state suppression of "progressive" NGOs in response to the demands of ethnoreligious nationalists are the dearth of institutions through which people can express their "counterhegemonic" views, and the social, economic, and political disorder resulting from the international state system's lack of accountability.

The crises of capitalism will result in continued limits on NGO interventions through state regulation and the commercialization of NGOs' own organizational cultures. These trends, however, will not prevent the opening of new frontiers, or society's demand for social justice institutions. If NGOs are to take advantage of opportunities and restore their credibility as effective agents of progressive social change, they must differentiate themselves not only in theory, but also in practice, both from the state and from for-profit organizations. To do so, they must develop a coherent counterhegemonic ideology and affirm their commitment to a political program capable of directly challenging capitalism. They need to re-envision the nature of the state, rather than accepting its form as predetermined by the class relations of capitalism. Class relations should be brought into the center of their praxis. Marx describes revolutionary praxis as "an active and social epistemology; the unity of theory and practice emancipates man from the contemplative, alienated existence that was forced on him."[50] Such an endeavor requires a serious moral commitment, and a strong political will to search for social and environmental justice outside the ideological and institutional parameters of capitalism.

To translate ideology into positive social praxis, NGOs must first demonstrate the ability and will to develop sustainable transnational solidarity centered on class inequalities. They must keep it in mind that class inequality is produced and sustained through all other social forms of inequalities. Second, NGOs must seek ideological and material ways to exceed the limits imposed by state sovereignty and transnational capital on NGO activities. Today, it is generally understood that social and economic relations are imperfect, and there is wide agreement that we can do much to improve them. Third, NGOs have helped us to understand the magnitude of the problems, and the contributions of NGOs are necessary for resolving them. But, despite their best intentions, they continually fail to achieve too many of their worthwhile goals. They seem to lack the political commitment and will necessary to bridge the gap between "knowledge for understanding" and "knowledge for action." This problem is well illustrated in St. Paul's letter to the Romans:

> For the desire to do what is good is with me, but there is no ability to do it. For I do not do the good that I want to do, but I practice the evil that I do not want to do. Now if I do what I do not want, I am no longer the one doing it, but it is the sin that lives in me.[51]

Let us imagine that "sin" and "evil" here refer to the oppressive forces that rupture just and equitable social relations. The challenge is fundamentally a moral one, though its foundations are consistently marginalized, misunderstood, and misarticulated in both "universalist" and "cultural relativist" discourses sympathetic to modernist and postmodernist perspectives on social change. Humanity's search for reference points, for an all-encompassing worldview to serve as a basis of moral judgments, will always bring the question of religion to the forefront of discussions of social justice. The centrality of morality in social discourse continues to create space for religion in social transformation, because

> whatever the excesses of secularism as political ideology, secularization as a cultural process does not seem to be at odds with the religious resurgence of today ... with the exception of a few notable cases, secularization has shed its hard-core tendency to draw on the prerogatives of state power to become a combative dogma.[52]

NGOs compel postmodernist and postdevelopmentalist social theorists to remember that structure and ideology not only limit, but also enable human agency. Bringing progressive universalist ideology into the center of praxis is essential if society is to "empower" people to address the problems of contemporary capitalism. Our choice of ideology should avoid the unproductive rhetoric of the "triumphalism of the Western agency and the strident claims of Third World victimization,"[53] and instead rest on firm moral foundations.

# Notes

## PREFACE

1. Smith (2004): 10.
2. Marx (1965): 58, quoted in Avineri (1968): 68.
3. Marx (1962): 403–4, quoted in Avineri (1968): 67.
4. Ibid., 67.
5. Ibid., 69.
6. Bebbington (1997): 10.
7. Fisher and Ponniah (2003): 29.
8. Hardt and Negri (2004): 20.
9. James (1963).

## INTRODUCTION

1. Jammer (1954/1993): xiii–xiv.
2. Steinberg (2001).
3. Ibid., 3.
4. Ibid., 4.
5. Nelson (1995); Paul (1996).
6. Geertz (1985): 218.
7. Thrift (1985): 366–403.
8. Korten (1990).
9. Uphoff (1993): 607–22; (1987): 145–60.
10. Stirrat and Henkel (1998): 66–80.
11. Korten (1990): 50.
12. Fernando (1995).
13. Wirsing (1977): 7.
14. Bourdieu (1972): 97.
15. Lewis (2001): 83–106.
16. Salmon (1993): 109–22.
17. Fisher (2003): 39–73; Korten and Qizon (1990).
18. Gledhill (1999): 135.
19. Salmon (1993): 110.
20. Ibid., 109–22.
21. Linklater (1998): 190.
22. Petras (2000): 27.
23. Sassen (1999): 233.
24. Ibid.
25. Laclau and Mouffe (1990): 175.
26. Ibid., 233.
27. Habermas (1989): 140.
28. Ibid., 48; see also Baker (1992).
29. Ibid., 184.
30. Ehrenberg (1999): 234.

31. Whaites (1996); see also Kean (1992), Edwards and Hulme (eds) (1992).
32. Ehrenberg (1999): 234.
33. Kean (2003): 7.
34. Eley (1993): 298.
35. Blair (1996): 25.
36. Ibid., 30.
37. Ibid., 41.
38. Jenkins (2000): 260.
39. Wood (1996): 83.
40. Ehrenberg (1999): 246.
41. Goodhand and Chamberlain (1996): 235.
42. World Court Project UK (2003).
43. Ibid.
44. Lowe and Lloyd (eds) (1997): 23.
45. Gowan (1999): 3.
46. Boyer and Drache (eds) (1996): 2.
47. Boli and Thomas (1999).
48. Ramonetthe (2004).
49. Ibid., 15.
50. Ibid., 16.
51. Ibid., 18.
52. Ibid., 48.
53. Ibid., 298.
54. Ibid., 196.
55. Ibid., 198.
56. Ibid., 298.
57. Steinmetz (1999): 26.
58. Hoogvelt (2001): 93.
59. Cummins (1999): 619–22.
60. Dicklitch (1998): 36.
61. Crosette (2003).
62. "America and the Rest" (2003).
63. Rashid (2002): 15.
64. Lobe (2003).
65. Bahumic (2003).
66. Meldrum (2002).
67. "End of International NGO Activity in the Gaza Strip?" (2003); Meldrum (2003).
68. McBride and Wiseman (eds) (2000); Sassen and Appiah (1998).
69. Hadiwinata (2003); Holloway (1999): 21; Lewis (2001).
70. Ibid., 13.
71. Fernando (1998).
72. Harvey (1996).
73. Mitchell (1999): 77.
74. Scott (1999).
75. Foucault (1991): 87–104.
76. Kerr (1999): 173–203.
77. Garland (1999): 15–45.
78. Marx (1859): 255.
79. Wolf (1982): 75.

80. Avineri (1968): 86–7.
81. Steinmetz (1999): 19.
82. Marx (1859); Avineri (1968): 69.
83. Wolf (1982): 77.
84. North (1990): 4.
85. Elster (1986/1994): 331.
86. Marx and Engels (1845–6/2003): 77–9.
87. Ibid.
88. Ibid.
89. Ibid., 21.
90. Ibid.
91. Hobsbawm (ed.) (1998): 44.
92. Ibid.
93. Harvey (2001): 86.
94. Ibid., 133.
95. Ibid., 134.
96. Marx quoted in Ehrenberg (1999): 134.
97. Marx (1956): 283.
98. Harvey (2000): 25.
99. Marx and Engels quoted in Ehrenberg (1999): 140.
100. Ehrenberg (1999): 221.
101. Marx and Engels quoted in Harvey (2000): 25.
102. Marx (1974): 69.
103. Jessop (1991): 157.
104. Ibid., 158.
105. Jessop (1991): 189.
106. Marx (1976): 814.
107. Marx quoted in Holloway (1992): 232.
108. Ibid., 236.
109. Ibid., 240.
110. Ibid., 236.
111. Ibid., 240.
112. Ibid., 241.
113. Marx (1967): 176.
114. Marx (1859): 272.
115. Ibid.
116. Ibid., 245.
117. Marx (1971b): 16.
118. Harvey (2000): 280.
119. Jessop (2006): 253.
120. Ibid.
121. Ibid., 256.
122. Gledhill (1997): 103–4.
123. Brown (1995): 103.
124. Ibid.
125. Kearney quoted in Gledhill (1994): 103.
126. Ibid., 104.
127. Ibid., 105.
128. Thompson (1991): 29.
129. Katznelson (1986): 14.

130.  Thompson (1991): 39.
131.  Harvey (1996):112.
132.  Jessop (2003): 26.
133.  Williams (1977).
134.  Smith (1984/1990): 109.
135.  Stewart (2001): 102.
136.  Arrighi (1994): 34.

## 1  THE EMERGENCE OF THE UNIFIED NATION-STATE: PRECOLONIAL NGOs IN BANGLADESH AND SRI LANKA

1.  Joshi (2001):187.
2.  Wijemanne (1996): 10.
3.  Fernando and de Mel (1991): 10; Perera (1998) 156–67; Wanigarathna (1998): 216.
4.  Sharma (1972): 49–50; Thapar (1969): 109–13.
5.  Eaton (1993): 232.
6.  See Bertoci (1970): 11–14; Hartman and Boyes (1983): 17; Spate and Learnomoth (1967).
7.  Eaton (1993): 26.
8.  Ibid., 234.
9.  Ibid., 226.
10.  During this period the *pirs*, and especially their descendants, were incorporated into the Mughal administrative structures. Their functions became routinized, and they were transformed into revenue collectors. See Eaton (1993): 256.
11.  Ibid.
12.  Cotton (1880): 3-4; Eaton (1993): 238.
13.  Ibid., 239.
14.  Eaton (1993): 266; Hosten (1910): 210.
15.  Eaton (1993): 100.
16.  Jenkins (2000): 260.
17.  Kaviraj (1972).
18.  Both were Sufi religious reformers. Taraqh-I-Muhammadiya is also known as Wahabis. For the history of the movement, see Khan (1984): 19–35.
19.  "Proceedings of Judicial Department-Criminal" (1847); "Zabanbandi of Manickchand" (1783); Eaton (1993): 236.
20.  Ziring (1992): 9.
21.  Forrester (1975): 7; Forrester (1974): 6.
22.  Forrester (1980): 78.
23.  Ibid., 59–60.
24.  Ibid., 90–1.
25.  Ibid., 119.
26.  Oddie (1998): 74.
27.  Oddie (1998): 120.
28.  Oddie (1998): 117.
29.  Ibid., 118.
30.  Bose (1987): 145–6.
31.  Ibid., 115.

32. Reply by Mr. Larmour, General Manager, Bengal Indigo Company, No. 2225, Report of the Indigo Commission. Cited in Bose (1987): 118.
33. Bose (1987): 146.
34. Ibid., 151.
35. Oddie (1998): 151.
36. David (1981): 80.
37. Ibid., 88.
38. Oddie (1998): 191.
39. "Some Thoughts on Present Discontent" (1907): 167–9; Panikkar (1953).
40. This was influenced by the outcomes of the ecumenical conference held in New York in 1900, which was attended by nearly 3000 missionaries including KajBaago, and called for speedy evangelization and unity among the missionaries. Baago (1965): 2–4.
41. Sarkar (1973).
42. Addy and Azad (1973) ; Joya (2002): 6.
43. Datta (1989).
44. McGuire (1983).
45. Ibid., 34.
46. Ibid.
47. Ibid., 38.
48. Ibid., 68.
49. Examples of associations: Atmitya Sabah (1815); Gaudiya Sabah, (1823); Academic Association (1928); Brama Samaj (1828); Bangaranji Sabah (1830); Jnanasandipani Sabah (1830); Dharma Sabah (1830); Debating Club (1830); Saratattwadipika Sabah, 1833; Bangabhashaprakashika Sabah (1836); Jnanchandrodaya Sabah (1836); Tattwavodhini Sabah (1839); Sadhran Jnanaparijika Sabah (1838); and British Indian Society (1843).
50. McGuire (1981): 78.
51. Ibid., 79.
52. Chandavarkar (1911): 86.
53. Raja (1817): 26.
54. Dutta (1992): 209–10.
55. Seal (1968): 57.
56. Sengupta (1971): 183.
57. Ibid., 185.
58. Ibid.
59. Ibid., 26.
60. McGuire (1983): 88.
61. Dutta (1992): 33.
62. Nur Afshan (July 6, 1900) quoted in S.V.N. Punjab (1900): 359.
63. McGuire (1981): 83.
64. Ibid.
65. Raychaudhuri (1988): 7–10.
66. Mani (1990): 112; Raja (1817): 477.
67. Joya (2002): 161.
68. Ibid., 14–15.
69. Pal (April 1909): 73.
70. Bose (1987): 165.
71. Joya (2002): 92–3.
72. Chakrabarty (1997): 197–203.

73. Greenough (1982); Gosh (1944).
74. Ray (2002): 186, 194.
75. Agarwal (1994): 439.
76. Mukherjee (1934): 23.
77. Ibid., 26.
78. Ibid., 29.
79. Ibid., 118.
80. Amin (1992): 757.
81. Risley (1969): 171.
82. Ibid., 115.
83. Kopf (1969): 208.
84. Heimsath (1964).
85. Amin (1992): 732; Jayawardena (1982): 81.
86. Major (1840): 68.
87. Rokeya S. Hossain quoted in Amin (1996): 13.
88. Borthwick (1984).
89. Rokeya S. Hossain quoted in Amin (1996): 27.
90. "The Present Position of Women," (1911): 196.
91. Everett (1976): 154.
92. Menon (1960): 162; Everett (1976): 130.
93. "The Rani and Mandi" (1929): 311; Everett (1976): 158.
94. Liddle and Joshi (1986): 22.
95. AIWC (1936): 31; Oddie (1998): 167.
96. Jayawardena (1995): 122.
97. Ibid., 239; Roy (1957): 124.
98. Minault (1981): 61.
99. Forbes (1996): 61; AIWC Annual Report (1947–1948): 62.
100. Forbes (1996): 141.
101. Chatterjee (1989): 249.
102. Pearson (1981): 175.
103. Government of Bengal Revenue Department (1941): 26.
104. Ibid., 12.
105. For a discussion on the collector's role in rural development, see Shawkat (1948); Shawkat (1982): 45–55.
106. Rai (1965): 644–59.
107. Jalal (1990): 76.
108. Ibid.
109. These included Babu Rakmal Mukharji Fund, Babu Gobind Law Funds, Central Relief Fund, and Indian Peoples Famine Trust Fund.
110. Government of Bengal Revenue Department (1941): 26.
111. Mathew (1988): 107.
112. Gulliford (1986): 168–9; Mathew (1988): 69.
113. Mathew (1988): 74.
114. Ibid.
115. Mehra (1977): 92.
116. Ibid.
117. Ibid.
118. Jalal (1990): 180–93.
119. For religious associations engaged in political developments see Ahmad (1972): 257–72.

120. Jalal (1990): 153.
121. *Civil and Military Gazette* (1950); Jalal (1990): 164.
122. Abdul Hye (1993): 128–71; Hussain (1996): 95–125;.
123. Hossain et al. (1982): 90–115.
124. Jahan (1972); Sobhan (1968); Westergaard (1985).
125. Blai (1972–73); Blai (1978): 65–82; Solaiman and Alam (1977).
126. Ibid.
127. Ibid., 34.
128. Hall (1985): 27–73.
129. Jalal (1990): 110.
130. For a discussion on the consequences of economic and regional disparities between West and East Pakistan, see Malik and Husain (1992, vol. 2): 500–73; Sobhan (1999): 706–80.
131. Guhathakurtha and Begum (1998): 39.
132. Sultana and Abdullah (1990): 5.
133. The APWA was founded in 1949 and headed by Begum Ra'ana Liaquat Ali Khan, a leading activist for women's rights.
134. Raman (1993): 52–3.
135. Khalid (1967): 277.
136. Timm (1997).
137. Ibid., 239.
138. Pope Paul VI wrote in *Octagesima Adveniens* (No. 34): "It should be illusory and dangerous to accept the elements in Marxist analysis without recognizing their relationship with ideology." Quoted in Timm (1997): 239.
139. Ibid., 257.
140. Guha (2000): 373–9.
141. Fernando and Henry (1991): 1; Perera (1998): 156–67; Wanigarathna (1998): 216–93.
142. Ariyarathna (1978, vol. 1): 52.
143. Gunasinghe (1990): 21–35.
144. Pieris (1953); Tambiah (1958); Yalman (1963).
145. Paranavithana (1931): 53.
146. Tiruchelvam (1984): 79.
147. Ibid., 125.
148. Samaraweera (1978): 1.
149. Bechert (1978): 200.
150. Ibid., 201.
151. Bechert (1978).
152. Bechert (1969–70): 761–78.
153. Ames (1964): 32–9; Obeyesekere (1966): 1–26; Obeyesekere (1963): 139–53.
154. Evers (1972).
155. Obeyesekere (1973): 142; Phadnis (1976): 18.
156. Rahula (1956): 164.
157. Evers (1972): 94.
158. Gunasinghe (1990): 88.
159. Gunasinghe (1990): 89.
160. Phadnis (1976): 41.
161. Quoted in Ibid.
162. Ibid., 82.
163. Ibid., 43.

164. Ibid., 92.
165. De Silva (1960): 62.
166. Malalgoda (1976): 109.
167. De Silva (1960): 65.
168. De Silva (1960): 380.
169. Peebles (1995).
170. De Silva (1965): 26–7.
171. Ibid., 26–7.
172. Ibid., 27.
173. Ibid., 34, 135.
174. Priyantha (1968): 175.
175. Ibid.
176. Ibid., 140.
177. O'Malley (1941): 157, 158, 688.
178. Root (2004): 13, 147.
179. *Missionary Herald* XXXIX (1843): 220, quoted in Priyantha (1968): 396.
180. *Missionary Herald* XXII (1926): 180–1, quoted in Priyantha (1968): 388.
181. *Missionary Herald* XXII (Appendix B), quoted in Harrison (1826): 404.
182. Meigs et al. (1854): 481, quoted in Priyantha (1968): 232.
183. Gogerly (1844) quoted in Priyantha (1968): 192.
184. Priyantha (1968): 195.
185. Ibid.
186. Ruberu (1962): 154–61.
187. *Missionary Herald* XXIII (1822): 105 quoted in Priyantha (1968): 51.
188. Wes. Mss. Cey., II Kesen (June 25, 1855) in De Silva (1965): 185.
189. De Silva (1965): 185.
190. De Silva (1965): 187–90.
191. Peebles (2006): 80.
192. De Silva (1981): 375.
193. Peebles (2006): 80.
194. Ibid., 76.
195. Ibid.
196. Ibid., 81.
197. Ibid., 274.
198. Ibid., 275.
199. Ibid., 281.
200. Ibid., 220.
201. Ibid., 237.
202. Gombrich and Obeyesekere (1988): 231.
203. Ibid., 233.
204. Ibid.
205. Malalgoda (1976): 238.
206. Ibid., 242.
207. Malalgoda (1976): 338.
208. Ibid., 240.
209. Malalgoda (1976): 245; *Old Diary Leaves* (1910): 120.
210. Obeyesekere (1970); Tambiah (1973); Wilson (1973).
211. Malalgoda (1976): 250.
212. Ibid., 201.
213. Rahula (1956): 101.

214. Ibid., 255.
215. Roberts (1982): 176.
216. Guruge (ed.) (1965).
217. Obeyesekere (1986): 231–58.
218. Roberts (1982): 241.
219. Jayawardena (1979).
220. *Kalaya* (1946): 1.
221. Tambiah (1992): 20.
222. *Ceylon National Review* (1907).
223. Jayasekara (1970): 323; Jayawardena (1979).
224. Obeyesekere (2008): 242.
225. Roberts (1982): 213–41.
226. Peeble (1995): 126.
227. Jayawardena (1995): 78.
228. Jayawardena, p. 79.
229. Ibid., 172–3; Ariyarathna (1973); De Silva (1981): 367, 396; *Hindu Organ* (27 April 1931).
230. Jayawardena (1972): 258.
231. Ibid.
232. Ibid., 60.
233. Ibid.
234. *Ceylon First Congress Literary Association* (1914): 8; De Silva (1981): 345.
235. *Ceylon Daily News* (March 14, 1930); Russell (1982): 33.
236. De Silva (1967); Russell (1982): 42.
237. Perinpanayagam (1939).
238. *Catholic Guardian* (March 5, 1936).
239. *Ceylon Daily News* (March 9, 1930).
240. Cheran (2009).
241. Nesiah (1981): 152.
242. Kearney (1967).
243. Russell (1982): 120.
244. Fraser (1963): 55; Russell (1982): 129.
245. Hansard (1939): 819.
246. Report of Jaffna Youth Congress Meeting (April 24, 1939).
247. Hansard (1936); Russell (1982): 132.
248. De Silva (1973): 233.
249. Panabokke, T.B. (1938)*The Autobiography of Tikiri Banda Panabokke* (unpublished) cited in Russell (1982): 26.
250. *Catholic Guardian* (February 15, 1935).
251. Russell (1982): 126.
252. Dickson (1871).
253. Russal (1871): 53.
254. "Crime Prevention" (1971): 7, quoted in Tiruchelvam Neelan (1984): 86.
255. Tiruchelvam Neelan (1984): 69.
256. Ibid.
257. Ibid., 72.
258. Research Council of the Department of Rural Development (1976): 70.
259. De Silva (1973): 29; Wanigarathna (1994): 6.
260. Hicks (1959): 107.
261. Warnapala (2001).

262. Blackton (1974): 40.
263. Kanesalingam (1971): 10–34.
264. The Government of Ceylon (1955): 6.
265. This information was gathered from interviews with the local government authorities and the villagers.
266. Sanjay (2001): 172.

## 2 WELFARE STATE TO NATIONAL SECURITY STATE: POST-INDEPENDENCE NGO–STATE RELATIONS IN SRI LANKA, 1948–2010

1. Corrigan and Sayer (1985): 21–2.
2. Shastri (1983a): 31.
3. Ibid., 12.
4. Tambiah (1992): 51.
5. Ibid., 52.
6. Phadnis (1976): 36.
7. Evers (1972): 27.
8. Brecht (1972): 251–95.
9. Jayawardena (1987).
10. *United National Party*, UNP (1947): 2, 119.
11. *Ceylon Daily News* (December 5, 1950): 120.
12. Ibid., 49.
13. Manor (1989); Tambiah (1992): 49.
14. See Shastri (1983): 34.
15. De Silva (1981): 518; Shastri (1983): 30; Wilson (1974).
16. Ibid., 34.
17. Phadnis (1976): 36.
18. Chandraprema (1991).
19. Phadnis (1976) : 235–41.
20. Peiris (1996): 64.
21. Ibid., 26.
22. Athukorala and Rajapatirana (1991): 15.
23. Ibid., 29.
24. Ibid., 24.
25. Athukorala (1993): 12–34.
26. Ibid., 33.
27. Ibid., 36.
28. Ibid., 152.
29. Laxman (1986): 35–63.
30. *The UNP Manifesto* (1977): 4.
31. Kemper (1992): 231.
32. Ibid., 178.
33. Amin (1980); Cardoso and Enzo (1979); Frank (1980); Ponnambalam (1980).
34. Shastri (1999): 57–77; also see Shastri (2004a & b).
35. Hellmann-Rajanayagam (1988–1989): 603–19.
36. Ibid., 633.
37. Author interview, Colombo, Sri Lanka (June 26, 1996).
38. Goulet (1981): 51.

39. Ariyarathna (1988): 48.
40. Author interview with employees at the Sarvodaya Headquarters in Anuradhapura (January 31, 1997).
41. Perera (1992): 162.
42. Ibid., 21.
43. Premadasa (1978): 1.
44. Perera (1992): 1992.
45. Government Commission on NGOs (1991).
46. "Sarvodaya Goes from Humble Village to Finance Big Time Commercial Ventures" (1991); "Sarvodaya Sells Lankan Children Abroad" (1992); "Sarvodaya Pours Millions into Black Holes" (1992).
47. ICJ Report quoted in Perera (1992): 35.
48. Perera (1992): 32.
49. Ibid., 105.
50. Ibid., 36.
51. Ibid., 36–7.
52. *The Sunday Island* (December 26, 1993): 1.
53. *Divaina* (July 7, 1992): 6.
54. NOVIB, letter to Dr. Ariyarathna from Hans Pelgrom (December 22, 1993), No. SRL-002-92-002, 2.
55. *Silumina* (February 2, 1992): 4.
56. *Dinamina* (December 30, 1991): 1.
57. Bond (1998): 35.
58. *Daily News* (July 21, 28, 1991).
59. Ibid.
60. Sarvodaya Shramadana Movement (November 1984): X; also see Ninth Monitoring Report of the Sarvodaya Donor Consortium (September 24–October 6, 1990); NOVIB (1994).
61. NOVIB (1994): 3.
62. NOVIB (1993).
63. "NOVIB Surprised by Christian Democrats Decisions to Withdraw" (1994).
64. NOVIB (1993); NOVIB (1994).
65. *Divaina* (January 25, 1994): 26.
66. "Six Hundred Sarvodaya Workers to the Road" (1993): 12.
67. "The Government to Mobilize and Coordinate NGO help for Front Line Men" (1991): 1.
68. Obeyesekere (1987): 31–2.
69. Ibid., 33–4.
70. Ibid,. 30.
71. Keerawella and Samarajiva (1995): 6.
72. Uyangoda (1976).
73. Ibid., 2.
74. Ibid.
75. Ibid., 4.
76. Ibid., 6.
77. Ibid., 8.
78. Orjuela (2004): 135–6.
79. Ibid., 167.
80. Appuhamy (2004): 167.
81. Gunathilaka (2004): 167.

82. News items appeared in all major newspapers: "A Secret Meeting of Foreign Voluntary Organizations at Bentota, To Call Upon the Government to Halt the Operation Rivirasa," *Lankadeepa* (November 14, 1995); "Angered by the Government Decision to Take Over Supply of Humanitarian Aid NGOs Prepare to Slander the Government," *Divayina* (November 14, 1995); "False Propaganda on Sending of Aid to Northern Refugees, NGO trying to Tarnish Sri Lanka's Image Abroad," *Daily News* (November 14, 1995); "Tiger Face of NGOs," editorial, *Divayina* (November 15, 1995); "Voluntary Organizations Give Terrorism a Human Face," *Divayina* (November 16, 1995); "The Meeting Which Was Unsuccessful in Bentota Held in Ratmalana Yesterday, The Participants of the Secret Meeting Fled Without a Beating," *Divayina* (November 17, 1995).

83. Reoch (1996).

84. "Be Fair, Tell Them All" (1994): 6.

85. NGO Forum on Sri Lanka (1995): 1–4.

86. *Sri Lanka's Economy* (1999): 1–11.

87. Wijesinha (2009).

88. Ibid.

89. Sri Lanka Ministry of Defence (2008).

90. Das (2005): 178.

91. Keenan (2006): 459.

92. Wickramasinghe (2006): 198.

93. Author interview with fishermen, Kirenda, Sri Lanka (June 25, 2004).

94. De Silva (2007): 26.

95. See the official website of the Sri Lankan government's secretariat for co-ordinating the peace process (http://www.peaceinsrilanka.org/).

96. "Minister Champika Ranawaka Violates the Constitution" (2008); see also Philips (2009).

97. Hussain (2009).

98. Jayawardena (October 21, 2007; April 15, 2009).

99. Seneviratne (2008).

100. Tamilnation.org (2009).

101. Jayatilleka (2005).

102. Athurugoda (2010).

103. "JVP Slams NGOs, Western Countries for Meddling" (2005).

104. Jayasoriya (2005).

105. "SPUR Opposes Peace Talks Based on the ISGA" (2005).

106. *LankaDissent* website (2009).

107. "Another religious leader/aid worker killed in Sri Lanka"; Samath (2008).

108. Reddy (2008).

109. Alles (2009).

110. "Religious Bigotry Used for Political Mobilization—Prof. Uyangoda" (2004).

111. Author interview with Charan in Toronto, Canada (March 22, 2010).

112. Kois (2007): 103.

113. Jayatilleka (August 2008).

114. Jayatilleka (July 2, 2008).

115. Wijesinha (February 29, 2008).

116. Ibid.

117. "Military victory is not the final solution, says Sri Lanka President" (2009).

118. *Tamils Against Genocide, Inc. vs. Timothy Geithner and Meg Lundsager* (2009).
119. U.S. Senate Committee on Foreign Relations (2009).
120. "Hillary discusses Sri Lanka issue with Norwegian Minister" (2009).
121. Dias (2009).
122. "Chomsky: West's self-interest reduces R2P to 'noble rhetoric'" (2009).
123. Lakbimanews (October 18, 2009).
124. Personal interviews conducted by the author in Sri Lanka.
125. Bhune (2009).
126. Lee (2009); Deen (2009).
127. "Non Violent Peace Force officer ordered to quit country: 5th officer in 3 months so ordered to leave" (2010).
128. De Silva (1997): 29; Wace (1961): 59.
129. See Anderson (2006).
130. Centre for Policy Alternatives (2010).

## 3   SECULARISM, RELIGION, AND PARALLEL STATES: POST-INDEPENDENCE NGO–STATE RELATIONS IN BANGLADESH, 1971–2010

1. Marx (1971): 42.
2. Riyaja (1994): 184.
3. Ibid., 212.
4. Ibid.
5. Ibid.
6. NGOs commissioned many studies that dealt with the issue of power relations. See Throp (1978); Timm (1983).
7. Timm (1974): 54.
8. Timm (1995): 54.
9. Timm (1994): 15.
10. Riyaja (1994): 183.
11. Sobhan (1968): 26.
12. Kochaneck (1993): 93; *World Bank Report* (1989): 1.
13. Parikh (1993): 177.
14. Kabeer (1991): 134.
15. Hannan (1980).
16. Moshin Kabeer (1983): 134–5.
17. Ibid., 136.
18. Ibid.
19. Rahman (1984): 240–9.
20. See Kochanek (1993): 3.
21. Subramaniam (1990): 25–6.
22. For an analysis of *upazila* reforms, see McCarthy (1987).
23. *The Bangladesh Times* (March 14, 1986).
24. Ibid.
25. Kabeer (1983): 129.
26. Choudhury (1992): 17.
27. Ibid., 19.
28. Reich (1994): 131.

29. Ibid., 133.
30. Ibid., 134.
31. Wolf and Gordon (1996): 82.
32. *Bangladesh Observer* (August 25, 1987); Kochanek (1993): 309.
33. Ibid., 19.
34. Ibid., 20.
35. Kochanek (1993): 238.
36. For a detailed study of NGO–GO collaboration, see Battacharya and Ahmed (1994).
37. Divine (1996): 36.
38. Hashmi (1995):106, quoted in Uphoff et al. (1998).
39. Personal communications with NGOs in Dhaka, Bangladesh (March 3, 1996).
40. The Directory of Organizations in Women's Development in Bangladesh (1994) lists 381 NGOs that are involved in women-related programs.
41. Kabeer (1983): 139.
42. Guhathakurtha and Begum (1998): 39.
43. Chowdhury (1996): 9.
44. Ibid., 3.
45. Bradly (1989): 1.
46. Canadian High Commission (1996).
47. Alam, J. (1993).
48. "NGOs create tremors among opposition parties" (1989). This statement was made by the Awami League in Manikgonj.
49. *Courier* (September 22–28, 1989): 4.
50. Ibid., 27-28; *Courier* (September 29–October 5, 1989): 28–30.
51. *Courier* (October 6–12, 1989): 24.
52. *Courier* (July 28–Aug 3, 1989): 29–30; (August 11–17): 31; (September 1–7, 1989): 19, 29; (September 29–October 5, 1989): 26; (October 13–19, 1989); (October 20–26, 1989): 30; (November 10–16, 1989).
53. Chowdhury (1996): 3.
54. *The Bangladesh Times* (December 7, 1990).
55. *Bangladeshi Observer* (December, 8, 1990): 6.
56. Author interviews with some prominent leaders of the NGOs.
57. Central Bank of Bangladesh (1995).
58. Ibid., 32.
59. Ali, R. (1994): 12.
60. Kochanek (1993): 708.
61. Central Bank of Bangladesh (1995).
62. Davis (1996–1999): 26.
63. Author interviews with NGOs representatives and tribal leaders in Madhupur, Bangladesh.
64. Author interviews, Association of Social Advancement, Dhaka, September 1995; Caritas, Dhaka, 1995.
65. *Bangladesh Observer* (September 15, 1990 and July 20, 1990).
66. "Pursuing Common Goals: Strengthening Relations Between Government and Development NGOs" (1996), Dhaka: University Press.
67. Daily Star (November 5, 1996): 1.
68. "Asian Development Bank: Institutional Strengthening for Government–NGO Cooperation Technical Assistance Project, Draft Inception Report" (June 1995); see also *Great Expectations* (1993).

69. Institutional Strengthening for Government/NGO Cooperation, ADB TA No. 2088.
70. "Pursuing Common Goals" (1996): 30.
71. The Meeting of the Bangladesh Learning Group on Participation (July 4, 1995).
72. Hashemi (1996): 13.
73. Alam (1995): 20.
74. Lovel (1992): 26.
75. Rashiduzzaman (1994).
76. *Review of Bangladesh Economy* (1995): 343.
77. Author interviews, December 2005, Dhaka, Bangladesh.
78. Westergaard (1992): 12–19.
79. Ibid., 20.
80. The Ford Foundation (September 26, 1994): 1.
81. Timm (1991): 26.
82. Ibid.
83. Chittagong Hill Tract Commission Report (1991); Samad (1990); Timm (1991): 12–14.
84. *Great Expectations* (1993): 18.
85. "NGO Bureau–NGO Relations" (1992): 2.
86. *Great Expectations* (1993): 18.
87. Ibid., 18.
88. The Ford Foundation (1992): 3.
89. See Kamaluddin (1993).
90. "Procedures to be followed by National and International NGOs receiving foreign funds" (1993).
91. Societies Registration Act, 1993, Company's Act 1913, Voluntary Social Welfare Agencies (Regulation and Control) Act 1961, The Foreign Donations (Voluntary Activities), Regulation Ordinance, 1978; Foreign Contributions (Regulation) Ordinance 1982.
92. ADAB Memorandum (1990): 3.
93. Ibid.
94. Ibid.
95. Ibid.
96. ADAB Position Paper (June 4, 1994).
97. "EC envoy says, agitation against the NGOs may scare the investors" (1994): 10. In 1994 the European Union established a separate liaison office in Bangladesh.
98. Daily Star (March 16, 1995): 12; (March 19, 1995): 1, 12; (March 16, 1995).
99. Mustafa (1995): 5.
100. *Daily Star* (April 2, 1995): 4.
101. Devine (1996).
102. Personal Interview, Dhaka, January 1994.
103. *The Times* (April 8, 1996): 13.
104. Choudhury (1996): 2.
105. Hossain and Marko (2002).
106. White (1996): 237–46.
107. Davis and McGregor (2000): 61–5.
108. Sanyal (1991): 136.
109. White (1999): 307–26; see also Lewis (2004): 300–21.

110. Stiles (2002): 835–46.
111. Haque (2002): 411.
112. Devine (2006): 43–59.
113. Ibid., 134.
114. Woods (1994).
115. Hashemi (1996): 123–31.
116. See Haque (2002); Gauri and Galef (2005); Kennedy (1999); Westergaard and Alam (1995).
117. World Prout Assembly website (April 16, 2009).
118. Pattaniak (2006); "NGOs with foreign funding fuelling militancy in Bangladesh" (2009).
119. Quamruzzmann (2010).
120. Gomes (April 1, 2009).
121. Hussain (2009).
122. Bangladesh Strategic and Development Forum (2007).
123. Kumar (2007).
124. "NGOs with foreign funding fuelling militancy in Bangladesh" (2009).
125. "Bangladeshi NGO leader arbitrarily arrested, potentially tortured" (2007).
126. UNHRC (2008); Mustafa (2007).
127. Gomes (April 6, 2009).
128. Feldman (2003): 21.
129. Gomes (April 16, 2009).
130. "The Economics and Governance of Non Governmental Organizations (NGOs) in Bangladesh" (2005).
131. Smillie (2006).
132. Gauri and Galef (2005): 2045–65.
133. Lewis (1998): 142.
134. Ibid.
135. Karim (2001).
136. Arzu (2010).
137. Choudhury (2010).

# 4 THE NGO INDUSTRIAL COMPLEX: MODERNIZING POSTMODERNITY

1. Miliband (1977): 67.
2. Quoted in Avineri (1968): 52; see also Marx (1963).
3. Lukacs (1993): 13.
4. Clarke (ed.) (1996): 181.
5. Ibid., 210.
6. Gramsci (1992): 276.
7. Observers since the nineteenth century including Alexis de Tocqueville, Karl Marx, Emile Durkheim, and Max Weber have noted the importance of the voluntary sector under democratic forms of governance, which serves as a counterpoint against the arbitrary use of power by the modern state. They argued that voluntary organizations are inconsequential in comparison with the power of the state and the markets, and that they provide only temporary solutions to social crises. For discussions of voluntary associations by classical

theorists, see Durkheim (1957), Marx and Engels (2002), Tocqueville (1945), and Weber (1978).

8. Bebbington (1997).

9. For galactic states, see S.J. Tambiah, *World Conqueror and World Renouncer*. This refers to a state system based on an overlord–tributary relationship, which was not necessarily exclusive. The distribution of powers is uneven between different units that pay tribute. The rulers play one "galactic unit" against another in order to minimize interference and threats to their own power. Burton Stein's highly contested notion of "segmentary states" captures the degree of fragmentation of the polity. Despite the controversies surrounding these two notions, they are useful for illustrating relations between state and society, particularly the ways in which state power is produced through various forms of decentralization. In segmentary state forms which lack extensive political power or pervasive military control over all its regional units, the rulers govern by establishing a ceremonial center that reinforces the authority of the leadership through tribute, rituals, festivals, parades, public architecture, and astronomical symbolism. See Burton Stein (1989) *New Cambridge History of India*, Vol. 1: Vijayanagara, Cambridge: Cambridge University Press; and Burton Stein (1977) "The segmentary state in South Indian history," in R.J. Fox (ed.) *Realm and Region in Traditional India*, Durham: Duke University Press: 3–51.

10. For a detailed discussion on the state–NGO relationship in development see Kamat (2002).

11. For a discussion of the characteristics of precolonial states, see Historian (1985); Kulke (1982): 237–64; Stein (1986).

12. Marx and Engels (1971): 41.

13. Marx (1853): 26.

14. Guha (1998): 35.

15. Sri Arubindo (September 17, 1907): 90.

16. Sarkar (1973): 84.

17. Sri Arubindo (November 21, 1907); Kruger (1989): 82.

18. Jayawardena (1988); see also Liddle and Joshi (1989).

19. Kandiyoti (1994): 387.

20. Ibid., 388.

21. Guha (1998): 130.

22. Ibid., 131.

23. Chatterjee (1986).

24. Hobsbawm (1989): 287.

25. Joshi (2001):187.

26. Ibid., 172.

27. Harvey (1991): 117.

28. Escobar (1994).

29. Ferguson (1994).

30. Fernando (2005); Rahman (2001); Rankin (2002).

31. I am thankful to my student Kevin Surprise for his insightful comments on microfinance and alienation under capitalism, Clark University, Worcester, MA, September 2008.

32. Hancock (2001): 871–903; Levine (2004); Johnston (2003); Midgley (2001).

33. Jayawardena (1988): 34.

34. Ibid., 10.

35. Gledhill (1994): 225.
36. Hilferding (1985).
37. Ramachandra (1999): 164.
38. For discussions on NGOs, neoliberalism, governmentality, neoliberal governmentality see Fisher (1997); Ferguson and Gupta (2002); Kamat (2003).
39. Ehrenberg (1989): 129.
40. Ibid.
41. Bottomore (ed.) (1981): 218; Marx and Engels (1920): 288.
42. Ibid., 35.
43. Marx quoted in Bottomore (1981): 94.
44. Marx cited in Bottomore (1981): 95.
45. Ludden (1992): 253.
46. Escobar (1994).
47. Ferguson (1994).
48. Tissanayagam (February 24, 2008).
49. See Ramonet (2008): 1–22.
50. Marx 34; Avineri (1968): 149.
51. The Holy Bible, King James Version (2006): 487.
52. Sanneh (2003): 9.
53. Ibid., 67.

# Bibliography

Abeysekera, Charles (1996) "The Role and Autonomy of NGOs," Annual Consultation, Coalition of NGOs, Colombo: Sri Lanka.

Abdul Hye, Hasnat (1993) "IRDP: Replication of An Experimental Project," in Md. Abdul Qudus (ed.) *Rural Development in Bangladesh: Strategies and Experiences,* Kotbari: Comilla. Bangladesh Academy for Rural Development.

ADAB Memorandum (1990) Dhaka: ADAB.

ADAB Position Paper (June 4, 1994) Presented at the Press Conference Organized by ADAB at the Dhaka Press Club on the Bangladesh Voluntary Activities (Regulation) Act, 1993 (Draft), proposed by the Social Welfare Ministry, Government of Bangladesh, April 1994.

Addy, Preman and Iben Azad (1973) "Politics and Culture in Bengal," *New Left Review,* Vol. 79 (May–June).

Agarwal, Bina (1994) *A Field of One's Own,* London: Cambridge University Press.

Ahamed, Shamsud-Din (ed. and trans.) (1960) *Inscriptions of Bengal,* Vol. 4.

Ahmad, Aijaz (1992) *In Theory: Classes, Nations, Literatures,* London: Verso.

Ahmad, Aziz (1972) "Activism of the Ulema in Pakistan" in Nikki R. Keddie (ed.) *Scholars, Saints, and Sufis: Muslim Religious Institutions Since 1500,* Berkeley: University of California Press.

"AID Groups Demand Access to Sri Lanka" (May 21, 2009) *Al Jazeera English,* http://english.aljazeera.net/news/asia/2009/05/20095218835185207.html.

AIWC (1936) 11th Conference.

AIWC Annual Report, 20th session, 1947–1948.

Alam, Jahangir (1993) "Rural Poverty in Bangladesh: The Impact of Non-Governmental and Governmental Organization," unpublished paper presented to National Seminar on Poverty Alleviation.

Alam, Mohammed Shahidul (1993) "GO-NGO management in Bangladesh," Dhaka: Bangladesh Public Administration Center, SAVAR. Unpublished paper.

Ali, A.M.M. Shawkat (1948) "ABC of Rural Reconstruction," Dhaka: East Bengal Government Press.

Ali, A.M.M. Shawkat (1982) "Field Administration and Rural Development in Bangladesh," Dhaka: Center for Social Studies.

Ali, Daud (2004) *Courtly Culture and Political Life in Early Medieval India,* London: Cambridge University Press.

Ali, Riza (1994) Unpublished paper delivered at the Symposium for South Asian Politics and Development, Dhaka.

Alles, Tyrone (April 20, 2009) "God help the Brits," *The Island Online,* http://www.island.lk/2009/04/20/opinion1.html.

"America and The Rest" (July 2003) *The Economist,* available at http://www.globalpolicy.org/intljustice/icc/2003/0702econ.htm. Accessed February 16, 2009.

American Board (1840) *Annual Report.*

Ames, M. (June 1964) "Magical Animism and Buddhism: A Structural Analysis of the Sinhalese Religious System," *Journal of Asian Studies,* Vol. 23.

Amin, Samir (1980) *Class and Nation,* New York: Monthly Review Press.

Amin, Samir (1997) *Capitalism in the Age of Globalization: The Management of Contemporary Society*, London: Zed Books.

Amin, Sonia Nishat (1992) "Women and Society," in Sirajul Islam (ed.) *History of Bangladesh 1704–1971*, Vol. III, Dhaka: Asiatic Society.

Amin, Sonia Nishat (1996) *The World of Muslim Women in Colonial Bengal*, London: E.J. Brill.

Anderson, Benedict (2006) *Imagined Communities*, New York: Verso.

"Another religious leader/aid worker killed in Sri Lanka" (2007) *Law and Society Trust*, http://www.lawandsocietytrust.org/PDF/Statement%20on%20killing%20 of%20Fr%20Ranjith-02Oct07.pdf.

Appuhamy, Durand (May 2001) "Manufacturing Consent for Eelam" in *The Island*, quoted in Orjuela (2004).

Ariyarathna, A.T. (1978) *Collected Works Volume 1*, Netherlands.

Ariyarathna, A.T. (1981) *Peace-making in Sri Lanka in the Buddhist Contexts*, Ratmalana: Vishva Lekha.

Ariyarathna, A.T. (1988) *Dharmic Cycle*, Ratmalana: Sarvodaya Vishva Lekha.

Ariyarathna, R.A. (1973) "Communal Conflict in Ceylon and the Advances Towards Self Government," Ph.D. Thesis, Cambridge University.

Arrighi, Giovanni (1994) *The Long Twentieth Century: Money, Power and the Origins of Our Times*, London: Verso.

Arzu, Alpha (January 26, 2010) "Over 20,000 NGOs to lose registration," *The Daily Star*.

Athukorala, Premachandra (1993) "Macro-economic Policy and the Trade Liberalization Outcome: Lessons from Sri Lanka's Experience," in *Essays in Honor of A.D.V. de S. Indraratna*, Kelaniya: Vidyalankara Press.

Athukorala, Premachandra and Sarath Rajapatirana (1991) "The Domestic Financial Market and the Trade Liberalization Outcome: The Evidence from Sri Lanka," *Policy Research and External Affairs Discussion Papers, WPS, 590*, Washington DC: World Bank.

Athurugoda, S. (March 6, 2010) "Rama Mani and the Gang," *Sri Lanka Guardian*, http://www.srilankaguardian.org/2008/03/rama-mani-and-gang.html.

*AVAB Newsletters*, Vol. I, No. 1, 1974; Vol. 1, No. 6, October 1974; AVAB News, Vol. I, No. 10, November 1975; Vol. I, No. 8, December 1974; Vol. I, No. 3, July 1974; Vol. I, No. 4, August 1974; Vol. I, No. 7, November 1974; Vol. I, No. 2.

Avineri, S. (1968) *The Social and Political Thought of Karl Marx*, Cambridge: Cambridge University Press.

Baago, Kaj (1965) "A History of the National Christian Council in India, 1915–1964," Nagpur India, The National Christian Council.

Baker, K.M. (1992) "Defining the Public Sphere in Eighteenth Century France: Variations on a Theme by Habermas," in Craig Calhoun (ed.) *Habermas and the Public Sphere*, Cambridge, MA: MIT Press.

*Bangladesh Observer* (August 25,1987).

*Bangladesh Observer* (September 15, 1990).

*Bangladesh Observer* (July 20, 1990).

Bangladesh Strategic and Development Forum (2007) "Strategic Relations Between Bangladesh and America," http://www.bdsdf.org/forum/index. php?showtopic=32932. Accessed September 25, 2010.

*Bangladesh Times* (March 14, 1986).

*Bangladesh Times* (December 7, 1990).

"Bangladeshi NGO leader arbitrarily arrested, potentially tortured" (February 2, 2007) *Bank Information Center* website, http://www.bicusa.org/en/Article.3128. aspx. Accessed April 16, 2009.

Battacharya, Debapriya and Salehuddin Ahmed (December 1994) "GO-NGO Collaboration in Human Development Initiative in Bangladesh," *Research Report*, No. 139, Dhaka: Bangladesh Institute for Development Studies.

Bebbington, Anthony (1997) "Social Capital and Rural Intensification: Local Organizations and Islands of Sustainability in the Rural Andes," *The Geographical Journal*, Vol. 163, 10.

Bechert, H. (1969–70), "Theravada Buddhist Sangha: Some General Observations on Ceylon: Historical Factors in its Development," *Journal of Asian Studies*, XXIX.

Bechert, H. (1978) "South Asian Politics and Dilemmas of Reinterpretation," in Bardwell L. Smith (ed.) *Religion and Legitimization of Power in Sri Lanka*, Chambersburg, PA: Conococheague Associates, Inc.

"Be Fair, Tell Them All," (November 13, 1994) *The Sunday Times*, Colombo, Sri Lanka.

Bertoci, Perter (1970) "Elusive Villages: Social Structure and Community Organizations in Rural East Pakistan," Ph.D. Thesis, Michigan State University.

Bhalla, S. and P. Glewwe (1986) "Growth and Equity in Developing Countries, A Reinterpretation of the Sri Lankan Experience," *The World Bank Economic Review*, Washington DC: The World Bank, Vol. 1 No. 1.

Bhattcharaya, Debapriya (1993) "Rural Development Poverty Alleviation in Bangladesh: An Overview of Programs," in Md. Abdul Qudus (ed.) *Rural Development in Bangladesh: Strategies and Experiences*, Kotbari, Comilla: Bangladesh Academy for Rural Development.

Bhaumik, Subir (June 18, 2003) "India Blacklists 800 NGOs," *BBC News*, http://news.bbc.co.uk/1/hi/world/south_asia/3001458.stm. Accessed February 16, 2009.

Blackton, John S. (1974) *Local Government and Rural Development in Sri Lanka*, Washington DC: USAID.

Blai, Harry W. (1972–73) "The Elusiveness of Equity: Institutional Approaches to Rural Development in Bangladesh," Ithaca: Cornell University Rural Development Program.

Blai, Harry W. (1978) "Rural Development, Class Structure and Bureaucracy in Bangladesh," *World Development* 1.

Blair, H. (1996) "Donors, Democratisation and Civil Society," in David Hulme and Michael Edwards (eds.) *NGOs, States and Donors: Too Close for Comfort?* New York: Palgrave Macmillan.

Bleanly, Michael (1976) *Under-Consumption Theories*, New York: International Publishers.

Boli, John and George Thomas (eds) (1999) *Constructing World Culture: International Nongovernmental Organizations since 1875*, Stanford, CA: Stanford University Press.

Bond, George (1998) *Buddhist Revival in Sri Lanka: Religious Tradition, Reinterpretation and Response*, Columbia: University of South Carolina Press.

Bond, George (2003) *Buddhism at Work: Community Development, Social Empowerment and the Sarvodaya Movement*, West Hartford, CT: Kumarian Press.

Borthwick, Meredith (1984) *Changing Role of Women in Bengal 1849–1965*, Princeton: Princeton University Press.

Bose, Sugatha (1987) *Peasant Labor and Colonial Capital*, London: Cambridge University Press.

Bose, Sugatha (1993) *Agrarian Bengal: Economy, Politics 1919–1947 (New Cambridge History of India)*, Cambridge: Cambridge University Press.

Bottomore, Tom (ed.) (1981) *History of Sociological Analysis*, London: MacMillan.

Bottomore, Tom (ed.) (1983) *A Dictionary of Marxist Thought*, Oxford: Blackwell.

Bourdieu, Pierre (1972) *Outline of a Theory and Practice*, Cambridge: Cambridge University Press.

Boyer, Robert and Daniel Drache (eds) (1996) *States Against Markets: The Limits of Globalization*, London: Routledge.

Bradly, Charles R. (November 25, 1989) "The Donor Perspectives on NGOs," Remarks by Representative, Ford Foundation, Bangladesh at the Meetings with President Ershad, International Conference Center, Dhaka.

Brecht, Heinze (1972) "Einige Fragen Der Religionssoziologie und des subasiatichen Buddhismus", Internationales jahrbuch fuer religionssoziologies, bd, 4 Kohln: West deutscher Verlag, 251–295 in Hance-Deiter Evers, *Monks, Priests and Peasants*, Leiden: E.J. Brill.

Bromley, Simon (1994) *Rethinking Middle East Politics: State Formation and Development*, Oxford: Polity Press.

Broomfield, J.H. (1968) *Elite Conflict in a Plural Society: Twentieth Century Bengal*, Berkeley: University of California Press.

Brothwick, Meredith (1984) *The Changing Role of Women in Bengal 1849–1905*, Princeton: Princeton University Press.

Brown, Wendy (1995) *States of Injury: Power and Freedom in Later Modernity*, Princeton, NJ: Princeton University Press.

Buchanan, Ruth and Sundha Pahuja (2004) "Legal Imperialism: Empire's Invisible Hand," in Paul Passavant and Jodi Dean (eds) *Empire's New Clothes*, London: Routledge.

Buhne, Neil (May 12, 2009) The United Nations and Humanitarian Coordinator, The Office of the Resident and the Humanitarian Coordinator, Colombo, Sri Lanka, letter to the Minister of Disaster Management and Human Rights.

Bhune, Neil (May 12, 2009) United Nations Office of the Resident and Humanitarian Coordinator, Colombo, memo to the Government of Sri Lanka.

Callinicos, Alex (2001) *Against the Third Way: An Anti-Capitalist Critique*, London: Polity Press.

Canadian High Commission (1996) Note to LCG donors from following the meeting of donor representatives with President Ershad (November 28, 1989), File # 38-6-1-2. Ford Foundation, Dhaka.

Cardoso, Fernando Henrique and Faletto Enzo (1979) *Dependency and Development in Latin America*, Berkeley: University of California Press.

*Catholic Guardian* (February 15, 1935).

*Catholic Guardian* (March 5, 1936).

Center for Policy Dialogue (1995) *Experiences of Economic Reform: Review of Bangladesh's Development*, Dhaka: University Press Limited.

Central Bank of Sri Lanka (1984) *Report of Consumer Finance and Socio-Economic Survey, 1981–1982*, Colombo: Central Bank.

Central Bank of Sri Lanka (1991) *Growth and Social Progress in Sri Lanka*, Colombo: Central Bank.

Centre for Policy Alternatives (2010) *CPA Statement on the Eighteenth Amendment Bill*, Colombo: CPA, http://www.box.net/shared/static/pcv68obari.pdf.

*Ceylon Daily News* (March 9, 1930).

*Ceylon Daily News* (March 14, 1930).

*Ceylon Daily News* (December 5, 1950).

*Ceylon Daily News* (July 21, 1991).

*Ceylon Daily News* (July 28, 1991).

Ceylon First Congress Literary Association (1914) Colombo: W.E. Bastian & Co.

Chabott, C. (1999) "Development INGOs," in John Boli and George Thomas (eds) *Constructing World Culture: International Nongovernmental Organizations since 1875*, Stanford, CA: Stanford University Press.

Chakrabarty, Bidyut (1992) "Social Classes and Social Consciousness," in Sirajul Islam (ed.) *The History of Bangladesh: Social and Cultural History*, Vol. 3, Dhaka: Asiatic Society of Bangladesh.

Chakrabarty, Dipesh (1993) "Marx after Marxism: Subaltern Histories and the Question of Difference," *Polygraph* 6/7.

Chanda, Nayan (1993) "Ershad Seeks a Role for the Army after a General Election: The March to Democracy," and "Parliament Must Rule," interview with H.M. Ershad, *Far Eastern Economic Review* (FEER) Vol. 121.

Chandraprema, C.A. (1991) *Sri Lanka: The Years of Terror, The JVP Insurrection, 1987–1989*, Colombo: Lake House.

Chatterji, Joya (2002) *Bengal Divided: Hindu Communalism and Partition, 1932–1947* (Cambridge South Asian Studies), Cambridge: Cambridge University Press.

Chatterjee, Partha (1986) *Nationalist Thought and the Colonial World: A Derivative Discourse?* Delhi: Oxford University Press.

Chatterjee, Partha (1989) "The Nationalist Resolution of the Women's Question" in Kum Kum Sangari and Sudesh Vaid (eds) *Recasting Women: Essays in Colonial History*, New Delhi: Kali for Women.

Chatopadhyay, Baudhaya (1981) *Notes towards Understanding of the Bengal Famine of 1943*, Calcutta: Transactions.

Cheran, P. (2009) *Pathways of Dissent: Tamil Nationalism in Sri Lanka*, New Delhi: SAGE.

Chipp-Kraushaar, Sylvia (1981) "The All Pakistan Women's Association and the 1961 Muslim Family Laws Ordinance" in Gail Minault (ed) *Extended Family, Women and Political Participation in India and Pakistan*, Columbia: South Asia Books, 262–85.

Chittagong Hill Tract Commission Report (1991) "Life is ours: Land and Human Rights in the Chittagong Hill Tracts," Bangladesh.

"Chomsky: West's self-interest reduces R2P to 'noble rhetoric'" (October 31, 2009) *TamilNet*, http://www.tamilnet.com/art.html?catid=13&artid=30537.

Choudhury, Dilhara (1992) "Women's Participation in the Formal Structure in Decision-making Bodies in Bangladesh" in Roshan Jahan et al. (eds) *Sultana's Dream and Selections from The Secluded Ones*, New York: Feminist Press.

Choudhury, Reshada (December 24, 1996) letter to colleague, ADAB, Association of Development Agencies in Bangladesh.

Choudhury, Salah Uddin Shoaib (April 9, 2010) "Encouraging State Repression in Bangladesh," *Blitz*, http://www.weeklyblitz.net/648/encouraging-state-repression-in-bangladesh.

Chowdhury, Dr. Zafarullah (1996) "State on the ADAB Exclusion," Memo, ADAM, Bangladesh.

*Christian Worker* (1981) (Third Quarter) Colombo: Christian Workers' Fellowship.

Church Missionary Society (1891–1892) Annual Reports.

"Citizens Report" (1992) Draft prepared by the NGOs and Country Position Paper, Ministry of Planning and Implementation, United Nations Conference on Environment and Development.

*Civil and Military Gazette* (May 16, 1950).

Clark, S. (1991) *The State Debate*, London: Palgrave Macmillan.

Comaroff, John L. (1992) *Ethnography and the Historical Imagination*, Westview, CT: Westview Press.

Corrigan, Philip and Derek Sayer (1985) *The Great Arch: English State Formation as Cultural Revolution*, Oxford: Blackwell.

Cosmos Indicipleustes (1860) *A Universal Christian*. Cited in Emerson Tennent, *Ceylon*, Vol. I: 562.

Cotton, H.J.S. (1880) *A Memorandum on the Revenue History of Chittagong*, Calcutta: Secretariat Press.

*Courier* (September 22–28, 1989).

Craig, John. C. (1951) American Vice Consul, Lahore, Dispatch no 28 (July 26) NMD. 842430, RG 84, Box 42, file 350-Pak. Pol.

Crosette, Barbara (August 18, 2003) "The Wrong Kind of American Exceptionalism," *The UN Wire*, http://www.globalpolicy.org/intljustice/icc/2003/0819except.htm. Accessed February 16, 2009.

Cummins, Stephen (1999) "NGOs: Ladles in the Global Soup Kitchen?" in D. Eade (ed.) *Development in Practice*, Vol. 9, No. 5.

*Daily Star* (March 16, 1995: 12; March 19, 1995: 1, 12; March 16, 1995; April 2, 1995: 5). Dhaka, Bangladesh.

Das, Samir Kumar (2005) *Peace Processes and Peace Accords*, New Delhi: Sage Publications.

Datta, Rajat (1989) "Agricultural Production, Social Participation, and Domination in the Late Nineteenth Century Bengal; Towards an Alternative Explanation," *Journal of Peasant Studies*, Vol. 17, No. 1.

Davis, Peter R. and McGregor, J. Allister (2000) "Civil Society, International Donors and Poverty in Bangladesh," *Commonwealth & Comparative Politics*, 38:1.

Davis, Rick (1996–1999) "Realizing the Potential for the PVDO Sector to Reduce Poverty in Bangladesh, A Proposal to Fund PRIP's Work," Ph.D. dissertation, University of Swansea.

Dayasri, Gomin (November 19, 2008) "Toasting the Terrorist," *The Eight Man Team* website, http://lrrp.wordpress.com/2008/11/19/toasting-the-terrorists-by-gomin-dayasri/. Accessed August 1, 2010.

"Deacons of Colombo to Dormieux," (October 23, 1880) Pro. of Comm. of Supt., Nov. 10, 1800, Factory Records, Ceylon, Vol. 39.

De Silva, Amarasiri, (2007) *Involuted Democracy: Tsunami Aid Delivery and Distribution in Ampara District*, United Nations Development Program: Bangkok, Thailand.

De Silva, Colvin R. (1941) *Ceylon Under the British*, Colombo: The Colombo Apothecaries' Co.

De Silva, K.M. (1960/61) "Buddhism and the British Government in Ceylon, 1840–1855," *Ceylon Historical Journal*, X.

De Silva, K.M. (1965) *Social Policy and Missionary Organizations in Ceylon, 1840–1855*, London: Longmans, Green and Co. Ltd.

De Silva, K.M. (1973) *University of Ceylon History of Ceylon*, Vol. III, Peradeniya: University of Ceylon.

De Silva, K.M. (1973) "The Reform and Nationalist Movement in the Twentieth Century," in *University of Ceylon History of Ceylon,* Vol. III, Peradeniya: University of Ceylon.

De Silva, K.M (1976) *Sri Lanka: A Survey,* London: C Hurst.

De Silva, K.M. (1981) *A History of Sri Lanka,* Oxford: Oxford University Press.

De Silva, K.M. (1997) "Resistance Movements in the 19th Century," in Michael Roberts (ed.) *Collective Identities Revisited,* Vol. I, Colombo: Marga Institute.

De Silva, K.M. (1997) *Sri Lanka: A History.* 2nd edition, New Delhi: Oxford University Press.

De Silva, Nalin (1997) *An Introduction to Tamil Racism in Sri Lanka,* Colombo: Chinthana Parshadaya.

De Tocqueville, Alexis (1945) *Democracy in America,* New York: Vintage Books.

Deen, Thalif (May 15, 2009) "Military Conflict vs. Propaganda War?" *Inter Press Service,* http://www.ipsnews.net/news.asp?idnews=46873. Accessed December 1, 2010.

Develtere, Patrick and An Huybrechts (2005) "The Impact of Microcredit on the Poor in Bangladesh," *Alternatives* 30.

Devine, Joe (1996) "NGOs: Changing Fashion or Fashioning Change?" Occasional Paper 02/96, CDS University of Bath.

Devine, Joseph (2006) "Bangladesh NGOs, Politics and Grassroots Mobilisation: Evidence from Bangladesh," *Journal of South Asian Development.*

Dias, Wije (October 31, 2009) "US makes cynical overture to Sri Lanka over war crimes," *World Socialist Web Site,* http://www.wsws.org/articles/2009/oct2009/sril-o31.shtml. Accessed December 1, 2010.

Dicklitch, Susan (1998) *The Elusive Promise of NGOs in Africa: Lessons from Uganda,* (International Political Economy Series). New York: MacMillan and St. Martin's Press.

Dickson, J.F. (1871) in *The Hansard* [Legislative Council].

*Dinamina* (December 30, 1991) Colombo: Lake House Publications Ltd.

*Divayina* (February 25, 1986; July 7, 1992; January 25, 1994) Colombo: Upali Newspapers Ltd.

Drexler, Anthony E. and Mirza Najmul Huda (1994) "Private Sector Philanthropy in Bangladesh," Bangladesh: PACT, Inc.

Durkheim, Emile (1957) *Professional Ethics and Civic Morals,* London: Routledge.

Dutta, Abhigith (1992) *Nineteenth Century Bengal and Christian Missionaries,* India: Minerva.

Dutt, Guru Sadaya (1929) *Women in India: Being the Life of Sarojini Nalini,* London: Hogarth Press.

Eagleton, Terry (1991) *Ideology: An Introduction,* New York: Verso.

Eagleton, Terry (May 13, 1999) "In the Gaudy Supermarket," *London Review of Books.*

Eaton, Richard M. (1993) *The Rise of Islam and the Bengal Frontier, 1204–1706,* California: California University Press.

"EC envoy says, agitation against the NGOs may scare the investors" (1994) *Bangladesh Observer* (July 9).

"The Economics and Governance of Non Governmental Organizations (NGOs) in Bangladesh" (August 2005) Poverty Reduction and Economic Management Sector Unite, South Asia Region, The World Bank, http://www.lcgbangladesh.org/NGOs/reports/NGO_Report_clientversion.pdf. Accessed April 16, 2009.

Edwards, Michael and David Hulme (eds) (1992) *Making a Difference: NGOs and Development in a Changing World*, London: EarthScan/Christian Children's Fund.

Ehrenberg, John (1989) *Civil Society: The Critical History of an Idea*, New York: New York University Press.

Eley, Geoff (1993) "Nations, Publics, and Political Cultures: Placing Habermas in the Nineteenth Century," in Craig Calhoun (ed.) *Habermas and the Public Sphere*, Massachusetts: MIT Press.

Elster, Jon (1986, 1994) *Making Sense of Marx*, New York: Cambridge University Press.

"End of International NGO Activity in the Gaza Strip?" (May 12, 2003) *Association of International Development Agencies*, http://globalpolicy.igc.org/ngos/state/2003/0512gaza.htm. Accessed February 16, 2009.

"Enter Ariyarathna: New Politics for '92" (December 29, 1991) *The Sunday Times*.

Escobar, Arturo (1994) *Encountering Development: Making and Unmaking of the Third World*, New Jersey: Princeton University Press.

Evers, Hans-Dieter (1972) *Monks, Priests and Peasants,* Leiden: E.J. Brill.

Everett, J. (1976) "The Indian Women's Movement in Comparative Perspective," Unpublished Ph.D. Dissertation, Ann Arbor: University of Michigan.

Fairehead, James and Mellissa Leach (1997) "Webs of Power and Construction of Environmental Policy Problems: Forest Loss in Guinea," in R.D. Grillo and R.L Stirrat (eds) *Discourses of Development: Anthropological Perspectives*, New York: Berg.

Feldman, Shelly (February 2003) "Paradoxes of Institutionalization: The Depoliticisation of Bangladeshi NGOs," *Development in Practice*, Vol. 13, No. 1.

Ferguson, James (1994) *The Anti-Politics Machine: "Development," Depoliticization and Bureaucratic Power in Lesotho*, Minneapolis: University of Minnesota Press.

Ferguson, James, and Akhil Gupta (2002) "Spatializing States; towards an Ethnography of Neoliberal Governmentality," *American Ethnologist* 29 (40:981–1002).

Fernando, Jude (June 25, 1994) Personal Interviews with fishermen, Kirinda, Sri Lanka.

Fernando, Jude (1995) Personal Interviews conducted in Anuradhapura, Sri Lanka.

Fernando, Jude (May 1998) "NGOs, Micro-Credit and Empowerment of Women" in *Annals of the American Academy of Political and Social Science*, Thousand Oaks: Sage, Vol. 536.

Fernando, Jude L. (2005) "Micro-Finance: Visibility without Power" in Jude L. Fernando (ed.) *Microfinance: Perils and Prospects*, London: Routledge.

Fernando, Vijitha and Henry de Mel (1991) *Non-Governmental Organizations (NGOs) in Sri Lanka: An Introduction*, Colombo: PACT.

Fisher, Julie (1997) *Nongovernments: NGOs and the Political Development of the Third World*, West Hartford, CT: Kumarian Press.

Fisher, William (1997) "Doing Good? Towards Politics and Antipolitics of NGO Practices." *Annual Review of Anthropology*, 26:439–64.

Fisher, William and Thomas Ponniah (2003) *Another World is Possible: Popular Alternatives to Globalization at the World Social Forum*, London: Zed Books.

Forbes, Major J. (1840) *Eleven Years in Ceylon*, London.

Forbes, Geraldine (1996) *Women in Modern India, New Cambridge History of India Series,* Cambridge: Cambridge University Press.

The Ford Foundation (August 13, 1992) Office of the Representative for Bangladesh, Memorandum, Subject NGO Bureau-NGO Relations.

The Ford Foundation (September 26, 1994) Inter-Office memorandum from Nancy Feller to Brenda Leggett.

Forester, Duncan (1974) "Indian Christians' Attitude towards Caste in the Nineteenth Century," *Indian History Review*, Vol. VII, No. 2.

Forester, Duncan (1975) "Indian Christians' Attitude to Caste in the Twentieth Century," *Indian Church History Review*, Vol. IX, No. 1.

Forester, Duncan (1980) *Caste and Christianity: Attitude and Policies of Caste of Anglo-Saxon Protestant Missions in India*, London: Curzon Press.

Foucault, M. (1991) "Governmentality" in G. Burchell, C. Gordon and P. Miller (eds) *The Foucault Effect: Studies in Governmentality,* Hemel Hempstead: Harvester Wheatsheaf.

Foucault, Michel (1999) "Governmentality," cited in George Steinmetz (ed.) *State/Culture: State Formation after the Cultural Turn*, Ithaca, NY: Cornell University Press.

Fowler, Alan (2000) "Relevance in Twenty-First Century: The Case for Devolution and Global Association of International NGOs" in Deborah Eade and Hazel Johnson (eds) *Development and Management: Selected Essays from "Development in Practice,"* London: Oxfam.

Frank, G. (1980) *Crisis in the World Economy*, New York: Holmes and Meier Publishers.

Frazer, J.G. (1922) *The Golden Bough,* London: NuVision Publications.

Fromm, Erich (1961/1964) *Marx's Concept of Man*, New York: Continuum.

Garland, D. (1999) "Governmentality and the Problem of Crime" in R. Smandych (ed) *Governable Places: Readings on Governmentality and Crime Control,* Aldershot: Ashgate.

Gauri, Varun and Julia Galef (December 2005) "NGOs in Bangladesh: Activities, Resources, and Governance," *World Development*, Vol. 33, No. 12, 2045–2065.

Geertz, Clifford (1985) *Local Knowledge: Further Essays in Interpretative Communities*, New York: Basic Books.

Ghosh, Shri Asoklal (1984) *British India's First Political Organization, in Public Associations in India*, N.R. Ray (ed.), Calcutta: Institute for Historical Studies.

Giddens, Anthony (1993) *The Nation State and Violence, Vol. II: A Contemporary Critique of Historical Materialism*, Berkeley: University of California Press.

Gledhill, John (1997) "Liberalism, Rights, and the Politics of Identity: From Moral Economy to Indigenous Rights," in Richard A. Wilson (ed.), *Human Rights, Culture and Context: Anthropological Perspectives*, London: Pluto Press.

Gledhill, John (1999) *Power and its Disguises: Anthropological Perspectives on Politics*, London: Pluto Press.

Gombrich, Richard and Gananath Obeyesekere (1988) *Buddhism Transformed: Religious Change in Sri Lanka*, Princeton: Princeton University Press.

Gomes, William (April 1, 2009) "Islamic NGOs: Shadow Government in Bangladesh," *Islam Watch*, http://www.islam-watch.org/Gomes/Islamic-NGOs-Shadow-Government-in-Bangladesh.htm. Accessed April 16, 2009.

Gomes, William (April 6, 2009) "NGOs in Bangladesh under Bureaucratic Dictatorship," Asian Tribune, http://www.asiantribune.com/?q=node/16572. Accessed April 16, 2009.

Goodhand, Jonathan and Peter Chamberlain (1996) "Dancing with the Prince: NGOs Survival Strategies in the Afghan Conflict," in D. Eade (ed.) *Development and States of War Reader*, London: Oxfam.

Gordon, Leonard A. (1998) "Wealth and Wisdom? The Rockefeller and Ford Foundations in India" in Jude Fernando and Alan Heston (eds) *The Role of NGOs: Charity and Empowerment*, New Delhi: Sage.

Gosh, Thushar Kanthi (1944) *The Bengal Tragedy,* Lahore: Hero Publications.

Goulet, Denis (1981) *Survival with Integrity: Sarvodaya at the Cross Roads,* Colombo: Marga Institute.

Government Commission on NGOs (March 10, 1991) "Public Sittings on 25th," *The Sunday Island.*

"The Government to Mobilize and Coordinate NGO help for Front Line Men" (May 29, 1991) *Daily News.*

Government of Bengal Revenue Department (1941) *The Famine Manual.*

Gowan, Peter (1999) *The Global Gamble: Washington's Faustian Bid for World Dominance*, London: Verso.

Gramsci, Antonio (1992) *Selections from the Prison Notebooks*, Quentin Hore and Geoffrey Nowell Smith (eds), New York: International Publishers.

*Great Expectations* (December 1993) Report of the Evaluation/Appraisal of The Association of Development Agencies in Bangladesh, submitted to ADAB Donor Consortium.

Greenough, Paul (1982) *Prosperity and Misery in Modern Bengal: The Famine of 1943–1944*, London: Oxford University Press.

Greg, Alling (1997) "Economic Liberalization and Separatist Nationalism," *Journal of International Affairs*, Vol. 51 (Summer).

Grillo, R.D. (1997) *Discourse of Development: View from Anthropology*, Oxford and London: Berg Publishers.

Grillo, R.D. and R.L. Stirrat (eds) (1997) *Discourses of Development: Anthropological Perspectives (Explorations in Anthropology)*, Oxford: Bergson Publication Ltd.

Guha, Ranajit (1998) *Dominance without Hegemony: History and Power in Colonial India Convergences: Inventories of the Present*, Cambridge: Harvard University Press.

Guha, Ranajit (1999) *Elementary Aspects of Peasant Insurgency in Colonial India*, North Carolina: Duke University Press.

Guhathakurtha, Meghana and Suriya Begum (1998) "Political Empowerment and Women's Movement," in Roshan Jahan et al. (eds) *Empowerment of Women: Nairobi to Beijing (1985–1995)*, Dhaka: Women for Women.

Gulliford, Rev. H (May 1986) "Neo-Hinduism and Christianity," *The Harvest Field.*

Gunasinghe, Newton (1990) *Socio-Economic Change in Kandyan Countryside*, Colombo: Sri Lanka Social Scientists' Association.

Gunathilaka, Susantha (February 10, 2004) "The Scramble for Sri Lanka: Peace Initiatives and Initiatives for Pieces in Lanka" in *The Island*, quoted in Orjuela (2004).

Gupta, K.P. Sen (1971) *Christian Missionaries in Bengal*, Calcutta: Firma K.L. Mukhopadhyay.

Guruge, A. (ed) (1965) *Anagarika Dharmapala; Return to Righteousness*, Colombo: The Government Press.

Habermas, J. (1989) *The Structural Transformation of the Public Sphere*, trans. P. Berger, Cambridge, MA: MIT Press.

Hadiwinata, Bob (2003) *The Politics of NGOs in Indonesia: Developing Democracy and Managing a Movement*, London: Routledge.

Hall, Peter Dobkin (1985) "Doing Well by Doing Good: Business Philanthropy and Social Investment, 1860–1984" in *Giving and Volunteering: New Frontiers of Knowledge*, Spring Research Forum Working Papers, United Way.

Hancock, Mary (2001) "Home Science and the Nationalization of Domesticity in Colonial India," *Modern Asian Studies, 35*:4.

Hannan, Shah Abdul (1980) "Women's Employment: Its Need and Appropriate Avenues" in *Thoughts on Islamic Economics*, Proceedings from Seminar, Dhaka: Islamic Economics Research Bureau.

*Hansard*, 1936.

*Hansard*, 1939, Col. 819.

Haque, M. Shamsul (June 2002) "The Changing Balance of Power between the Government and NGOs in Bangladesh," *International Political Science Review*, 23, 4.

Haque, M. Shamsul (2002) "The Changing Balance of Power Between the Government and NGOs," *Voluntas: International Journal of Voluntary and Nonprofit Organizations*, Vol. 13, No. 2.

Hardt, Michel and Antonio Negri (2004) *Multitude: War and Democracy in the Age of Empire*, New York: Penguin Press.

Hardiman, David (1981) *Peasant Nationalists of Gujarat: Kheda District 1917–1934*, Oxford University Press, New Delhi.

Harrison, Udivil (1826) "Appendix B", *Missionary Herald*, XXII.

Hartman, Betsy and James Boyes (1983) *A Quiet Revolution: A View From a Bangladesh Village,* London: Zed Press.

*Harvest Field*, Vol. V (December 1893).

Harvey, David (1991) *The Condition of Postmodernity: An Inquiry into the Origins of Cultural Change*, London: Wiley-Blackwell.

Harvey, David (1996) *Justice, Nature and the Geography of Difference*, New York: Blackwell.

Harvey, David (2000) *Spaces of Hope*, Los Angeles: California University Press.

Harvey, David (2005) *A Brief History of Neoliberalism*, Oxford: Oxford University Press.

Hashemi, S. (1996) "NGO Accountability in Bangladesh: Beneficiaries, Donors and the State," in M. Edwards and D. Hulme (eds) *Beyond the Magic Bullet: NGO Performance and Accountability in the Post-Cold War World*, West Hartford, Conn: Kumarian Press.

Heimsath, Charles (1964) *Indian Nationalism and Hindu Social Reform,* Princeton: Princeton University Press.

Hellmann-Rajanayagam, Dagmar (1988–1989) "Tamil Militants, Before and After," *Pacific Affairs*, Vol. 61, No. 4 (Winter).

Hicks, Ursula (1959) "Local Government and Finance in Ceylon" in *Papers by Visiting Economists*, Colombo: Planning Secretariat.

Hilferding, Rudolf (1985) *Finance Capital: A Study in the Latest Phase of Capitalist Development*, London: Routledge.

"Hillary discusses Sri Lanka issue with Norwegian Minister" (April 7, 2009) *Business Line*, http://www.thehindubusinessline.com/blnus/10071051.htm. Accessed April 15, 2009.

*Hindu Organ* (April 27, 1931).

Historian, J.C. (1985) *The Inner Conflict of Tradition: Essays in Indian Ritual, Kinship, and Society*, Chicago: University of Chicago Press.

Hobart, M. (1993) *An Anthropological Critique of Development: The Growth of Ignorance*, London: Routledge.

Holloway, Richard (January 1999) "Freeing the Citizens Sector from Global Paradigms and Trying to Get a Grip on the Moral High Ground," paper presented at "NGOs in Global Future" Conference, University of Birmingham, UK.

Holloway, John (1980/1991) "The State and Everyday Struggle," in Clarke (ed.) *The State Debate*, London: Macmillan.

*The Holy Bible*, King James Version (2006) Ohio: Barbour Publishing.

Hoogvelt, Ankie (2001) *Globalization and the Post-Colonial World: The New Political Economy of Development*, 2nd edition, London: Palgrave.

Hossain, Farhad and Marko Ulvila (2002) "Development NGOs and Political Participation of the Poor in Bangladesh and Nepal," *Voluntas: International Journal of Voluntary and Nonprofit Organizations*, Vol. 13, No. 2.

Hossain, Mahabub et al. (1982) "Participatory Development Efforts in Rural Bangladesh: A Case Study of Experiences in Three Areas" in Amit Bhaduri and MD Ansuir Rahaman (eds) *Studies in Rural Participation*, Dhaka: Dhaka University Press.

Hossain, Rokeya S (1988) "Sultan's Dream" in Roushan Jahan (ed.) *The Secluded Ones*, New York: Feminist Press.

Hosten, S.J. (July–December1910) "The Earliest Recorded Episcopal Visitation of Bengal, 1715–1721," *Bengal Past and Present 6*.

Hulme, David and Michael Edwards (eds) (1996) *NGOs, States and Donors: Too Close for Comfort?* New York: Palgrave Macmillan.

Hussain, Izeth (2008) "Sarath Fonseka Statements Reek of Sinhala Triumphalism," transCurrents website, http://transcurrents.com/tc/2008/11/post_76.html. Accessed April 15, 2009.

Hussain, Md. Zaker (1996) "Village and Industrial Development: (V-AID) Program," in Md. Abdul Quddus (ed.) *Rural Development in Bangladesh: Strategies and Experiences,* Comilia: Bangladesh Academy for Rural Development.

Hussain, Muhammad (January 2, 2009) "Will Women Prevent Bangladesh's Descent to Islamism?" BC Politics website, http://blogcritics.org/archives/2009/01/02/215441.php. Accessed April 16, 2009.

"Indictment Against Sri Lanka: Sri Lanka's Undeclared War on Eelam Tamils ... in the Shadow of the Ceasefire," *Tamilnation.org*, http://www.tamilnation.org/indictment/shadow_war/index.htm. Accessed April 15, 2009.

"In this land of the most compassionate Lord Buddha..." *LankaDissent*, http://www.lankadissent.com/. Accessed April 15, 2009.

Institutional Strengthening for Government/NGO Cooperation, ADB TA No. 2088.

Islam, Sirajul (ed.) (1992) *History of Bangladesh*, 3 Vols, Dhaka: Journal of the Asiatic Society of Bangladesh.

Jabber Zacki (March 30, 2009) "Government consider to temporarily suspend attacks [*sic*]," Lanka-e-News, http://www.colombopage.com/archive_09/April7142959JV.html. Accessed April 15, 2009.

Jabber, Zacki (April 7, 2009) "International Pressure Stopped Army's March Into No Fire Zone," *The Island*, http://www.asianewsnet.net/news.php?id=5046&sec=1. Accessed April 15, 2009

Jaffna Youth Congress, *Hand Book*.

Jaffna Youth Congress (April 24, 1939) Meeting Report.

Jahan, Ronaq (1972) *Pakistan: Failure of National Integration,* New York: Columbia University Press.

Jahan, Roshan (1981) "Biographical Introduction" in *Inside Seclusion: The Avaradh Basini of Rokeya Shakwat Hossain,* Dhaka: Dhaka University Press.

Jalal, Ayesha (1989) *The State of Martial Rule: The Origins of Pakistan's Political Economy of Defense,* Cambridge: Cambridge University Press.

James, C.L.R. (1963) *The Black Jacobins,* New York: Vintage Books.

Jammer, M. (1954/1993) *Concepts of Space: The History of Theories of Space in Physics,* Cambridge MA: Dover.

Jameson, Frederic (1991) *Postmodernism, or, the Cultural Logic of Late Capitalism,* Durham, NC: Duke University Press.

Jayasekara, P.V.J. (1970) "Social and Political Change in Ceylon 1900–1919," Ph.D. Thesis, London.

Jayasoriya, Jagath (2005) "Government must not fall into 'Venus Trap' set by LTTE," http://www.asiantribune.com/oldsite/show_news.php?id=13517.

Jayathilaka, Dayan (April 29, 2005) "The Murder of Sivaram," *AsianTribune,* http://www.infolanka.com/ubb/Forum2/HTML/001043.html. Accessed December 1, 2010.

Jayathilaka, Dayan (August 2008) "Sri Lanka's Foreign Policy: The Way to Go," FEDERALIDEA Web site, http://federalidea.com/fi/2008/08/sri_lankas_foreign_policy_the.html. Accessed April 15, 2009.

Jayathilaka, Dayan (2008) "60th Year of Independence, Personal Perspective: Make 2008 the Year of Victory!" http://www.defence.lk/new.asp?fname=20071225_05. Accessed April 15, 2009.

Jayathilaka, Dayan (September 9, 2008) "The Politics of Winning in the Vanni," Groundviews website, http://www.groundviews.org/2008/09/09/the-politics-of-winning-in-the-vanni/. Accessed April 15, 2009.

Jayawardena, Kumari (1972) *The Rise of the Labor Movement in Ceylon,* Durham, NC: Duke University Press.

Jayawardena, Kumari (July 1, 1979) "Bhikkhus in Revolt, Part 3: Buddhist Radical Labor Movement," *Lanka Guardian.*

Jayawardena, Kumari (1979) "Some Aspects of Class and Ethnic Consciousness in Sri Lanka in the Late 19th and Early 20th Centuries," in *Ethnicity and Social Change in Sri Lanka: Papers Presented at Seminar Organised by the Social Scientists Association December,* Colombo: Social Scientists Association, 74–92.

Jayawardena, Kumari (1988) *Feminism and Nationalism in the Third World,* London: Zed Books.

Jayawardena, Kumari (1995) *The White Woman's Other Burden: Western Women and South Asia During British Rule,* London: Routledge.

Jayewardena, J.R. (1987) quoted in James Hughes, "Buddhist Monks and Politics in Sri Lanka," paper presented at the Institute for Social Science Research, University of Chicago, http://www.changesurfer.com/Bud/Sri/Sri.html. Accessed April 14, 2009.

Jenkins, Rob (2000) "Mistaking 'Governance' for 'Politics': Foreign Aid, Democracy, and the Construction of Civil Society," in Sudipta Kaviraj and Sunil Khilnani (eds) *Civil Society: History and Possibilities,* Delhi: Cambridge University Press.

Jessop, Bob (1991) "Accumulation Strategies, State Forms and Hegemonic Projects," in Simon Clark (ed.) *The State Debate,* New York: St Martin Press.

Jessop, Bob (2003) *The Future of the Capitalist State,* Cambridge: Polity Press.

Johnston, Anna (2003) *Missionary Writing and Empire, 1800–1860*, Cambridge: Cambridge University Press.

Joshi, Sanjay (2001) *Fractured Modernity: Making of a Middle Class in Colonial North India*, New Delhi: Oxford University Press.

"JVP Slams NGOs, Western Countries for Meddling" (April 6, 2005) *TamilNet*, http://www.tamilnet.com/art.html?catid=79&artid=14625. Accessed April 15, 2009.

"JVP's War on NGOs and Fears of Neo Colonialism" (April 27, 2005) *Daily Mirror*, http://www.tamilnation.org/forum/sivaram/050427.htm. Accessed April 14, 2009.

Kabeer, Naila (1991) "The Quest for National Identity: Women, Islam and the State in Bangladesh" in Deniz Kandiyoti (ed.) *Women, Islam and the State*, Philadelphia: Temple University Press.

Kabeer, Naila (1991) "The Quest for National Identity" in Rafiuddin Ahmed (ed.) *Islam in Bangladesh*, Dhaka: Dhaka University Press.

Kabir, Shariar (ed.) (1995) "Resist Fundamentalism: Focus on Bangladesh, Nirmul Committee: Committee for Resisting Killers and Collaborators of Bangladesh Liberation War of 1971," Dhaka: Dhaka University Press.

*Kalaya* (December 12, 1946) Vol. 1, No. 38.

Kalecki, M. (1967) "Observations on Social Formation and Economic Aspects of Intermediate Regimes," *Coexistence*, 4, 1.

Kamaluddin, Syed (April 22, 1993) "Donors are Critical: Paris Donor Consortium Meets," *Holiday*.

Kamat, Sangeeta (2002) *Development Hegemony: NGOs and the State in India*, New York, Oxford University Press.

Kamat, Sangeeta (2003) *The NGO Phenomenon and Political Culture, Third World Development* 46 (1)88–93.

Kandiyoti, Deniz (1994) "Identity and Its Discontents: Women and the Nation," in Patrick Williams and Laura Chrisman (eds), *Colonial Discourse and Post-Colonial Theory: A Reader*, New York: Columbia University Press.

Kanesalingam, V. (1971) *A Hundred Years of Local Government in Ceylon*, Colombo: Modern Plastic Works.

Karim, Lamia (May 2001) "Politics of the Poor? NGOs and Grass-roots Political Mobilization in Bangladesh," *PoLar: Political and Legal Anthropology Review*, Vol. 24, No. 1.

Katznelson, Ira (1986) *Working Class Formation*, Princeton, NJ: Princeton University Press.

Katz, Stanley (March 15, 1985) "The History of Foundations" in *Giving and Volunteering: New Frontiers of Knowledge,* Spring Research Forum Working Papers, United Way (working draft).

Kean, Jean (1992) *Civil Society: Old Images, New Visions*, Cambridge: Polity Press.

Kearney, Michael (March 1991) "Borders and Boundaries of State and Self at the End of Empire," *Journal of Historical Sociology*, Vol. 4, No. 1.

Keenan, Alan (2006) "Building a Democratic Middle Ground: Professional Civil Society and the Politics of Human Rights in Sri Lanka's Peace Process," in Julie Mertus and Jeffrey W. Helsing (eds), *Human Rights and Conflict*, Washington, DC: U.S. Institute of Peace Press.

Keerawella, Gamini and Rohan Samarajiva (February 1995) "Sri Lanka in 1994: Mandate for Peace" in *Asian Survey*, Vol. 25, No. 2.

Kemper, Steven (1992) *The Presence of the Past: Chronicles, Politics, and Culture in Sinhala Life*, Ithaca: Cornell University Press.

Kennedy, Charles H. (Winter 1999) "Reconsidering the Relationship between the State, Donors, and NGOs in Bangladesh," *Pakistan Development Review* 38: 4, Part I.

Kerr, D. (1999) "Beheading the King and Enthroning the Market: A Critique of Foucauldian Governmentality," *Science and Society*, 63: 2.

Khalid, Mohammed (1967) *Welfare State: A Case Study of Pakistan*, Karachi: Royal Book Co.

Khan, Muin-ud-Din Ahamad (1982), "Muslim Struggle for Freedom in Bengal: From Plassey to Pakistan AD 1757–1947," Dhaka: Islamic Foundation of Bangladesh.

Kiernan, Victor G. (1995) *Imperialism and Contradictions*, New York: Routledge, quoted in Lazarus (1999) *Nationalism and Cultural Practice*.

Kopf, David *(1969) British Orientalism and the Bengal Renaissance,* Berkeley: University of California Press.

Kochaneck, Stanley A. (1993) *Patron-Client Politics and Business in Bangladesh*, Dhaka: University Press Limited.

Kois, Lisa, (2007), "Traversing the Global Village: Violence against women, discourses, dialectics, and dialogues" in Nimanthi Perera, Lisa Kois, and Rizvina Morseth De Alwis (eds) *Feminist Fragments with Violence: Contingent Moments From Sri Lanka*, Colombo: International Center For Ethnic Studies

Korten, David C. (1990) *Getting to the 21st Century: Voluntary Action and the Global Agenda*, Hartford, CT: Kumarian Press.

Korten, David C. and Antonio B. Qizon (1990) "Government, NGOs, and International Agency Cooperation: Whose Agenda?" Kuala Lumpur: Asian Pacific Development Center.

Kruger, Horst (1989) "Hinduism and National Liberation Movement in Hinduism Reconsidered" in Günther D. Sontheimer and Hermann Kulke (eds) *Hinduism Reconsidered*, New Delhi: Manohar Publications.

Kulke, H. (1982) "Fragmentation and Segmentation versus Integration: Reflections on the Concepts of Indian Feudalism and the Segmentary State in Indian History," *Studies in History,* Vol. 4, No. 2.

Kumar, Anand (May 22, 2007) "Bangladesh: Islamist Terror and the Caretaker Government," Paper No. 2252, South Asia Analysis Group, South Asia Group, http://www.southasiaanalysis.org/%5Cpapers23%5Cpaper2252.html. Accessed April 16, 2009.

Laclau, Ernesto and Chantal Mouffe (1990) *Hegemony and Socialist Strategy: Toward a Radical Democratic Politics*, New York: Verso.

*Lakbimanews* (October 18, 2009) Vol. 3, number 8, Sumathi Newspapers, Colombo, online edition, http://www.lakbimanews.lk.

Laxman, W.D. (1986) "State Policy in Sri Lanka and its Economic Impact 1970–85" in *Growth and Equity in Developing Countries, A Reinterpretation of the Sri Lankan Experience*, Washington, DC: The World Bank.

Lazarus, Neil (1999) *Nationalism and Cultural Practice in the Post-Colonial World*, Cambridge: Cambridge University Press.

Lee, Matthew Russell (May 20, 2009) "On Sri Lanka, IMF Said Ready to Lend, Dodges Ethnic Cleansing, Where Are Obama, UK?" *Inner City Press*, http://www.innercitypress.com/imf4srilanka052109.html. Accessed November 28, 2010.

Lenin, Vladimir (1969) "State and Revolution" in *Selected Works,* London: Lawrence and Wishart.

Levine, Philippa (2004) *Gender and Empire*, Cambridge: Cambridge University Press.

Lewis, D. (1988) "NGOs, Donors and State," unpublished paper, London School of Economics.

Lewis, David (Winter 1998) "Nongovernmental Organizations, Business, and the Management of Ambiguity," *Nonprofit Management and Leadership*, Vol. 9, no. 2.

Lewis, David (2001) *The Management of Non-Governmental Development Organizations*, New York: Routledge.

Lewis, David (2004) "On the difficulty of studying 'civil society': NGOs, state and democracy in Bangladesh," *Contributions to Indian Sociology*, 38 (3), 299–322.

Liddle, Joanna and Rama Joshi (1986) *Daughters of Independence: Gender Caste and Class in India*, New Jersey: Rutgers University Press.

Linklater, Andrew (1998) *Transformation of the Political Community*, Cambridge: Polity Press.

Lobe, Jim (12 June 2003) "U.S. Conservatives Take Aim at NGOs," *One World Net*, http://www.commondreams.org/headlines03/0612-09.htm. Accessed February 16, 2009.

Lovel, Catherine H. (1992) *Breaking the Cycle of Poverty: The BRAC Strategy*, West Hartford, CT: Kumarian Press.

Lowe, Lisa and David Lloyd (eds) (1997) *The Politics of Culture in the Shadow of Capital*, North Carolina: Duke University Press.

Ludden, David (1992) "India's Development Regime," in N.B. Dirks (ed.) *Colonialism and Culture*, Ann Arbor: University of Michigan Press.

Lukacs, George (1993) *History and Class Consciousness: Studies in Marxist Dialectics*, New Delhi: Rupa & Co.

Luxemburg, Rosa (1968) *Accumulation of Capital*, New York: Monthly Review Press.

MacPhail, James M. (1910). *The Heritage of India*, Calcutta: The Association Press.

"Mahinda, Dullas and 8 Others Should Also Be In the Cage, of [sic] I Am Imprisoned for Betraying Country by Signing the Ceasefire Agreement" (April 9, 2009) Lanka-e-News, http://www.lankaenews.com/English/news.php?id=7450. Accessed April 15, 2009.

Majid, Anouar (2000) *Unveiling Traditions: Post Colonial Islam in a Polycentric World*, North Carolina: Duke University Press.

Malalgoda, Kithsiri (1976) *Buddhism and Sinhalese Society 1750–1900: A Study of Religious Change*, Berkeley: University of California Press.

Malik, A.R. and Anwer Husain (1992) "Political Basis of Bengali Nationalism," in Sirajul Islam (ed.) *History of Bangladesh: Political History*, Vol. 2, Asiatic Society of Bangladesh.

Malik, Vijay (1985) *Commentary on the Societies Registration Act, 1860*, Lucknow: Eastern Book Company Law Publishers & Book Sellers.

Mani, Lata (1990) "Contentious Traditions: The Debate on Sati in Colonial India" in Kum Kum Sangari and Sudesh Vaid (eds) *Recasting Women: Essays in Indian Colonial History*, New Jersey: Rutgers University Press.

Manor, James (1989) *The Expedient Utopian: Bandaranaike and Ceylon*, Cambridge: Cambridge University Press.

Marshman, John Clark (1859) *The Life and Times of Carey, Marshman, and Ward: Embracing the History of the Serampore Mission*. 2 Vols, London: Longman, Brown, Green, Longmans and Roberts.

Marx-Engels Gesamtangabe (MEGA) (1920) Berlin, I/33.

Marx, Karl (August 8, 1853) "The Future Results of British Rule in India," *New York Daily Tribune*.

Marx, Karl (1859) "A Contribution to the Critique of Political Economy" in *Collected Works*, Vol. 29.

Marx, Karl (1962) "Thesis III on Feuerbach," *Selected Works, II*, Moscow and London, excerpted in Avineri (1968) *The Social and Political Thought of Marx*.

Marx, Karl (1963) *Early Writings*, Tom Bottomore (trans.) London: Watts.

Marx, Karl (1965) *The German Ideology*, London: Institute of Marxism Leninism.

Marx, Karl (1967) *Capital*, Vol. 1 London: Dent (Everyman).

Marx, Karl (1967) *The Communist Manifesto*, New York: Penguin.

Marx, Karl (1971) *Critique of Hegel's Philosophy of Right*, Cambridge: Cambridge University Press.

Marx, Karl (1971b) "On the Jewish Question," in *Early Texts*, D. McLellan (ed.), Oxford: Oxford University Press.

Marx, Karl (1972) *Capital*, New York: Vintage.

Marx, Karl (1973) *Grundrisse*, New York: Vintage Press.

Marx, Karl (1974) *Political Writings, Vol. 1: The Revolutions of 1848*, David Fernbach (ed.), New York: Random House/Vintage.

Marx, Karl (1984) *Capital*, New York: International Publishers.

Marx, Karl (1988) "The Inaugural Address of the Working Men's Association," London: The Bee-Hive Newspaper Office, cited in Tom Bottomore et al., London: Blackwell Publishing.

Marx, Karl "On the Jewish Question," quoted in Ehrenberg (1989) *Civil Society*.

Marx, Karl (February 13, 1866) Letter to Engels, in Marx and Engels, *Selected Correspondence* (1942), Moscow Publishers, 1975.

Marx, Karl and Friedrich Engels (1942/1975) *Selected Correspondence*, Moscow Publishers.

Marx, Karl and Friedrich Engels (1971) *Articles on Britain*, Moscow: Progress Publishers.

Marx, Karl and Friedrich Engels (1989) *The German Ideology*, quoted in Ehrenberg (1989) *Civil Society*.

Marx, Karl and Friedrich Engels (1998) *The Communist Manifesto: A Modern Edition*, Eric J. Hobsbawm (ed.), New York: Verso.

Marx, Karl and Friedrich Engels (2002) *The Communist Manifesto*, Baltimore: Penguin.

Marx, Karl and Friedrich Engels (2003) "Thesis on Feuerbach" in *Collected Works*, 1845–6, cited in Robert Antonio (ed.) *Marx and Modernity: Key Readings and Commentary*, London: Blackwell Publishing.

Mathew, A. (1988) *Christian Missions, Education, and Nationalism: From Dominance to Compromise, 1870–1930*, Delhi: Anamika Prakashan.

McBride, Stephen and John Wiseman (eds) (2000) *Globalization and Its Discontents*, London: Macmillan Press.

McCarthy, Florence (1985) *An Evaluation of the Intensive Rural Works Program*, Dhaka: IRWP.

McCarthy, Florence (August 1987) "Upazila Government in Bangladesh," unpublished paper, Cornell University.

Mcgrawth, Allen (1996) *The Destruction of Pakistan's Democracy*, Karachi: Oxford University Press.

McGuire, John (1981) *The Making of a Colonial Mind, A Quantitative Study of the Bhadralok in Calcutta, 1857–1885*, Australian National University Monograph on South Asia, No. 10.

Mehmet, Ozay (1995) *Westernizing the Third World: The Eurocentricity of Economic Development Theories*, London: Routledge.

Mehra, Rekha (1977) *The Impact of American Private Philanthropy*, Ph.D. dissertation, University of Florida.

Meldrum, Andrew (October 17, 2002) "Zimbabwe Banned Food Aid Charities" *Mail and the Guardian*, http://www.globalpolicy.org/ngos/aid/2002/1017aid.htm. Accessed February 16, 2009.

Mendelson, Sarah Elizabeth and John K. Glenn (eds) (2002) *The Power and Limits of NGOs*, New York: Columbia University Press.

Menon, Ammu K. (1960) "Mahatma Gandhi's Contribution to Social Welfare in India: A Study of Three Major Programmes," Ph.D. dissertation, Columbia University.

Midgley, Clare (2001) *Feminism and Empire, Women Activists in Imperial Britain, 1719–1865*, London: Routledge.

Miliband, Ralph (1977) *Marxism and Politics*, Oxford: Oxford University Press

"Military victory is not the final solution, says Sri Lanka President" (May 19, 2009) *Colombo Page*, http://www.colombopage.com/archive_091/May1242741695CH. html. Accessed May 19, 2009.

Minault, Gail (1981) *The Extended Family: Women and Political participation in India and Pakistan*, New Delhi: Chanakya Publications.

Minault, Gail (1981) "Sisterhood or Separatism? The All India Muslim Ladies Conference and the Nationalist Movement," in Gail Minault (ed.) *The Extended Family: Women and Political participation in India and Pakistan*, New Delhi, Chanakya Publications.

Minault, Gail (1981) "The Indian Women's Movement: A Struggle for Women's Rights or National Liberation?" in Gail Minault (ed.) *The Extended Family: Women and Political participation in India and Pakistan*, New Delhi, Chanakya Publications.

"Minister Champika Ranawaka Violates the Constitution" (October 18, 2008) Lanka-e-News, http://www.lankaenews.com/English/news.php?id=6548. Accessed April 14, 2009.

"Ministry of Disaster Management & Human Rights," The Democratic Socialist & Republic of Sri Lanka website, http://www.dmhr.gov.lk/english/information. php. Accessed April 14, 2009.

*Missions and Governments* (1910) World Missionary Conference, New York: Fleming H. Revell Company.

Mitchell, Timothy (1999) "Society, Economy, and the State Effect" in George Steinmetz (ed.) *State/Culture: State formation After the Cultural Turn*, Ithaca: Cornell University Press.

*Morning Star* (June 30, 1930; May 3, 1934).

Moshin, K.M. (1983) "Trends in Islam in Bangladesh" in Rafiuddin Ahmed (ed.) *Islam in Bangladesh*, Dhaka: Dhaka University Press.

Mukherjee, K.K. (1994) *Voluntary Organizations: Challenges and Responses*, Ghaziabad: Gram Niyojan Kendra.

Mukherjee, Subhas (January 1934) "Communist Party-Organ," *People's Age*.

Murphy, Brian (2000) "International NGOs and the Challenge of Modernity," in Deborah Eade and Hazel Johnson (eds) *Development and Management: Selected Essays from "Development in Practice,"* London: Oxfam.

Mustafa, Sabir (March 23, 1995) "Confusion Amid Commitments," *The Financial Express*, Dhaka.

Mustafa, Sabir (April 5, 2007) "Bangladesh at a crossroads," BBC News South Asia website, http://news.bbc.co.uk/2/low/south_asia/6530781.stm. Accessed April 16, 2009.

Nelson, Paul J. (1995) *The World Bank and NGOs: The Limits of Apolitical Development*, New York: St. Martin's Press.

"NGO Bureau-NGO Relations," (August 13, 1992) Memorandum, The Ford Foundation.

NGO Forum on Sri Lanka (November 17, 1995) *Annual Consultation: Chronology of Events*, Colombo: Inform.

"NGOs create tremors among opposition parties" (April 10, 1989) *The New Nation.*

"NGOs with foreign funding fuelling militancy in Bangladesh" (March 19, 2009) *Deccan Herald*, http://www.deccanherald.com/Content/Mar192009/scroll20090319125012.asp. Accessed April 16, 2009.

Ninth Monitoring Report of the Sarvodaya Donor Consortium (September 24–October 6, 1990).

"Non Violent Peace Force officer ordered to quit country: 5th officer in 3 months so ordered to leave" (September 18, 2010) *Lanka E-News*, http://www.lankaenews.com/English/news.php?id=10023. Accessed November 30, 2010.

North, Douglas (1990) *Institutions, Institutional Change, and Economic Performance: Political Economy of Institutions and Decisions*, Cambridge, Mass: Cambridge University Press.

"NOVIB Surprised by Christian Democrats Decisions to Withdraw" (April 12, 1994) NRC Handelsblad, *Weekeditte Voor Het Buitenland,*

NOVIB (December 22, 1993) Letter from Hans Pelgrom to Dr. A.T. Ariyarathna, No. SRL-002-92-002, 2.

NOVIB (December 29, 1993) Letter from Dr. A.T. Ariyarathna to Hans Pelgrom.

NOVIB (January 28, 1994) Letter from Hans Pelgrom to Dr. A.T. Ariyarathna, Ref. ZOAI, 28.01.94.

NOVIB (June 29, 1994) Letter from Hans Pelgrom to Dr. A.T. Ariyarathna, June 29, 1994, ZOA2/94-SRL- 002-92-001.

Obeyesekere, Gananath (February 1963) "The Great Traditions and the Little in the Perspective of Sinhalese Buddhism," *Journal of Asian Studies*, Vol. 22.

Obeyesekere, Gananath (1966) "The Buddhist Pantheon and Extensions," in M. Nash et al. (eds), *Anthropological Studies in Theravada Buddhism*, New Haven: Yale University Press.

Obeyesekere, Gananath (1970) "Religious Symbolism and Political Change in Ceylon," *Modern Ceylon Studies*, Vol. I.

Obeyesekere, Gananath (1988) "Sinhala Buddhist Identity," in George de Vos and Lola Romanucci Ross (eds) *Ethnicity, Identity, Cultural Continuity and Change*, Palo Alto: Mayfield, California Co.

Obeyesekere, Gananath and Richard Gombrich (1973) *Buddhism Transformed: Religious Change in Sri Lanka*, Princeton: Princeton University Press.

Obeyesekere, Gananath (2008) *Land Tenure in Village Ceylon*, Cambridge: Cambridge University Press.

Oddie, Geoffrey A. (1998) *Religious Traditions in South Asia: Interaction and Change*, New York: Curzon.

*Old Diary Leaves*, IV (1887–1892), (1910).

O'Malley, L.S.S. (ed.) (1941) *Modern India and the West: A Study of the Interaction of their Civilization*, London: Oxford University Press.

Orjuela, Camilla (2004) *Civil Society in Sri Lanka: Peace Work and Identity Politics in Sri Lanka*, Goteborg, Sweden: Department of Peace and Development Research, Goteborg University.

Pal, Bipin Chandra (1909) *Nationality and Empire*, London: Swaraj.

Palmer, Nicole (2005) "Defining a different War Economy: The Case of Sri Lanka," Berghof Research Center for Constructive Conflict Management, http://www.berghof-handbook.net/uploads/download/dialogue3_palmer.pdf. Accessed December 10, 2010.

Panikkar, K.M. (1953) *Asia and Western Dominance*, London: George Allen and Unwin Ltd.

Paranavithana, S. (1931) "The Village Communities of Ceylon," *Ceylon Literary Review Register*, third series.

Parikh, Ashokh (1993) "Bangladesh, 1973–85," in Sheila Page (ed.) *Monetary Policy in Developing Countries*, London: Routledge.

Pattaniak, Smruti S. (November 9, 2006) "The Neutral Caretaker Government Interregnum in Bangladesh," IDSA Strategic Comments, IDSA website, http://www.idsa.in/publications/stratcomments/SmrutiPattanaik091106.htm. Accessed April 16, 2009.

Paul, James (1996) "The World Bank and NGOs," http://www.globalpolicy.org/ngos/int/bwi/1996/worldbank.htm. Accessed February 22, 2009.

"Vision Statement," Peace in Sri Lanka: The Official Website of Sri Lankan Government's Secretariat for Coordinating the Peace Process, http://www.peaceinsrilanka.org/. Accessed April 14, 2009;

Pearson, Gail (1981) "Nationalism, Universalization and the Extended Female Space," in Gail Minault (ed.) *The Extended Family*, Columbia: South Asia Books.

Peebles, Patrick (1995) *Social Change in Nineteenth Century Ceylon*, New Delhi: Navrang.

Peebles, Patrick (2006) *History of Sri Lanka*, Connecticut and London: Greenwood Press.

Peet, Richard with Elaine Hartwick (1999) *Theories of Development*, New York: Guilford Press.

Peiris, Gerald (1972) "Agricultural Growth through Decentralization and Popular Participation: A Survey of DDC Farm Projects in Kandy District, 1971–1973" in *Modern Ceylon Studies*, Vol. 2, No. 6.

Peiris, Gerald (1996) *Development and Change in Sri Lanka: Geographical Perspectives*, New Delhi: Macmillan.

Perera, Jehan (1992) *People's Movement Under Siege*, Ratmalana: Sarvodaya.

Perera, Jehan (1998) "Sarvodaya Shramadana Movement," in David Hulme and Michael Edwards (eds) *NGOs, States and Donors: Too Close to Comfort*, New York: St. Martins Press.

Perera, Nihal (2002) "Indigenising the Colonial City: Late 19th-Century Colombo and its Landscape, 1703–1721," *Urban Studies*, Vol. 39, No. 9.

Perinpanayagam, S.H. (1939) "Jaffna" (cyclostyled manuscript).

Petras, James (March 2000) "The Third Way: Myth and Reality," *Monthly Review*, Vol. 51.

Petras, James and Henry Veltmeyer (2001) *Imperialism in the 21st Century*, London: Zed Books.

Phadnis, Urmila (1976) *Religion and Politics in Sri Lanka*, New Delhi: Manohar.

Phadnis, Urmila (July–September 1979) "Ethnicity and Nation Building in South Asia: A Case Study of Sri Lanka," *India Quarterly*, Vol. 35, No. 3.

Phelps, Rev. L.R. (1887) *Poor Law and Charity*. Oxford.

Philips, Rajan (October 24, 2008) "India, Sri Lanka, Tamil Nadu and the LTTE," FEDERALIDEA website, http://federalidea.com/fi/2008/10/post_25.html. Accessed April 14, 2009

Pieris, Ralph (1953) *Sinhalese Social Organization*, Colombo: Ceylon University Press.

Pilapitiya, R.A. (ed.) (1987) "At This Moment the Nation Needs Your Services," in *A.T. Ariyarathna Lekhana Samhithiya*, Vol. 1, Ratmalana: Sarvodaya Vishva Lekha.

Pinto Jayawardena, Kishali (October 21, 2007) "Blind Refusal to the See the Realities for What They Are," *Sunday Times Online*, http://sundaytimes.lk/071021/ Columns/focus.html. Accessed April 15, 2009;

Ponnambalam, Satchi (1980) *Dependent Capitalism in Crisis: The Sri Lankan Economy, 1948–1980*, London: Zed Press.

"Posters against LTTE's evacuation of NGOs," (January 7, 2008) Lanka-e-News, http://www.lankaenews.com/English/news.php?id=5178. Accessed April 15, 2009.

Premadasa, R. (February 4, 1978) "Address delivered at the inauguration of the International Conference of Sarvodaya and World Development," Ratmalana: Sarvodaya Shramadana Movement.

Priyantha, C. (1968) *American Education in Ceylon, 1816–1875: An Assessment of Its Impact*, Ann Arbor: University of Michigan.

"Procedures to be followed by National and International NGOs receiving foreign funds," People's Republic of Bangladesh, Prime Minister's Secretariat, *Circular* No. 22.433.1.0.46.93-478, 12/4/1993 (Bangla) 27/7/1993 (English).

"Proceedings of Judicial Department-Criminal" (April 7, 1847).

"Pursuing Common Goals: Strengthening Relations Between Government and Development NGOs" (1996) Dhaka: University Press.

Quamruzzmann, A.M.M. (2010) "The Militia Movement in Bangladesh: Ideology, Motivation, Mobilization, Organization, and Ritual," Master's Thesis, Queen's University, http://qspace.library.queensu.ca/bitstream/1974/5702/1/ Quamruzzaman_AMM_201005_MA.pdf.

Rahman, A, (2001) *Women and Microcredit in Rural Bangladesh: An Anthropological Study of Grameen Bank Lending*, Boulder, CO: Westview Press.

Rahaman, Atiur (November 1983) "Rural Power Structure: A Study of Union Parishad Leaders in Bangladesh," *Journal of Social Studies*.

Rahman, Md. Ataur (February 1984) "Bangladesh in 1983: A Turning Point for the Military," *Asian Survey*, Vol. 25, No. 2.

Rahula, Walpola (1956) *History of Buddhism in Ceylon. The Anuradhapura Period: 3rd Century BC–10th Century AD*, Colombo: Gunasena & Company Ltd.

Rahula, Walpola (1974) *The Heritage of the Bhikkhu*, New York: Grove Press, Inc.

Rai, Haridwar (1965) "Institution of the District Collector," *India Journal of Public Administration*, Vol. 11.

Raja, Rammohun Roy (1817) "Address to Lord William Bentinc," *The English Works of Raja Rammohun Roy*.

Rajapaksa, Reginald (1973) "Christian Missions, Theosophy and Trade: A History of American Relations with Ceylon 1815–1915," Ph.D. dissertation in History, University of Pennsylvania.

Ramachandra, Vinoth (1999) *Faiths in Conflict: Christian Integrity in a Multicultural World*, Secunderabad, Andhra Pradesh India: OM Books.

Raman, A.T.R. (1993) *Voluntarism and Nation-Building for Bangladesh*, Dhaka: Academic Publishers.

Ramonet, Ignacio (2008) "A Hundred Hours with Fidel" in Fidel Castro and Ignacio Ramonet, *Fidel Castro: My Life. A Spoken Autobiography*, New York: Scribner.

Ramonethe, Sgnacio (2004) *21st Century: New Threats New Fears*, Melbourne: Ocean Press.

"The Rani and Mandi" (January 12, 1929) *The Indian Social Reformer*.

Rankin, Kathrine, (2002) "Social Capital, Microfinance and Politics of Development," *Feminist Economics*, 8:1, 1–24.

Rashid, Ahmed (2002) *Taliban*, New Haven: Yale University Press.

Rashiduzzaman, M. (November 1994) "The Liberals and the Religious Right in Bangladesh," *Asian Survey,* Vol. XXXIV, No. 11.

Ray, Subhajyoti (2002) *Transformations on the Bengal Frontier*, New York: Routledge.

Raychudhuri, Tapan (2006) *Europe Reconsidered: Perceptions of the West in Nineteenth Century Bengal*, New Delhi: Oxford University Press.

Reddy, B. Muralidhar (August 8, 2008) "Cut of NGOs' aid to LTTE," *The Hindu*, online edition, http://www.hindu.com/2008/08/08/stories/2008080861981500.htm. Accessed April 15, 2009.

Reich, Michael R. (1994) "Bangladesh Pharmaceutical Policy and Politics," *Health Policy and Planning*, Vol. 9, No. 2.

"Religious Bigotry Used for Political Mobilization—Prof. Uyangoda," (January 30, 2004) *TamilNet*, http://www.tamilnet.com/art.html?catid=13&artid=11088. Accessed April 15, 2009.

Reoch, Richard (February 1996) letter from the Chair, NGO Forum on Sri Lanka.

*Review of Bangladesh Economy* (1995) Dhaka: Center for Policy Dialogue.

Rew, Alan (1997) "The Donor Discourse: Official Social Development Knowledge in the 1980s," in Ralph and Grillo and Jock Stirrat (eds) *Discourses of Development: Anthropological Perspectives*, Oxford: Berg.

Risley, Sir Herbert Hope (1969) *The People of India*, Second edition, Delhi: Oriental Books.

Riyaja, Ali (1994) *State, Class and Military Rule: Political Economy of Martial Law in Bangladesh*, Dhaka: Nadi New Press.

Roberts, Michael (1982) *Caste Conflict and Elite Formation: The Rise of a Karava Elite in Sri Lanka, 1500–1931*, Cambridge: Cambridge University Press.

"The Role of Rural Development Societies in Sri Lanka" (1976) Research Council of the Department of Rural Development.

Root, Helen I. (2004) *A Century in Ceylon: A Brief History of the Work of the American Board in Ceylon: 1816–1916*, The American Ceylon Mission.

Russal, H.S.O. (1871) in *The Hansard* [Legislative Council].

Russell, Jane (1982) Communal Politics under the Donoughmore Constitution, 1931–1947, Dehiwala: Tisara Prakasakayo.

Ryan, Bryce (1953) *Caste in Modern Ceylon: The Sinhalese System in Transition*, New Brunswick: Rutgers University Press.

Sachs, W. (ed.) (1992) *The Development Dictionary: A Guide to Knowledge as Power*, London: Zed Books.

Saleem, Samad (1990) "Political Analysis and Ethnic Problems in Chittagong Hill Tracts," unpublished paper.

Salmon, Lester (1993) "The Rise of the Non-Profit Sector," *Foreign Affairs*, Vol. 73, No. 4.

Samaraweera, Vijaya (1978) "Litigation, Sir Henry Main's Writings and the Ceylon Village Communities Ordinance of 1871" in Leelananda Prematilleke Karthigesu Indrapala and J.E. van Lohuizende Leeuw (eds), *Senarat Paranavitana Commemoration Volume, Studies in South Asia Culture*.

Samath, Feizal (August 11, 2008) "Sri Lankan government targets foreign NGOs," *One World South Asia*, http://southasia.oneworld.net/todaysheadlines/sri-lankan-government-targets-foreign-ngos. Accessed November 20, 2010.

Sanneh, Lamin (2003) *Whose Religion is Christianity? The Gospel Beyond the West*, Cambridge: William B. Eerdmans Publishing Company.

Sanyal, Bishwapriya (1991) "Antagonistic Cooperation: A Case Study of NGOs, Government and Donors," *World Development*, Vol. 19, No. 10.

*Sarasavi Sandarasa* (May 28, 1899) Colombo.

Sarkar, Sumit (1973) *The Swadeshi Movement in Bengal, 1903–1908*, Delhi: People's Publishing House.

Sarkar, Sumit (1989) "The Kalki-Avatar of Bikrmapur: A Village Scandal in Early Twentieth Century in Bengal," in Ranajit Guha (ed.) *Subaltern Studies VI*, New Delhi: Oxford University Press.

"Sarvodaya Goes from Humble Village to Finance Big Time Commercial Ventures—Third Generation NGOs in the Third World," (October 3, 1991) *Sunday Observer*, Provincial Edition.

"Sarvodaya Pours Millions into Black Holes" (April 12, 1992) *Sunday Observer*.

"Sarvodaya Sells Lankan Children Abroad," (April 4, 1992) *Sunday Observer*.

Sarvodaya Shramadana Movement (November 1984) "Report of the CIDA Review Mission."

Sassen, Saskia and Kwame Anthony Appiah (1998) *Globalization and its Discontents: Essays on the New Mobility of People and Money*, New York: New Press.

Scott, James (1999) *Seeing Like a State*, New Haven: Yale University Press.

Seal, Anil (1968) *The Emergence of Indian Nationalism: Competition and Collaboration in the Late Nineteenth Century*, Cambridge: Cambridge University Press.

Seneviratne, Malinda (November 2008) "The Man Behind Country's Defense Strategy", *Business Today*, http://www.btoptions.com/def_sec.pdf.

Sengupta, K.P. (1971) *Christian Missionaries in Bengal*, Calcutta.

Shah, A.B. (ed.) (1977) *Letters and Correspondence of Pandita Ramabai*, Bombay: Maharashtra State Board for Literature and Culture.

Shahi, Husain (1965) *Bengal, 1494–1584 A.D.: A Socio-Political Study*, Dacca: Asiatic Society of Pakistan.

Sharma, Brinjendra Nath (1972) *Social and Cultural History of Northern India, C. 1000–1200 A.D.*, New Delhi: Abhinav Publications.

Shastri, Amita (1983a) "Formation of the Contemporary Political Formations in Sri Lanka," *South Asia Bulletin*, 3(1).

Shastri, Amita (1983b) "The Political Economy of Intermediate Regimes: The Case of Sri Lanka 1956–1970," *South Asia Bulletin*, 3(2).

Shastri, Amita (Feb. 1999) "Material Basis for Separatism, Tamil Eelam Movement in Sri Lanka," *Journal of Asian Studies*, Vol. 9, No. 41.

Shastri, Amita (2004) "The United National Party of Sri Lanka: Reproducing Hegemony" in Subrata K. Mirta, Mike Eskat and Clemens Speib (eds) *Political Parties in South Asia*, London: Praeger, 236–258.

"Six Hundred Sarvodaya Workers to the Road," (December 11, 1993) *Aththa*.

Smillie, Ian (2006) *BRAC: Words and Deeds*, Dhaka: BRAC.

Smith, Neil (1984, 1990) *Uneven Development: Nature, Capital, and the Production of Space*, Atlanta: University of Georgia Press.

Smith, Neil (2004) *The End Game of Globalization*, New York: Routledge.

Sobhan, Rehman (1968) *Basic Democracies, Workers Program and Rural Development*, Dhaka: University of Dhaka, Bureau of Economic Research.

Sobhan, Rehman (1983) *The Crisis of External Dependence: Political Economy of Foreign Aid to Bangladesh*, Dhaka: University Press Limited.

Sobhan, Rehman (1999) "Economic Basis of Bengali Nationalism," in *History of Bangladesh: Economic History 1704-1971*, Dhaka: Asiatic Society of Bangladesh.

Solaiman, M. and M. Alam (1977) "Characteristics of Candidates for Elections in Three Union Paraishads in Comilla Kohwall Thana," Comilla: Bard.

"Some Thoughts on Present Discontent" (May 1907) *The Harvest Field*.

Spate, O.H.K. and A.T.A. Learnomoth (1967) *India and Pakistan: General Regional Geography*, 3rd edition, London: Methuen.

S.P.G. MSS., Ceylon 1840–55, Bishop Chapman to S.P.G., November 12, 1847.

Spivak, Gayatri Chakravorty (1998) "Cultural Talks in the Hot Peace: Revisiting the Global Village," in Pheng Chea and Bruce Robbins (eds) *Cosmopolitics*, Minneapolis: University of Minnesota Press.

Spivak, Gayatri Chakravorty (1999) *A Critique of Post-Colonial Reason: Toward a History of the Vanishing Present*, Cambridge, MA: Harvard University Press.

Sri Arubindo (September 17, 1907) "Liberty and Our Social Laws," in *Bande Mataram*.

Sri Arubindo (November 21, 1907) "Tragedy in Lisbon," in *Bande Mataram*.

*Sri Lanka's Economy* (1999) Colombo: Institute for Policy Studies.

"Sri Lanka's War Secretariat?" (November 22, 2007) *TamilNet*, http://www.tamilnet.com/art.html?catid=79&artid=23831. Accessed April 15, 2009.

Sri Lanka Ministry of Defence (2008) "Using UN to Fulfil NGOs Agendas" http://www.defence.lk/new.asp?fname=20080309_03. Accessed November 30, 2010.

Stein, B. (1986) *Peasant State and Society in Medieval South India*, Oxford: Oxford University Press.

Steinberg, Natalie (December 2001) "Background Paper on Gongos and Quango's and Wild NGOs," World Federalist Movement Papers, http://www.globalpolicy.org/ngos/intro/defining/2001/0112wild.htm. Accessed February 22, 2009.

Steinmetz, George (1999) *State/Culture: State/Formation After the Cultural Turn (The Wilder House Series in Politics, History, and Culture)*, Ithaca: Cornell University Press.

Stewart, Angus (2001) *Theories of Power and Domination*, London: Sage.

Stiles, Kendall (2002) "International Support for NGOs in Bangladesh: Some Unintended Consequences," *World Development*, Vol. 30, No. 5.

Stirrat, R.L. and Heiko Henkel (November 1998) "Development Gift: Problem of Reciprocity in the NGO World," in Jude Fernando and Alan Heston (eds) "The Role of the NGOs: Charity and Development," *Annals of the American Academy of Political and Social Science 554*, Thousand Oak, CA: Sage.

Subramaniam, Venkateswarier (1990) *Public Administration in the Third World*, Westport, CT: Greenwood.

Sultana, Maheen and Tahrunnesa Abdullah (May–June 1990) "Study of Voluntary Organizations, Resource Organizations in Bangladesh," *ADAB News*.

*The Sunday Island* (December 26, 1993) Colombo: Upali Group Publications.

Tambiah, S.J. (1958) "The Structure of Kinship and its Relationship to Land Possession and Residence in Patha Dumbara, Central Ceylon," *Journal of the Royal Anthropological Institute*, 88.

Tambiah, S.J. (1973) "Buddhism and Third-World Activity," *Modern Asian Studies*, Vol. VII/I 8.

Tambiah, S.J. (1992) *Buddhism Betrayed? Religion, Politics, and Violence in Sri Lanka*, Chicago: University of Chicago Press.

*Tamils against Genocide, Inc. vs. Timothy Geithner and Meg Lundsager* (2009) Available at http://www.tamilsagainstgenocide.org/IMFLawsuit.html. Accessed April 15, 2009.

Tampoe, Manel (1997) *The Story of Selestina Dias, Buddhist Female Philanthropy and Education*, Colombo: Social Scientists' Association.

Tandon, Rajesh (2000) "Riding High or Nosediving: Development NGOs in the New Millennium," *Development in Practice*, Vol. 10, Numbers 3 & 4, August 2000.

Thapar, Romila (1963) "History of Female Emancipation in South Asia," in Barbara Ward (ed.) *Women in South Asia*, Paris: UNESCO.

Thapar, Romila (1969) *A History of India*, Vol. 1, London: Penguin.

Thompson, E.P. (1991) *The Making of the English Working Class*, London: Penguin Books.

Thrift, N. (1985) "Flies and Germs: Geography of Knowledge," in Derek Gregory and John Urry (eds) *Social Relations and Spatial Structures*, London: Macmillan.

Throp, John (1978) *Power Among the Farmers of Daripalla*, Dhaka: CARITAS.

*The Times* (April 8, 1996) Dhaka, Bangladesh.

Timm, Fr. R.W. CSC, (1974) "Reminiscence in Grassroots," *AVAB Quarterly*, July-December, Vol. IV, No.XII-XIV.

Timm, R.W. (1983) *Power Relations in Rural Development: The Case of Bangladesh*, Hong Kong: Center for the Progress of People.

Timm, R.W. (December 1991) "The Adivasis of Bangladesh," *Minority Group International Report*.

Timm, R.W. (June 1994) *Building a Just Society*, Dhaka: Caritas Bangladesh.

Timm, R.W. (1995) *Forty Years in Bangladesh: Memoirs of Father Timm*, Bangladesh: Caritas.

Tiruchelvam, Neelan (1984) *Ideology of Popular Justice in Sri Lanka: Socio-Legal Study*, New Delhi: Vikas Publishing House.

Tissanayagam, J.S. (February 24, 2008) *Telescope*, Sunday Vol. 42, No. 39, Wijeya Newspapers Ltd. Colombo, Sri Lanka, available at http://tissa102.blogspot.com/. Accessed September 2010.

Tvedt, Terje (1998) *Angels of Mercy or Development Diplomats: NGOs & Foreign Aid*, New Jersey: Africa Press.

Ullah, A.K.M. Ahsan and Jayant K. Routray (2007) "Rural poverty alleviation through NGO interventions in Bangladesh: how far is the achievement?" *International Journal of Social Economics*, Vol. 34, No. 4.

*United National Party, UNP* (September 26, 1947) Vol. I, No. 29.

UNHRC (2008) "Aide-Mémoire: Bangladesh,7th Session of the UN Human Rights Council (March 3–28), http://forum-menschenrechte.de/cms/upload/

PDF/ab_05-2008/aides_memoires/Bangladesh_-_ai-Misereor-DW.pdf. Accessed April 16, 2009.

Unithan, Maya and Kavita Srivastava (1997) "Gender Politics and Women's Agency in Rajastan Maya," in R.D. Grillo and R.L. Stirrat (eds) *Discourses of Development: Anthropological Perspectives,* Oxford: Berg.

*The UNP Manifesto* (1977) Colombo: United National Party.

Uphoff, N. (1987) "Third Generation NGO Strategies: A Key to People-Centered Development," *World Development,* Vol. 15.

Uphoff, N. (1993) "Grassroots Organizations and NGOs in Rural Development: Opportunities and Diminishing States and Expanding Markets," *World Development,* Vol. 21, No. 4.

U.S. Senate Committee on Foreign Relations (February 24, 2009) "Recent Developments in Sri Lanka," Hearing before the Committee on Foreign Relations, United States Senate, 111 Congress, First Session, http://foreign.senate.gov/hearings/2009/hrg090224p.html. Accessed April 15, 2009.

Uyangoda, Jayadeva (1976) "NGOs, Politics and Questions of Democracy," lecture given at the Annual Consultation, Colombo, Sri Lanka.

Van Rooy, Alison (2000) "Good News! You May Be Out of a Job: Reflections on the Past and Future 50 Years for Northern NGOs" in Deborah Eade and Hazel Johnson (eds) *Development and Management: Selected Essays from Development in Practice,* London: Oxfam.

Wace, Cyril (1961) *A Concise History of Ceylon,* Colombo: Ceylon University Press.

Wanigarathna, Ranjith (June 1994) "NGO Relationship: Rights, Interests and Accountability," unpublished paper, Colombo: Mahaweli Authority of Sri Lanka.

Wanigarathna, Rangith (1998) "The State–NGO Relations in Sri Lanka," in David Hulme and Michael Edwards (eds) *NGOs, States and Donors: Too Close to Comfort,* New York: St. Martins Press.

Wiswa, Warnapala (2001) Local Governments, Participation and Development in Sri Lanka at the Village Level, International Academic Publications.

Weber, Max (1978) *Economy and Society,* Berkeley: University of California Press.

Weerawardana, I.D.S. (1951) *Government in Politics of Ceylon,* Colombo: Ceylon Economic Research Association.

Wesleyan Missionary Notices (1891) Vol. VI, 171; W.M.S. Cooling to Walton, February 5, April 9, April 16.

Westergaard, Kirsten (1985) *State and Rural Society in Bangladesh,* Scandinavian Institute for Asian Studies Monographs Series, No. 49, London: Curzon Press.

Westergaard, Kirsten (July 1992) "NGOs, Empowerment and the State in Bangladesh," CDR working paper 92.2.

Westergaard, Kirsten and Muhammad Mustafa Alam (1995) "Local Government in Bangladesh: Past Experiences and Yet Another Try," *World Development,* Vol. 23, No. 4.

Whaites, Alan (1996) "Let's Get Civil Society Straight: NGOs, the State, and Political Theory," *Development in Practice,* Vol. 6, No. 3.

White, Sarah C. (February 1996) "Depoliticising Development: The Uses and Abuses of Participation," *Development in Practice,* Vol. 6, No. 1.

White, Sarah (1999) "Civil Society, and the State in Bangladesh: The Politics of Representing the Poor," *Development and Change,* Vol. 2, No. 30.

Wickramarathna, U.C. (1993) *The Conservative Nature of the British Rule of Sri Lanka with a Particular Emphasis on the Period 1796–1802,* New Delhi: Navrang.

Wickramasinghe, Nira (1995) *Ethnic Politics in Colonial Sri Lanka: 1927–1947*, New Delhi: Vikas.

Wickramasinghe, Nira (2006) *Sri Lanka in the Modern Age*, Honolulu: University of Hawaii Press.

Wijemanne, Adrian (1996) *War and Peace in Post-Colonial Ceylon 1948–1991*, Delhi: Orient Longman.

Wijesinha, Rajiva (February 29, 2008) "Radhika Coomaraswamy Resigns from GCR2P Advisory Board," *SCOPP Report*, http://www.peaceinsrilanka.org/peace2005/Insidepage/SCOPPDaily_Report/SCOPP_report290208.asp. Accessed April 15, 2009.

Wijesinha, Rajiva (March 14, 2009) "Amnesty International Bombs South Asia," http://www.peaceinsrilanka.org/peace2005/Insidepage/SCOPPDaily_Report/SCOPP_report140309.asp. Accessed April 15, 2009.

Wijesinha, Rajiva (March 18, 2009) "The Great NGO Game," http://www.peaceinsrilanka.org/peace2005/Insidepage/SCOPPDaily_Report/SCOPP_report180309_1.asp. Accessed April 14, 2009.

Williams, Raymond (1977) *Marxism and Literature*, Oxford: Oxford University Press.

Wilson, A.J. (1974) *Politics of Sri Lanka, 1947–1973*, London: Macmillan.

Wilson, Howard A. (1973) "An Anatomy of the Buddhist Renaissance in Ceylon in the Work of K.N. Jayathilaka," *Ceylon Compass*, Vol. XX/2201.

Winslow, D. and M. Woost, "The Economy in Conditions of Intense Civil War: Sri Lanka 1994–2000," in *Economy, Culture, and Civil War in Sri Lanka*, Indiana: Indiana University Press.

Wirsing, Robert G. (1977) *Socialist Society and Free Enterprises Politics*, South Carolina: Carolina Academic Press.

"The Woes of the Middle Class" (August 1, 1869) *National Paper.*

Wolf, Eric (1982) *Europe and the People Without History*, Berkeley: University Of California Press.

Wolf, Sydney and Benjamin Gordon (1996) Public Health Research Group, letter to Harman Kirby, Deputy Assistant Secretary (Acting), Department of State, Washington.

Wood, Geoffrey (1996) "States without Citizens: The Problem of the Franchise State," in David Hulme and Michael Edwards (eds) *NGOs, State, and Donors: Too Close for Comfort?* New York: Palgrave Macmillan.

Woods, G.D. (1994) *Bangladesh: Whose Ideas, Whose Interests?* Dhaka: University Press.

*World Bank Development Report* (1989) Washington DC: World Bank.

World Court Project UK (January 23, 2003) "Blair, Hoon and Straw to be Investigated for War Crimes," Press Release, http://www.cnduk.org/index.php/press-releases/2003/blair-hoon-and-straw-to-be-investigated-for-war-crimes.html. Accessed February 16, 2009.

World Prout Assembly website, http://www.worldproutassembly.org/archives/2007/03/bangladesh_arbi.html. Accessed April 16, 2009.

Yalman, N. (1963) *Under the Bo Tree: Studies in Caste, Kinship and Marriage in the Interior of Ceylon*, Berkeley and Los Angeles: University of California Press.

Ziring, Lawrence (1992) *Bangladesh from Mujib to Ershad: An Interpretive Study*, New Delhi: Oxford University Press.

# Index